# Hauling
### BY
# Hand

*The Life and Times of
a Maine Island*

Other books from Islandport Press

*My Life in the Maine Woods*
by Annette Jackson

*Contentment Cove*
by Miriam Colwell

*Stealing History*
by William D. Andrews

*Shoutin' into the Fog*
by Thomas Hanna

*down the road a piece: A Storyteller's Guide to Maine*, and
*A Moose and a Lobster Walk into a Bar*
by John McDonald

*Windswept*, *Mary Peters*, and *Silas Crockett*
by Mary Ellen Chase

*Nine Mile Bridge*
by Helen Hamlin

*In Maine*
by John N. Cole

*The Story of Mount Desert Island*
by Samuel Eliot Morison

*Here for Generations: The Story of a Maine Bank and its City*
by Dean Lawrence Lunt

*The Cows Are Out! Two Decades on a Maine Dairy Farm*
by Trudy Chambers Price

*A History of Little Cranberry Island, Maine*
by Hugh L. Dwelley

These and other Maine books are available at:
www.islandportpress.com.

# Hauling
## BY
# Hand

*The Life and Times of*
*a Maine Island*

**by Dean Lawrence Lunt**

## ISLANDPORT PRESS

NEW GLOUCESTER • FRENCHBORO • MAINE

First Printing, December 1999
Second Printing, October 2000
Third Printing, July 2007

Library of Congress Catalog Card Number: 2007930072

ISBN 1-934031-07-0

Designed in Yarmouth, Maine by Michelle A. Lunt and Dean L. Lunt
Edited by: Dean L. Lunt, Michelle A. Lunt and Nancy E. Piccin
Copyediting: Ann Parrish
Design and Production: Michelle A. Lunt and Dean L. Lunt

Cover photo of Sanford L. "Dick" Lunt, 1936
Cover design by Karen Hoots, Hoots Design
Author photo by John Ewing

Islandport Press Inc.
P.O. Box 10
Yarmouth, Maine 04096
www.islandportpress.com
info@islandportpress.com

## The Grandfather

The grandfather stands on the wharf.
Spirits of ancestors walk the paths, the docks, the shores.
The island wind whispers their names in the night.
While their voices still echo in the morning mist,
marking the tide of time, the flow of generations.

The eldest son of a fisherman closes his eyes.
He sees a childhood of little, now gone.
A boyhood of work, near forgotten.
One marriage, one house, one home still strong.
And a life, stubborn, proud, tireless, that marches on.

The grandfather stands on the wharf.
The dock he built and rebuilt
after fall days on the ocean hauling traps,
after summer nights on the sea watching seine.
Passed to the son, it reaches ever outward, solid, secure.

He watches the sun glint on the ageless, rippling harbor.
He sees grandsons, great-grandsons and great-granddaughters.
Boats, skiffs, rowboats, slip in and out.
Ever bigger, ever faster, ever changing.
They flicker like decades through the mind.

The grandfather stands on the wharf
stooped in the September of life.
The air chilled in the way of fall.
But he does not shiver, he just stands.
And watches what his life has wrought.

Dean Lawrence Lunt
Frenchboro, Maine 1996

# Preface

*Hauling by Hand* is the product of four years of research and writing — frequently interrupted by life. The book, much longer than orginally intended, consists of four distinct parts.

Part I is mostly a research-driven history of the 19th century — including island settlement and the building of a community — that I hope sheds light on not only Long Island and its people, but the Maine coast and a way of life. At times details were scarce or nonexistent, yet several historical finds clarified and sometimes revealed parts of Long Island history that had long been forgotten. Historical information about Maine and Blue Hill Bay in the pre-Long Island settlement era was gleaned from other publications that I encourage history buffs to read.

Part II mostly chronicles the 20th century. It is more sweeping and anecdotal than Part I. It includes personal recollections of various island residents and myself.

Part III, the appendix, is a resource of mostly vital statistics and census records. Island vital statistics were reconstructed from a variety of sources to aid researchers of family history and interested parties. This was not an easy task and is ongoing, given the missing, conflicting and ambiguous information that exists for Long Island. Most original Long Island records from the 19th century were either lost or accidentally destroyed by fire. U.S. census records are not presented verbatim, either. I corrected many errors, mostly incorrect or inconsistent names, although some surely remain.

Finally, Part IV is a photographic history. These pictures, roughly 180 in all, were chosen not to just highlight people and physical structures, but to provide insight into island life.

While this book attempts to serve many purposes, at its core it is a local history with a level of detail befitting the genre. I also hope the prologues, historical context and voices of islanders provide an interesting read for more casual observers. I intended to write a book that did not collapse under too much minutiae, but which also did not rely merely on anecdotes, and thus fail to provide context or historical insight. It was neither my plan to write a chamber of commerce valentine to Long Island nor to expose all its rumors and skeletons.

The book, to some extent, is written so it can be picked up and read at any point. Therefore, some facts are repeated for the reader's convenience.

Before I could finish, I had to realize that historical research, regardless of subject, is continuous and fluid. No matter how much I discovered, I knew that some new fact or source of information was still out there. Knowing that is annoying to a writer trying to provide a complete history, but also exciting, as it means other discoveries await the persistent.

I encourage anyone who finds mistakes or omissions, who can clarify issues or provide further details related to Long Island or island families, to contact me. Eventually, I hope to learn more about the island's original Pomroy, Rich and Davis families, whose roots have proven elusive. And my one great dream concerning island history is to find a picture or portrait of Israel B. Lunt Sr. I am convinced that one exists. The Islandport mailing and e-mail addresses are printed elsewhere should anyone have information.

# Acknowledgments

While I was researching and writing *Hauling by Hand*, many people provided invaluable help.

Foremost is my grandmother, Vivian Davis Lunt, who virtually pioneered research of Frenchboro's history, encouraged (and promoted) me ceaselessly and waited patiently for upwards of 15 years for me to start and finish this book. My parents, to whom I owe a great debt in general, were encouraging and helpful in many ways. My wife, Michelle, allowed me time to research and write, and then was crucial in the editing, layout and design process.

My grandfather, Sanford "Dick" Lunt, whose life and memories stretched back two decades further than any other island man, provided wonderful details of a bygone era. Sadly, Dick passed away in October, just as *Hauling by Hand* was in the final preparation for printing.

Nancy E. Piccin, whom I met and worked beside during my days at the *Union-News* in Springfield, Massachusetts, edited and critiqued the manuscript. Her professional opinion and assistance were critical. Karen Hoots, a Massachusetts-based free-lance designer, designed the beautiful book cover and jacket using a photograph of my grandfather taken in 1936. Peter Ralston, the best photographer of the Maine coast working today (see *Sightings* or www.pralston.com for proof), generously allowed me to use several of his photos.

Numerous family members and friends were critical to the final manuscript, providing memories, photographs and a wealth of other information. One discovery came courtesy of Marjorie (Dalzell) Giamo. Marjorie, looking through some belongings of her late mother, Vera (Ross) Dalzell, found old papers that included original handwritten island deeds and business agreements, helping shed some light on the early 1800s.

Interviews included: Ben S. Davis Jr., Verna B. Dobson, Marjorie D. Giamo, Michael Holland, Phoebe Horton, Lillian J. Lunt, John R. Lunt Jr., Robert A. Lunt, Earlene F. Lunt, Carroll W. Lunt, David L. Lunt, Sandra Lunt, Russell Lunt, Rebecca J. Lunt, Ella V. Lunt, Barbara A. Sawyer and June E. Thompson. Also, Ben, Ella, June, Marjorie, Sandra, Verna, Vivian, Lorena Beal, Joseph Blackburn, John Ewing, Donna Hasal,

Pamela Pierce, Jill Rabine, *The Bar Harbor Times* and the Frenchboro Historical Society all provided photographs. And special thanks to Lillian J. Lunt for making available her wealth of family photographs. Michael Nasuti, art director for the *Union-News*, drew three illustrations, including one of Blue Hill Bay. Additional help came from: Bessie Black (my grandmother), Gregory Rec, Tina Lunt, Marcia Priestley and many others.

In the museums and libraries of Maine and Massachusetts, I stumbled across many unexpected treasures. I don't believe the historical resources available to the citizens of Maine are used enough. (However, I must complain that some archives simply do not offer convenient or even reasonable hours of access.) The Maine Historical Society library in Portland is a gem. In addition to published records, I found there the priceless journals of Amos Coffin Lunt Sr., which contained sporadic entries from the early 1800s through the 1840s. These provided a first-hand account of life on Long Island during the pioneer era. Thank you to Stephanie Philbrick and Nicholas Noyes for their help.

Other important repositories include: Maine State Library and Archives; Congregational Library of the American Congregational Church in Boston; The American Baptist — Samuel Colgate Historical Library in New York; Miller Library Special Collections at Colby College (Valerie Mitchell and Maili Bailey); Raymond H. Fogler Library at the University of Maine; Franklin Trask Library at Andover Newton Theological School (Diana Yount); Portland Public Library; Osher Map Library and the Smith Center for Cartographic Education at the University of Southern Maine; Penobscot Marine Museum (John G. Arrison); Massachusetts State Archives; Newburyport Historical Society; and the National Archives.

Researchers who helped either directly or indirectly included: the late Jean Ward and her mother, Shirley Rhodes, who transcribed 19th century *The Ellsworth American* and *The Ellsworth Herald* obituaries and marriages; the late Thomas S. Lunt, whose genealogy of the Lunt family to 1906 contained critical information. I am further indebted to all the historians and writers (see bibliography) whose research and books provided information about other islands, Blue Hill Bay and Maine.

I sincerely thank you all.

Dean   Lawrence   Lunt

# Table of Contents

# Introduction

*Hauling by Hand* is a local history about two intimately entwined subjects: an island and a family. An island is a special place, often invested by both its residents and outside observers with an identity, a life and a personality. People talk and whisper, defend and attack, brag and condemn an island as if the landmass were a friend, family member or nemesis.

I don't know why islands inspire such personification or generate such strong opinions. Some people, including friends and relatives of mine, have stepped off the shores of Long Island and never again returned. Others leave for several years before coming back. And still others leave, but no matter how young they were when they sailed from Lunt Harbor, they still consider Frenchboro "down home."

Certainly, some spiritual justification exists for all this. An island does seem to possess, and can potentially lose, a unique life force. Some 300 year-round Maine island communities, although many consisted of no more than a few families, have died over the past century or so.

I find it strangely sad to read about the historic deaths of these once common island communities, killed by progress and a changing way of life, during the 19th and early 20th century. Many have vanished without a trace.

Some days as I stand in my father's lobster boat and sail past the now deserted Placentia and Black Islands and even the summer colony of Great Gott Island in Blue Hill Bay, I am enveloped by a sense of melancholy.

On Black, I envision the railways that once carried granite from quarries to waiting vessels. I imagine old man Benjamin Dawes, an island pioneer in the early 1800s, ambling across the shore to his fishing boat. Or my great great great grandmother, Lydia Dawes, building castles as a child on the sandy beach along Black Island pool. Knowing a community once existed makes the island seem even older and more lifeless — almost like a floating cemetery. Or maybe like the once-bustling house on the corner that stands silent and empty, save for drawn curtains and dusty dishes stacked in cobwebbed cupboards. You just know that life will never return.

*Long Island looking across Lunt Harbor and Blue Hill Bay toward Mount Desert Island. The entire population of Frenchboro, the island's village, is clustered around Lunt Harbor.*

I sometimes feel the same way while standing in the stillness on Long Island's Richs Head. I know a small village thrived here for about 80 years. I know houses stood strong against the winter chill, that settlers plowed this field into gardens and that wharves once stretched into the waters of Eastern Cove.

Today, a handful of shallow, hand-dug cellars, barely discernible even at close range, and broken rock walls are all that remain. Scattered somewhere amongst the tall grass and encroaching spruce lie the unmarked graves of settlers and children, their locations long ago lost to the living world.

With all this as a spiritual backdrop and constant warning, Long Island, and its sole village, Frenchboro, has survived.

I no longer live in Frenchboro; college, work and life have carried me across New England and New York to explore other places for awhile. This exploration has been fun and enlightening and no doubt provided some clarity to island life, something to which I someday will return. Still, for nearly 23 years Long Island fit me like a second skin. I knew its landscape by touch, smell and intuition. From the well-trodden woods behind my house to the deer paths that wound through huckleberry bushes to the Salt Ponds to the tumbled beach rocks of Big Beach, I knew the land. I knew the smell of moss, the hidden brooks, the cracked ledges, the shoreline and the unique trees.

I was baptized in the harborside church, engaged on the sloping granite of Gooseberry Point, educated in the one-room school and consumed by daydreams on Lookout Point.

Yet even more than an island or hometown, Long Island is a family and heritage.

I was born an eighth-generation islander. I am unapologetically proud to say my family built the island community and has helped sustain it for 180 years.

The family flourished and failed and feuded on the shores of Long Island. They were keen business operators, tireless workers, layabouts, bandits, alcoholics, church workers, community leaders, detached, mean, congenial and fun-loving along the banks of a harbor that bears the family name and on hillsides that contain the bodies of their forebears.

It is a heritage that to people from other states — and even other parts of Maine — sometimes inspires a certain amount of intrigue, bewilderment and snobbery. One time a newspaper colleague and friend of mine learned about a year into our friendship that I grew up on a small island of less than 50 people and attended a one-room school. Not only that, but it was in Maine! She looked at me and without any intentional condescension, said somewhat quizzically, "But you seem so well adjusted, socially."

The myths, both positive and negative, about islands — and Maine itself, for that matter — are legion. Residents of both are alternately portrayed as crusty fisherman, sturdy woodsmen, wizened sages or drunken, backward hicks.

Most stereotypical reactions are rooted in ignorance and the unknown. Some myths are certainly inspired by writers and visitors who have spun romantic or mythical tales. Even writers who delve into the "real" Maine often reinforce its image as a backwater state. It is probably best to say that to some extent it is all true; and it is all false. It is the endless shades of gray that are always missed.

My view of island reality is a heritage of endless labor, the sea, raw winter days, glorious summer mornings and crisp fall afternoons on the Atlantic Ocean. Of long days and short nights, of nature's elements, sewing circles and Christmas dinners. Of one-room schools, cribbage games and family. It is a heritage of the ultimate independence and the ultimate dependence. Of great joy and daily sacrifice. Of frustrating attitudes and joyous honesty. Of great isolation and suffocating closeness.

It is to honor that heritage that this book is written.

It is written for island pioneers Amos Sr., Amos Jr., Israel B. and Abner Lunt along with my other 19th century ancestors such as Capt. William Davis, William Rich, Thomas Rice and William Pomroy so their work, lives and legacy may be resurrected from historical obscurity.

It is for the pioneer women such as Nancy and Eliza Pomroy, Priscilla Butler, Jane Dawes, Mary Beal and Eleanor Rice, who raised families and built island homes under most trying conditions.

It is for my great-uncles Cecil and Clarence and Vincent, who, may they rest in peace, helped provide the texture of a childhood. For my great-aunts Lillian and Rebecca and my great-uncle John, who still do. For my grandparents, Vivian and Sanford, and parents Sandra and David, who provided the heart and soul. And for my entire family both immediate and extended, and all the people who have moved onto or visited the island over the years and thus helped sustain it.

And it is in no small part the first payment on a father's debt to my own young daughters, Emily Ann and Eliza Rose. So they, no matter where life leads them, no matter what roads they travel, will know where they came from.

An island and a family.

Dean Lawrence Lunt
Autumn 1999

*Photo by Dean L. Lunt*

*Emily A. and Eliza R. Lunt, August 1999.*

# Hauling By Hand

*Part I*

# Chapter One

# Long Island, Maine

More than 250 years after it first appeared on nautical charts and nearly two centuries after settlers built the first log cabins, Long Island survives. Out "amid the ocean's roar," as one writer put it, Long Island is one of only 15 Maine islands that still support a year-round community — down from more than 300 a century ago. And it is one of the smallest and most remote.

The island itself lies in Blue Hill Bay roughly eight miles southwest of Mount Desert Island, but a world away from the tourist-driven economy of Bar Harbor and the posh estates of Northeast Harbor and Seal Harbor.

The working-class village surrounding Bass Harbor is the closest mainland port and the one most frequently used by Long Islanders. On the run from Bass Harbor to Long Island, three main islands are clustered in the first four miles: Great Gott Island, Placentia Island and Black Island. All three once supported year-round communities, but now Great Gott has summer residents only, Black has one house and Placentia is abandoned.

Between Black Island and Long Island, the second half of the boat trip, sit five smaller islands: Drum Island, the two Green Islands, Crow Island and Harbor Island.

This last stretch of ocean, exposed to the open Atlantic, can grow nasty when heavy seas roll in unobstructed from offshore. Many a passenger and more than a few captains have breathed a sigh of relief after making Crow Island Head and the more protected final run that follows.

*Photo by Joseph Blackburn*

*The Starburst at its mooring on a calm day in Lunt Harbor.*

In the summertime, even on foggy days, that final stretch with Crow Island and Harbor Island to the right and Northeast Point to the left is unmistakable. Suddenly, the cold, clear air off the open ocean gives way to the warm, sweet-scented breezes off the islands.

Because of its spot along the outermost line of Maine islands, Long Island was usually called Outer Long Island and sometimes Lunt's Long Island in the 1800s to distinguish it from a similarly named island closer to Blue Hill. Starting in the 1890s, the village on the island became known as Frenchboro, named after a Tremont lawyer who helped establish the island's first post office.

The town of Frenchboro, not officially incorporated as a town until 1979, is made up of 12 islands that run from Pond Island southeast to Placentia Island and Black Island, southeast to Great Duck Island and then back westward to Long Island. About 15 miles southeast of Long Island is Mount Desert Rock — a lonely outcropping of ledge that features the state's most remote lighthouse. The Rock is part of Frenchboro. The other islands of Frenchboro are: Harbor, Crow, the two Green Islands, Little Duck and Drum.

Long Island also sits about four miles southeast of Swans Island. The harbor at Burnt Coat, sometimes called Old Harbor, is actually the closest port to Long Island. The daily mail still runs from Burnt Coat, but the harbor is not commonly used by Long Islanders.

Long Island itself is irregularly shaped, and generally considered about

*Lunt Harbor and the village of Frenchboro, looking toward Mount Desert Island, 1989.*

*Daniel L. Lunt and son, Nathaniel D. Lunt, 1989.*

three miles by three miles. It is a generous measurement.

The community of about 50 year-round residents sits on or near the sloping banks of Lunt Harbor, a long horseshoe-shaped inlet that provides protection from all weather but a northeast wind. The sheltered and accessible harbor is one reason why Long Island has survived for more than 180 years while other island communities have died.

Lunt Harbor opens toward Mount Desert Island with the Mount Desert hills looming ghostlike on the horizon. On summer nights, you can sit on a wharf and watch headlights from cars full of tourists as they climb to the peak of Cadillac Mountain, high above Acadia National Park.

The banks make sharply away from Lunt Harbor, providing a perch for mostly modest homes to sit in quiet observance of the daily goings and comings.

The island has just over one mile of paved road that starts at the ferry pier and runs around the cove to Lunt & Lunt Lobster Co., the island's only full-time business. Along the way, the road passes the Frenchboro Post Office, the Frenchboro Historical Society, Becky's Boutique, the Long Island Congregational Church and the Frenchboro Elementary School. The church and school were built in 1890 and 1907 respectively. There is no general store.

Leaving the harbor, paths and dirt roads wind through sometimes-pristine spruce forests, past bogs, lichen-covered ledges and small mossy patches where evergreen branches have given way to occasional glimpses of sunlight. There is little warning before these paths empty onto the island's granite shores, and suddenly the confining, sometimes claustrophobic woods give way to the mighty Atlantic.

The main trails are actually old logging roads. These dirt roads run to Eastern Beach, the Beaver Pond, Southern Cove and partway to Richs Head. A walking trail runs to Northeast Point.

One other dirt road, known locally as the Bennie June road, cuts through the woods, past a small camp, apple trees and cranberries to Gooseberry Point, where smooth, sloping ledges disappear into the ocean on the island's southwestern side.

Looking out from Gooseberry, Swans Island sits off to the right while the hills of Isle au Haut, which helped guide the great European explorers, are visible roughly 12 miles to the southwest. On stormy days here, foam from the churning sea combs across these ledges and fills the small, ratty spruce like angel hair on a Christmas tree.

Counter clockwise from Gooseberry is Little Beach, an aptly named rocky inlet set between solid ledge. Many a driftwood-fueled bonfire has been started here for hotdog roasts and marshmallow toasts. A marsh, occasionally a stream during a wet spring, snakes from Little Beach to the head of Lunt Harbor. About half way along is the old "Meadow." Once popular for ice-skaters, the Meadow has been overtaken by clumps of grass

*©Peter Ralston, 1999*

*John R. Lunt Jr. (left), April (Davis) Wiggins, and Paul "Rusty" Crossman.*

Harbor Island
Lookout Point
Steamboat Beach
Western Point
Lunt Harbor
Salt Ponds
Ferry Pier
Northeast Point
WEST SIDE
Gooseberry Point
EAST SIDE
Eastern Beach
The Meadow
Little Beach
Beaver Pond
House Point
Yellow Head
Big Beach
Burnt Hills
Southwest Point
Eastern Cove
Southern Cove (Deep Cove)
Bluff Head
Carrying Place
NORTH
Western Cove
Sheep Yard
Eastern Point
Richs Head
Flat Point
Union Point

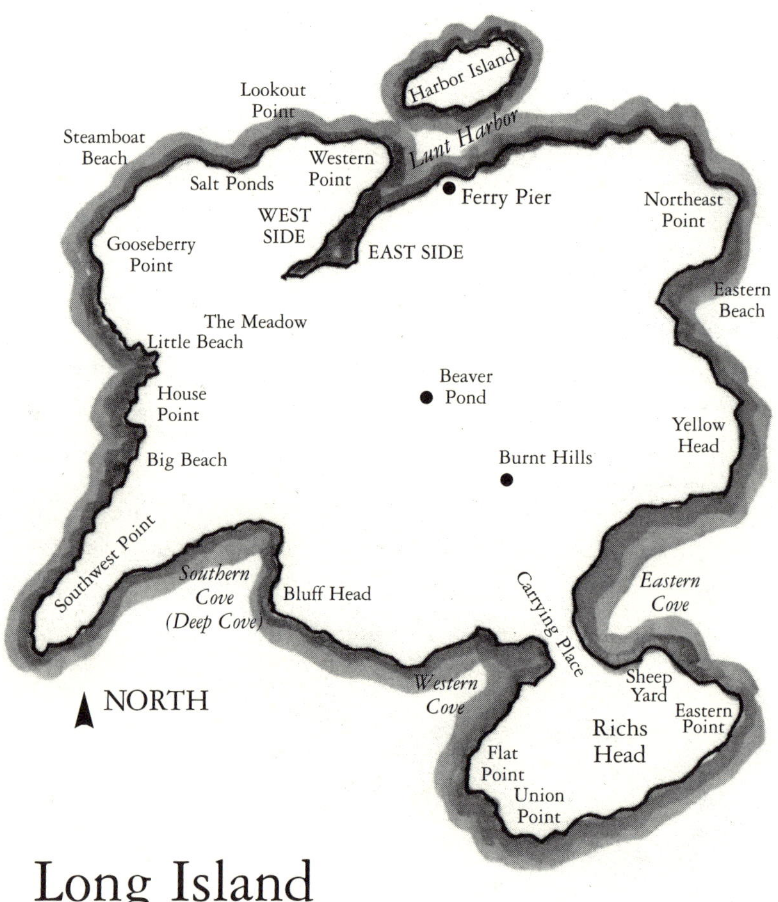

# Long Island

and other growth. It is now better named the Bog.

Next to Little Beach is Middle Beach. Next to Middle Beach, of course, is Big Beach.

Continuing on, Southwest Point, which has trapped a few unsuspecting vessels, juts out to the south like an index finger. On the far side, Southwest Point dissolves into Southern Cove.

The island's most distinguishing geographic feature is Richs Head, the island's easternmost point. The roundish Head is connected to the main island by a narrow neck of rocks, sometimes called the carrying place. On one side of the neck is Eastern Cove; on the other side is Western Cove. Like all beaches and points with Southern views, the Head is exposed to the open sea.

Richs Head, settled by William Rich and his family in the 1820s, hosted the island's only other village for almost 80 years. It was abandoned by the turn of the century. Only the slight depressions of hand-dug cellars near former farmland suggest that three generations of pioneers lived, worked and raised families there.

©*Peter Ralston, 1999*

*Genevieve (McKown) Osier, late 1980s.*

Continuing past Eastern Cove and Yellow Head is Eastern Beach, a popular, although buggy, picnic spot. The stones found here are gloriously polished after tumbling against each other with each retreat and advance of the sea for centuries. The soothing sound of tumbling rocks under the gentle whoosh of the tide is as unmistakable as the cry of seagulls breaking a quiet dawn.

Many island visitors have carried one or two of these stones home to their gardens, patios or mantels. These stones, found at several island beaches, also made their way into the cobblestone streets of growing Eastern cities during the 1800s.

The island's interior is mostly wooded. And mostly spruce at that. One exception is the Beaver Pond, the only natural fresh water pool on the island. The Beaver Pond's main tributary flows over and through a series of smaller beaver dams before running into Southern Cove.

Island animals are few. However, white-tailed deer proliferate, chomping their way through island flower and vegetable gardens and practically shaking the apple trees in the fall.

Meanwhile, bald eagles commonly soar overhead. Seagulls and mallard ducks are everywhere. Loons sometimes swim through the harbor and blue heron remain a common sight. Rabbits have come and gone and come again over the years, as have squirrels, minks and other small animals.

On ledges just off island shores, seals often sun themselves when they are not diving into the ocean then popping just their heads above water to watch the watchers. Sailors may also spot the fins of porpoises as they run across the bay. Further offshore, puffins reward the persistent and ambitious.

*Photo by Lillian J. Lunt*

*A deer washing a house cat on Long Island.*

For two months in July and August, Lunt Harbor is filled with yachts, their passengers taking advantage of the relatively easy and scenic walking trails. Or they might have stopped for a lobster dinner at Lunt's Dockside Deli. Or they might just sit and soak in the nighttime quiet broken only by the lapping of water against hull or the occasional clanging of Harbor Island bell.

On such crisp island evenings, which require sweatshirts even in August, you can look up into the clear night sky, and see more stars than you ever knew existed. In fact, they seem so numerous and hang so close it seems you can almost reach out and touch Heaven itself.

# Chapter Two

# Explorers and Pioneers

Not until the 18th century did Europeans seriously begin to settle and develop the vast and mostly unorganized territory that was known as the District of Maine. Likewise, as pioneers pushed further eastward into the district, which was still controlled by Massachusetts, they finally began settling the islands along the coast of what is now Hancock County. The islands in Penobscot, Blue Hill and Frenchman Bays boasted close access to fishing grounds, vacant land, fertile soil and crucial timber to help supply the developing mainland. During this era, water routes remained the fastest, most effective means of transporting goods to population centers. Overland roads, where they existed, remained slow and cumbersome.

The largest and most famous island in these bays is Mount Desert Island, with its soaring mountains, clear lakes and sheltered harbors. Mount Desert Island faces the Atlantic Ocean with Frenchman Bay to its left and Blue Hill Bay curling around to its right. Mount Desert Island serves as a natural hub for the smaller islands that extend more than eight miles into the Atlantic from its outer shores. As a result, many of the smaller islands did not support thriving communities of their own until Mount Desert Island was settled — which took time.

Indeed, despite the island's magnificent beauty and abundant natural resources, it took roughly 250 years of European exploration and contact before settlers established a permanent community on its shores.

During and long before this evolution, Native American Indians and prehistoric man roamed the landscape and coastline of what is now Maine. Shell heaps and other ancient artifacts found at various sites in Hancock County place man in Maine thousands of years ago.

The modern-era Indians in what is now Maine, as well as Vermont, New Hampshire and large parts of Canada, were collectively considered the Wabanaki — "the people of the dawn." Under the Wabanaki umbrella existed several major tribes whose names, alliances and territories vary slightly depending on the source. However, according to the Smithsonian Institution, the Wabanaki included the Western Abenaki, Eastern Abenaki, Maliseet-Passamaquoddy and Micmac.

While parts of Maine were considered the territory of other groups — Western Abenaki in southern Maine and the Passamaquoddy in parts of northern and eastern Maine — the Eastern Abenaki controlled the largest amount of territory, including the mighty Penobscot River and Mount Desert Island (Snow, *Handbook of North American Indians*, ix). In 1600, some estimates place the total Eastern Abenaki population in Maine at about 10,000 people (Snow, 138).

The Eastern Abenaki chose locations for their camps based on the season and other factors. The summer usually found them on rivers and the coastline where they ate lobsters and clams and hunted porpoises and seals. In the fall, they began to move upstream to harvest and hunt game. Winter might find them in the deep woods hunting moose, while the spring thaw brought them back downriver for planting. (Rolde, *Maine: A Narrative History*, 8). In the 1600s, the Eastern Abenaki also emerged as important fur-trading partners with the English and French, including the colonists at Plymouth.

Despite some apparent common heritage, during the 1500s and 1600s not all Wabanaki tribes coexisted peacefully either within the group or with neighboring Indians. Among the wars during this area was the so-called Tarrantine War that pitted the Micmac (based in what is now Canada) against the Eastern Abenaki. That war, which lasted from roughly 1607 to 1615, included frequent Micmac raids as far west as the Kenduskeag. It ended when a Micmac raiding party killed Bashabes, the great leader of the Eastern Abenaki (Snow, 142).

The confusion that gripped the Eastern Abenaki following Bashabes' death was soon overshadowed by far greater events. Early European explorers unknowingly brought diseases that the Indian immune system was unable to fight. "The Great Dying" that followed wiped out entire Indian coastal villages between 1616 and 1619.

From the Eastern Abenaki also emerged the Penobscot Indians, who by the 1700s were the most powerful tribe in Maine. It was the Penobscots who met the early European visitors to Mount Desert Island and who were among those who visited the islands of Blue Hill Bay each summer.

## The European Explorers

Given the advancing technology and the push for exploration emanating from Europe in the 15th and 16th centuries, it was inevitable that explorers would soon set their sights on what is now the Americas.

The first European definitely known to visit the Maine Coast was the Italian explorer Giovanni de Verrazano in 1524. Verrazano, sailing for the king of France, first struck America in South Carolina. He then sailed northward along the Atlantic seaboard and eventually hit the coast of Maine (Judd, *Maine: The Pine Tree State from Prehistory to the Present,* 37).

The first European known to describe Mount Desert and the surrounding islands in any detail was Estevan Gomez, a former boat commander in Magellan's fleet. Gomez, a Portuguese sailor in service for Spain, crossed Blue Hill Bay in 1525 while searching for a strait to the Pacific (Morison, *The Story of Mount Desert Island,* 7).

The most significant early explorer was Samuel de Champlain, who visited Mount Desert Island in 1604 and named it "l'Isles des Monts-deserts." Champlain, the father of New France, eventually founded and built fortresses at Quebec and gave his name to Lake Champlain on the New York and Vermont borders. In 1604, Champlain worked as a pilot and a guide serving the Sieur de Monts who possessed a grant to "La Cadie," from Henri IV, king of France. La Cadie (translated to Acadia) covered France's North American claim that extended from what is now Philadelphia to Montreal (Morison, 8).

The de Monts expedition sought to establish a French foothold on the new continent. As his first order of business, de Monts built a trading post and ill-fated colony on the St. Croix River. He then sent Champlain further west to continue exploring the coast. In part, Champlain also searched for Norumbega, a mythical walled and wealthy city believed to sit on the banks of what is now the Penobscot River (Morison, 8).

Many explorers left European ports seeking this fabled city, but to no avail. In truth, the city of Norumbega was a myth created by local Indians and embellished by Europeans. In some stories Norumbega was filled with furs and ivory and chunks of gold as big as a fist. The houses were said to sit on pillars of gold, silver and crystal. In some instances, the name Norumbega referred to the entire region around the Penobscot, also hailed in Europe as a proverbial land of milk and honey (Judd, 39).

During his voyage, Champlain passed and named "Ille Haut" or Isle au Haut. He also sailed past the Fox Islands and up the Penobscot (or Pentagoet) River as far as modern Bangor. He encountered tribes of the Eastern Abenaki, but found no city of gold.

In 1607, Champlain again sailed off the coast of Mount Desert. On a manuscript map of 1607, he shows Mount Desert in fairly accurate detail. The two Duck Islands are also shown. Historian Samuel Eliot Morison suggests that since Deer Isle and the Fox Islands are shown somewhat inaccurately, Champlain probably did not sail directly past them, but instead chose a more clear route past Isle au Haut and Matinicus.

Regardless, Champlain unquestionably saw and passed near Outer Long Island during his trips. Unfortunately, Champlain does not list many islands in detail and actually names only a few. Outer Long Island does not appear on nautical charts for another century.

In 1613, Mount Desert Island was briefly settled by the Saint-Sauveur Colony, a French Jesuit expedition also searching for Norumbega. The Jesuits, led by Father Biard, planned to build a colony on the Penobscot. Instead, the expedition first landed on Mount Desert where Chief Asticou, a leader of the Penobscots, persuaded them to remain. Biard's group set up a colony on what is now Somes Sound. However, the colony was driven out within weeks by the English, who learned of the settlement and sent a gun ship from Virginia. At the time, the English and French were battling over claims to the New World. The English did not want the French establishing an outpost on Mount Desert (Morison, 11-15).

Among the other explorers of the Maine Coast was Capt. John Smith, an Englishman from the Virginia Colony. The legendary Smith sailed as far east as the Penobscot River in 1614 and spent several weeks on Monhegan Island.

Gov. Winthrop, sailing on the *Lady Arbella*, drew the first sketches of the Mount Desert hills as he passed them en route from England to settle the Massachusetts Bay Colony in 1630.

Despite all these explorers, no Europeans attempted to settle Mount Desert or its smaller island neighbors for nearly 150 years after the failure of Saint-Sauveur. The reasons are varied and include the island's general isolation and the near-constant conflict between the English and the French and Indians. Many Maine settlements were abandoned during the various New England wars. In fact, because of attacks and fear of attack, Castine was the only permanent community established along the eastern section of the Maine coast between the 1670s and the 1760s (McLane, *Islands of the Mid-Maine Coast*, 9).

## European Foothold

In 1761, the first permanent European settlers with continued descendants on Mount Desert Island — Abraham Somes and James Richardson of Gloucester — built homes in what is now Somesville. At roughly the same time, other pioneers settled the Cranberry Islands, located a short distance beyond Somes Sound.

The Somes and Richardson settlement came as several factors conspired to boost migration to Maine and open the region to settlement, igniting the only eastern migration of families in this country's history.

For one, the various French and Indian Wars were slowly drawing to a close, ending the threat of coastal raids that caused so many English settlers to abandon their villages. Starting in 1758, Lord Jeffrey Amherst took Louisburg, General James Wolfe defeated Marquis de Montcalm on the Plains of Abraham to capture Quebec, and soon Montreal fell to the English as well. The ensuing Treaty of Paris in 1763 essentially eliminated France as a power in the New World. With the defeat of France, its Indian allies, weakened by decades of war and the ravages of disease, also retreated from the coast. Eventually, only the Penobscots, who remained in villages on the Penobscot River, and the Passamaquoddy maintained any significant presence in Maine.

Meanwhile, immigration to Mount Desert Island itself increased after Francis Bernard, Governor of the Province of Massachusetts Bay, became the island's sole proprietor. He encouraged settlement — in fact, he helped entice both Somes and Richardson to settle in the area by offering free land.

In September of 1762, Bernard visited Mount Desert Island in the official sloop *Massachusetts*. He anchored at Southwest Harbor, where he found a handful of settlers. He also found families on Great and Little

Cranberry Islands and Stephen Richardson at Bass Harbor. Bernard surveyed the land and laid out lots and pastures at Southwest. He hoped to establish a thriving community and even built several houses (Morison, 24). However, the American Revolution thwarted Bernard's plans. During the war, his lands were confiscated and he fled to England.

This remained an era of hardship on the sparsely populated frontier. Settlers in the 1780s complained that the Commonwealth provided little help, especially regarding defense and clear land titles. They also complained about the lack of help building adequate schools and churches. Settlers in 1786 described an existence during the prior 25 years that included houses burnt and plundered, cattle killed and fellow settlers captured as prisoners of war.

The period of trouble described included the Revolutionary War. During the war, British warships patrolled the waters, sometimes harassing local fishermen and coastal villages. British troops also occupied Castine for several years and frequently stopped on outer islands for food and other supplies. Despite these problems, the effects of war were relatively short-lived.

Within a few years of the war's end, ownership of Mount Desert Island was divided in half. Essentially, the western half, which now includes Tremont and Southwest Harbor, went to Sir John Bernard. Although he was the son of former Gov. Bernard, John remained loyal to the American cause and was rewarded with a land grant in 1785. Bernard quickly mortgaged the property to a Bostonian and returned to England.

In 1786, the eastern half went to Madame Barthelmy de Gregoire, granddaughter of Sieur de Cadillac. Cadillac had possessed a claim to the island that had been granted by King Louis the 14th. Madame de Gregoire sold lots to settlers, but mixed results forced her to sell most of her holdings to Henry Jackson of Boston. Jackson, who also owned Great and Little Duck Islands, in turn sold much of the property to William Bingham of Philadelphia in 1796. Bingham, a wealthy land speculator, at one point owned two million acres of Maine land.

## *The Islands*

By this time, many smaller islands in the waters around Mount Desert Island were also sprouting tiny communities, usually started by one or two families. By 1785, Isle au Haut boasted five households. Other islands with settlements by the 1780s included another Long Island, near Blue

Hill; Bartlett Island; Robinson's Island, later Tinker; Placentia Island; Gotts Island, and Swans Island (McLane, *Blue Hill Bay*).

Outer Long Island, among the outermost ring of islands on the Maine coast, remained unsettled during this era of island exploration, although explorers and fishermen certainly saw and visited the island for decades. Among its lures was an easily accessed, well-sheltered harbor with a fresh-water spring.

The island first appeared and was named "Long Isle" on charts of the 1720s and 1730s. Those charts used the island's three-hill silhouette, as seen from the southwest, as a key navigational tool. Sailors lined up the hills of Outer Long Island in front of the hills of Mount Desert Island to identify their position while sailing offshore.

The first known reference appears in the the *Coasting Pilot* charts published between 1729 and 1734. The *Pilot* charts were made by Capt. Cyprian Southack who sailed for the crown for Great Britain. The Southack charts also name Duck Island, Mount Desert Rock and "Little Persance" or Placentia. However, the outlines of these islands are very inaccurate.

In 1776, the *Atlantic Neptune* charts compiled by J.F.W. Des Barres show Long Island and the other bay islands in good detail, providing a leap forward in coastal navigation. This collection, with many charts based on surveys by Samuel Holland and engraved and composed by Des Barres, shows several households in the area, including four in Somesville, two in Southwest Harbor, four on the Cranberries and one on Bartlett Island.

The Des Barres maps also show the outline of Outer Long Island in good detail. On the map, Lunt Harbor, Richs Head, Gooseberry Point, Southern Cove, the Salt Ponds and Eastern Beach, although not yet named, are easily discernable. However, both Harbor Island and Crow Island remain unnamed.

Elsewhere on these charts, Johns Island is named, the Sister Islands are called the Seal Islands, Great and Little Duck are named correctly, and Swans Island is mistakenly called Burnt Coal Island instead of Burnt Coat Island. Also, the Green Islands are called the Calf Islands, Eastern Black Island is called Black Island, Placentia Island is called Great Placentia Island, Great Gott Island is called Little Placentia and Little Gott Island is called Barr Island.

To the North of Outer Long Island, Pond Island is named Thrum Cap Island, Opechee is named Charles Island and Eastern Black Island is

*Illustration by Mike Nasuti*

*Blue Hill Bay, 1990s. The islands shown that are part of the town of Frenchboro include: Long Island, Great Duck Island, Black Island, Placentia Island, and Pond Island. The village of Frenchboro is located on Long Island.*

named Grass Island. Regardless of the names used, the important issue is that with these islands identified and accurately outlined on charts, the coast was better primed for growth.

Indeed, with the Des Barres maps in hand and new settlers streaming into Maine after the Revolutionary War, activity on the bay increased dramatically. The islands were finally springing to life. The potential of the islands did not go unnoticed in Boston. And soon much of Blue Hill Bay would be owned by a single man: James Swan.

## *The Island Empire of Col. James Swan*

Following the Revolutionary War, Massachusetts actively pursued land sales in the District of Maine — known as the Eastern Lands — to not only encourage settlement but to help the Commonwealth pay its massive war debts. Taxes were not only inadequate to pay these debts, they were resisted by many rural farming towns, leading to anti-tax uprisings such as Shay's Rebellion in western Massachusetts.

To boost revenues, Massachusetts Gov. John Hancock turned to the 17 million acres of the largely unsettled and unsurveyed land in Maine. Hancock called for land sales as a substitute for taxation and saw Maine as a nearly inexhaustible source of such cash. Starting in 1783, the Commonwealth established a succession of committees dedicated to selling tracts of Maine land.

An early committee in Lincoln County, which covered what is now Hancock and Washington Counties, included men whose names appear in many early coastal deeds: Samuel Phillips Jr. of Andover; Nathaniel Wells of Maine; and John Brooks of Massachusetts. Brooks later became governor of Massachusetts. In 1785, Rufus Putnam, a Maine surveyor, joined the committee. Putnam soon undertook an historically important survey of island settlers from Eastport to Penobscot Bay.

The effort by Massachusetts ushered in the era of land speculation as men of wealth and privilege acquired large tracts of land hoping to establish individual empires. Or at least get rich.

Under these circumstances in 1786, the wealthy, but ill-fated, Colonel James Swan bought Burnt Coat Island (now Swans Island) and 24 surrounding islands, including Outer Long Island. (Two books on Swans Island provide a detailed accounting of Swan's attempts to develop the island and his personal troubles. They are: H.W. Small's *History of Swan's*

*Island, Maine* and Perry Westbrook's *Biography of an Island*. Most information on Swan's life came from those books.)

Swan was born in Fifeshire, Scotland in 1754. He came to America as a young boy in 1765. By the time he turned 22, he was an author, merchant, soldier and politician. As a member of the "Sons of Liberty," he participated in the Boston Tea Party in 1773 and was later wounded at the Battle of Bunker Hill in 1775. He watched George Washington march into Boston in 1776, became Secretary of the Massachusetts Board of War in 1777 and was a member of the Massachusetts Legislature in 1778. Among his books were: *A Dissuasion to Great-Britain and the Colonies, from the Slave-Trade to Africa* in 1773 and *National Arithmetick: or, Observations on the Finances of the Commonwealth of Massachusetts* in 1786.

He amassed great wealth partly through his own dealings and partly through "shady" inheritances, according to the Historian H.W. Small.

In one case, William Dennie, an elderly friend and businessman, left his entire estate to Swan at Swan's behest, instead of to the sons of Dennie's business partner as originally intended. Swan also inherited property from his brother-in-law, who named Swan executor of his will as well as his nephew's guardian. However, Swan failed to follow his brother-in-law's instructions about how to divide investments and property. By the start of the Revolution, Swan owned more than 2.5 million acres, much of it in Pennsylvania, Virginia and Kentucky.

Swan also owned considerable property in Boston after buying land confiscated from Tories (British loyalists) during and after the war. His property included estates on Tremont Street in Boston and in Dorchester where he dined with the likes of Count de Rochambeau, Marquis de Lafayette and Gen. Henry Knox.

In the early 1780s, Swan saw an opportunity to establish a personal island empire in Maine, so he asked for a group of islands. In 1784, the Commonwealth passed a resolve, signed by both Samuel Adams and Hancock, ordering a committee to survey and set a price for Burnt Coat. That November, the Commonwealth sent a man on a 32-day mission to record all observations of Burnt Coat in preparation of its sale to Swan.

Swan, now in his early 30s, purchased the Burnt Coat Group in 1785 and received his deed in 1786.

Swan had grand designs for his new island domain. He built a mansion on the renamed Swans Island. He built a gristmill for corn and barley, built a lumber mill at the millpond and advertised for settlers. He offered deeds of 100 acres to anyone who would come with his family, build a home, cultivate the land, and stay for seven years. His entreaties drew settlers from Mount Desert Island, Sedgwick, Deer Isle and other communities along the coast. Many early residents worked in his lumber mills or in the woods cutting and hauling timber.

Also arriving was Joseph Prince, Swan's primary agent in Maine. Prince built a home on Harbor Island, just outside Burnt Coat Harbor, to oversee the budding community. Prince also built a boat on the island for his use, the 95-ton, 64-foot schooner *Swan* in 1797 (Penobscot Marine Museum, Applebee papers).

But Swan's dream quickly unraveled. He soon found himself consumed by debt as business dealings elsewhere went awry.

In 1787, Swan headed to France. There, with the help of Lafayette, he rebuilt his fortune through government contracts to supply naval stores and salt meat to the army. He also gained control of U.S. debt to France and made money through a complex exchange of notes, supplies and stock.

At one point, he became active in the French Revolution. During this tumultuous era of revolt, Swan attempted to ship proscribed French nobility to America, thus saving them from the guillotine. While his efforts failed and many were executed, some of their belongings, including elegant furniture, tapestry and paintings, passed to America and adorned Swan estates, according to Small.

In the late 1790s, after briefly returning to the United States, Swan again went to France. This time, his ventures proved less successful. By 1808, Swan was confined to the French prison St. Pelagie, buried under crushing debt. A Frenchman claimed Swan owed him 2 million francs, a claim Swan denied. Instead of paying the debt, he chose to remain in prison on principle, according to Small.

What transpired on the Maine coast during the five decades after Swan's original purchase was a complex unraveling of ownership as Swan attempted to pay off his debts, extricate himself from trouble and shelter holdings through mortgages, transfers and sales.

Swan first sold the islands to his agent Prince in 1790 for 300 pounds. In 1795, Prince dealt the islands to another man, who in turn sold them back to Swan within a year, still carrying a price tag of 300 pounds (*Bangor Historical Magazine*, Picton Press, Vol. 1-3, 499-504).

While back in control on Feb. 28, 1798, Swan gave Prince the power of attorney for these islands. This time, Prince also promised 10 acres of land to any fisherman owning his own fishing boat who would settle on the island with his family. To receive the land, settlers had to stay seven years. Prince also moved to convey land to some settlers on Swans Island who had already fulfilled their seven-year commitment.

Prince left Swans Island soon after 1800. He returned to Massachusetts, leaving Swan's property neglected. Eventually the mills closed and the buildings, including the grand mansion, decayed.

Meanwhile, Swan's personal problems grew worse.

By October of 1812, Swan's debtors included Michael O'Maley, a Baltimore businessman and friend. As security for payment, Swan, now in prison, mortgaged 13 islands of the original Burnt Coat Group, including Outer Long Island, to O'Maley. Small speculates the mortgage was given in friendship to protect the property from other debtors. In addition to Outer Long Island and Swans Island, the mortgage included Marshall, Black, and Great and Little Placentia, as well as such property as the grist-mill, farms, stores and mansion.

Whatever the true reason for the O'Maley mortgage, Swan obviously no longer had any personal involvement in the islands and he never saw them again after being imprisoned in 1808. Swan, 76, was released with other debtors on July 28, 1830 by Louis Philippe, King of France. According to Small, Swan did not want to leave prison and tasted freedom for only three days. During his release he fulfilled one wish, to again embrace his friend Lafayette. Swan died as he prepared to return to jail.

In his will, Swan left large sums of money and other forms of wealth to his children and the city of Boston. However, they received little or nothing because Swan's estate was declared hopelessly insolvent (*Bangor Historical Magazine*, 499-504).

Meanwhile, on the coast of Maine, far from French prisons or Boston estates, Swan's legacy was rather simple: a group of islands in a tangled legal mess.

# Chapter Three

# Island Settlement

Despite the business failures and personal misfortunes of Col. James Swan, the islands he purchased and attempted to settle were becoming increasingly active, even while the man himself sat in a French debtor's prison. With most islands closer to Mount Desert Island inhabited by the 1790s, Outer Long Island[1] soon followed.

While no Europeans settled on Outer Long Island during the 1700s, Maine Indians visited seasonally for decades, if not centuries. Shell heaps at Eastern Beach were likely deposited by Wabanaki tribes who spent summers on the various islands. The Wabanakis, which included the Penobscot tribe, frequently summered along the coast during the 17th, 18th and even 19th centuries. Numerous shell heaps and burial grounds have also been found on neighboring Swans Island (Westbrook, 32). A small island just north of Swans Island is named Orono in honor of a great leader of the Penobscots.

According to Outer Long Island legend, Penobscots kept a camp on Yellow Head, not far from Eastern Beach, into the 19th century. The Penobscots also spent time at camps on the banks of Lunt Harbor. They collected island sweetgrass from fields near the present-day ballfield to

---

[1] The name for Long Island has evolved over the years. During most of the 1800s, Long Island was popularly called Outer Long Island to distinguish it from other inhabited Long Islands closer to the mainland. In keeping with that theme, the name will appear most frequently as Outer Long Island in Part One of this book. The name Frenchboro did not exist until the 1890s.

weave baskets. One seasonal camp, located near the house owned in 1999 by Marjorie (Dalzell) Giamo, still stood when the first settlers arrived in the early 1800s, according to island legend. A cellar hole can still be identified.

Regardless of legend, it is documented that Indians paddled into Lunt Harbor in birch bark canoes until at least 1839, nearly two decades after the island emerged as a year-round community.

## *Long Island Pioneers*

The settling of Outer Long Island was spurred in part by its timber, which early settlers harvested and shipped to feed the growing demand for wood at mainland markets. The local waters also teemed with such fish as cod, halibut and sole, providing both food and income. The fish, caught in open boats using lines and hooks, were either eaten or dried and shipped to Boston and other ports.

The island's soil, unlike that of some other Blue Hill Bay islands such as Pond and Bartlett, was not very fertile. There is no evidence of large farms until the Rich family settled what became known as Richs Head in the 1820s. Even the Rich farm was considerably smaller than those on neighboring islands.

Details of the island's earliest settlers remain shrouded.

William Davis is believed to be the island's first temporary settler in 1797 (Small, 75). Davis originally settled on Swans Island in 1794, but moved to Outer Long Island about three years later. He stayed for only a short time, and was apparently gone by 1800. No census record places Davis or anyone else on Outer Long Island in 1790, 1800 or 1810. Other than Small's book, no primary account, record or deed yet found confirms that Davis lived on the island during this era.

Later in the 1800s, other Davises, likely descendants or relatives of either William Davis or John Davis (John Davis lived on Placentia in 1820) reappeared on the island and played important roles in island life.

During the second decade of the 1800s, island activity picked up.

Early traders frequented the island seeking to harvest its timber. The men who claimed property or built log cabins during the first decade or so were likely seasonal or transient residents who also kept homes on the mainland. Outer Long Island didn't develop a thriving, sustained community until the Lunt family, led by brothers Israel B. Lunt and Amos Coffin Lunt Jr., arrived in 1822.

However, through 1820, a handful of pioneers helped tame the island. These men included John Perkins, Samuel Allen, John Walls, William Post, William Stevens and Jacob Lunt.

*John Perkins* — Perkins laid claim to a 100-acre lot at the head of the harbor by 1812. He eventually built a house and probably lived on the island for at least several months of the year, but little is known of his activities. George B. Perkins joined him on the island. A prominent coastal family who lived in Castine and Bangor during the early 1800s had the surname Perkins. John and George probably were members of that family.

John Perkins maintained ties to Outer Long Island for more than a decade, signing several documents as a witness there in the early 1820s. He sold his house and property to Israel B. Lunt in 1826 and doesn't appear again in the island's history. Neither John nor George ever appear in island census records.

*John Walls* — Even less is known about the early activities of John Walls. Walls claimed about 75 acres on the island's east side as early as 1809. John Walls is mentioned on a later deed, but no other documents or records have been found that place him on the island during this era. The Walls land was eventually sold to Abner Lunt, then to Abner's son Israel Lunt II and later to a William Davis in 1858. While census records do not show a John Walls on Outer Long Island during this era, they do place him on Placentia in 1820 and on Black Island in 1830. An Abigail Walls, a widow who later married Richard Lunt, is listed on Outer Long Island in 1840. A Capt. John Walls did marry Israel B. Lunt 's daughter Amanda in the late 1840s. However, that John Walls was still only 25 when he died in an 1851 shipwreck.

*Samuel Allen* — Samuel Allen claimed at least 100 acres on the west side in 1819. For a short time during the early 1800s, Western Point was known locally as Allen's Point. Allen sold part of his land to John Rich and Abner Lunt and then to Bartholomew Russell Lunt in 1833. Samuel Allen does not appear in island census records of either 1820 or 1830.

*William Post and William Stevens* — William Post laid claim to land on the harbor's west side. Post may have lived on Long Island even before Perkins. A brief island history written by an unknown grammar school student several decades ago mentions Post as the island's first settler in the early 1800s. Where that information came from is unknown. In the mid-

1820s, Post was involved in a legal fight over land claims with agents of James Swan. In 1822, Post rented a house on the island owned by a man named William Stevens (sometimes spelled Stephens). Stevens, of Georgetown, Maine, owned about 100 acres on the west side of the harbor. Stevens sold his claim in 1823 for $40. It is unknown whether Stevens lived there, but his land included a house. Neither Post nor Stevens ever appear in an island census.

*Jacob Lunt, the first* — Jacob Lunt 1st staked a claim to about 100 acres on Northeast Point in 1812. His land included Eastern Beach. Jacob's ownership is referred to in a deed between himself and William Davis in 1852. (Over the years multiple men named William Davis lived on the island. Given the timeframe, it is extremely unlikely this William Davis is the same man who allegedly lived on Outer Long Island in 1797. But which William Davis is unknown). Jacob Lunt 1st was an uncle to Israel B. and Amos Jr.

Given the 1812 date, Jacob was likely the first Lunt to claim land on Outer Long Island. Despite this, he does not appear on any island census until 1850, by which time he lived with his brother Abner. Jacob probably lived on the island with his relatives earlier, but only the heads of households were named in census records until 1850. Jacob never married and died an island bachelor. (Despite his lack of children, Jacob was called Jacob 1st to differentiate him from his nephew Jacob.)

While it is unlikely any of these men lived year-round on the island, or brought their families, they did open the island to trade, activity and civilization, thus blazing a trail for future permanent settlers.

## First Settlers

Regardless of what the early pioneers did, by 1820, Outer Long Island had three households and a population of 19, according to census records. The three houses were headed by William Pomeroy, Thomas Pomeroy (sometimes spelled Pumroy, and later Pomroy) and Asa Smith.

Asa Smith, who claimed 100 acres of land on the island's west side, did not stay on Outer Long Island for long. Smith (likely Asa Smith 2nd) had family on Swans Island and returned there by 1824. He never reappears in an island census. Smith also owned Harbor Island just off Outer Long Island until 1827. He built a landing on that island and continued to conduct business there even after he moved.

Like Smith, neither William Pomroy nor Thomas Pomroy reappear in a town census after 1820. However, three of William's daughters — Nancy, Eliza and Laurania — all married Lunts and remained on, or returned to, Outer Long Island.

Two male descendants of William — John and Abner — both sea captains, lived on Outer Long Island into adulthood before moving to West Tremont in the mid-1800s.

Another Pomroy, Francis, married Israel's half sister, Jerusha (sometimes spelled Jerushia). Francis must have been related to the above five Pomroys, but apparently was not a sibling.[2]

William Pomroy, who lived on the island with his wife Mary (also called Polly), cut cordwood and built a fishhouse on the harbor's east side during his stay. He leased part of his fishhouse to Israel starting in 1823 and then sold all or most of his land to Israel in 1825. Mary (Beal) Pomroy, who lived on Long Island in 1850, is buried in West Tremont. William is buried in Massachusetts.

### Israel B. and Amos Coffin Lunt Jr.

Israel B. Lunt Sr. arrived on the shores of Outer Long Island with his brother Amos C. Lunt Jr. in 1822 (see Chapter Four) and they quickly became the driving forces behind island growth. Israel and Amos married two island sisters, Nancy and Eliza Pomroy, respectively. It is unknown whether they met the women on Long Island or met them on Mount Desert and then became more familiar with Long Island after visiting their future father-in-law. The two young men may also have visited the island with their Uncle Jacob who staked a claim to island land in 1812.

In any event, the two brothers were soon followed to Outer Long Island by their father, Amos C. Lunt Sr., and his brother, Abner Lunt, and their families.

With the arrival of the Lunts, a community set roots. The Rich family,

---

[2] The Pomroy genealogy, like that of the Rich family, remains difficult to understand. A bible kept by Agnes Joyce Bridges Davis lists her grandmother as Nancy Pomroy Lunt and names Nancy's sisters as Eliza Lunt, Maria Tinker, Laurania Lunt, Emily Brown, Caroline and Sarah Dix and lists her brothers as John and Abner Pomroy. A Pomroy family history compiled by Rhoda Murphy Hamor in 1984 changes Maria to Harriett and omits Eliza, Emily and Caroline. However, the Hamor history names their parents as William and Mary (Beal) Pumroy (Pomroy). A handful of nagging questions concern the Pomroy family, including the parentage of Francis. For one thing, the 1820 census places all but one child in the household of Thomas Pomroy, not William Pomroy. Second, why is there a discrepancy between the two family accounts of Nancy's siblings.

who moved to Maine from Massachusetts in the late 1700s, settled and claimed land on what became Richs Head also in the early 1820s. That family sold their last pieces of land on Richs Head in 1899. Members of the Rice family also settled there in the 1820s.

Exactly when Richs Head was settled is unknown. Neither Rich nor Rice is listed in the 1820 census, but Rich was clearly on the island by 1823. No pictures have been found that clearly show how many, or what style houses were built on the Head either. In the 1970s, the remains of seven shallow cellars were clearly identified, but some may have been from barns or outbuildings. A map in 1860 shows only three households on Richs Head. However, enough children lived there during the mid-1800s to warrant keeping school. There were at least two farms on The Head during the 1800s.

*Photo by Dean L. Lunt*

*Richs Head, 1990s. The far point, "Sheep Yard," is where settlers herded sheep to shear. The Head wharf was near this cove and the houses were built near this field.*

Meanwhile, on the main harbor, Israel B. Lunt soon purchased the stakes of Pomroy, Perkins, Stevens and others. He also started a business shipping wood, paving stones and dried fish. He eventually purchased title to the entire island in 1835. Early islanders sold all or some of the goods they harvested to Israel, who in turn shipped them down the coast.

Following is an agreement with William Rich, the earliest yet found of Israel's emerging island business. The deed, signed in 1823, was witnessed by Israel's brother Amos Jr., Asia (Asa) Smith and George Perkins.

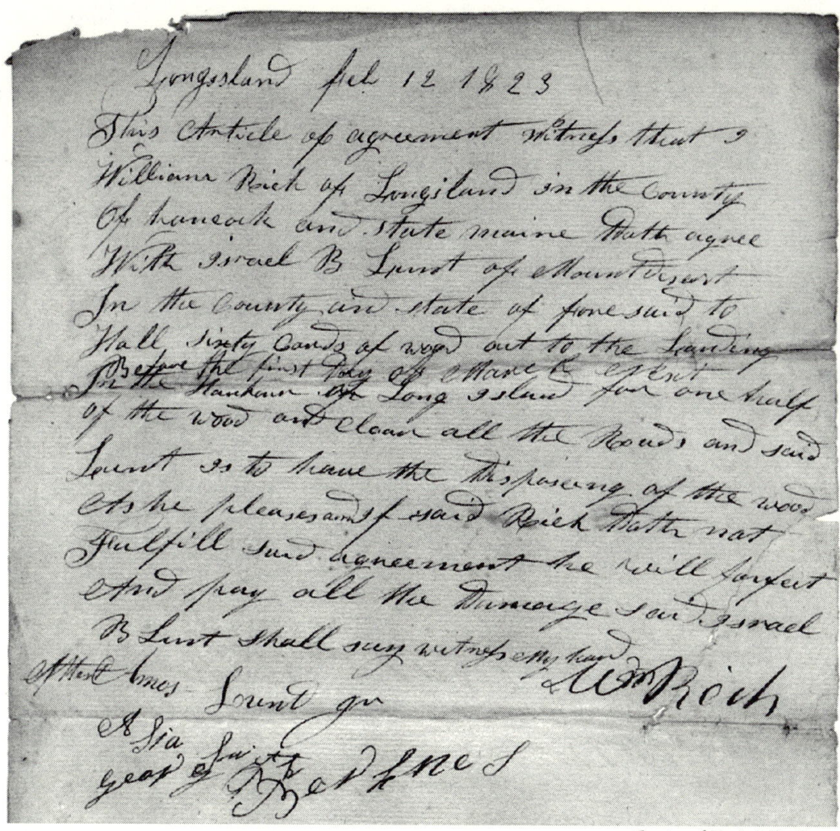

*Courtesy of Marjorie D. Giamo*

*In this business agreement dated Feb. 12, 1823, William Rich agreed to deliver 60 cords of wood to Israel B. Lunt.*

Long Island, Feb. 12, 1823
This article of agreement witnesses that I William Rich of Long Island in the County of Hancock and State of Maine doth agree with Israel B. Lunt of Mount Desert in the County and State of foresaid to hall sixty cords of wood before the first day of March out to the Landing in the harbor of Long Island for one half of the wood and (unreadable) and said Lunt is to have the disposing of the wood as he pleases and if said Rich doth not fulfill said agreement he will forfeit and pay all the damages said Israel B. Lunt shall say witness my hand.

Wm. Rich.

attest Amos Lunt Jr., Asia Smith, George B. Perkins

The following agreement between Israel and his father-in-law, William Pomroy, was signed about two months later. Franklin Spofford was an early business partner of Israel. While the preceding document was a deal involving wood, this one is for fish, illustrating Israel's market expansion and need for additional storage.

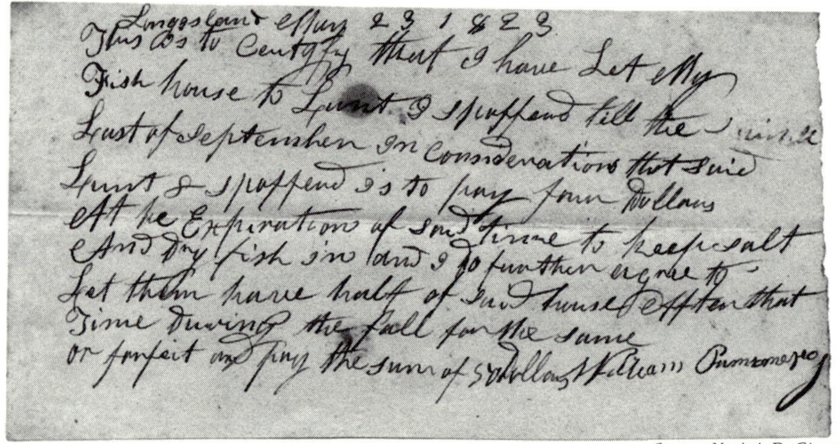

Courtesy Marjorie D. Giamo

*In May 1823, Israel B. Lunt and his partner Franklin Spofford rented a fish house from William (Pomroy) Pumeroy to store salt and dry fish.*

Long Island May 23, 1823
This is to certify that I have let my Fish house to Lunt & Spofford till the last of September in consideration that said Lunt & Spofford is to pay four dollars at the expiration of said time to keep salt and dry fish in and I do further agree to let them have half of said house after that time during the fall for the same or forfeit and pay the sum of 5 dollars. — William Pumeroy.

And so an island community was born.

Israel B., Amos Jr., Amos Sr. and Abner Lunt, along with William Rich and Thomas Rice, headed the six households on the island in 1830. The population was 42. These settlers, their families, in-laws and descendants (along with the soon-to-arrive Davis family) formed the island's backbone, spurred its growth and shaped its development well into the next century. They set in motion the forces that transformed the island from a wilderness outpost to an organized plantation to a town that now survives as one of only 14 year-round island communities.

## *The Aftermath of Col. Swan*

As Outer Long Island began to emerge as a full-fledged community, one nagging problem remained from its pioneer days: the fallout from Col. James Swan's financial turmoil. Swan originally purchased Burnt Coat and 24 surrounding islands in 1786. His financial problems left him jailed in France by 1808 and he never returned to the United States again. But his agents lurked around the islands and harassed settlers for decades. Executors of his will still worked to dispose of his possessions in the 1840s.

The Swan situation presented several problems for islanders; most crucially it created an uncertain state concerning rightful land claims.

On March 10, 1817, Rufus B. Allyn of Belfast, a lawyer representing Michael O'Maley, went to Swans Island and other islands to notify settlers in O'Maley's name that he was taking possession of their property. O'Maley was a friend and former business partner of Swan who received some of Swan's islands as security for a debt. The Allyn visit was probably a legal move intended to pave the way for future legal action if necessary.

Indeed, despite the ownership changes and financial intrigue that had transpired since Swan's original purchase, settlers continued to arrive on the islands, stake claims and build homes. Some were probably drawn by Swan's original promise of free land, while others came because land seemed available. Still others had purchased lots from earlier settlers and believed they now had rightful ownership.

With these residents ensconced on the islands, Allyn returned in the 1820s demanding payments. He executed several deeds and mortgages between 1823 and 1839. But some people refused to pay, believing they were entitled to the land as original settlers.

Among the deeds executed were several to lots on Swans Island, and other islands that became part of Long Island Plantation. The parties and transactions included: Moses Bridges of Sedgwick, who bought Eastern Calf Island in 1823; Peter Powers, who bought Western Calf Island in 1822; Robert Mitchell, who bought land on Placentia in 1824; and Daniel Hamblen, who bought land on Placentia in 1825 (Small, 39-40).

O'Maley took action against some settlers who either did not pay or refused to leave. It seems unlikely O'Maley actually wanted the land, but instead he simply tried to squeeze islanders for as much cash as he could. Among those he took to the Court of Common Pleas over land were

Alexander Staples of Burnt Coat Island, Benjamin Daws (Dawes) of Black Island and William Post of Outer Long Island.

The Post case involved six acres and O'Maley sought damages of $300 in the lawsuit. Post was served notice on Long Island by a deputy sheriff in December of 1824 (Maine State Archives, Court of Common Pleas).

When the case went to court in March 1825, Post — like both Staples and Daws — failed to appear. The judge ruled Post should vacate the property and pay court costs of $12.58. He did not award damages.

Exactly what happened in the wake of the court decision is unknown, but O'Maley and his agents did not go away. Neither did Post, who, while forced to give up his claim, remained on Outer Long Island or at least maintained ties to the island into the latter 1820s.

In the spring of 1834, O'Maley filed a lawsuit against Israel B. Lunt. By 1834, 36-year-old Israel was a successful business owner and a man who had purchased the claims of numerous early settlers. After about 12 years as a settler, he was the dominant figure on Outer Long Island.

O'Maley accused Israel of wrongful possession and the lawsuit covered Israel's house, wharves and buildings. It also encompassed land Israel had purchased from other settlers, including 20 acres formerly occupied by Franklin Spofford, William Pomroy and Joseph Remick.

The case, originally set for April of 1834, was continued until October. For the hearing, Israel hired Hezekiah Williams to argue his case against O'Maley's lawyer, Allyn. The court found against Israel, but the young businessman vowed to fight on. He immediately appealed to the Supreme Judicial Court in Castine.

However, neither party appeared at the SJC when the case was called in 1835. Instead, the two men reached an out-of-court settlement in which Israel purchased the entire island for $600.

The purchase not only cleared up any claims O'Maley may have had against Israel, but also any claims O'Maley may have had against other island settlers.

Israel eventually transferred about 400 acres to settlers around the harbor. Unlike O'Maley, he also recognized existing claims as legal, and eventually either transferred ownership of that land or simply let the claims stand.

His purchase no doubt eliminated any unease about the validity of claims and no doubt O'Maley was happy to be clear of unproductive and unwanted property. Israel later purchased several smaller islands from the executors of Swan's will.

Israel's deed brought Outer Long Island, thought to contain 1,132 acres based on Swan's original deed, into its present-day cycle of title, ownership and control. Most importantly, it officially and forever vanquished O'Maley, Allyn and the remnants of Swan's would-be empire from the shores of Outer Long Island.

The text of the original deed[3] follows:

> Know all men by these presents that I Michael O'Maley of Baltimore in the State of Maryland a citizen of the United States, at present a resident of Paris in the Kingdom of France, in consideration of six hundred dollars to me paid by Israel B. Lunt of an unincorporated place called Long Island in the County of Hancock in the State of Maine Trader the receipt whereof is hereby acknowledged, do hereby grant, sell and convey unto him said Israel B. Lunt his heirs and assigns, a certain parcel of land situate in the County of Hancock aforesaid, being Long Island containing one thousand one hundred thirty two acres 130 rods and being one of the islands formerly conveyed to James Swan formerly of Boston Esquire by Samuel Philips Junr. Nathaniel Wills and John Brooks Esquire, a committee in behalf of the commonwealth of Massachusets by deed bearing date the seventh day of July in the year of our Lord 1786 and recorded in the land Office of Massachusetts volume first Page 409 — To have and to hold the premises hereby granted to him said Israel B. Lunt his heirs and assigns to his & their use and behalf forever. And I said Michael O'Maley do hereby covenant with said Israel B. Lunt that I will to the extent of the aforesaid consideration warrant and defend the premises hereby granted to him said Israel B. Lunt his heirs and assigns against the lawful claims of all persons lawfully claiming under said commonwealth of Massachusets or said James Swan or me the said Michael O'Maley or lawfully claiming by virtue of taxes heretofore lawfully assessed on same premises by the author-ity of the State of Maine but against no other claims whatsoever. —

---

[3] A copy of this deed can be found in the Hancock County Registry of Deeds in Ellsworth. This deed is taken from the original handwritten deed kept by Israel B. Lunt. The deed was kept over the years by Israel's descendants and recently rediscovered by Marjorie Giamo amongst the belongings of her late mother, Vera (Ross) Dalzell. Marjorie has donated the deed and other papers to the Frenchboro Historical Society.

In witness whereof I Rufus B. Allyn of Belfast in the County of Waldo in the State of Maine Esquire authorized by a letter of attorney & a letter of substitution recorded in the registry of deeds in said County of Hancock have hereunto set the name and seal of Michael O'Maley this thirtieth day of June in the year of our Lord Eighteen hundred and thirty five.

Signed, Sealed and delivered
in the presence of us                     Michael   O'Maley
F.B. Morgan

Hancock SS June 30, 1835. The aforementioned Michael O'Maley appeared by the said Rufus B. Allyn his attorney and acknowledged this instrument to be the free act and deed of him the said Michael O'Maley

Before me           Francis B. Morgan
                              Justice of the Peace

Rec'd July 1st 1835 & Entered by F.B. Morgan Regr.
    A true copy as of record Vol. 60. Page 422
    Attest J.S. Lord Regr.
    Pr. A. A. Bartlett Clerk.

*Chapter Four*
# The Lunts

S oon after settlement, Outer Long Island was often called "Lunt's Long Island" to further differentiate it from similarly named islands and in deference to its leading family.

Starting in the 1820s with the four original Lunts who brought their families — Israel B., Amos Jr., Amos Sr. and Abner Sr. — the overwhelming majority of island residents for the next century were either Lunt descendents or Lunt in-laws. Those four pioneers alone produced 52 children, many of whom lived on the island. The prominent island surnames who married into the family during the 1800s included: Pomroy, Rich, Rice, Davis, Teel, Dalzell, Ross and Van Norden. By the early to mid-1900s it was difficult to find any island resident, regardless of last name, who didn't have ties to those four original Lunts.

But, while the names Lunt and Long Island quickly became synonymous in the early 1800s, the family's journey to the island and its determined building of a community actually began 250 years earlier when America's first Lunt, 21-year-old Henry, stepped off the English ship *Mary and John* and onto the shores of the New World.[1]

---

[1] Most information on the Lunt family prior to 1800 comes from either *A History of the Lunt Family in America* by Thomas S. Lunt or *The Ancestry of Abel Lunt* by Walter Goodwin Davis. Both books deal strictly with genealogy. Information on family and events was extracted and written into a narrative by the author. It was combined with information from other sources such as church and town records and deeds. The T.S. Lunt book — an invaluable resource on the Lunt family, despite some gaps and mistakes — includes a crucial 600-word excerpt (p. 68-70) from a now-lost memoir of Abner Coffin Lunt's eldest son, Amos. That excerpt briefly details his father's life.

## Settling Massachusetts

Henry Lunt, possibly of South Marston, Wiltshire, sailed from the River of Thames in London during March of 1634, according to Walter Goodwin Davis in *The Ancestry of Abel Lunt*. Henry, like many of his fellow passengers, was likely prompted to emigrate by three influential Puritan pastors. The group landed in Ipswich of the Massachusetts Bay Colony two months later. Most who arrived on the *Mary and John*, commanded by Robert Sayres, became the original settlers of Newbury. Henry, who married Anne (last name unknown) in 1638, was given several acres of land on the banks of Quascaqunquen — now the Parker — River and became a successful farmer. He took the Freeman's Oath May 2, 1638. After his death in 1662, Henry left his estate to Anne and their seven children (Davis, 6).

---

### The First Six Generations of Lunts in America

1. Henry Lunt, d. 1662, m. Anne. First Lunt to America
2. Daniel, 1641 - 1702, m. Hannah Coker
3. Henry Jr., 1669 - 1738, m. Elizabeth (Wood) (Chute) Stickney
4. Abner, b. 1707, m. Hannah Stickne (Stickney?)
5. Abner Jr., b. 1732, m. Merriam Coffin
6. Abner Coffin Lunt, 1752-1792, m. Elizabeth Hodgdon. Moved to Maine, 1769. First Lunt to Mount Desert Island, 1789
   - A. Amos Coffin, 1772 - 1851, m. Mary Bartlett, m. Priscilla Butler. To Long Island between 1825 and 1827
   - B. Miriam, b. 1774, d. infancy
   - C. Elizabeth (Betsy), b. 1778, m. Amos Allen
   - D. Abner, 1781 - 1855, m. Jane Dawes. To Long Island, between 1825 - 1827
   - E. Jacob, b. 1784, unmarried. To Long Island, 1812 - 1827
   - F. Micajah, 1787 - 1804
   - G. Bartholomew Russell, 1790 - 1825
   - H. Mary, b. 1792

---

Henry's oldest son Daniel, who married Hannah Coker, left the farm for the sea — the first of many generations of Lunts who became mariners and sea captains. Daniel ran a coasting vessel that among other things carried malt to a Newbury innkeeper and iron to Boston (Davis, 9).

Starting with Daniel, some Lunts rose to prominence on the ocean as either traders or soldiers. For example, Cutting Lunt served as a lieutenant to John Paul Jones on the famed *Bon Homme Richard*, and Benjamin Lunt sailed a privateer during the Revolutionary War. Still others died as young men simply trying to earn a living from the sea.

Three generations after Daniel in the 1760s, Abner Lunt Jr. and Merriam (Coffin) Lunt still lived in Newbury. The young couple were raising five children: Abner Coffin, Miriam, Jacob, Mary and Micajah. But Abner Jr., while commanding his vessel on a return voyage from the West Indies, died in stormy seas off Cape Ann. Abner's death left Merriam to raise five children alone.

## Journey to the Maine Coast

A short time after Abner Jr.'s death, his eldest son, Abner Coffin Lunt, sought new frontiers to the north. The 18-year-old boarded a ship and sailed for the district of Maine, landing in Scarborough in about 1769. In that coastal town, Abner met Elizabeth Hodgdon and they married Sept. 13, 1771 at the Second Parish Congregational Church.

While living in Maine, Abner fought in the Revolutionary War, and was present at the siege of Castine. There are four listings for Abner Lunt of Scarborough in *Massachusetts Soldiers and Sailors in the War of the Revolution*, all presumed to be one person. Abner served in Captain John Rice's Company in the 31st Regiment of foot soldiers. He also marched into Boston following its siege by the British and marched from both Fort Ticonderoga and Fort George.

Abner Coffin Lunt's younger brother, Capt. Micajah Lunt, also participated in many battles, including partaking in the ill-fated expedition to the Penobscot River. During the Penobscot expedition, Micajah served on the *Vengeance* with Capt. Thomas. The ship, and the rest of the American fleet, was driven up river by the British and burned.

Following the war, Micajah, after whom Abner named one of his children, lived with Abner for two years in Scarborough, before returning to Massachusetts where he became a prominent merchant and importer. His son, also Micajah, later headed shipping companies, steam mills and banks and served as a state senator in Massachusetts.

Abner chose to remain in Maine.

However, after about 13 years in Scarborough, Abner and Elizabeth, and their children Amos Coffin Lunt, 12, Elizabeth or "Betsy," 7, Abner, 4, and 8-month-old Jacob, continued their journey along the coast. (A first daughter, Miriam, died as an infant in 1774). The family sailed for North Fox Island (North Haven) on June 2, 1785 and landed at Bartlett Harbor seven days later. Abner spent two years living in a log home on more than 262 acres cutting wood, farming and trading goods. He and Elizabeth had their fourth son, Micajah, while living on North Fox.

While on North Fox, Abner also bought half interest in a 70-ton sloop, *Industry*, and started a coasting business. But the *Industry* was ill-fated from the start, kicking off several business misfortunes for Abner, now in his mid-30s. The *Industry* was first cast away on Georges Island (Presumably Georges Island in Muscongus Bay) during a snowstorm. Following repairs and several successful coasting trips, he hired a crew and set sail for Boston loaded with cordwood. En route, the *Industry* was rammed by another schooner and sunk. Abner then bought part interest in the schooner *Betty* using cordwood as payment, but he was soon forced to give up the ship to cover his remaining debt.

Following that loss, Abner sold his 260 acres near Bartlett Harbor to John Williams and Cyril Brown on July 9, 1787 (*Bangor Historical Magazine*, Vols. 4-6, 1257). He moved to a 150-acre lot on South Fox Island (now Vinalhaven) and lived there with his family until December 1789.

Finally, 37-year-old Abner, his wife Elizabeth, who was six months pregnant with Bartholomew Russell Lunt, and their children, Amos, 17, Betsy, 11, Abner, 8, Jacob, 5, and Micajah "Cager," 2, sailed out of Penobscot Bay and arrived on Mount Desert Island. The family lived on 100 acres of land in Pretty Marsh that Abner purchased from Samuel Milliken. They were the first Lunts on Mount Desert Island.

Meanwhile, Abner continued his ambitious and ill-fated ventures, earning a little money through labor and drive, then losing it.

In early 1790, four months after arriving in Pretty Marsh, Abner traveled to Rhode Island to collect on some debts. He used the money to purchase a 20-ton schooner. But fate again stepped in. Abner's new schooner sank in a spring storm off Cape Cod, killing his one crew member. Abner then headed to Salem, Massachusetts where he started work on a vessel bound for the Penobscot River after salmon.

During his various trips, Abner remained absent from his family for lengthy stretches — a situation that apparently didn't go unnoticed by the early fathers of Mount Desert. Abner's family was officially "warned out" of Mount Desert in July of 1790. Being "warned out" was not a notice to leave, but a formal way for the town to tell individuals, usually recent settlers or sojourners, that they were not the legal responsibility of the town and the town would not support them if the family could not pay debts or care for themselves. The warning, as it appears in Alice MacDonald Long's *Vital Records of Mount Desert Island Maine and Nearby Islands 1776 - 1820* (page 80):

Hancock SS To Stephen Richardson one of the Constables of the Town of Mount Desert in said County.
GREETING
You are in the Name of the Commonwealth of Massachusetts Derected to Warn and give Notice unto Abner Coffin Lunt of Newbery in the County of Essex and Rubin Noble of Northyarmouth in the County of Comburland Labourer who has Latly Come into this Town for the purpose of abiding therein not having Obtained the Towns Consent therefor that they Depart the limets thoreof with their wives and Children and all under there Care within fifteen Days. And also Sarah Meder likwise the Negro that is called by the Name of Nippe Together with Robart Scott & his wife and child And of this Precept with your doings thereon you are to make Return into the Office of the Clark of the Town within twenty Days next coming that such further Proceedings May be had in the premises as the Law Directs. Given under our hands Seals at Mount desert this third Day of July A: Domini 1790
Ezra Young
Thomas Richardson
Daves Wasgatt
Selectmen for Mount desert
Return July ye. 20th 1790 Agrable to the above Warrant I have warned Rubin Noble with his wife and Children Viz Pressallah Sarah born at Northyarmouth Susana Nathan and Mary born at Dear Island, also Abner Coffin Lunt & his wife & Children Viz Amos Elizabeth & Abner & Jacob born at Scurbrough & Cager born at Venalhaven; also the Negro called Neppe; also William Scott with his wife & child from Nove Scotta; and also Sarah Meder of Salom in the County of Essex.

Stephen Richardson Constable
Mount Desert August ye. 16th 1790

While Abner worked his way home from Rhode Island, his son Amos Coffin Lunt took a job paying $40 per year to help support his mother and his five brothers and sisters.

After finally returning home in August, Abner began yet another business venture. That fall, he and Amos cut and hauled about 50 cord of wood, which they exchanged for a small fishing schooner. Using that boat they sailed from Pretty Marsh to tiny York Island, located just off Isle au Haut. On York, father and son built a log cabin and spent the winter cutting wood, hunting and trapping.

Scraping together money after a year on York, they stepped up in vessel class, buying a two-masted schooner to continue fishing. Part of their business was making barrels of oil from dogfish livers.

In brief memoirs cited by T.S. Lunt, Amos does not mention visiting Outer Long Island. However, the island is visible from Isle au Haut and the other areas where Abner and Amos sailed. It is conceivable the two men used the harbor at Outer Long Island for shelter and that Amos later told his sons about it.

Amos and his father worked together on York Island for two years, but Amos was soon forced out on his own. In the spring of 1792, after 21 years of helping blaze a trail on the frontiers of Maine, Abner died.

Amos wrote (T.S. Lunt, 69): *"He took off his flannel shirt and put on a fine linen shirt, dressed up, and went to Deer Island to sell his cord wood. While there he was taken with Pleurisy and died, May 4, 1792, aged 39 years, 7 months, 2 days."*

## *Amos Coffin Lunt*

Abner's family — Betsy, 14, Abner, 11, Jacob, 8, Micajah, 5, and Bartholomew Russell, 2 — remained in Pretty Marsh, now supported by 20-year-old Amos. Elizabeth, two months pregnant with Mary when her husband died, remained in Pretty Marsh for another 32 years until she moved to Vinalhaven in 1824.

Life for coastal pioneers was difficult and hazardous.

Like Abner, some of his children died young. Micajah drowned in 1804 while hunting in a birch bark canoe at Mount Desert. He was 17. Abner's youngest son, Bartholomew Russell Lunt, whose name reappeared in later generations, was lost at sea with his entire crew in 1825. He was 35.

The Lunt homestead and farm in Pretty Marsh was near the landing for Bartlett Island, founded and settled by Christopher Bartlett in 1762. Christopher's daughter, Mary, was born on Bartlett Island around 1771. Sometime after his father's death, Amos began courting Mary. Their marriage intentions were published by the town clerk on Dec. 3, 1795 and a certificate was probably issued the following January (Long, 55).

Mary and Amos produced nine children, including eldest sons Israel Bartlett Lunt, born in 1796, and Amos Coffin Lunt Jr., born in 1798. Both men later became the crucial forces behind building a community on Outer Long Island.

The name Israel did not appear in earlier generations of Lunts. Instead, Israel was likely named after either Mary Bartlett's uncle, who had followed Christopher to Maine from Rhode Island, or Mary's brother, who disappeared in England (Binnewies, *A History of Bartlett's Island*, 123).

At At time when many pioneers could neither read nor write, Amos Coffin Lunt Sr. was clearly educated, undoubtedly self-taught and deeply religious. In his journal (see Chapter Five)[2], he recorded details, including biblical passages and the names of speakers at the Baptist Church in Mount Desert and later at the Baptist Church on Outer Long Island. Amos also recorded deaths, births and major events taking place around him in Pretty Marsh, such as the arrival of small pox in 1821 and the burning of the Pretty Marsh meeting house in 1822.

On Mount Desert Island, Amos was among the 15 men and women baptized on Sept. 12, 1816 and organized into the first Baptist Church in what became Tremont (Thornton, *Traditions and Records of Southwest Harbor and Somesville*, 58). In this church, he undoubtedly solidified many of his religious beliefs. Four years later, in November 1820, Elder Lemuel Norton was received into that church, becoming the first settled Baptist minister of Mount Desert. Norton married Israel B. Lunt and Nancy Pomroy on Outer Long Island in 1823. Norton left the Baptist Church in 1828 because of his concerns about Calvinist tenets such as closed communion and predestination.

Like Amos Sr., his children were educated and touched by religion. They too joined early Pretty Marsh prayer meetings and later the Baptist Church. The few surviving journals and letters of Amos' descendants contain poetry, often spiritual in tone, or love letters. Israel B. wrote verse in the early 1820s that frequently espoused the importance of being a good Christian. Most of Israel's voluminous journals have been destroyed. However, the surviving lines penned by him seem to contradict the

---

[2]The surviving journals of Amos Coffin Lunt are part of a collection held by the Maine Historical Society. Most of the papers related to the Lunts of Mount Desert Island and Long Island are in three folders under the names Cyrus King Lunt and Israel B. Lunt. An unnamed donor donated the papers in the 1960s. Some papers are actually official town and church records of Long Island, as kept by Amos. Excerpts from the journal appear in Chapter Five.

stereotypical Maine frontiersman, fisherman, entrepreneur and islander. In 1821, while stopped in Boothbay, the 25-year-old Israel wrote (Maine Historical Society, Israel B. Lunt papers):

> *May thy good spirits guide my youth*
> *And lead me to the ways of truth*
> *Disclose the evils of my heart*
> *Direct me how with sins to part*
> *O Let me not thy spirit grieve*
> *Come let me now thy grace receive*
> *Kindly thy pardning love bestow*
> *So that I may my Savior know.*

A short time later he wrote (see illustration):

> *There favored with the wind and tide,*
> *And on the ocean we sweetly glide.*
> *No harm or danger seems to attend.*
> *No storm to agitate our minds.*
> *As love and peace and harmony,*
> *Here dwells in our ships company.*
> *Dear friend these lines which I now write,*
> *Unto the girl where I take delight,*
> *Now while I am on the stormy sea*
> *Tis pleasure when I think of thee*
> *Our love if lasting proves to be*
> *No one but you will wed with me*

In the early 1800s, Israel and his younger brother Amos Jr. were moving out into the world. Israel helped support the family, bringing home the money he earned working on the Union River. He and Amos Jr. also helped tend their father's gardens and animals on the family farm in Pretty Marsh. The official family cattle mark in 1805 was a hole through the right ear (Long, 75).

Amos C. Lunt Sr. wrote: *"Lords Day, October 20th, 1816. Israel come home from Union River. Got home at dark or after ... Israel brot home 15 dollars in money. Paid Mr. Wait two dollars and Alex Hodgdon 50 cents on Monday morning."*

*"The 21st Day of October, 1816. Israel brot one wool hat for Amos & 1 shaul for Betsy Obear & a testament and 1 quill of paper and a parcel of small books and some cloth, India cotton, to make him a shirt and 1 qt. jug of wine."*

*Copy of a love poem written by Israel B. Lunt in the 1820s to his wife, Nancy.*

Unfortunately for the family, more sorrow lay ahead.

In 1818, Amos Sr. left this simple journal entry: *"Mrs. Mary Lunt, the wife of Amos C. Lunt, died Tuesday morning at day break, Oct. 20, 1818 in the 47th year of her age."*

Despite the sparse words, which characterize nearly all of his writing, Amos did not immediately forget Mary's death. For some time, nightmares tormented him.

In October of 1820, he wrote: *"I dreamed last night of digging a grave and coming out of it that I was going to attend a funeral, that it was my wifes and she was not willing to be entered there and seeing Mr. Grindall go by me and water come in the grave & Miriam was crazy."*

Miriam was a daughter.

About three years later, Amos Sr. remarried. He filed intentions to marry Priscilla Butler on Sept. 21, 1820. With Priscilla, Amos Sr. had eight

### Amos C. Lunt's children with Mary Bartlett:

Israel Bartlett (May 16, 1796 - Oct. 2, 1861), m. Nancy Pomroy (1806-1871)

Amos Coffin Jr. (March 15, 1798 - Aug. 27, 1863), m. Eliza Pomroy (1809 - 1884)

Freelove, b. June 25, 1800. unm.

Miriam, b. about 1803, m. George B. Lunt

Elizabeth, b. Sept. 4, 1805, m. Hezekiah Treworgy

Lucy, b. April 14, 1807, unm.

R. Hannah (Oct. 28, 1810 - Jan. 10, 1895), m. Joseph D. Lunt

Rebecca, b. July 18, 1813, d. young

Cyrus King Lunt (July 23, 1816 - April 17, 1848), unm.

### His children with Priscilla Butler:

Z. Sophia, b. Dec. 19, 1821, m. William Nutter

Andrew P. (June 6, 1823 - Nov. 23, 1897), m. Laurania Pomroy

Mary (April 10, 1825 - Feb. 15, 1827)

Jerushia (Jerusha), b. July 11, 1827, m. Eben Walls. m. Francis Pomroy

Joshua (John) Sylvester, b. Dec. 18, 1829, m. Rebecca Walls

Rufus Babcock (April 13, 1832 - July 2, 1858)

Roland H.N. (March 23, 1834 - July 2, 1858), m. Nancy Thurston

(Daniel) Baron Stow (Feb. 18, 1837 - Feb. 5, 1864), m. Mary A. Dawes.
  m. Lydia A. Leach

more children, the last being Daniel Baron Stow Lunt in 1836 when Amos was 53. Several of Priscilla and Amos' children were born on Outer Long Island. In total, Amos Sr. had 17 children by two wives over the course of 41 years. Twelve of his children lived on Long Island at least into adulthood.

## Outer Long Island

Israel B., a budding merchant and entrepreneur, arrived on Outer Long Island with his younger brother Amos, both in their mid-20s, no later than 1822. Israel and Amos Jr. married Pomroy sisters, Nancy and Eliza, respectively. Nancy and Eliza were the daughters of William and Mary (Beal) Pomroy, two early island settlers (see Chapter Three).

Amos C. Lunt Sr. did not follow his sons to the island immediately, instead he remained on the farm in Pretty Marsh until probably about 1825 or 1826.

Regardless of the exact date, by the mid-1820s, the Lunt family had moved en masse to Outer Long Island, including the families of Amos Jr. and Israel B., the family of their father Amos Sr., the family of their Uncle Abner, and their unmarried Uncle Jacob.[3]

---

### The Children of Israel B. Lunt and Nancy Pomroy:

Albion K.P. Lunt (Dec. 29, 1823 - May 9, 1884), m. Matilda Clark
John R. Lunt (Dec. 30, 1831 - Nov. 14, 1874), m. Katie Lopaus
Amanda S. (1833 - 1851), m. John Walls
Edward P. (1835-1851)
Mary A., b. 1838, m. Reuben Joyce
Rhoda Z.M., May 15, 1839, m. William J. Teel
Hortense B. (Oct. 20, 1841 - March 8, 1909), m. Marston Pinkham,
    m. William A. Van Norden.
Nancy H., b. 1843, m. Rastus Clough (or Clow?)
Freelove, b. 1844, m. George E. Brewer
Israel B. Jr. (March 11, 1846 - Dec. 27, 1912), m. Isora Rich (Gilbert
    Rich & Mary Walls)
A. Victoria, b. 1847, m. Byron Wilson
Fannie E., b. Feb. 7, 1849, m. Edward Clossen

---

[3]Jacob Lunt was most likely the first Lunt on Long Island (see Chapter Three). Jacob claimed about 100 acres, including Whale Beach, Northeast Point and Eastern Beach, in 1812. However, he probably did not move to the island year-round until the 1820s.

---

### *The Children of Amos Coffin Lunt Jr. and Eliza Pomroy:*

Charles H. Lunt, b. 1826, m. Rhoda Lurvey

Joseph Warren (April 27, 1828 - Jan. 18, 1891), m. Alice A. Twist
(George Twist & Mary Rice)

Freeborn G., b. 1831

William P., b. 1836, m. Helen Clark

Maria L., April 27, 1839, m. Robert Dix

Hiram H., b. April 1, 1841

Caroline M., b. 1843

Mary Ann, b. 1845, d. young

Matilda, stillborn

Emma Frances, b. 1851

George Washington (1848 - 1938), m. Abbie F. Clark.

---

In 1827, the now 45-year-old Amos Sr. wrote this letter from Outer Long Island to his daughter Elizabeth, who remained on Mount Desert Island with her sisters Lucy and Freelove (Maine Historical Society collections, Cyrus K. Lunt papers).

*Long Island, October 20th, 1827*
*Dear Daughters,*
*Set down and take thy pen in hand to write a few lines to you to inform you that I have not forgotten you, if you have us - I hope these lines will find you well and in good health and enjoying peace and comfort of mind. We all want to see you very much, but my business is so I can not come to see you, but I often think about you and the rest of my children, wishing you all well and enjoying peace and comfort in religion. I suppose you heard of the heavy affliction we met with in losing our dear little Mary. Her death was very cutting to me. But I had to be reconciled to the will of God and say with Job, the Lord giveth & taketh, he takes but what he gives. She was 1 year and 10 months and 5 days old when she died the 15th day of February 1827 at 7 o'clock in the evening. Andrew was very sick at the same time, but he now is in good health again. But I did not expect he would live for sometime. But we are all in good health now, as usual through the great goodness and mercy of God. I should be glad to have you take an opportunity and come down and see us and Lucy likewise. I don't know as ever I shall see any of you my children again*

*that are absent but I hope I shall. Miriam lives here at home and your aunt Polly is here. Your Uncle Abner and his family lives on this island and are all well and your Uncle Jacob. We have another daughter born July 11, 1827 we call her name Jerusha - We have been to Sedgwick this fall to your Aunt Betsy Allens, last week. They are all well. Your Aunt Betsy has been down here and Mr. Allen and Mrs. Rebecca Patterson have been to see us this summer. Mr. Patterson is here now, his family is all well. Mr. Patterson lost one of his small children and John Hodgdon lost one of his last year. Both carried to their grave on one bier.*

*Israel and Amos is both here and are well and are doing very well in business. We all remember our love to you and Freelove and Lucy and tell them from me I wish them well if you should see them. I expect to come up to Beach Hill to Mr. Isacc Somes this fall to get Freelove to come down here to do some weaving for us after we get in our new house that we are building. I have got the letter bug. I started - and expect to git in course of 4 or 5 a week - Write me a letter and send me as often as you can. I remain your affectionate father and well wisher.*

*To Elizabeth Lunt*

*Amos C. Lunt*

As the Lunts arrived, William Rich and Thomas Rice also settled on the island with their families. Rice and Rich, who both settled on Richs Head about two miles from the main village on Lunt Harbor, are names that appear in Amos' journal from Mount Desert (as well as in the history of other islands in Blue Hill Bay) and likely were friends or acquaintances. All three families would eventually become in-laws. The four Lunts, Rich and Rice headed the six island households in 1830.[4]

By 1840, seven of Outer Long Island's 17 households were headed by Lunt men, three others by members of the Rich family and still others by married Lunt daughters. In 1850, Lunt men headed 13 of the 25 households. Brothers Abner and Amos Sr. each headed one household, while their sons headed 11 others.

On Outer Long Island, some Lunts worked locally for either themselves or Israel, while others sailed the sea, stopping at ports such as New York, Florida, Boston and the West Indies, or fishing on grounds off Canada such as those in the Bay of Chaleur or off the Magdalan Islands.

[4]Complete U.S. Census records for Long Island can be found in the Appendix.

Throughout the community's formative years, Amos C. Lunt Sr. served as island elder. He was the first town clerk, first church clerk, helped teach children, led Sabbath School and hosted prayer meetings. In 1842, Amos Sr. donated land on the east side for the first schoolhouse, which doubled as the island chapel.

## *Rehoboth Hannah Lunt*

In many ways Amos' daughter, Rehoboth Hannah Bartlett Lunt — known almost exclusively as Hannah — followed in her father's footsteps. She emerged as the island's first leading lady and a force for building the community. Hannah kept Sabbath school classes, frequently led early religious meetings, taught the earliest schools in island homes, and was named to the first School Committee. She was likely the only female to serve as an elected official until well into the 20th century — and one of few island woman to own a schooner, *A.T. Haynes*, during the 1800s. Her son, Zaphnath P., served as the captain of the *A.T. Haynes*.

Hannah later donated land intended for a Baptist Church, although the land was eventually used for a building, located near the present-day Frenchboro Historical Society, that served as the second schoolhouse and sometimes church. She and her husband, Joseph, also provided the land where the Congregational Church now sits. The couple, who were cousins, lived in a house built near the church and Donald Osier's house.

Hannah's niece, and Israel's daughter, Rhoda, also served as an island schoolteacher, teaching the children living on Richs Head. Rhoda wrote poetry in a style common to the era, but perhaps, like her father, defying some island stereotypes. Following are short excerpts from her poems (Maine Historical Society collections, Cyrus K. Lunt papers).

It must be remembered that no formal school existed on the island until the 1840s, and many islanders of her generation grew up illiterate.

Excerpts from *"Woman's Love"*

*Tell him, sister, when you see him*
*That I never ceased to love;*
*That I, dying, prayed to meet him*
*In a better home above;*
*Tell him that I ne'er upbraided,*
*Never a word of censure spoke,*
*Through his silence and his absence*
*My heart had well night broke.*

*Tell him that I watched him coming,*
*When the noon-time sun was high,*
*And when at eve the angels*
*lit their star lamps in the sky;*
*And when I saw he come not,*
*Tell him that I did not chide,*
*But that I ever loved him*
*That I blessed him when I died.*

### Forever Thine

*Forever thine; how blest the words*
*that breathe such bliss untold,*
*How rich the promise they extend,*
*How better far than gold.*
*Though others live in gilded halls,*
*And flaunt in silken pride,*
*What care I, so I own thy love -*
*What can I want beside?*

*Forever thine; the constant son*
*Which daily walks the skies,*
*Is no more faithful to its trust*
*Than love that fades nor dies.*
*Thy faults are virtues to my sight,*
*Thy joys are all my own;*
*Thy voice is sweeter to my ears*
*Than music's dulcet tone.*

*Forever thine; through time and space -*
*Through varying weal and woe,*
*Our hearts in unison will beat,*
*Nor e'er estrangement know,*
*As clings the vine around the oak,*
*In sunshine or in shade,*
*to trusts my love in thy true heart;*
*Nor trusts to be betrayed.*

*Forever thine; nor time nor death*
*Can change my constant heart,*
*E'en though the might monarch's law*
*May call on us to part;*
*But on that bright and farthest shore*
*Where joys supernal reign,*
*We'll meet to bind the broken links*
*of loves electric chain.*

## *The Rehabilitation of Bartholomew Russell Lunt*

On the other side of the family, Bartholomew Russell Lunt also became a 19th century island force, serving as a Justice of the Peace, community leader and family patriarch. Bartholomew, sometimes called Russell and nicknamed "Judge," lived on the west side in a home just north of the house formerly owned by Vincent A. Davis. As a J.P. he married many islanders, both on Outer Long Island and Mount Desert Island, and emerged as a leader in both town government and the church. He led the first drive for township status and appealed to Baptist organizations for increased guidance when the original island church was withering from inattention.

Bartholomew's life may also be one of the island's great resurrection stories. Like most islanders, Bartholomew, son of Abner Lunt and Jane Dawes, was relatively poor as a young man on Outer Long Island.

Bartholomew married Asenath Allen of Sedgwick in November of 1832. Almost immediately after his marriage, he and his brother Abner Jr. were caught shoplifting at a Long Island store owned or operated by Joshua Trask. Punishments meted out in the early 1800s were obviously more severe than those imposed in the 1900s. Bartholomew, although only 18 years old and with Asenath pregnant at home, was sentenced with his brother to one year of hard labor at the state prison in Thomaston. Bartholomew's first child, Hezekiah W. Lunt, was born while Bartholomew was in jail.

---

### *The children of Abner Lunt Sr. and Jane Dawes:*

Jacob, b. Nov. 3, 1807, m. Sally Allen
Abner Jr. (Aug. 4, 1809 - 1871), m. Abigail R. Tinker
George B., (1811 - 1881), m. Miriam Lunt
Richard (about 1812 -1889), m. Abigail
Bartholomew Russell (May 3, 1814 - Dec. 20, 1886), m. Asenath Allen
Jane., b. about 1815, m. John Rich
Julia Ann (Juliann), b. June 22, 1817, m. Jonathan Tinker 2nd., m.
    Anderson Lewis
Benjamin, b. 1820, m. Mary (Polly) Davis
Joseph D. (May 27, 1821 - Sept. 14, 1894), m. R. Hannah Lunt
Nancy B., m. Livset Pinkin (Pinkham?)
William D. (March 1823 - Oct. 31, 1888), m. Mary Elizabeth Allen
Israel (1825 - May 2, 1883), m. Dorcas Rice

---

However, the two brothers apparently were not problem youths. A letter from the town fathers in Mount Desert, including Simeon Milliken and Jacob Somes, stated the two never caused trouble while living in that town as pre-teens. John Lovejoy of Thomaston and a group of men soon petitioned the governor and the governor's council requesting a pardon for the two men, in part so they could help support their family. The petition (Executive Council Reports 1833) read: "Mercy is a devine attribute, we ask of your honorable body for a discharge of the youths from the place where they are sentenced to the arms of an afflicted family."

The Standing Committee on Pardons recommended, and the governor granted, the pardons. Bartholomew was a free man. He apparently never looked back, rising to prominence as a town leader. By 1862, a year after Israel died, the island looked to Bartholomew to solve the increasing problems caused by rowdy fishermen from visiting fishing vessels.

William Rich and 40 other island men petitioned the governor in November 1862 seeking help. The petition described the quality of the harbor, its role as a fishing port and told the governor that many visiting fishermen were transients prone to "rows and fighting." However, despite their crimes, these men went unpunished for lack of island law. They asked the governor to appoint Bartholomew as a special trial justice so he could quell the problems by arresting and sentencing troublemakers. The governor obliged and "Judge" Russell took control. His wharf, the old Alexander Davis home, served as the island's makeshift jail.

Bartholomew died Dec. 20, 1886. He is buried with most of his family in unmarked graves on the hills of the island's west side.

Bartholomew's siblings also played island roles. Among them, Bartholomew's sister, Juliann, whose first husband was Jonathan Tinker 2nd, hosted early island temperance meetings. Jacob Lunt 2nd, Bartholomew's brother, became a frequent lay preacher before and during the formation of the island's Baptist Church. Likewise, George B. served as a community and church leader for years in the 1800s.

## The Squire, Israel B. Lunt

While many people played important roles, the dominant islander of the 1820 - 1860 era — from an overall economic and leadership standpoint — was Israel B. Lunt.

Israel, a religious man like his father, was often identified as Esquire, and known in some circles as Squire, an old English term that described the principal landowner of a town as well as a Justice of the Peace. Israel was both. As a commissioned J.P. he married numerous settlers, including residents of Black Island, and authorized many early island documents.

Israel, an ambitious and skilled coastal merchant, practically built the island economy starting in the 1820s and quickly dominated the landscape. He purchased[5] land claims from settlers such as William Pomroy, John Perkins and William Stevens in the early 1820s, sometimes by himself and sometimes with Franklin Spofford, an early partner.

Soon after he first arrived, Israel rented a fishhouse from William Pomroy to store dry fish and salt, while building his business. Israel soon opened an island store, a crucial source of goods for islanders and fishing vessels, and built a prominent business shipping cordwood, kilnwood, dry fish and paving stones down the coast, often to Boston. Through I.B.L. & Co., he bought and shipped wood harvested by islanders such as William Rich and William Pomroy, and bought goods from nearby islands. Israel bought fish from local fishermen, the fishing fleets of coastal Maine and caught them in his own vessels.

During a three decade span from the 1820s to the 1850s, Israel owned or was part-owner of at least 16 schooners. These schooners included the 88-ton, 67-foot *Napoleon*, the 65-ton, 60-foot *Cornelia*, and the 99-ton, 72-foot *Aurora* of Sedgwick. His first registered schooner was the *Arcade*, a 125-ton, 79-foot schooner he built on either Swans Island or Outer Long Island in 1827 (Penobscot Marine Museum, Applebee papers). These vessels also brought goods for his store on their return trips.

On an island that was generally poor, many family members and other islanders worked for Israel hauling fish to the flakes (drying racks) to dry, unloading wood, fish and supplies, haying islands such as Duck, and planting acres of potatoes on not only Outer Long Island, but on Crow Island as well. They also operated his vessels, which in some cases they co-owned.

---

[5]One island story, that has survived, but never been proven, suggests Israel bought land or expanded his business through considerable good fortune. According to this legend, Israel and Capt. William Davis were spearing flounder for lobster bait in Eastern Cove when they spotted a rusted iron chest on the cove's bottom. The two hauled the chest up and buried it on the beach until dark. After dark, they retrieved the chest, supposedly lost from a steamship that sunk off Richs Head, and carried it to Davis' house. There, they pried it open and found it brimming with gold coins. Telling no one, Lunt supposedly used his half of the treasure to build his business, while Davis supposedly used his half to start a boat building and shipping business. While an interesting story that would help explain why these two men seemed to have more land than other islanders, it is not only highly suspect but many facts and general circumstances directly dispute its validity. Chalk it up to the famous "island gossip."

Israel's main wharf was the wharf owned in 1999 by Benjamin S. Davis Jr. but he probably owned and used others on the harbor as well. Israel's homestead was the house owned for years by Norma Teel and purchased in 1999 by Paul Charpentier.

In 1835, Israel became the first official landowner on Outer Long Island. He paid $600 to Michael O'Maley for the entire island, thought at the time to have 1,132 acres based on the earliest deed provided to Col. James Swan by the Commonwealth of Massachusetts (see Chapter Three). The earlier claims Israel purchased were apparently unofficial ones staked by settlers. The claims of those settlers, although possibly lured to settle by Swan's offer of free land, were apparently not recognized by Swan's subsequent agents.

While Israel bought the entire island, he transferred lots — totalling at least 400 acres — to other settlers and family members, or simply let stand some existing claims. He kept his homestead lot and the unsettled areas.

Eventually, Israel owned at least six other islands in Blue Hill Bay including Johns Island, Eastern and Western Sister Islands, Crow Island and the Green Islands. He bought Johns and the two sisters from Charles J. Abbott of Castine for $200 in 1841. Abbott had been appointed the administrator of Swan's estate in 1837. Abbott worked to settle parts of that estate, including the sale of Swan's former islands, to help pay debtors.

Although hailed as generous, Israel did protect his unsettled tracts, taking some people, including his own relations, to court for trespass. For example, in 1850 Israel took William Rich, and then William Davis, Bartholomew Russell Lunt and Amos C. Lunt Jr. to District Court for cutting trees without permission.

In the William Rich case, Israel accused Rich of cutting 500 spruce, 500 hemlock, 500 hardwood, 500 pine trees and 500 other trees between 1843 and 1849. Rich was found guilty and Israel was awarded $800.30 in damages and $46.32 in court costs (Maine State Archives, District Court Records). He made roughly the same case against Davis and his two Lunt relatives.

Israel's land holdings were such that in 1850, his property was valued at $1,600[6] in the federal census. The next largest island landowners were his brother, Amos Jr,. and his sister, Hannah, both with property valued at $75. His father's property was valued at $65. Property values for other settlers fell quickly from $65. The average property value, excluding Israel,

[6]In 1999, 850 acres of Israel's original property, which excludes the village, Richs Head and the west side, was on the market for nearly $3 million.

*East side probably in the mid-1800s. The structure at lower right is Israel B. Lunt's wharf. The house at right is his homestead. The house at left is probably the Joyce house, later owned by Clarence McIntire.*

was $41, with some pieces of property valued as low as $15. By 1860, the land value discrepancies were considerably less marked than in 1850.

In the waning years of his life, Israel turned most assets over to his oldest sons, John R. and Albion K.P., and his wife, Nancy, for safekeeping. Exactly why is unknown, but he apparently grew sick. Family legend also says that a partner cheated him. Israel's obituary makes reference to problems caused by his generosity.

Clearly, something happened. In 1858 and 1859, around the time he transferred assets to his sons, Israel was sued by several Boston businesses for unpaid debts, totaling hundreds of dollars (Maine State Archives, Hancock County Supreme Judicial Court records). The courts approved many of the lawsuits, although at a reduced amount. A former partner, William Smith, was also named.

Regardless of what transpired, Israel died Oct. 2, 1861 with most of his holdings intact. He died the most dominant figure in island early history.

Israel's obituary from *The Ellsworth American* of Oct. 18, 1861 reads:

"Long Island, Israel B. Lunt, Esq., age 65 years, 7 months, 16 days. Esq. Lunt will be missed very much by the inhabitants of Long Island and vicinity, as well as his numerous family. He has been a man of considerable business and influence; and in this one trait particularly marked his character, a ready disposition to help others, especially the poor and needy, and that to an extent injurious to himself, so that in his later days he could not control his affairs to his best intention and desire. In his social capacity, Esq. Lunt was modest yet affable, agreeable and pleasant. Domestically, he was generous and hospitable in a very marked and noticeable degree. Strangers from every quarter found with him a generous and hospitable entertainment; to clergymen, a comfortable home; friends, a cordial reception; and the hungry, an amiable spread table for their wants. Quite early in life he embraced the salvation preferred by the Gospel and maintained a steady unwavering faith in Christianity and its institutions and utility of practical religion. In 1843 under the pastoral labors of the Rev. Mr. St. Clair, he was baptized and united with the Baptist Church, of which he lived and died an acceptable member. In his last sickness he was resigned, sub-missive, trusting in the sustaining hand of

---

### My Father

Lines on the death of Israel B. Lunt Esq. of Long Island, Me.

*Peacefully they've made him*
*A grave on the hill;*
*Mournfully they've laid him there,*
*So silent and still;*
*Gently they've placed*
*The sods on his breast;*
*Tenderly and sweetly*
*They've laid him to rest.*

*Softly the moonbeams*
*Fall on his bed;*
*Brightly the stars gleam*
*Where low lies his head;*
*Moonbeams and starlight*
*Disturb not his rest.*
*Calmly he's sleeping*
*The sleep of the blest.*

*Sickness and death,*
*With him now are o'er,*
*Trials and troubles*
*He'll see never more;*
*Sweetly he'll sleep*
*'Till the last day,*
*While angels will keep*
*Guard o'er his clay.*

Rhodie M. L.
(*The Ellsworth American*, March 21, 1862)

*Photo by Dean L. Lunt*
*The island gravestone of Israel B. Lunt*

Omnipotence and the sufficiency of his grace to bear him triumphantly over the Jordan of death. Also, affectionate and impressive in his last remarks, ready and willing to die and thus departed in peace in the hope of a blessed immortality. A large procession of weeping relatives and sympathizing friends followed him to his last resting place, Long Island, October 5, 1861."

## *A New Era*

By 1860, the island's population had increased to more than 150 residents, but many of the original settlers were growing old or dying. Amos C. Lunt Sr. had died in 1851 at the age of 78. His brother Abner died in 1855 after more than two years of home confinement following a stroke. Israel B. would die in 1861 and Amos Jr. in 1863.

With the four original patriarchs either gone or aging and given the island's large families and limited opportunities, Lunt family descendents followed ever more diverging paths. Certainly, economic and social circumstances for the various family offshoots varied greatly from the start, but it is likely some unifying forces were also at work during the pioneer era. As patriarchs died, it appears that divergence accelerated. Some Lunts moved away, some stayed. Some lived relatively well and others lived hand-to-mouth in virtual poverty. Some were well-educated, some illiterate. Some were upstanding citizens and leaders, others were essentially bandits. In some quarters, alcohol remained or became a serious problem.

Obviously, such general descriptions apply to all island families, but the Lunts accounted for more than half the population during this era.

The Lunt family did not always get along, either. Feuds were as legendary within the family as they were between families. Perhaps because of these feuds, or some other unknown reason, a false story that passed down into the late 20th century claimed that Outer Long Island actually had two completely separate and unrelated Lunt families.

Also, among the Lunts of Long Island in the 1860s were at least eight men who fought in the Civil War (see Chapter Eleven). They included long-time islanders Joseph Warren Lunt, Hezekiah Wills Lunt and George Colliver "Colver" Lunt, all buried on the island. In addition, Jacob Jr., Henry L. and James H. Lunt fought during the war and survived. William T. and Daniel Baron Stow Lunt went to fight and never returned home.

## *The Aftermath of Israel's death*

Just as Israel's life helped build the island, his death caused long-lasting problems.

Israel's oldest sons, John R. and Albion K.P., both sea captains, left Outer Long Island for West Tremont in the mid-19th century. Albion left in the 1850s and John in the 1860s.

Both built houses and lived surrounded by family members and former Outer Long Island residents on the banks of Goose and Duck Coves. Their neighbors included John and Abner Pomroy, two brothers (and John and Albion's uncles) who once lived with them in Israel's house on Outer Long Island. Albion built the "Bayview House" on a 27-acre lot on the north side of Goose Cove.

Several family members are buried in the Hillrest Cemetery in West Tremont, including Amos C. Lunt Jr.'s wife Eliza, and their son George Washington Lunt. Three island-born brothers: John R., Albion K.P., and Andrew P. are also buried there.

Unfortunately for Outer Long Island, John and Albion took some of their father's money and vessels with them. This no doubt damaged the Outer Long Island economy. The island simply wasn't large enough or economically diverse enough to comfortably withstand the withdrawal of prime capital and money from its shores, especially during a time when the state's fishing economy was starting to suffer.

Albion and John did keep watch of the family land.

It was technically under their watch that much of Israel's land was officially transferred to settlers, although under their father's instructions.

They also protected that land. In 1873, for example, the brothers sued a Brooklin man for cutting 5,000 spruce, 3,000 gray birch, 1,000 fir, 300 maple and 300 "hackmatack" trees. They sued for $1,500 and were awarded $400 plus expenses (Maine State Archives, Court of Common Pleas records).

However, neither man lived long after their father died, causing still further problems.

Albion, who married Matilda Clark, grew mentally ill during the final decade or so of his life, rendering him incapable of making his own decisions. The courts placed him under the care of Franklin W. Lunt, his adopted son. According to West Tremont historian Raymond Robbins (*A History of the Houses of West Tremont, Maine*), Albion rarely left his room during his final years and then usually only to complain about the children making too much noise. He died at 60 in 1884.

The death of John R. in 1874 triggered a dispute between John's brothers and sisters and his widow, Katie P. (Lopaus), over family land. Katie wanted to sell the "unproductive" land, including John's half of all property on Outer Long Island and the other islands. She wanted the money.

John's surviving island siblings protested. His brothers and sisters — Mary A. Joyce, Rhoda Z.M. Teel, Hortense Pinkham (later Van Norden), Israel B. Lunt Jr., A. Victoria Wilson and Francis E. Lunt — all believed their father's land and other property was placed in John and Albion's hands for safekeeping only, and was not to be sold (Hancock County, Probate Court records). It was, they believed, supposed to be conveyed back to Israel or to his widow and children as outlined in his will.[7]

The dispute, pitting the family against John's widow, was resolved either in court or through some type of settlement. But regardless of the exact details, the tricky aftermath of John's death helped unravel the last of Israel's land holdings on Outer Long Island and the other islands in Blue Hill Bay.

Some islands were sold at public auction, some were just sold outright, some land fell to specific heirs and some was divided into eighths. While some land remained in family hands and Israel's island relatives, it was no longer held and controlled by a unified force.

In the late 1800s and early 1900s, much of Israel's former property was reassembled by businessman Clarence E. McIntire and eventually bought by David Rockefeller in the 1960s. For example, some 25 years after the original dispute, two of John's children, Basil R. Lunt and Cora E. Clark, were among several people who sold their part-shares to McIntire.

Meanwhile, a different branch of the Lunt family controlled much of the west side property and the land located around the head of the harbor. This land was largely owned by Abner's descendents, including George B., Bartholomew, Jane (Lunt) Rich, Joseph D. and Israel II. At some point, land also came down through the family of Joseph Warren Lunt, who probably acquired it from Capt. William Davis.

The specific identification of controlling land interests after the mid-1800s is far too complicated to detail in any understandable way here. The

---

[7]The sale request made by Katie P. Lunt can be found in legal notices published in *The Ellsworth American*, including on July 6, 1876. The protest filed by John's siblings can be found in the records at Hancock County Probate Court. However, I have located neither a court decision nor Israel's actual will.

number of heirs and offspring grew exponentially after the families arrived in 1822 and some land seemed to transfer often.

After all, while the four original Long Island Lunts produced 52 children, many of their offspring also produced large families as well.

Bartholomew had 12 children, including Hezekiah Wills Lunt, who had 13. Israel B. Lunt Jr. had five, and Amos C. Lunt Jr.'s son, Joseph Warren, had nine children. And Hezekiah alone had more than 50 grandchildren.

## The 20th Century

By the turn of the century, Long Island was in the throes of an economic depression triggered both by national events and a struggling local fishing economy. The family, including a large number of in-laws, still dominated the island scene, although circumstances continued to vary. Given the sheer numbers it is impossible here to detail the activities and contributions of every family member. Although, many of their contributions and activities are detailed elsewhere in this book.

Today, many descendants continue active roles on the island. About half the population are descendents of the original Lunts, as are a large number of the landowners and seasonal homeowners.

Descendents who are also Long Island homeowners include Benjamin S. Davis Jr., Marjorie (Dalzell) Giamo, Ellsworth T. "Derry" Rundlett III,

*Courtesy of Jillane Rabine*

*Isora (Rich) Lunt and Israel B. Lunt Jr., early 1900s.*

W. Kenneth Osier, Verna "Bunny" (Mitchell) Dobson, William "Billy" Lunt, Donald Lunt and Kim and Steve Brown.

So are Donna (Howard) Hasal and Ross T. Giamo, who spend several months on the island each year with their spouses Gerd Hasal and Paula Sue Giamo, respectively.

*The Children of Hezekiah W. Lunt and Lydia M. Dawes:*
1. Adelbert W., b. 1859, m. Rosanna Murphy
2. Cora H., b. 1862, m. Geoge Hardy
3. Sabra A., b. 1866, m. Samuel Rice
4. Flora A., b. 1868, m. Charles E. Rice
5. Mary Susan, b. 1870, m. Hiram A. Lunt
6. Hezekiah W. Jr., b. 1871, m. Cora A. Lunt
7. Elizabeth "Lizzie" M., b. 1874, m. James H. Thurlow
8. Edwin Spears, b. 1876.
9. Asenath M., b. 1878, m. Charles L. Wallace
10. Calvin B. "Cade," b. 1880, m. Bertha L. Lunt
11. Charles K., b. 1882, Mary E. McFarland
12. Jessie M., b. 1884
13. LeForest Glendon, b. 1889, m. Mary E. McFarland

*Courtesy of Frenchboro Historical Society*

*The William Sanford Lunt family, 1906. Fourth Row: Everett (left), Nellie, Charles and Ben "Dib." 3rd Row: Leonard "Nardy" and Lida. 2nd Row: Flora E., William Sanford, Orrin "Birge" and Edna (Rich). 1st Row: Irving "Pean," Guy E. and Margaret.*

*Courtesy of Frenchboro Historical Society*

*Hezekiah Wills Lunt Sr. and Lydia M. (Dawes) Lunt, about 1910.*

*Photo by Dean L. Lunt*

*Sanford L. "Dick" Lunt hauling traps in the Sundance, early 1990s.*

*©Peter Ralston, 1999*

*David L. Lunt at the Lunt & Lunt wharf, 1989.*

*Photo by Dean L. Lunt*

*Daniel L. Lunt aboard the Zachary Nathaniel, late 1980s.*

*Photo by Dean L. Lunt*

*Nathaniel D. Lunt, early 1990s.*

Island residents who are descendants include:

Barbara (Lunt) Sawyer, daughter of Cecil and Lillian (Davis) Lunt, who lives with husband Randall, an island fisherman and town selectman. Their youngest son, Christopher, is also an island lobster fisherman.

Sisters Vivian (Davis) Lunt and Lillian (Davis) Lunt, led the church for about four decades and built the Frenchboro Historical Society.

Donald K. Osier, a lifelong fisherman and sometimes town official.

John R. Lunt Jr., a lifelong island fisherman, long-time fire chief and community leader, lives on the island with his wife Rebecca (Reed), the long-time "Frenchboro News" columnist for the *The Bar Harbor Times*.

April (Davis) Wiggins, John and Rebecca's granddaughter, lives on the island with husband, Tim, a lobster fisherman, and their son, Elijah.

Sanford L. "Dick" Lunt, who died in October at 89, was an island fisherman who lived on Long Island for nearly half its existence as a community. He lived with his wife, Vivian.

Dick started a lobster-buying firm, now Lunt & Lunt Lobster Co., in 1951 and it remains the island's only major business.

Lunt & Lunt is now operated principally by Sanford and Vivian's only son, David L. Lunt. David, who married Sandra Morris, has expanded the business and added a seasonal restaurant. David has served as a key political and business leader for decades and continues to serve the island in numerous capacities.

Also active in civic affairs beyond Long Island, he serves as a trustee for The Island Institute, serves on the advisory board for Acadia National Park and on the

*Courtesy of Frenchboro Historical Society*

*Back Row (left): Sadie L. (McKusick) and Alphonso L. "Fon" Lunt, about 1903.*
*Front Row: Gertrude and Leonard A. Lunt.*
*Fon was the son of Israel B. Lunt Jr.*

advisory board of the Maine State Ferry Service. In fact, David, a seventh-generation islander, has had a hand in virtually every major island decision during the last 40 years, working as a key architect of the island's groundbreaking Homestead Project in the 1980s.

Two of his sons, David W., who married Debbie Herbest, and Daniel L., who married Tina LeMoine, are both island lobster fishermen, as is David W's son, Travis W.

David L's third son, Dean (the author), who married Michelle Priestley, is an island landowner and clerk of the island church, as well as a journalist and historian living in Southern Maine. He has two pre-school children, Emily A. and Eliza R.

David's remaining four grandchildren — Zachary D., Nathaniel D., Kristi L., and Joseph W. — are all in either junior high school or high school on Mount Desert Island.

The grandchildren represent the ninth generation of Lunts to live on Long Island.

*Photo courtesy of Sandra Lunt*

*Travis (left), David W., and Debbie A. Lunt aboard the original Starburst, early 1980s.*

*Joseph W. Lunt and Steven B. Davis, 1990s, both direct descendants of the island's original Lunt settlers.*

# Chapter Five

# Journals of Amos Coffin Lunt Sr.

mos Coffin Lunt Sr. was born Aug. 8, 1772 in Scarborough, Maine, the son of Abner Coffin Lunt and Elizabeth Hodgdon. Over the next five decades, Amos moved to North Fox Island (North Haven), South Fox Island (Vinalhaven) and Pretty Marsh on Mount Desert Island. In the mid-1820s, he followed his sons Israel B. and Amos Jr. to Long Island where he helped build a community.

With his first wife, Mary Bartlett, Amos had nine children. Mary, daughter of Christopher Bartlett, founder of Bartlett Island, died in 1818 at 47. In 1821, Amos, living in Pretty Marsh, married Priscilla Butler. Amos and Priscilla had eight more children, at least six born on Long Island. All told, Amos had 17 children over a 41-year span.

Amos, a religious man, was active in the Baptist Church throughout his life, serving as both a delegate and clerk. He also served as the first clerk of Long Island Plantation when it was organized in 1840.

Amos kept a daily journal, faithfully recording the events taking place around him. His surviving papers provide an intriguing look at daily life on Long Island and the Maine Coast during the first half of the 19th century, although they provide little interpretation of those events. His journal includes some official plantation and church records, as well as entries from Pretty Marsh prior to 1825. The Pretty Marsh entries are less developed than the Long Island entries.

The journal entries from Long Island start in 1839 when Amos was 66 years old and end in 1848 when he was 75, about three years before his death on May 18, 1851.

Amos' journal is stored at the Maine Historical Society museum on Congress Street in Portland. It is among the Cyrus K. Lunt papers donated by an unnamed benefactor to the society in the 1960s. Unfortunately, by that time, most of his journals and other papers were apparently lost or destroyed.

Entries in this chapter have been edited slightly — especially punctuation, which Amos used sparingly — to improve readability. My goal was to provide a look at island life during this period; thus readability was the overriding factor as opposed to a strict verbatim transcription. That said, the changes made are slight, with nearly all spelling and most grammatical mistakes left uncorrected. Most entries have also been shortened. Amos provided a weather description each day and followed reports of all religious meetings with bible citations and quotes; most of those have been omitted. And, of course, only selected entries are presented.

Some entries in Chapter Six also appear in other chapters to illustrate specific themes. However, Amos' oldest found letter, written to his daughter Elizabeth from Long Island in 1827, appears in Chapter Four only.

Most of Amos' family and his extended family make appearances in his journal. The names of Amos' immediate family are listed below. Other family trees, which include many people mentioned in this chapter, can be found in other chapters. They are: Abner on page 54; Israel on page 49 and Amos C. Lunt Jr. on page 50.

Amos' children (and their spouses who appear in this chapter) are:

Israel B. Lunt, b. 1796, m. Nancy Pomroy
Amos C. Lunt Jr., b. 1798, m. Eliza Pomroy
Freelove, b. 1800
Elizabeth, b. 1805, m. Hezekiah Treworgy
Lucy, b. 1807
R. Hannah, b. 1810, m. Joseph D. Lunt
Rebecca, b. 1813 d. young
Miriam, b. 1811, m. George B. Lunt
Cyrus, b. 1816
Z. Sophia, b. 1821
Andrew P., b. 1823, m. Laurania Pomroy

Mary, b. 1825, d. 1827.
Jerusha (Jerushia), b. 1827, m. Francis Pomroy
Joshua (John) Sylvester, b. 1829, m. Rebecca Walls
Rufus B., b. 1832
Roland H.N., b. 1834
(Daniel) Baron Stow, b. 1837

Regarding other names mentioned in this chapter — especially Rich and Walls — I do not yet know many of the familial connections.

Frequently mentioned is James T. Davis. By the end of this chapter, James marries Abigail Milliken of Mount Desert. James and Abigail are the parents of Emily (Davis) Gilman and the grandfather and grandmother of Emily's first son, James H. Thurlow. James Davis' mother was Rebecca Davis.

Also frequently mentioned are Abner and John Pomroy (spelled Pumroy in most entries). Abner and John are the sons of early settlers William and Mary (Beal) Pomroy. Abner and John are also brothers to Eliza and Nancy (Pomroy) Lunt. Both moved to West Tremont in the late 1840s. Abner married Caroline Rich, also of Long Island.

## *Pretty Marsh, Maine 1810 - 1824*

Hannah Lunt was born Sunday October 28th, 1810.

---

Old Mr. John Rich died October 16, 1811.

---

Mr. Ebeneezer Ball was hanged at Castine October 31st, 1811.

---

Lords Day October 20th, 1816 Cloudy weather with S.E. wind. Israel come home from Union River. Got home at dark or after. ... Israel brot home 15 dollars in money. Paid Mr. Wait two dollars and Alex Hodgdon 50 cents on Monday morning.

---

The 21st Day of October, 1816 Israel brot 1 wool hat for Amos & 1 shaul for Betsy Obear & a testament & 1 quill of paper & a parcel of small books & some cloth India cotton to make him a shirt and 1 qt. jug of wine.

---

Lords Day November 24th, 1816 Cloudy with cold N. wind. I & Israel & Amos & Freelove went to Thomas Heath to a private meeting. Sally

Bartlett stayed here all night. 5 or 6 inches of snow fell.

Samuel Obears saw mill burnt January 22d, 1818.

Capt. Jonathan Tinkers child died the 14th or 15th of April 1818.

Joanna Richardson and son were found dead in their barn about the 30th of May 1818. Daughter of Thomas Richardson.

Mrs. Mary Lunt, the wife of Amos C. Lunt, died Tuesday morning at day break Oct. 20, 1818 in the 47th year of her age.

Wm. Reeds child died Monday November 16, 1818. David Robinsons child died about a week before at Burnt Coat.

Old Mr. Abraham Somes died Tuesday Sept. 7, 1819. Aged 87 years.

William Rich Jr. was drowned in Seal Cove Falls Thursday night Oct. 14th, 1819 was found dead Saturday night the 16th.

Lucy Lunt went away to live with Mr. Benjamin Friend at Blue Hill Saturday Jan. 29th, 1820.

Mr. Stephen Richardsons son of Beach Hill was drowned in the ripples May 31st 1820. One of his twins, his name was Henry.

Mr. Christopher Bartlett died Thursday August 10, 1820 on Bartletts Island.

Oct. 14, 1820 I dreamed last night of digging a grave and coming out of it that I was going to attend a funeral, that it was my wifes and she was not willing to be entered there and seeing Mr. Grindall go by me and water come in the grave & Miriam was crazy.

Capt. Abraham Rich and son died Sept. the 22d or 23d, 1820.

John Rich was married to Rhoda Dodge Thursday Nov. 30, 1820.

The small pox brot into Cranberry Island and Mount Desert and Eden in January 1821.

Cyrus King Lunt cut his left foot very bad with an axe Saturday March 24th, 1821.

A shock or an earthquake Saturday May 5, 1821.

Amos C. Lunt was published to Priscilla Butler Sept 10, 1821.

Mr. John C. Somes was baptised and taken into the Baptist Church in full communion by Elder Lemuel Norton. Lords Day June 30, 1822.

Mr. James Thurstons wife died on Gotts Island Monday August 26, 1822. A sudden death.

The Pritty Marsh meeting house was burnt Thursday Sept. 19th, 1822.

Old Mr. Jonathan Dawes died Sunday November 24, 1822 on Robinsons Island at Capt. Jon Tinkers.

Mr. John Walls Jr. died at Mount Desert Thursday May 8th, 1823. Aged about 24 years.

Mr. Joseph Basset of Hingham died on Long Island township of Swans Island July 5, 1823.

Andrew Lunt was born Friday June 6th, 1823.

Hannah Rehobeth Lunt was received by the Baptist Church as a candidate for baptism Saturday Aug. 31, 1823.

Freelove Lunt was baptized and received into the Baptist Church at Mount Desert Lords Day October 5th, 1823 by Elder Lemuel Norton.

Mr. John Tinker Jr. was drowned at Union River the latter part of April 1824.

Mother went away to Vinalhaven with Mr. Eben Calderwood and Mr. Elijah Glover Sept. 15, 1824.

## Long Island 1839

Wednesday March 13th, 1839 — Cyrus & Andrew carried some rockweed from the beach after they came off from Sister Island from helping Ross land Sch. Native. Capt. Pumroy[1] began to load Sch. Napoleon with Israels cordwood at Israels landing in the harbor. Amos and James Davis hall'd out 2 sled loads of fencing, 1 over in my field & 1 I have by the shore.

Friday March 15th, 1839 — Clear'd off last night with a light N.W. breeze. Most calm & very pleasant. Rufus & Rowland went to school[2] today. Cyrus & Andrew chopt firewood for Israel. Amos C. Lunt Jr. birthday, 41 years. Reading the memoir of Rev. John Robert McDowell of upper Canada the first of this week. He became a preacher at New York.

Saturday March 16th, 1839 — Cyrus & Andrew chopt firewood for Israel for spring & summer. Priscilla making Andrew a pair of trousers. I was sick a bed all day. John Pumroy loaded Sch. Napolean here with Israels cordwood.

L.D. March 17th, 1839 — Clear and pleasant. No meeting today here. Hannah went away somewhere with her bible was gone all day. James Davis went away to go to Duck Island, they said. News of the death of Lemuel Norton Jr. and Thomas Manchester, last week. Hannah kept a day of fasting and prayer by herself.

Monday March 18th, 1839 — Cyrus helpt hall fencing in forenoon for Israel with Amos. Andrew work'd helping load Sch. Napolean for Stillman Bridges. Hannah was here all day. Schooner Cornelia arrived here, Samuel Alley, master.

Tuesday March 19th, 1839 — Thick of snow the forenoon. Clear'd off after dark with northerly wind, but moderate. Andrew tapt[3] Albeons & Stillmans boots. No work with Oxen. Hannah was here all day. Priscilla

---

[1] Amos spelled Pomroy as Pumroy in many of the early entries.

[2] No formal school or dedicated schoolhouse existed on the island in 1839. Some island children attending school occasionally in the homes of island residents (see Chapter Eight). For the most part, education was a family affair.

[3] To tap a shoe was to repair it by adding a thickness of leather, usually to the heel or sole.

finish'd a pair of trousers for Andrew, but too large & let Israel have them for Cyrus.

---

Wednesday March 20th, 1839 — Andrew helping Amos[4] hall fencing for Israel. Hannah wrote a letter last night & this morning to send to Boston to her sisters Elizabeth & Lucy by Abner Pumroy & Israel in Schooner Napoleon. I remain very unwell to keep my bed. Cyrus cutting firewood for Israel in the woods to hall with oxen. Hannah kept school again. Rufus & Rowland & Rodney[5] went to school. News yesterday of the death of Mrs. Katherine Kent, widow of Samuel Kent of Burnt Coat. Died the first of this month at Swans Island, Burnt Coat. Napoleon hall'd off into the harbor.

---

Thursday March 21st, 1839 — Rufus & Rowland & 2 of Israels children went to school. The schooner Napoleon of Long Island sail from here bound for Boston. Israel went in Sch. N after goods with John Pumroy. Andrew let Cyrus have his new trousers.

---

Lords Day March 24th, 1839 — Blow heavy last night from N.N.W. & clear off. The Schooner Palm of Newburyport, Rogers, master, was in here. News of the death of Old Mr. John Perkins of Newburyport. Hannah held a meeting to Mr. Abner Lunts, spoke from 1 Thessalonians 2 Chap & had a prayer meeting in the evening by candlelight.

---

Monday March 25th, 1839 — Hannah had 10# of nails was 80 cts & 1 peck of white beans was 50 cts & 4 1/2# of pork was 45 cents of Capt. McCready all came to $1.75 cents. Amos hall'd up the bords from the flake yard[6] to bord my house & Joseph Davis & Cyrus & Andrew & James Davis borded the roof of my house up on the hill. Joseph Davis & Andrew Lunt[7] agreed to go a fishing with Capt. Rogers of Newbury in Schooner Palm; Joseph for 20 dollars pr month and Andrew for eleven dollars pr month. Priscilla done a large washing of clothes for Caroline Bridges. Andrew bot

[4]Amos Coffin Lunt Jr.

[5]John Rodney Lunt, Israel's oldest son.

[6]Flakes were wooden racks that were used to dry split fish. An area covered by a large number of flakes was called a flake yard.

[7]Andrew was only 15 years old at this time, but was already beginning to work full-time, like many island boys at his age. Notice the small amount of start-up provisions he purchased cost him more than two weeks wages. A frock is a type of long work coat or shirt that typically hung to the knees.

him a striped frock was $2.25 cents & one calico shirt was $1.25 cts & 1 pair of stockings was 33 cts & 1 comb was 10 cts & paid James Davis $2.50 for a pair of trousers & 1 white plate was 6 1/2 cts all came to $6.56 cents. Capt. Edward Rogers master of Sch. Palm give us 6# of beans & 5 or 6lb salt beef.[8]

---

Wednesday March 27th, 1839 — James Davis kill'd our veal calf. James Davis & Cyrus carried rocks & clay up to my house to build a chimney. Ezra Davis work'd for Hannah on my house on the hill fixing the outside door casing and cutting out doors. I let Nancy, Israels wife, have a hind quarter of veal weighing 9 1/2 lbs. I let Capt. McCready[9] have my calf skin weighing 5 1/4 lbs. I had 3 knives and 3 forks of Capt. McCready.

---

Saturday March 30th, 1839 — James Davis & Cyrus helpt to make mortar. John Rich to work on his schooner. Hannah went down to Mr. Riches at most night in order to hold a meeting tomorrow. Hannah had 2 quarts of molasses & 2.2 oz. pepper & 2 oz. of spice & 2 blue plates & 2 small white plates of Capt. McCready.

---

Lords Day March 31st, 1839 — Priscilla and myself went down to old Mr. Riches[10] to meeting. Hannah held a meeting, spoke in the forenoon from Jeremiah 13 ch. and the afternoon from Isaiah.

---

Tuesday April 2d, 1839 — Ezra Davis finished my chimney and put steeples in entry. James & Cyrus got moss to chink in the cracks. James and I went over to Eastern Beach to find slabs. Hannah had of Capt. McCready 5 lbs bord nails, 40 cents; 1 lbs coffee, 17 cents; 2 quarts molasses, 25 cents; and 1 candle, 2 cents.

---

Wednesday April 3d, 1839 — Ezra Davis made an outside door & cut a window and put a nine square window in the north end. James went over to Salt Pond round to George Lunts to find slabs, but did not find any. Then he & I & Br. Jacob went over to Jacobs camp. Br. Jacob let me have

---

[8]Bartering was a common part of the early island economy. Numerous entries describe the exchange of goods, not money, for other goods, services or help provided.

[9]Capt. William McCready was either a business parter or full-time employee of Israel B. Lunt.

[10]Old Mr. Rich, William Rich, lived on Richs Head, a small settlement that was roughly a two mile walk from the main harbor. The John Rich mentioned in the previous entry married Jane Lunt.

28 long slabs & 38 short slabs & James & Cyrus back'd[11] over in the afternoon. Hannah had 2 lbs of clapboard nails & 1/2 lbs of McCready, was 21
cents. Caroline Bridges had a daughter born about 10 o'clock in evening.

---

Lords Day April 7th, 1839 — Schooner Napoleon arriv'd from Boston
with Israel B. Lunt with his goods for I.B.L. & Co. Abner Pumroy arrived
from Boston in Sch. Lucy that he & John Pumroy has bot. Hannah Lunt
held a meeting in my new house. Spoke forenoon from St. Luke XIX. Also,
spoke in afternoon. Old Mr. Rich & his wife & Thomas Rice & Mary Twist
& Sally Rice & Ezra Davis & James Davis all got dinner here with us.

---

Monday April 8th, 1839 — Israel B. Lunt Esqr. & Co. landed their goods
at their store here on Long Island. 200 bushels of corn & meal & about 30
bushels of flour & bread. I had from Boston by I.B.L. 12# of sugar and 2#
of tea.

---

Tuesday April 9th, 1839 — Hannah had 2 lbs more nails & 2 lbs bord
nails & 2 qts molasses & 1 qt soule fish & 5 candles of Capt. McCready &
I.B.L. Ezra Davis laid a closet floor & put up the petition to closet & made
a closet door & a book shelf & part of window sash for chamber window.
James Davis cut 25 fence poles, he said, for me. James has cut 86 poles for
me. Cyrus helpt Abner Pumroy load Sch. Lucy with paving stones[12] down
in Riches South Cove. John Pumroy went away to loading down in Riches
Cove. Amos Lunt Jr. went with John Pumroy in Sch. Napoleon.

---

Wednesday April 10th, 1839 — I had 8 pounds of cheese of Israel out of
the 18 lbs piece that I.B.L. brot from Boston for me. I let him have 10
pounds of cheese for a pair of shoes. James Davis birthday, 23 years old.
Cyrus helping Abner Pumroy load Sch. Lucy down in Riches Cove. Ezra
Davis cut out a chamber window sash & batten the north gable end & put
in 2 beams & hung closet door & mended school benches. James Davis
began to bord here with us this morning for nine shillings per week or
$1.50 cents.

---

[11]Back'd was a word that meant carry. Originally, most heavy materials such as wood and stones were
carried on an island man's back, thus the term "backed."

[12]The smooth roundish stones found on several Long Island beaches were loaded into the holds of
schooners and shipped to cities, such as Boston, to make cobblestone streets. Stones, along with kilnwood
and cordwood, were an important part of the early island economy.

Saturday April 13th, 1839 — Hannah & Priscilla quilting our quilt up to our new house. I was reading in Mr. Rices bible that we have here today & yesterday. Rufus B. Lunts birthday. 7 years old today. Rufus B. Lunt was born Friday April 13, 1832.

L.D. April 14th, 1839 — I fell yesterday down by the middle brook and hurt my thigh and side bad. Hannah Lunt held a meeting in the afternoon. Spoke from Proverbs 1 Chap 24 to 32 verses.

Monday April 15th, 1839 — Rained stormy weather with N.E. wind. No work done here except to git a little firewood.

Wednesday April 17, 1839 — Mr. Abner Lunt arrived here last night & John Rich this morning from Thomaston in Schs. Mary & Amelia.

Mrs. Mary Rice & Mary Twist[13] & Juliann Tinker & Hannah were all helping Priscilla quilting up in our new house.

Sch. Fawn went to Ellsworth after boards, shingles & hay. Capt. McCready & Jonathan Tinker 2d & Charles Lunt went in Sch. Fawn. Mr. Rice & Jacob Rice was here to dinner & all the quilters.

Thursday April 18, 1839 — Snow this morning. Priscilla & Hannah finished quilting our quilt up to my new house. Cyrus got 9 quarts of molasses off Israel yesterday & Amos hall'd the last of his hay over from Jacobs field. Napoleon in this harbor with about 30 tons of paving stones on bord.

Saturday April 20th, 1839 — I wrote a recommendation for Hannah Lunt to carry to Boston. The Sch. Napoleon, John Pumroy, sail'd in the afternoon from Riches Cove for Boston with stones.

L.D. April 21st, 1839 — Ezra Davis & Wm. Davis & G. Twist & Gilbert Rich all left this island to go to the Magdalen[14] on a fishing cruise for herring. Israel B. Lunt went away with Capt. Wm. Smith to attend court at Ellsworth.

---

[13]Mary Twist, whose maiden name was probably Rice, was the wife of George Twist and mother of Alice Twist. Mary, a young widow, later married Capt. William Davis.

[14]During this era some islanders sailed on schooners to the Magdalen Islands and the coast of Labrador, both in Canada's Gulf of St. Lawrence, on long fishing trips.

Monday April 22d, 1839 — John Rich, Samuel Alley & Cyrus Lunt went on to Duck Island[15] after hay. Hannah & Priscilla went down to Mrs. Riches to get some hens. Brot 2 hens home 1 for Hannah & 1 for Priscilla. John Rich, Samuel Alley, Cyrus Lunt, Richard Lunt got back from Duck Island at night, got one ton & 3 hundred lbs of hay off Mr. Lurvey. Let John Rich have 5 hundred, they said.

---

Thursday April 25th, 1839 — S. Alley finished plowing the old piece of ground between the Pumroy house & Israels house & fenc'd some. Cyrus went away with Jona Tinker to load Sch. Fawn to Burnt Coat[16] after he finish'd the hen house. Br. Jacob was here most all day. Philip Remic & Ben Milliken stay up in my new house last night.

---

Friday April 26th, 1839 — Abner Pumroy arrived from Boston saw his brother. James Davis went to Boston with him got back today. Cyrus got back from Burnt Coat with Jona Tinker in Sch. Fawn, could not get their kilnwood[17] for Harey was gone to Boston. Alley plowing Green Sword. James Davis begun to bord here again.

---

Saturday April 27th, 1839 — Cyrus & James Davis helpt Abner Pumroy load Sch. Lucy down in Riches Cove today. Hannah went to Mt. Desert with Jacob Lunt 2d[18] in Sch. Mary-Ann. Eliza, Amos Lunt Jrs wife, had a daughter[19] born this morning at daylight, 14 day of moons age. Warren Lunts[20] birthday, 11 years old today.

---

Lords Day April 28th, 1839 — No meeting on this island today. Mrs. Jane Rich had a son born last night on this island about one o'clock this morning.

---

[15]Residents of Long Island frequently utilized the small nearby islands, such as Duck, the Sisters and Crow, in Blue Hill Bay for hay, wood or planting. Israel B. Lunt owned some of these islands.

[16]Swans Island

[17]Kilnwood was a term usually used to differentiate it from cordwood. Kilnwood was typically used to fire limekilns, like those at Rockland and Thomaston. Cordwood usually referred to wood that would be used to heat homes and businesses. Both, like paving stones, were important to the early island economy.

[18]Jacob Lunt 2d was Abner Lunt's son, not the son of Jacob Lunt 1st, who never married. Jacob married Sally Allen of Sedgwick. Two of their children, like at least 10 other islanders, fought in the Civil War (see Chapter Twleve).

[19]Maria L., later married Robert Dix.

[20]Joseph Warren Lunt, son of Amos C. Lunt Jr. and Alice Twist.

Monday April 29th, 1839 — James Davis helpt Abner Pumroy load Sch. Lucy today. Jonathan Tinker 2d went away to go to Castine to take out fishing papers for Sch. Fawn of this island. Charles Lunt went with Capt. Tinker.

---

Wednesday May 1st, 1839 — James went to help Abner Pumroy finish loading Sch. Lucy after breakfast over to Salt Pond shore. Cyrus helpt Samuel Alley again today plowing in Green Sword[21] and planting potatoes in the old ground piece between Israels house and the Pumroy house.

---

Thursday May 2d, 1839 — Old Skipper Clark and John Young Jr. catch'd 240 fish today up between Money Ledge and the Western Sister, all Cod but 7 they said.

---

Friday May 3d, 1839 — Priscilla and I went down to John Riches to see their sick child. Cyrus helpt Israel get his potatoes ashore and into the store chamber. Israel paid Cyrus in pork for his forenoon work. Then Cyrus helpt Alley plow the rocks in the afternoon by the hovel[22]. James Davis cut bushes up on my hill to plant him some potatoes by his mothers fence.

---

Saturday May 4th, 1839 — Mr. Samuel Alley work'd framing his house frame. John Wintworth, his boy, hall'd up the bords for his house. Cyrus chopt firewood for us and hall'd one sled load with the oxen. James Davis and I measured off 3 acres of land for Mrs. Davis, his mother.[23]

---

Sunday May 5th, 1839 — Abner Pumroy sail'd for Boston after breakfast. Stillman Bridges and James Davis went with Abner Pumroy in Schooner Lucy. Priscilla and I went down to John Riches to see their sick child. Hannah Lunt held a meeting at Mount Desert, Seal Cove.

---

Monday May 6th, 1839 — Cyrus cut fencing up in the little spruce swamp in the forenoon. Priscilla and I went over to Miriams after dinner to see their sick child Micajah and Cyrus stay'd in the house with our children in the p.m. Snow squalls at night.

---

[21] Amos frequently refers to planting in the "Green Sword." Sword may have been a misspelling of Sward. From descriptions it seems that Green Sword ran from near Israel's house toward the present-day ballfied.

[22] A hovel is usually a low, open shed used to shelter animals or store supplies.

[23] Rebecca Davis. There were several women named Rebecca Davis on the island during the 1800s.

Wednesday May 8th, 1839 — Froze ice and froze the ground last night and this morning. Cold to the season. John Rich grounding the Amelia on the pint of the beach and painting. I sold him 20 eggs.

Thursday May 9th, 1839 — I unloaded a sledload of stones up in the head of Israels field then went up where Cyrus cut fencing poles. Then came home went over to Miriams and got some soup that she owed Priscilla. John and Jane Riches youngest child died this afternoon aged 11 days.

Friday May 10th, 1839 — Cyrus went down to old Mr. Riches to dig a grave for Jane Riches child that died yesterday. Old Mr. Rich come up here after Cyrus to go down to dig the childs grave.

Saturday May 11th, 1839 — Cyrus went and found Israels cow and calf. Drove them home. Cyrus dug John and Jane Riches childs grave yesterday and it was buried yesterday. Cyrus went on to Green Island with Israel and John Wintworth and burnt it over, the old grass that was not mowed last year. Hannah Lunt got back to this island from Mt. Desert in Sch. Congress with Capt. Andrew Lopaus.

Sunday May 12th, 1839 — Hannah was over to Miriams and came over and went down to Mr. Riches to see Jane. John Rich went to Sedgwick after Doctor Hall for his wife Jane.

Tuesday May 14th, 1839 — Capt. John Pumroy sail'd for Boston in Sch. Napoleon. Hannah Lunt went with Capt. Pumroy to go to Boston. Israel B. Lunt Esq. went away with John Ross in Sch. Native to go to Castine and Belfast.

Wednesday May 15th, 1839 — Jacob Lunt & I went over to Br. Jacobs hovel & we brot over 2 slabs. Jacob let me have 8 slabs to help batten my house off his hovel. Capt. McCready & one of the whalemen went to Mt. Desert in a whale boat after a doctor for Nancy. Cyrus went down after old Mr. Rich for Nancy Lunt, Israels wife. Nancy Lunt had a daughter[24] born today the 2d day of the moons age. Doctor Damon came on this island to Nancy Lunts and Julia-Ann Tinker. Cyrus went after Mrs. Davis cow that had been gone 2 or 3 days and found her.

[24]Rhoda M., an island school teacher. Later married William J. Teel.

Thursday May 16th, 1839 — Priscilla had a large washing of clothes to wash for Nancy today. Israel B. Lunts birthday, 43 years old.

Friday May 17th, 1839 — Cyrus & I back'd over some slabs from Jacobs hovel. David Cain stay'd here last night. Samuel Alley cross plowing & planting potatoes down by Israels house. Mr. D. Cain helpt plant for Israel & Cyrus work the afternoon for Israel & Co. salting fish, Capt. James Tinker & Thomas Rice catch'd. Priscilla had 2 yards of cloth of Nancy for washing clothes, was 25 cts per yard.

Lords Day May 19th, 1839 — James Davis arrived back from Boston in the morning. Had dinner and supper here and begun to bord here again with us. He brot Priscilla 5 yards of sheeting cloth toward her work washing & mending his clothes. Israel got back from Castine with Mr. Abner Lunt 1st. Brot 1/2 ton of hay in Sch. Mary.

Monday May 27th, 1839 — Cyrus work for Israel and Co. carrying rockweed onto the potato ground and work'd all day. I planted potatoes for Israel B. Lunt & Co. in forenoon and some in the afternoon. James Davis & his mother catch'd a boat load of haddock. James had 1 barrel and nearly one-half barrel, salted them for himself.

L. D. June 2d, 1839 — Abner Lunt & his wife was here to dinner. Priscilla washed some clothes yesterday for Mr. Merithew of Schooner Albert of Beverly and sold him 1 qt. of milk. James Davis got 1/4 lbs of tea yesterday was 10 cents. He sold his salt haddock to Israel & took his half for 50 cents worth of cotton shirt.

Monday June 3d, 1839 — Mr. Alley finished planting his green sword piece to the path that goes to the hovel that parts it from my piece. Cyrus work'd 2 hours for the Capt. & Israel carrying out fish onto the flakes. Cyrus & I planted most a pail full of seed potatoes by Elizas hen house. James Davis bot the Fog boat of Israel & Co. & 2 old cod lines was 1 dollar & a basket was 25 cents.

Tuesday June 4th, 1839 — I planted potatoes for Israel to the half in Green Sword by Elizas hen house. James Davis & Silvester went out a fishing. Silvester catch'd 24 fish, come to 31 cents weighed 24# of cod & 14# of haddock. James catch'd 216 in number, he said. James Davis sold all his fish to Israel B. Lunt & Co. come to 3 dollars & 56 cents.

---

Thursday June 6th, 1839 — Andrew P. Lunt birthday, he is 16 years old. Cyrus and I planted potatoes for ourselves by Elizas henhouse. James Davis brot up one bushel of potatoes for us to eat. I had 2 dozen of small buttons of Capt. McCready was 10 cents per dozen on credit. Rowland had his new jacket and trousers finished today. Mr. S. Alley put the roof on his house frame and borded some of the walls and ends.

---

Friday June 7th, 1839 — The Peacock, Capt. Savage, arrived here from the Magdalen loaded with herring. Cyrus work'd for Israel B. Lunt & Co. carrying out fish to the flakes with John Wintworth & Jacob Lunt 1st & Gilbert Rich & George Twist. James Davis catch'd 159 lbs of cod fish and 90 lbs of soule fish. Came to $2.04 cents.

---

Monday June 10th, 1839 — Mrs. Pumroy and Jason Alley came to this island today. Ezra Davis got home today from the Magdalen. James Davis catch'd 51# of codfish and 81# of haddock - come to 91 cents. I cut 5 bushels of seed potatoes for I.B.L. & Co. in store chamber.

---

Saturday June 29th, 1839 — Abner Pumroy sail yesterday for Boston in Sch. Lucy. James Davis went out fishing alone and catch'd 10 cents worth of fish. Sold them to I.B.L. & Co. Took it all up in calico for a shirt. He bot 4 yards of calico 24 cents per yard was 1 dollar.

---

Thursday July 4th, 1839 — Clear'd off. Nearly calm. Very Pleasant. Independence Day was kept by firing small arms. James Davis bot one pound of powder of I.B.L & Co. Miriam was over here to dinner & her children.

---

Wednesday Sept. 25th, 1839 — I wrote a letter for Mrs. Mary Rice to send to her son William Rice. James Davis catch'd 150 cents worth of fish sold them to I.B.L. & Co. Bot us 2 lbs of pork was 2 shillings turned in toward his bord. Old Mr. Walls to work cutting house pieces to put him up a house on this island.

---

Thursday Sept. 26th, 1839 — Hannah sick a bed with cough. Russell Lunt[25] tapt & heel tapt one of my shoes.

[25]Bartholomew Russell Lunt.

Saturday Sept. 28th, 1839 — News came Mr. Pollard and Jason Alley be killed blowing rock at Mt. Desert. Jason Alley was not killed, but wounded very bad. Cyrus and James Davis helping Mr. John Walls putting up his house above Mrs. Davis hovel on this island. Mr. Samuel Alley went off to Mt. Desert to see his brother Jason.

Monday Sept. 30th, 1839 — Mr. Alley got back from Mt. Desert last night. Jason Alley lost one arm, they said, had to be cut off. Mr. John Walls moved his family onto this island.

Thursday Oct. 3d, 1839 — A Bangor boat loaded a quantity of tin ware at I.B.L. & Co. store. Three Indians in a birch canoe came on this island to the store of Israel B. Lunt & Co.

Friday Oct. 4th, 1839 — A doctor Indian was here to Hannah & Nancy & Eliza & little Wm. Lunts. Two other Indians with the doctor. Cyrus had half pound of tea at I.B.L.

Saturday Oct. 5th, 1839 — The Indians went away off this island with Mr. Wm. Stanly to Burnt Coat.

L. D. Oct. 6th, 1839 — Jacob Lunt & his father held a meeting in my new house. Hannah did not go. Hannah taking the Indian doctors medicine.

L. D. Oct. 27th, 1839 — Abner Pumroy arrived from Boston at night. Brot news of Andrew being in Cape Ann harbor, lost their mast and jib. Hannah held a Sabbath School in the forenoon and a meeting in the afternoon in my house. I helpt teach the children at the Sabbath School.[26]

Thursday Oct. 31, 1839 — John Pumroy arrived here last night in Schooner Napoleon from New York. I was digging my cellar drean. Hannah wrote a lengthy letter yesterday to send to Boston to Elizabeth and Lucy Lunt. Sent it today by Miss Eleanor in Sch. Dolphin of Long Island, John Dix master.

Saturday Nov. 2d, 1839 — Cloudy with snow squalls. Wild geese flew to the southard. I work'd on the drean of my celler got 60 feet of drean

---

[26]As with the school, there was no dedicated building for a church in 1839. Sabbath School, like prayer meetings and lay services, was held in island homes.

cover'd. Cyrus went over to little southern cove with Albeon.

---

## *Long Island 1840*

Saturday November the 28th, 1840 — The Schooner Native from East Thomaston, Eben Walls & Jerusha B. Lunt & James Davis & John Walls come home in said Sch. Native of Long Island, all well. James Davis brot me 1/2 quill paper & James had 1 meal with us.

---

Monday November 30th, 1840 — Native went over to Sisters Island, but could not land, there was so much sea. Eben Walls helpt kill Israels black cow in the forenoon. The schooner Mahala of Mt. Desert arrived from Boston, Gilbert Rich, master, John Rich & Wim. Rich 2d, hands on bord. News of Schooner Mary-Ann of Long Island, Joseph Davis, master, and Cyrus K. Lunt & Stillman Bridges, hands on bord and Andrew P. Lunt on bord, passenger, with his goods; flour & meal. Andrew P. Lunt brot me out of his wages 2 barrels of flour was nine dollars, 2 bushels of meal was $1.30, 1 bag was .20 cents, 6 galons molasses was $1.50.

---

Wednesday December 2, 1840 — Priscilla wash'd clothes again for Mrs. Rhoda McCready. Eben Walls went onto Sister Island again and took on part of his load in Sch. Native. Mr. S. Alley & Jacob Rice went away to go to Bartletts Island in Sch. Mary-Ann after hay. Andrew P. Lunt got his & Cyrus flour & meal ashore, out of Sch. Mary, up to our house today.

---

Tuesday December 8th, 1840 — Cyrus K. Lunt & James Davis went onto Sister Island with Mrs. Davis and brot off a boat load of Mrs. Rebecca Davis' hay for Mrs. Davis in Israel B. Lunts large boat.

---

Thursday December 10, 1840 — Eben Walls & Andrew P. Lunt & John Walls[27] & Cyrus K. Lunt was loading Sch. Native with kilnwood in this harbor. James Davis was helping Joseph Davis load Sch. Mary-Ann down in Riches Cove. News of the death of Uncle Micajah Lunt[28] of

---

[27]This John Walls from all indications was a young man and possibly the son of the Old Mr. (John) Walls mentioned earlier. The young John eventually married Amanda Lunt, daughter of Israel and Nancy Lunt. He died in the infamous "Yankee Gale" of 1851 of Canada (see Chapter Eleven).

[28]Uncle Micajah Lunt, a revolutionary war veteran, was the brother of Abner Coffin Lunt (see Chapter Four).

Newburyport, died last fall of 1840, aged about 78 years.

---

Monday December 21, 1840 — Capt. G. Dix loading Sch. Lucy down in Southern Cove with kilnwood. Eben Walls & John Walls got their victuals with us yesterday & Eben today. Eben Walls helpt git firewood on hand sled. Israel B. Lunt & the rest got back from Bangor in Sch. Fawn. Abner Lunt 1st sail'd in Sch. Mary for Thomaston.

---

Monday December 28th, 1840 — Ebenezer Walls & Andrew P. Lunt mended Schooner Natives jib & hall'd Sch. Native out into this harbor again. John Walls gits his vituals with us and Eben Walls also.

---

Tuesday December 29th, 1840 — Overcast & calm. Albeon K.P. Lunts birthday, seven years old today. Eben Walls & Andrew P. Lunt sweeping for Sch. Natives anchor. Priscilla my wife down to Mrs. McCreadys washing clothes. Priscilla had a nine pence & 4 1/2 pence of Mrs. McCready toward her washing clothes, makes 18 3/4 cents.

---

Wednesday Dec. 30th, 1840 — Joseph Davis finish'd loading Sch. Mary-Ann down toward Yellow Head with cordwood. James Davis & his mother went out a fishing catch'd about 100 fish, they said, in forenoon. Then James helpt load Schooner Mary-Ann at Yellow Head. Eben Walls and Andrew P. Lunt went down into Riches southern cove and took into Schooner Native most her hold full of kilnwood.

---

Thursday December 31st, 1840 — About a foot or more of snow on the ground now. Eben Walls & John Walls went a gunning. Eben Walls kill'd & got four coots. Schooner Mariner arrived her from Boston with I.B. Lunt & Co. goods, Maurice Rich, master.

## Long Island 1841

Saturday January 2d, 1841 — Stillman Bridges[29] moved his family onto this island yesterday into his framed house that Samuel Alley built.

---

L.D. January 3d, 1841 — Mrs. Harriet Bung was here going onto Mt.

---

[29]Stillman Bridges moved to Outer Long Island from Opechee (Calf) Island. John Ross, also mentioned in this journal, was also a resident of Opechee.

Desert Rock to settle up for tending the light on the rock. Schooner James, Daniel Robinson, was in this harbor going onto Mount Desert Rock carrying Mr. Wards family.

---

Monday January 5th, 1841 — John Walls went to I.B. Lunts to work helping cut firewood. Abner Lunt Jr. & Joseph Lunt was here in the evening. Eben Walls & Andrew Lunt went over to Eastern Beach in the evening to scate & slide.

---

Thursday March 18th, 1841 — Eben Walls & George Twist & Cyrus K. Lunt went down to Riches Cove in Schooner Native to load George Twists kilnwood, but could not take any wood there was such a sea.

---

Friday March 19th, 1841 — Joseph Davis and Betsy Davis publishment put up to Burnt Coat or Swans Isle.

---

Saturday March 20th, 1841 — The Schooner Cornelia sail'd from this Long Island up the bay to Mt. Desert loaded with cordwood bound to Cape Ann or Boston. Andrew P. Lunt & Abner Pumroy & Amos Lunt Jr. & Stillman Bridges & John Pumroy all went in Sch. Cornelia & Albion K.P. Lunt went in Sch. Cornelia. They stopt at Mr. Trasks to take in John & Abner Pumroys dry fish.

---

Monday March 22d, 1841 — Abner Lunts birthday, 60 years old. He was born in 1781.

---

Friday March 26th, 1841 — Eben & John Walls went a gunning but kill'd no birds. Hannah B. Lunt & Israel B. Lunt Esqr. was here talking again about building a school house.

---

Thursday April 1, 1841 — (see journal graphic on next page) Thick weather with brisk S.W. wind. Abner Lunt Jr. moved his family onto this Long Island yesterday.[30] Eliza P Lunt had a son. Child born this morning the 10th day of the moons age. Cyrus & Eben Walls cut fencing poles part of the forenoon to day upon the hill near Richs road.

---

[30]Abner Lunt Jr. moved his family from Placentia to Long Island, as did George Twist earlier and possible the elder John Walls. Walls had also spent time on Black Island.

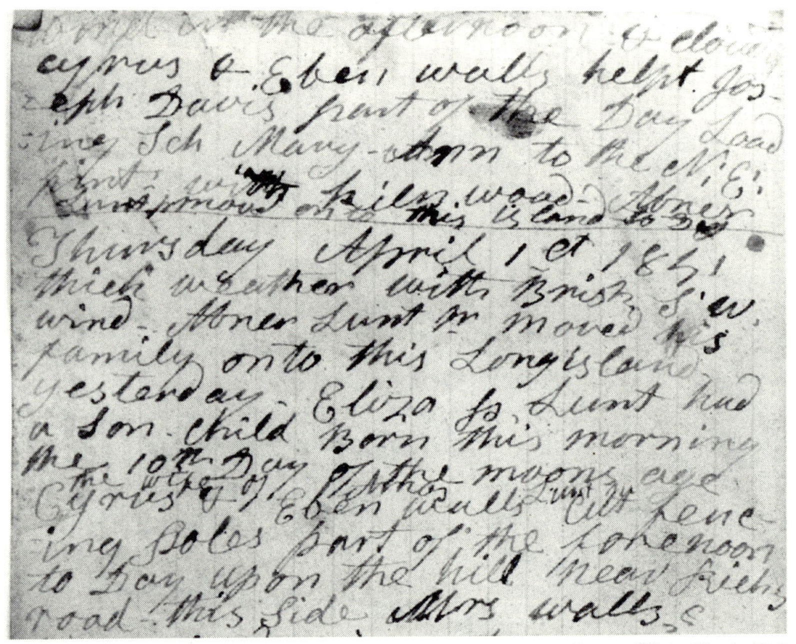

Courtesy of Maine Historical Society

*A page from the journal of Amos Coffin Lunt, including an entry for April 1, 1841.*

## Long Island 1842

Friday April 1, 1842 — A N.N.W breeze of wind & cold. Simeon Milliken Esqr and Capt. Isaac Ober came onto this Long Island as a committee appointed to regulate matters respecting building a School House on this island. Part of the male inhabitants met at the dwelling house of Joseph D. Lunt & acted on the following proposals, 1st choose Hannah B. Lunt for first committee and John Rich second committee and Israel B. Lunt Esqr third committee, and likewise proposed on two places to set the School House & then left it to the committee to say on whether of the places it should be built.

---

Saturday April the 2d, 1842 — I went down to I.B. Lunts Esqr and done the writing respecting the meeting of last evening at Joseph D. Lunts. I recorded it and drew a coppy for Esqr Milliken & Capt Ober to take with them. The majority thought proper to have the School House built down

near my share in my field or a little to the southard and westward of my
lower field fence.

Saturday April 23d, 1842 — Clear & Cold. Mr. Eben Torrey was here to
see if we wanted to buy a spinning wheel.

L.D. April 24th, 1842 — Clear & pleasant with a Northerly breeze in the
forenoon and a S.W. breeze in the p.m. Mr Eben Torrey held a meeting in
Mr Jonathan Tinkers 2ds new house today. Read a discourse of Dr. Edward
Paysons in the a.m. and a sermon in the p.m. of Rev. Abiel Abbots. The
text was "what is highly esteemd among men is an abomination in the
sight of God." Eben Walls & Andrew P. Lunt & Abner Pumroy came down
from Mt Desert, they have been to Lubec.

Monday April 25th, 1842 — I went with Hannah B. Lunt over to the
Western Beach to help her carry Josephs dinner where Joseph was loading
Sch. Mary with kilnwood.

Tuesday April 26th, 1842 — Overcast with a lite breeze from the eastward. Andrew & Eben & Abner Pumroy went away again up to Mt. Desert
to go on bord Brig[31] Etrunion to go to New York. John Walls got home
come to stay with us this afternoon. Brot his mother a barrel of flour & 2
bushels of meal & 4 lbs of coffee & 3 galons of molasses. Brot home 13
dollars in cash.

Monday May 2d, 1842 — Thick foggy weather today. It rain'd most all
last night. James went to Mount Desert with Jacob Lunt & Betsy Tinker.
I.B. Lunt got home yesterday from Ellsworth. A trader, Capt. Mansfield,
lying in the dock trading.

Tuesday May 3d, 1842 — I bot some needles & thread of the trader. Paid
in cotton rags.

Saturday May 7th, 1842 — Jerusha came home from Mt. Desert with
Abner Pumroy. Andrew P. Lunt agreed to go in Capt. Jonathan Tinkers
new brig for 12 dollar per month. The brig Gulinair, John Tinker, master
& Andrew Lopaus, mate.

---

[31]A brig or brigantine is a two-masted vessel with square-rigged sails.

Monday May 9th, 1842 — I went down to Hannahs & put some papers on her library books stating The Long Island Seamans Library. Please return in fourteen days.

---

Tuesday May 10th, 1842 — A topsail schooner belonged to Waldoborough got ashore on Harbor Island point & lay all day. Loaded with lumber. Amos Lunt Jr. helpt Cyrus fence some in the afternoon moving our field above our last years cow yard. Cyrus work'd last Friday & last Saturday for Israel B. Lunt Esqr. putting fish on bord Sch. Mary Jane and Saturday he worked on Crow Island clearing & burning.

---

Wednesday May 11th, 1842 — John Walls and Samuel Rice went away to go to Cranberry Island to go a fishing with Captain Bunker. I went over to Eastern Beach & to N.E. Point after our cow.

---

Wednesday & Thursday May 18th & 19th, 1842 — Cyrus & myself was putting up the fence at Eastern part of my field. I back'd out some of the fence poles. I went down to old Mr. Riches to hire his plow. Israel B. Lunt Esqr went to Boston from Bangor in the steamboat last Monday.

---

Friday May 27th, 1842 — Amos Lunt brot 12 bushels more of potatoes home last night. Cyrus work yesterday & today for I.B.L on Crow Island planting potatoes. James Davis & Ezra Davis & Joseph Davis & Stillman Bridges all went away with Captain Thomas Bunker to Cranberry Islands to go a fishing this year. James Davis and Ezra been to Boston with Capt. Bunker brot home flour, molases & coffee.

---

Saturday May 28th, 1842 — Brig from Liverpool went out of this Long Island harbor and was cast away between the Gooseberry Point & the Western beach on the Southwest point of this island, partly loaded with beech and rock maple cord wood.

---

L.D. May 29th, 1842 — Israel B. Lunt Esqr & Amos Lunt Jr. & John Pumroy & John Rich & Cyrus K. Lunt & Albeon K.P. Lunt & Warren Lunt all over helping get off the Brig Swan of Liverpool, Nova Scotia.

---

Monday May 30th, 1842 — All the men except Albeon & Warren over to work on bord the cast away brig helping git her sails & riggin round to the harbor. I brot some cordwood round by water. The Capt. & hands stript the said Brig and cut away her masts. She entirely a wreck.

---

Wednesday June 1st, 1842 — My daughters Elizabeth and Lucy arrived here on Long Island with Capt. Isaac Gott Jr. Brot me 2 bushels of meal, 1 pair of shoes, 6 yards of red flannel, 1 orange, some cheese, half a pound of tea and 2 oz. & one galon of molases & 2 lbs of coffee & 2 lbs of sugar & 29 cents in money to buy a milkpan & pay Mr. Rich for the use of his plow. I paid Mr. William Rich 1st 12 cents.

---

Thursday June 2d, 1842 — Lucy Lunt stay'd here with us last night. I feel better today. Cyrus & Priscilla planting potatos to the S.W. of the house. Israel & Capt. Collis of Brig Swan went to Mount Desert to enter a protest.

---

Friday June 3d, 1842 — Mr. Gregory Brown one of the hands of Brig. Swan of Liverpool tapt a pair of shoes for Jerusha. The men brot the deck & stern of the wreck of the Brig Swan round into this harbor & burnt & finished getting the iron out of the wreck.

---

L.D. June 12th, 1842 — The Castine cutter in this harbor took on bord the sails, rigging, chains & Capt. & men of the wreck of Brig Swan of Liverpool to carry it to Castine to have the sails, rigging, chains, black iron sold at public auction. Israel B. Lunt Esqr went to Castine in the cutter with them. No meeting here today.

---

Tuesday June 14th, 1842 — Overcast & rain in the forenoon. We planted potatoes in the afternoon. John Pumroy & George Twist went away to go after I.B. Lunt Esqr to Castine. Cyrus sick.

---

Thursday June 16, 1842 — Thick weather. Rain'd by spells. Lucy Walls helpt Jerusha & Silvester bring dung from Mrs. Davis's hovel for us & we planted down to the easy ground below the stone piles today. We let Lucy Walls have a pair of shoes for her work.

---

Tuesday June 21st, 1842 — Clear with a westerly breeze. George Twist kill'd I.B. Lunts calf for veal & I helpt him dress the calf. Nancy let us have a piece of the veal. Eben Walls went up last night in Brig Atlas got to Mt. Desert this morning and came down home today. He brot 20 dollars & 25 cents in silver money & 14 dollars in paper money.

Thursday September 8th, 1842 — Elder Samuel Macomber[32] came onto this Long Island today and preach'd a sermon on bord of Capt. Harts sloop in this evening by candlelight from Psalms XLIX & 14th & 15th Verses. Cyrus worked for I.B. Lunt at fish house & flake yard. Jerusha & Silvester pick about six quarts of blackberries today.

L.D. September 11th, 1842 — I was sick. Mr. Gott held a meeting to Abner Lunt Jrs.

Tuesday September 13th, 1842 — Priscilla & I went a blackberrying a spell this forenoon. Then I went to the shore and got a quarter of lb. of tea at I.B. Lunt Esqr makes half a pound we had of I.B. Lunt & 1 galon of molases on Elizabeth Lunts acct. & one peck of meal.

Wednesday September 14th, 1842 — Cyrus was helping get Mr. Snows and I.B. Lunts dry fish on bord Mr. Trasks boat at I.B. Lunts wharf today to carry to Bangor. I am considerable unwell today. Priscilla & Jerusha & Lucy went a blackberrying in the a.m. down on the southern ledge after Jerusha came home from Gilbert Riches. We had some of our carrots stole last night.

Thursday September 15th, 1842 — I cut a few alder bushes in the lower field today. Betsy Davis & Lucy Walls had a dreadful quarrel today.

Friday September 16th, 1842 — Charles Davis & Charles H. Lunt & John Walls & Sam'l Rice all got home today from Labrador, they arrived at Cranberry Island, they said last Tuesday, with what they called 300 quintals[33] of fish with Mr. Amos Bunker. Mr. Hezekiah Truworthy was here to my house this afternoon, took supper with us, agreed to frame Eben Walls house & to come down a week from next Monday. Israel B. Lunt & Mr. Trask & Mr. Snow & his son Anthony all sail'd in Mr. Trasks boat today for Bangor with a load of fish.

Tuesday, November 1st, 1842 — I went to the store. I.B. Lunt give me an

---

[32]Samuel Macomber was a Baptist missionary (see Chapter Six).

[33]A quintal is a unit of measurement equal to 100 pounds.

almanack for 1843 edited by Daniel Robinson of Holowell called the Maine Farmers Almanac. He also give me 24 apples. I cut some bushes in my field with my jack knife.

---

Thursday November 3d, 1842 — Mrs. Sally Birch was here making a dress for Jerusha, a red striped flannel. Mr. Alfred L. Harper & Mark Hodgdon was here took dinner with us. A prayer meeting into Mrs. Davises. I was there.

---

Friday November 4th, 1842 — I cut some more bushes out to the east of my field fence. Cyrus carrying out cord wood for Albion K.P. Lunt over toward Yellow Head. There was a prayer meeting last evening into Mrs. Davis by candlelight or lamplight. Polly Davis was into my house this morning to talk & pray with us. A great revival on Swans Isle commonly called Burnt Coat.

---

## Long Island 1847

Elder C.P. St. Clair[34] came on to this Long Island, Wednesday August the 11th Day A.D. 1847.

---

Elder St. Clair preached in the evening in the schoohouse August 12th Thursday 5 o'clock p.m. from 11 Kings IV Chapter & 26 Vers.

---

Saturday afternoon Elder C.P. St. Clair preached from Zachariah XIII. Chap & 1st and 6 verses. "In that day there shall be a fountain opened to the House of David and to the inhabitants of Jerusalem for sin and for uncleaniness." The above was preached August the 14 1847, Saturday.

---

The next is Elder C.P. St. Clair text preached in the School House on Long Island to a large number of fishermen & mackerel catchers on Tuesday 3 o'clock p.m. August the 17th, 1847. His text was in Hebrew XII Chap. & 25 verse. "See that ye refuse not him that speaketh."

---

Elder C.P. St. Clair preached again in the School House on Long Island in the afternoon 3 o'clock, Wednesday August 18th, 1847. His text was in Acts XXVI Chapter. Then there was a Church meeting the same afternoon

[34]C.P. St. Clair was a Baptist missionary.

and delagates chosen to go to the Association meeting that was holden in Sedgwick 2 Church on the Bay meeting house the first Tuesday in September which was the 7, 8 & 9th days of the month, Sept. 1847. The delagates that was chosen was Amos C. Lunt, Israel B. Lunt, Thomas Rice, Jacob Lunt 2d & Albeon K.P. Lunt. Chose Amos C. Lunt, church clerk. Richard Lunt was excluded from this Baptist Church on Long Island. James Davis & John Richs case entered into the church & Jacob Lunt 2ds case was entered but not acted upon.

---

Thursday in the forenoon we attended the association Sept. 9th, 1847.

---

Friday September the 10th day 1847 — We, Jacob Lunt 2d, & myself come down to Long Island, found all well.

---

Sunday September 12th, 1847 — Jacob Lunt 2d held a meeting, he preached in the forenoon from XII Chap. & 32 vers. In the p.m. Jacob spoke from Zachariah 10 Chap. & 4 vers.

---

Dr. Spear was on this island today Monday Oct. 4 1847 to Nancy Lunt, wife of I.B. Lunt Esqr.

---

In the afternoon 4 o'clock we attended the weding of James T. Davis who was married to Mrs. Abigail Morrison, daughter of Mr. Samuel Milliken of Mount Desert. Married by Israel B. Lunt Esqr. Sunday November the 7th Day, 1847.

---

Mr. Thomas Turner of Deer Isle or Isle au Haut, the trader, arrived here at Long Island harbor Sunday November the 7th Day A.D. 1847 with apples and goods.

---

There was our monthly conference meeting held in the schoolhouse on Saturday p.m. November the 13th day 1847. Only 6 members present. James Davis & Abigail Walls applied to be restored to the church. Was received under the watch care of the church until Elder Macomber visits us again, he expects to be 5 weeks.

---

The next is Elder Sam'l Macombers text preached in the School House Sunday forenoon November the 14th A.D. 1847.

After the services was over some business was attended to. A committee of three was chosen to see & look up the disorderly members of this church to see if they wanted to withdraw from this Baptist Church or not and to report when Elder S. Macomber does visit us again. At a church meeting the committee chosen was Amos C. Lunt, Israel B. Lunt and Jacob Lunt 2d.

---

Charles Henry Lunt was married to Rhonda Lurvy, Thanksgiving Day, November the 25th A.D. 1847.

---

Francis Pomroy building a chimney in Jerushas house Nov. 26th.

---

Jacob Lunts 2d text preached in the schoolhouse on Long Island L.D. December 12th, A.D. 1847 in the forenoon. He spoke from Proverbs 28th Chap. & 26 Vers. "He that trusteth in his own heart is a fool; but whoso walketh wisely, he shall be delivered."

---

Francis Pomroy killed his cow Dec. 15th 1847.

---

Schooner Exchange, Henry Clark, sail'd from this harbor, Long Island, Wednesday night about 8 o'clock December the 15th A.D. 1847 bound to New York & West Indies. John Pomroy, mate, Charles H. Lunt, Freeman Lurvey, Andrew P. Lunt, hands. Joshua Sylvester Lunt, cook.

---

Elder Macombers text preached in Charles Davis's house Friday evening by candle light December 17, 1847. Text from Revelations VI Chap. 17 verse. "For the great day of his wrath is come and who shall be able to stand?"

---

Elder Macomber went down to Mr. Richs to hold a meeting there Sunday evening December 19th, 1847.

---

Elder Macomber left here Dec. 20th, 1847.

---

Mr. Nathaniel Truorgy from Surry was here brot a phial of Balsom of Life & Hoar Hound Herbs that Elizabeth my daughter, sent to Cyrus. Cyrus very sick with cough. Dec. 22d day 1847.

---

Benjamin Lunt was married to Mary Davis Thursday Dec. 23d, A.D. 1847 by Israel B. Lunt Esqr.

L.D. December 26th, 1847 — No meeting on Long Island for public worship today. Cyrus continues out of health. Confined to the house.

## Long Island 1848

Tuesday January 11th, 1848 — This day Little Charles St. Clair Rich died here on Long Island, son to Gilbert Rich and Paulina Rich. The child was 5 years and 2 months old, lacking 5 days.

Little Charles P. St. Clair Rich was buried on Long Island Thursday January 13, A.D. 1848 on the N.W. side of the harbor. Jacob Lunt 2d spoke at the funeral from Job III. chap. and part of the 11th verse. "Why died I not from the womb? Why did I not give up the ghost?" In the evening of the same day, Thursday January 13th, A.D. 1848 Sarah M. Rice was married to Peter Stanly of Swans Isle by Israel B. Lunt Esqr on Long Island.

Received letters from Andrew P. Lunt & Sylvester Lunt & Charles H. Lunt from New York dated Jan. 1st & 2d, January 16th 1848. And from Elizabeth Treworthy at night, by Mr. Nathaniel Lamos, rec'd 2 quilts, 2 blankets, one pillow, 2 pillow cases, drawers, 1 dress for Miriam, 2 pair of mittens, 1 pair for Cyrus & 1 pair for me. Some rice & cheese & letters received January 16th A.D. 1848, Sunday.

William D. Lunt was married to Mary Elizabeth Allen of Sedgwick on Long Island by Israel B. Lunt Esqr Thursday January 20th, 1848.

There was a temperance meeting held by Mr. Nathaniel Lamos at the dwelling house of Julia Ann Tinker on Tuesday evening January 25th, A.D. 1848.

Mr. Henry Pomroy was joined in marriage to Mrs. Caroline Bridges, Saturday evening by Israel B. Lunt Esqr. January the 29th, 1848 on Long Island.

Jacob Lunt 2d preached in the schoolhouse on Long Island Sunday January 30th, 1848 in the forenoon from Hebrews 2d Chap. & 3 vers. In the afternoon he spoke from Ephesians VI Chap. 24 vers.

February 24 Thursday evening Rebecca Walls & we received a letter from Joshua Sylvester Lunt dated at East Florida in Jacksonville, January the 26th A.D. 1848.

---

Schooner Exchange arrived in to S.W. Harbor Mount Desert Tuesday March 7th, 1848 in the p.m. from East Florida, Jacksonville. Andrew & Sylvester got home here to Long Island about eleven o'clock at night, Tuesday night March the 7th, 1848. Sylvester brot me one barrell of flour & 1 pair of shoes for me & one pair for his mother.

---

Andrew P. Lunt & Joshua Sylvester Lunt & Rollin H.W. Lunt sail'd in Schooner Oscar for Cape Ann Friday morning March 31st, 1848. Sch. Mary-Ann, Abner Pomroy & Francis Pomroy & Henry Pomroy sail'd for Castine March the 31st, 1848. Sch. Leader sail'd for Cape Ann, Albion K.P. Lunt and John Rodney Lunt Friday March 31st, A.D. 1848.

---

Cyrus King Lunt died on Long Island, Monday morning a little after daylight, April the 17th A.D. 1848. Aged 31 years, eight months and 25 days. Buried on Long Island April 18th, Tuesday p.m.

---

Rufus B. Lunt begun with Mr. Elisha Friend in Schooner Oscar, Wednesday April 19th, 1848.

---

Joshua Sylvester entered on bord of Schooner Mary Ann with Abner Pomroy Friday morning April the 21st A.D. 1848.

---

Sylvester Lunt brot us two galons of molasses when he returned from Cape Ann about the 15th of April 1848.

---

The widow Abigail Walls was married to Richard Lunt by William Fife Esqr on Swans Isle (they say) Saturday April the 22d day or evening A.D. 1848. Both of Long Island.

---

Thursday May the 18th, A.D. 1848 This day I published John Dawes to Elizabeth Gott, both residents of Black Island & of the Plantation of Long Islands. Amos C. Lunt, Plantation Clerk.

---

Schooner Leader sail'd for Castine Friday May the 19th Day, A.D. 1848.

I.B. Lunt Esqr went in her.

May the 27th, 1848 — Rollin sail'd in Schooner Mariner with Albion K.P. Lunt for Boston this morning. The first time that ever Rollin H.N. Lunt went to go to Boston. They have a moderate pleasant fair wind today.

Baron Stow Lunt fell out of a skiff or float Saturday June the 3rd Day A.D. 1848 and came very nigh being drowned in Long Island harbor.

I.B. Lunt Esqr went off with Mr. John Daws Saturday June 10th A.D. 1848 to Black Island and married Mr. John Daws to Miss Elizabeth Gott, residents of the Plantation of Long Island.

Schooner Helen Gray of Addison went a shore on the Western Shore of Long Island on Monday morning 2 o'clock (they said) June the 19th, A.D. 1848. Cotton, master. Not much on board, 4 barrels of flour and vessels stores. They cut away the masts Thursday June 22d, A.D. 1848. She is a wreck indeed, getting rigging on shore.

Schooner Mary Ann arrived Thursday night about sunset June 22d A.D., 1848 with 200 quintils fish they say.

# Chapter Six

# Coastal Missionaries

## The Baptists

Religion, in the form of prayer meetings and lay services, took root on Outer Long Island even as the first permanent settlers built their homes on the banks of Lunt Harbor. Island elder Amos Coffin Lunt Sr., active in the Mount Desert Baptist Church in Pretty Marsh, emerged as a driving force in religious life after moving to Outer Long Island in the mid-1820s.

His son Israel B. Lunt also arrived with an ingrained religious spirit, if not his father's zeal. Rehoboth Hannah B. Lunt, Israel's sister, was baptized into the Mount Desert Baptist Church as a 10-year-old in 1823. She also emerged as a central figure in the island's spiritual life, leading religious services in island homes, teaching Sunday school, and at times walking to back shores, bible in hand, to pray.

In his journal (Maine Historical Society collections, Cyrus K. Lunt papers), Amos Lunt Sr. wrote: *"L.D. March 17, 1839 — No meeting here today. Hannah went away somewhere with her bible, was gone all day. News of the death of Lemuel Norton Jr. and Thomas Manchester last week. Hannah kept a day of fasting and prayer by herself."*

Amos' nephew Jacob 2nd, son of Abner Lunt, took to the island's figurative pulpit for years, first preaching in island homes and later in the schoolhouses that doubled as chapels starting in 1843.

The Lunts brought religious beliefs fashioned largely in the Mount Desert Baptist Church, which practiced a strict brand of Calvinism. What brought Amos and his family into the Baptist Church is unknown. His father was married in a Congregational Church and his American ancestors, starting with Puritans who sailed from England to Massachusetts in 1634, also were members of a different denomination.

Amos was one of the original 15 men and women baptized in the Mount Desert waters and embodied into a church when it was formed in 1816. Even before the formal church existed, Amos attended various religious meetings held in Pretty Marsh homes and the surrounding area. During the first official church ceremony, Elder Isaac Case, a prominent Baptist missionary along coastal Maine, administered the sacrament of the Lord's supper. Other original members included Davis Wasgatt, Ezra H. Dodge and Simeon Milliken, all prominent early settlers of Mount Desert.

The early Baptist church had no full-time clergy until Elder Lemuel Norton, a former sailor, accepted a request from Mount Desert Island residents and moved his family from Brooksville to an island farm. Before receiving that request, Norton had planned to teach school in the island's "Cape District," but instead settled in as the church's first permanent minister in 1820 (Norton, *Autobiography of Lemuel Norton*, 137-140).

However, Norton slowly decided that some Calvinist tenets such as predestination and closed communion, which forbade the taking of sacraments even by those of other Protestant denominations ran contrary to his beliefs. Within eight years, Norton grew so troubled he revealed his concerns from the pulpit, creating a split between himself and both the congregation and mother church. He left the Calvinist Baptists in 1828 to organize a more liberal Free Will Baptist Church, also on Mount Desert Island.

By the time of the Norton/Baptist schism, Amos had already moved across the bay. So it was from the original Calvinist-based background that Amos and his family brought early religion to Outer Long Island.

Sabbath meetings occurred throughout the 1830s. They often included a morning service followed by candlelight evening meetings led by Hannah or Jacob in homes of island residents such as Jonathan Tinker 2nd, Charles Davis and the Rich family on Richs Head.

Amos C. Lunt Sr. entered typical Sunday entries such as these in his journal:

*"Lord's Day March 24th, 1839 — Hannah held a meeting to Mr. Abner Lunts; spoke from 1 Thessalonians 2 Chapter & had a prayer meeting in the evening by candlelight."*

*"Lord's Day Oct. 6, 1839 — Jacob Lunt and his father (Abner) held a meeting in my new house."*

*"L. D. Oct. 27, 1839 — Hannah held a Sabbath school in the forenoon and a meeting in the afternoon in my house. I helpt teach the children at the Sabbath School."*

With a growing population on Outer Long Island and its increasing stability as a community, more formal religion arrived on island shores as the 1830s faded into the 1840s.

The earliest missionaries, usually carried across the bay by islanders or mainland residents willing to ferry them, hailed from the Hancock Baptist Association, part of the Maine Baptist Convention. The Baptists were already making inroads on other islands such as Swans Island and Deer Island when missionaries, including Elders A. Cummings, S. Allen, D. Dodge, and Samuel Macomber, visited Outer Long Island in the 1840s.

On September 8th, 1842, Amos wrote: *"Elder Samuel Macomber came onto this Long Island today and preac'd a sermon on bord of Capt. Hart's sloop in the evening by candlelight from Psalms XLIX & 14th & 15th Verses."*

## The First Island Church

While the earlier visits may have sparked interest, the most important event took place in the winter of 1843 when 29-year-old Rev. C.P. St. Clair walked up from the harbor hoping to save island souls.

Rev. St. Clair, a native of Freedom, Maine, and an earnest advocate of church missions and temperance, quickly baptized 35 islanders. Those 35, combined with 10 people baptized earlier by Brother David Nutter, were organized into the island's first church Feb. 23, 1843.

The island's first schoolhouse, which doubled as a chapel, provided an island meeting house and encouraged that formal movement. The school was built in 1842 on land donated by Amos C. Lunt Sr. It sat on the east side between property owned in 1999 by Daniel and Tina Lunt and Lorena and Wyatt Beal.

Minutes from the 1844 annual meeting of the Maine Baptist Convention provide this description of the joint school and church (p. 17):

"On this island there is now erected a building which is provided with a bell, and used both as a school and meeting house. Thus on this most outward of islands on this coast, there is a house of God, and a church of Jesus, provided with a bell to call these poor people (for poor they are, as to this world's goods) to the worship of the one living and true God. But they have no one to administer to them the ordinance of the gospel, or to preach to them the word of life."

The Baptists were pleased with their progress on Outer Long Island, which now served as the Baptist's most remote island outpost. However, in the hyperbolic style of much missionary writing, the helplessness and poor conditions they found on the islands and in the small towns of Maine were usually exaggerated, as was the glorious aftermath of their visits. This created a record of communities that experienced frequent and wild swings from towns of desperation and wickedness to towns of peace and piety. Still, there is much truth in the early writings. Missionaries surely found often isolated communities, overall poor conditions and sometimes poverty. And despite their obvious slant, the reports and letters do provide important insights into 19th century island communities.

In the aftermath of the church's formation and St. Clair's revival, the Baptists (Millet, *A History of the Baptists in Maine*, 364) said:

"Although in years past, these islanders were blessed with the occasional visiting and preaching ... they were notorious for their profanity, general wickedness, and intemperance; and when the work of God commenced, opposition to it was strong among them. But a stronger than they was there, and most of the twenty-three families now resident on the Island are praying families. How changed the scene! Piety, peace, order and harmony now reign, where once sin, infidelity and polluting habits degraded society."

This description clearly contrasts with the entries made in Amos Lunt's journal that described candlelight prayer meetings and lay services, long before Rev. St. Clair arrived. Although certainly not everyone attended those early meetings.

Through September 1843, St. Clair spent a combined nine weeks on 11 islands including Outer Long Island, Black Island, Great Gott Island and Swans Island. During his trips he visited 150 families and preached 66 sermons, in addition to attending prayer and conference meetings. In October and November, St. Clair spent another three weeks on the various islands visiting 46 families and delivering 18 more sermons.

Come winter, the association continued its interest in the islands, particularly Outer Long Island, and sent St. Clair back to continue his mission.

St. Clair combined religious teachings with basic education, a common practice by Baptists and other missionaries of the era. They often taught islanders to read through Scripture. In fact, for most of the 19th century and early 20th century, the church, whether Baptist or Congregational, was critical to education on the island. The Maine Baptist Convention minutes of 1844 (p. 18) read:

> "The board also appointed Bro. S to visit these islands in the winter, with the understanding that he would teach school during the week and preach on the Sabbath. Accordingly, he spent nine weeks in this way, chiefly on Long Island. He had an interesting school composed of persons of all ages, from the infant to the man of grey hairs, all of whom were anxious to learn to read the word of eternal life."

During this stay, St. Clair, who later died destitute after 30 years of debilitating illness, preached 28 times, held 12 prayer meetings, kept school two months, and attended one funeral.

St. Clair, who like other missionaries boarded with island families, was well received by the islanders, and their collections supported his efforts. The minutes from the 1844 Maine Baptist Convention meeting read: "$63.57 were received from the people, and truly we may say, that in paying that sum, 'their deep poverty abounded to the riches of their liberality.' Instead of paying $63, they needed to have been paid, in charities, $500 to make their families comfortable, through the last most terrible winter experienced on this coast."

Despite missionary zeal and grand intentions, the great failing of the Baptists on Outer Long Island, and seemingly in other towns scattered across Hancock County, was its lack of permanent pastoral presence. The beleaguered clergy, overwhelmed by the sheer number of towns and people, bemoaned this lack of constant nurturing. Their efforts on Outer Long Island came in enthusiastic spurts, followed by years of silence during which the island church maintained little or no connection with its parent association.

The island's situation was not unique. In 1844, Brother David Nutter pleaded for help in Hancock County (Maine Baptist Convention 1844, 18):

> "If the Society can make an appropriation, or send a missionary to this District, it would find a large field to occupy on the islands of the sea, and in the back settlements. These islands have been very much neglected, and yet there are no people who are more ready to receive the gospel and do what they can towards supporting a missionary than they."

Nine years later, the situation was little improved. While thirty-one churches belonged to the Hancock Association, only a "small number of, however, can be regarded as efficient, active organizations."

Still, throughout the 1840s, the Baptist Church was a presence to many islanders who apparently remained quite pious at times. In 1847, six island church members were excluded for unknown reasons. The congregation became plagued by dismissals and alleged disruption.

Amos Sr. wrote: *"Saturday, August the 21st, 1847 — There was a church meeting for business. First, after singing and prayer, William D. Lunt and Israel Lunt the second withdrew Fellowship from this Baptist Church on Long Island. Then the Church withdrew their fellowship from them and they were excluded from our Fellowship of this church and recorded in the church book. Then James Davis and Rebecca Davis and John Rich were excluded from our Fellowship in this Baptist Church and recorded in our Church book. It being Saturday, August the 21st day of 1847. Deacon John Pomroy and Caroline Pomroy his wife was dismissed by letter to join the Baptist Church on Mount Desert."*

And later that fall, he wrote: *Sunday forenoon November the 14th A.D. 1847 — After the services was over some business was attended to. A committee of three was chosen to see & look up the disorderly members of this church to see if they wanted to withdraw from this Baptist Church or not and to report when Elder S. Macomber does visit us again. At a church meeting the committee chosen was Amos C. Lunt, Israel B. Lunt and Jacob Lunt 2nd."*

Rev. St. Clair, ordained as an evangelist on Vinalhaven in 1820, regularly visited Outer Long Island until the fall of 1847 when Rev. Samuel Macomber became the island's chief missionary. During Macomber's and St. Clair's missions, services were held daily, often with A.M. and P.M. sermons delivered in the schoolhouse or island homes.

In 1847 — perhaps the height of the Baptist influence on Outer Long Island — the island church sent five delegates to the Hancock Baptist Association's annual meeting in Sedgwick. The five delegates were: Amos C. Lunt Sr., Israel B. Lunt, Thomas Rich, Jacob Lunt 2nd and Albion K. P. Lunt.

By this time, however, islanders understood the difficulty in sustaining a vibrant church with only sporadic attention from dedicated clergy. They sought more regular service.

Amos Sr. wrote in late September 1847: *"There was meeting Sunday Evening after the other services to see what the church & inhabitants would do respecting on hiring Elder Samuel Macomber a third of the time for one year to see if this Long Island together with Placentia and East Black Island and Gotts Island would agree to pay him 33 dollars and 33 cents or one-third of 100 dollars for his services to preach here on these islands one third of the time of the ensuing years. A committee was chosen to see what the inhabitants would do as to paying him the salary proposed by the association. It was proposed by the association that if Deer Isle Church and Swans Isle and Long Islands and Gotts Island would pay Elder Samuel Macomber $100 that they would pay him another $100 for the year ensuing. The committee chosen was Amos C. Lunt, Amos Lunt Jr., and Jacob Lunt 2nd."*

Macomber was never hired.

## *An Unalterable Decline*

The undermanned Baptist missionaries and some island residents continued their efforts to keep the church going for the next 40 years, but membership and activity generally declined starting in 1847.

The island church offered no report of its activities in either 1850 or 1851.

In 1852, with Amos C. Lunt Sr. dead and his nephew George B. Lunt serving as the church delegate, a new island pastor, Rev. Glover, visited many islands, including Outer Long Island. Glover (Hancock Baptist Association 1852, 18) said, "They speak of having had to contend with the evils of intemperance, and of great improvement having taken place on the Island, in this respect."

But also by 1852, the Association grew increasingly concerned about Outer Long Island's lack of connection and sent a committee to investigate. The Hancock Baptist Association said in 1853, "although we did not find the condition of things so favorable as we could wish, yet as Rev. W. Glover is the pastor of this church, and well received, and has evidently been instrumental of good among the people, we deemed it the most prudent course, after having given them the advice we thought necessary, to dismiss the whole subject."

Glover was soon gone, and the Baptists did not make another strong attempt at reviving the Outer Long Island church until 1861 when N. C. Everett arrived to find a church that, after seven drops, two dismissals, six exclusions and one death, had 27 members. Still, Everett was welcomed and Bartholomew Russell Lunt, church clerk, told the association, "While we have been sitting and hearing the gospel we have been refreshed, and our prayer is that the Head of the Church will bless the labors of our pastor in saving souls."

However, 1861 was another temporary burst. During the next seven years membership fell from 27 to 17, largely through deaths and exclusions.

Again, the Outer Long Island experience was not unique. In 1870, the Baptists wrote of their Hancock Association: "Great destitution of pastors, about 17 churches without preaching ... many churches feeble and dying."

That certainly described Long Island. After members failed to report between 1868 and 1872, the Hancock Baptist Association voted Wednesday morning, Sept. 10, 1873 to "drop the Long Island and the Second Franklin Churches from the Association."

Still the island made one last gasp. In 1874, with James T. Davis, an enthusiastic lay preacher, serving as deacon and Ebenezer Nelson Pierce, a 22-year-old native of Plymouth, Massachusetts, attending to pastoral duties for the remaining 14 members, the church sought readmission: "A letter was read from the Long Island Church which was dropped last year for failing to report, and after some remarks from Bro. Benj. Dodge, that church was restored to membership in the Association."

However, Pierce neither rekindled a Baptist spirit nor increased membership, prompting Bartholomew Russell Lunt to solemnly write in 1876, "We feel like sheep without a shepherd. No Special Int."

Without that interest, membership dwindled to eight members by 1886 on an island with more than 150 residents. By this time, most of the settlers active in building the early Baptist Church had died, contributing to the unalterable decline.

Finally, the Hancock Baptist Association voted for the last time in 1889 — 46 years after the church was founded in the dead of winter by Rev. St. Clair — to drop the Baptist Church of Long Island.

# The Congregationalists

Baptists were not the only missionaries poking around the islands of Maine in the 19th century. The second denomination to take an interest in Outer Long Island represented a different, somewhat less rigid branch of Protestantism: Congregationalists. Their missionaries not only planted the seeds from which sprouted the current church, but also played a critical role in the birth of the interdenominational Maine Sea Coast Missionary Society.

Congregational Church missionaries worked the islands of Hancock County early in the 19th century, including visits to Isle au Haut as early as 1816. The first known Congregational missionary on Outer Long Island was Rev. Joshua Eaton in 1858.

When Eaton, a long-time minister on Isle au Haut, made his first visit to Outer Long Island, the Baptist Church maintained a presence there and operated a church with 35 members. Even when the Congregational Church finally developed in the late 1880s, the Baptist Church, though virtually gone, remained, so technically the island had two religious denominations. It is unknown whether any factions or divisions existed between the islanders over the two churches. Most likely, by the 1880s, islanders seeking spiritual guidance reached out to any branch that showed interest.

Rev. Eaton returned to Long Island a second time in 1860, one year before Everett made his short-lived attempt to reenergize the Baptist Church. Eaton wrote with little hyperbole of his 1860 visit (Clark, *History of the Congregational Churches in Maine, Volume One,* 133):

"I found them morally in a prostrate condition. No stated preach-ing, except a few Sabbaths the last Winter, since I visited them two years ago. They have a commodious harbor, and fishing vessels come in considerable numbers; more than fifty were in the harbor at one time. A convenient house, which answers the double purpose of a meeting house and school, with a small bell which calls the people together as it rings out to the whole harbor. Here I preached Sabbath days and evenings to 30, 40, 60, 100, 150 and even more of eager, attentive listeners. Most, of course, were strangers, for the population of the island is 184. I tarried there five Sabbaths with the four intervening weeks, preaching 28 discourses, visiting all the families, and distributing tracts among them. Several persons who obtained a hope two and a half years ago, when Mr. Wallace (a pious layman) was among them, appear well, though unconnected with any church. My labors were cordially and thankfully received. The most of them were very poor. But they paid me for three Sabbaths. They are hoping that Mr. Wallace will visit them again, but have no settled plans for the future. Some of them expressed a desire that a Congregational church might be formed there."

## *A Refreshed Spirit*

More than 20 years passed before an active Congregational Church began to take shape.

That movement, although initially slight, began in the early 1880s after Captain George W. Lane, of the Atlantic Coast Sunday School Missionary, sailed into Lunt Harbor in his open boat *Pilgrim*. Lane, dubbed the "Coast Missionary," was a businessman turned evangelist who sailed the coast starting Sunday schools. His missionary style, one that was copied by most who followed, was somewhat paternalistic in nature.

After starting such a school on Outer Long Island, he visited once or twice each summer for about five years despite seeing little success. Indeed, interest in his services remained poor and attendance sporadic until the summer of 1886 when islanders finally warmed to the persistent Lane.

By the summer of 1888, interest was such that Lane decided a more formal and organized church was necessary to continue fostering the island's religious development.

Overall, 1888 became a watershed year for religion on Outer Long Island as several forces and people converged to accelerate the drive towards a second organized church and the island's first devoted chapel. Through many of those same forces, the year also became important in the education of island children and development of the elementary school.

In August, I.P. Warren, editor and proprietor of the influential Portland weekly newspaper *The Christian Mirror*, accompanied Lane on his rounds, including stops at Deer Island, Swans Island and Outer Long Island. His descriptions — although written in a style designed to elicit help from readers — provide further glimpses of island life during a difficult economic period.

In the August 18 edition of his newspaper, under the headline "The Mission Work on Our Coast," Warren wrote:

*On Board the "Pilgrim" Head Harbor Island, July 31, 1888.*

*On this picturesque coast, among its many islands, nearly all of great beauty because of the diversity of surface, God in his loving kindness has permitted me to spend a little time this summer in company with the "coast missionary," Capt. George W. Lane, and his wife. Under the auspices of the Congregational Sunday-school and Publishing Society of Boston, he is working to-day, and I wish that it was possible for all who are represented by this society to follow him in his travels. I am convinced that they would unhesitatingly say that he has been chosen by God for this work as sure as Paul was raised up for his great and peculiar mission.*

*Leaving the steamer in Rockland, we found the captain waiting for us, and were soon on the "Pilgrim" under sail for Burnt Cove, Deer Isle; but ere long the impenetrable fog came closing in about us, and we were obliged to anchor in Rockport harbor. How often we have wished, as the fog and patience-trying calms hindered our progress, for steam. How much more time could be given to the islanders if we had it! But the captain is well-pleased with the beautiful little yacht furnished him by the society, and God is good in tempering the winds and waves, and we anchored in Burnt Cove safely Saturday, July 21st, and spent a happy, though rainy, Sabbath with the people. Here we found a church, a well-attended Sunday-school and an earnest pastor, who, we found, not only ministered to this, but to some of Swan's Island people's needs, which island is on our route between Deer and Long Island."*

*On our way, we stopped at "Green's Landing," where, seven years ago, Capt. Lane found a Sunday-school in a very discouraged state, having very scanty means to sustain it. From his treasury of books and papers he then supplied them, and helped the superintendent to bring the people back into it and to-day the new pastor, who came from Bangor Seminary to them about six weeks ago, told us that it still continues. They have a church edifice, but it has an uncared-for look, needing paint sadly;*

*not surprising, if one knows the fact that there is not church organization here, although the inhabitants number about one thousand. The pastor told us that he had crowded audiences every Sabbath since he had been here, and astonished us by saying that a society of Christian Endeavor meets regularly every Tuesday evening.*

*This is a rendezvous for large numbers of seamen, and the stone quarries bring together very many men, who need religious influences to keep them from intemperance and vice. We are very glad for them that they have such a leader in their new pastor for he seems like a very earnest man. Going from there through the "thoroughfare," we passed many rocky points, and came within a mile of Long Island, when dense fog caused us to anchor and stay all night in the bay.*

*Entering the cove (Long Island harbor) at daybreak, we were impressed with the poverty of the place. On our right, scattered over the rocky projections, were houses so small, so black, they looked hardly habitable, three only of these had any paint on them. On the left, only two bore any signs of comfort.*

*Anchoring, we were soon greeted by the fishermen in the harbor, and when once the islanders realized that Capt. Lane was there, their enthusiasm was great, nor did it diminish a particle during his stay. They seem to look upon him as a father and I do not wonder when I hear them tell what under God, he has done for them. Mothers told me that years ago they prayed, asking God to send them a teacher, a leader and they look upon the captain as the answer to those prayers. They number in all about one hundred and fifty, and a kindlier, more gentle, reverent people it would be hard to find. About seven years ago, intemperance and consequent vice made this island a desert to live in, but now, how changed!*

*A school-house, formerly forbidding because of its dirty condition, has received the blessing of cleanliness to the extent of fresh paper on the walls and an oil-cloth for its floor. This is used for church as well as school purposes. While there is no church organization here, the people seem all ready to unite in one, for last year there were many who came out on the Lord's side, and at the six meetings recently held many more expressed their convictions and desired to follow Christ. As if to encourage in the good work God gave the captain this year the chief of the island, who has been a sinner above all sinners the islanders say. Fine-looking, noble-hearted in many ways, if he serves God half as well as he has Satan, he will surely be the means of good to hundreds of his brother fishermen, for he is so widely known.*

*With two or three exceptions, these people are very poor. May I ask you to go into two or three of their houses with me? We shall see two ten by twelve rooms on the ground floor; no plaster on the walls, old blackened newspapers and flaming posters taking its place. A ladder steep as the wall it rests against, furnishes access to the loft above. In one such place lived an old couple who had three grown sons, two of whom were lame, the third supporting the family. Looking in any direction here I saw nothing but discomfort. How they exist under such circumstances is a mystery. And these are not exceptions; there are many such. ...*

## Maine Missionary Society

Also in 1888, Lane and island residents petitioned the Maine Missionary Society for aid. Rev. Jonathan Edwards Adams, secretary of the society, fielded their request. The 66-year-old Adams was a long-time missionary not only in the outposts of Maine, but in the still developing nation. He started in a church in Boothbay and eventually helped care for Civil War soldiers on the battlefields of 1863.

Earlier in 1888, Adams recognized the opportunity and the need on the islands and in the rural towns of Maine. He pressed for support of these outposts (Maine Missionary Society *1888*, 250):

"We find the new fields, called destitute communities, where no organized churches exist or have been desired. It is a sad and shameful fact that there are multitudes of rural neighborhoods, some considerable villages and not a few whole townships, of this sort in our beloved state. There is no way to reach such communities but by the voice of the living evangelist. He must be a traveling herald, like Paul and Barnabas of early days, one who can 'become all things to all men, that by any means (he) may save some.'"

With that issue fresh in his mind, the request from Long Island recently in hand and a familiarity with the missionary work of Capt. Lane, Rev. Adams headed for Outer Long Island in October 1888 to decide what aid his missionary society might provide. In the Nov. 3, 1888 edition of *The Christian Mirror*, he wrote:

*"Several weeks ago I had a petition from outer Long Island, some nine*

*miles to the south of Mount Desert, to which sixty-seven names were signed, praying that "a man of God might be sent, to lead them to a better life." At length it happened that a visit could be made. A boatman was found willing to brave a fresh breeze and the dashing waves, if I could stand the "oiling up," and the wetting sure to come. So in our full suits of rubber, "south-westers" and all, we started from Bass Harbor under double reefs, and in one hour reached our destination, dry as to our under clothing, thanks to "the oils."*

*We found the island about two miles long and one mile wide, with a convenient harbor and wharves, where fishing vessels find shelter and the paraphernalia for curing fish upon the shores. On either side of the harbor were dwellings, which gave shelter and some comfort to about twenty-five families, numbering in all one hundred and forty souls. A school house tolerably well situated to convene the scholars, showed up as the only public building at the place.*

*Capt. Lane, now of the missionary yacht Alert, visited them some four years ago and found them in a sadly neglected condition and without any religious privileges. The people, young and old, were considered to be quite immoral and intemperate. Capt. Lane called them together, organized a school, gave them books and papers, secured their confidence by other means and continued his visits from time to time, till he reached their hearts and moved them to better hopes and better lives.*

*I inquired as to their present condition and was told that a number of the men and women hope they are Christians, that six persons are reliable for Sunday-school and prayer meeting work, and that the evening before though stormy, twenty-five were in attendance and it was one of their best meetings. They have a temperance organization, and a weekly Saturday evening gathering.*

*On the Sabbath they have a Sunday-school and a religious service in which they are often assisted by Christian fishermen who happen to harbor there. But their great desire is to have "a man of God' with them for several months at least to teach them in Bible truths and tell them how to live. My heart went out towards them, was pained for them and cried for direction or suggestion as they looked to me for advice and possible help. ...*

*My mind turned to their school. There are forty or more scholars, who get about three months of summer and three months of winter teaching. The winter teacher comes from abroad. They pay twenty-five dollars a month*

*Courtesy of Ella V. Lunt*
*William Sanford Lunt (1862 - 1936)*

*and board. A thought and a question comes in a breath — why not let us send your teacher, a Christian man, and a half preacher, perhaps better, you paying the twenty-five dollars and board? Why not? they say. And so it stands the one who shall undertake this mission is to be envied for his rare opportunity to do good, and to get a rich experience in self-sacrifice, and a genuine Christian ministry. I have admired Capt. Lane for years and feel more than ever before like endorsing his Sunday school work on the Atlantic Coast.*

Rev. Adams quickly searched for someone to both teach school and lead church meetings that winter.

He found Alexander P. MacDonald.

MacDonald, a sophomore at Bowdoin College and a fiery minister in the making, arrived Dec. 1, 1888 and stayed for three months. MacDonald, who later founded the Maine Sea Coast Missionary Society, stayed with various town residents.

His early December meetings, held in the island's second schoolhouse near the site now occupied by the Frenchboro Historical Society, were lightly attended and the congregation predominantly women. Those residents attending from the start included: Thomas and Almenia S. (Davis) Osier, Mary T. (Rice) Davis, Mrs. Samuel Allen, Abbie (Davis) Rich, Mary Lunt, Rhoda (Lunt) Teel, Calvin C. and Kate (Dawes) Lunt and Alice (Twist) Lunt.

Then, two days before Christmas, William Sanford Lunt, great-grandson of Amos Coffin Lunt Sr., offered his confession of faith, helping spur a fruitful two months that saw 20 people join the church and more than 60 attend services (See Appendix B).

Nearly two months after William Sanford's confession, MacDonald wrote a letter to *The Christian Mirror* answering questions originally posed by I.P. Warren. The letter appeared March 2 and, although not without its missionary flourishes, offers a relatively realistic depiction of the island.

*From Outer Long Island, Maine*
*Feb. 12, 1889*
*To the Editor of The Christian Mirror*
*Dear Sir:*

*In answer to your letters inquiring into the condition and needs of the people on this island, and a description of my winter's work, I can say that God has indeed blessed me and that this has been the happiest winter of my life.*

*It will be remembered by most readers of the Mirror that Rev. J.E. Adams, secretary of the Maine Missionary Society, visited the Island last fall and called for someone to lead the people in spirituality, and to teach the children. It will also be remembered that Long Island is the farthest island out, it being 12 miles from the mainland.*

*The area of the island is about three square miles. The population, about 25 families, numbers in all upward of 150 souls. Fishing is the principal occupation. Although the coast of the island is rocky, rough and a dangerous place for vessels, yet it possesses a good harbor which is often sought by vessels out in a storm. The whole surface of the island is rough, and mostly covered with wood. Very little of the land can be cultivated on account of the rocks and ledges. One of the greatest inconveniences is that the nearest post office is three miles away on another island.*

*The people are all kind hearted, and as a rule, industrious. The majority are poor, yet not to be helped or pitied much. Last summer was a bad season for their business, so some families may be reduced in means, but I have not seen any suffer here this winter for want of food or clothes. Many in all our cities fare worse than the poorest here.*

*Capt. G.W. Lane, the Sunday-school coast missionary, has visited the island off and on, every summer for eight years. No interest was manifested in the gospel till within three years, when the people were led through the influence of Capt. Lane to support a Sunday school which he organ-*

*ized for them. For 12 years back, the people had no one to preach the gospel to them and it is not strange that when found by our missionary the majority of the people were given to intemperance and vice, and that the Sabbath was little regarded. When Capt. Lane visited here last summer, he found his efforts blessed. A Sunday school had been kept along, a temperance organization had sprung up among the people, and efforts had been put forth to banish intemperance from the island. For the last three months not a glass of liquor has been sold here and the inhabitants feel determined that there never shall be a glass sold here again.*

*When I came here the first of December, I found their temperance meetings were supported. I also found a Sunday school of 50 scholars, with little or no order of work, and about eight Christians who could be depended upon to help in meetings.*

*I at once arranged the Sunday school on the plan suggested to them by Capt. Lane, procured from the Missionary Society, the International Lessons leaves for the quarter and from Mr. E.J. Phelps of Rockland, Mass., a picture roll illustrating each lesson, which I find to be a great help in impressing the lesson on the minds of children. We have a teachers meeting every Tuesday evening in which the Sunday school teachers and all others who wish, study the lesson for Sunday.*

*The Sunday school and temperance meetings were the only meetings held regularly. I appointed devotional exercises for Sunday; preaching in the morning, Sunday school in the afternoon, and prayer and praise services in the evening and also arranged for a prayer meeting Wednesday evening. All the meetings are well attended, especially the evening services. The people take great interest in singing and are very thankful to the Winter Street church of Bath for the "Gospel Hymn" books sent to them. The Lord has seemed to bless my efforts from the very first. I had scarcely spent a month here before many began to inquire "the way to eternal life." Many of them confessed that they had tried to live better lives since Capt. Lane talked to them.*

*There are now 45 who take part in meetings and who are seeking after Christ, and among them are some of the oldest men on the island. "The old settlers" who never cared for religion and who never attended meetings have come now to be a great help to our meetings. One thing in which these people would be an example for many of our city Christians to follow is in taking part in the meetings. Each does willingly his part.*

*The winter's work has been especially blest among the young men, thirteen of whom are now striving to follow Christ. A few days ago eight of them left on a fishing trip down east to be gone for a month. On departing nearly everyone took his Bible and hymn book. "What a contrast!" I have heard some of the people say; "a year ago each took a bottle of rum and left half drunk."*

*There are many other points I might speak of in regard to our meetings and what the Lord has been doing among us. Now about the needs; they are not clothing or food. The people are all healthy, hardy and rugged; there has scarcely been a case of sickness in the last three months. The need above all is a place of worship: all our meetings are held in the old schoolhouse which serves as town hall, temperance hall, and for everything in general.*

*If the people could have help in building them a church, and could have Christian people from the mainland visit them more in the summer months, they would soon be in circumstances to help themselves and maintain their own preacher.*

*The island is one of the prettiest and quietest places on the whole coast, and if good Christian people would direct their steps this way in the summer months, they would not only help these people to a higher life, but would also receive a blessing to themselves, as I have.*

*I thank the Maine Missionary Society for sending me here. I feel that God has truly been my strength. I trust the day is not far distant when I can see the 45 seekers members of a church here on Long Island.*

*Yours truly, A.P. MacDonald.*

In May 1889, Rev. Edwin Alphonso Harlow, general missionary of the Maine Missionary Society, visited for one week to see what progress MacDonald had made. Impressed with the results he saw, Harlow recommended the Society organize a church on the island.

Seeing the results of the missionary work, heeding Harlow's words and bowing to requests from islanders, the Missionary Society sent MacDonald to the island again in June of 1889. He stayed three months, adding more members and reenergizing the faithful. Most importantly that summer came the culmination of work begun less than a year earlier: the Congregational Church of Outer Long Island was organized.

*Alexander P. MacDonald, early 1900s.*

During high tide on the morning of July 23, 1889, Rev. Harlow led ten people into the cove at the head of Lunt Harbor to the strains of "My Faith Looks Up to Thee." One by one, Henry W. Lunt, Agnes (Joyce) Davis, Hiram A. Lunt, Constantine Carter, Bartholomew R. Lunt, George C. Lunt, Mary E. Lunt, James T. Davis, Katie Lunt and Calvin C. Lunt were dunked under the ocean in the sandy cove near Sam Rich's fish-house and baptized.

The new church quickly developed its organizational structure. On the night of the 22nd, Thomas N. Osier, Calvin C. Lunt and Bartholomew Russell Lunt were chosen to lead a committee on the Articles of Faith, Covenant, Constitution and By-Laws. The committee met at Osier's house the next day and adopted the articles of faith. Hiram Lunt, Frank Gilman, Hortense Van Norden, Katie Lunt and Constantine Carter were chosen as the nominating committee, while Rev. Harlow and Rev. G.A. Hood served as the Congregational Council.

The first church officers were William Van Norden, clerk; William J. Teel, treasurer; and Calvin C. Lunt, William Sanford Lunt and Thomas Osier, all deacons.

The momentous day ended that evening when 15 more residents were baptized. Rev. Hood led the services, and Scripture was read by Rev. Pierce, a former Baptist minister on Outer Long Island who had since moved to a church in Colrain, Massachusetts.

In *The Christian Mirror* of Aug. 3, 1889, Rev. Harlow described the event:

"The communion service was administered by Rev. Messrs Hood and Harlow, and the meeting was brought to a close with a sort of Congregational love feast, which was a very tender, joyful testimony meeting. Tears of joy were in many eyes and much grateful mention was made of Capt. Lane, who had been God's instrument in beginning the good work, and of Mr. McDonald, under whose charge last winter the precious revival culminated. The revival spirit is still with the people, and Sunday evening last three confessed the purpose to strive to live the new life."

## *The Fisherman's Chapel*

While organizing the formal church was a crucial step, the membership took the penultimate step in the island's religious evolution four days later, July 27, 1889, when it voted to take any action necessary to procure land and build a chapel. The clerk was instructed to contact Joseph D. Lunt about acquiring a piece of his property. The membership also voted to take a collection each Sunday for building funds, and voted a $1 tax on each church member to pay the pastor's board.

That December, Alexander P. MacDonald's brother, Angus, arrived to keep the spirit alive during the cold winter months.

The membership broke ground in the spring of 1890 with the island men digging the cellar and building the church while Alexander P. MacDonald oversaw construction, which eventually cost $1,325.

The 1890 annual report of the Maine Missionary Society (p.197-198) read:

"Outer Long Island has come to the notice of almost every one during the year, and adds to the interest of our missionary results. Some $500.00 are in the treasury of the society for a chapel, and it

*Courtesy of Frenchboro Historical Society*

*Long Island Congregational Church, 1890 - 1904. The parsonage and schoolhouse were not yet built. Note original steps and steeple.*

will be built at once. It will cost about $200 more than has been estimated, but we feel sure the friends will add to the amount in hand. These gospel privileges are of exceeding value to the isolated families of this lone isle of the sea, and they open to them the promise of a new life. Mr. A. P. MacDonald is there now for the summer."

The church, the focal point of island life for more than a century, was dedicated Sept. 10, 1890, with 10 children and one adult baptized. Rev. Salem Town, Dr. Adams, Rev. Porter, Rev. Lewis and Alexander MacDonald all blessed the event. The guests were presented with a bountifully laden table of chowder and lobster.

The Missionary Society (Maine Missionary Society, *Annual Report 1891*, 147) wrote later: "All is now complete and paid to the last cent. We doubt if any other object has touched the churches as has this "fisherman's chapel," or if money has come so readily and cheerfully before, or if any house has been built at any missionary station, with less friction and trouble."

The first sermon in the newly erected church was led by Rev. Harlow who preached from Acts 2:1, while Rev. Lewis read from the sixth chapter of 2nd Chronicles:

"Then said Solomon, the Lord hath said that he would dwell in the thick darkness. But I have built an house of habitation for thee, and a place for thy dwelling for ever."

Courtesy of Frenchboro Historical Society

*Lunt Harbor and the Long Island Congregational Church (left) between 1890 and 1904.*

*Chapter Seven*
# 19th Century Education

Some early island settlers were relatively well educated, almost certainly self-taught or taught by family members who recognized the importance of education. Others grew up illiterate. Even by 1870, about one-quarter of the adults 16 or older could not write and about 10 percent could not read. Typically, the people who could not write were clustered in specific families.

The island's rare semi-formal classes in the 1830s were driven by a mix of secular and religious forces. Classes were taught by residents or missionaries often using the Bible. In such cases "students" ranged from young children to adults, or as one Baptist missionary wrote in the early 1840s, "from the infant to the man of grey hairs."

This link between education and religion foreshadowed the future. Religion, while struggling to establish spiritual roots, played a critical role in developing formal education on the island throughout the 19th century. Amazingly, the church did not abandon this role until the late 1960s.

## The Family School

The Lunt, Rich, Rice and Pomroy men who settled on Long Island in the 1820s were the first to raise families on the island and begin building the community.

The number of island children increased dramatically over the next decade as other settlers arrived and as a younger generation began having their own children. By 1830, the island population was 42, including more than 20 school-aged children. By 1840, the population surged to more than 120 people living in 17 households. Those households included more than 40 youths between 5 and 20 years old, and another 29 children younger than 5.

Given the practical needs and the generally poor conditions of rural Maine, many young men started work as teenagers or younger to help support often large families. Likewise, daughters, who also tended family gardens and animals, typically helped raise and care for their numerous siblings. This island dynamic lasted into the 1900s, helping keep some teens out of school and lessening the perceived importance or at least the practicality of formalized education. During this era, there were neither mandatory school attendance laws in Maine nor even minimum school-year requirements.

Despite such circumstances, some did emphasize education. Rehoboth Hannah B. Lunt, daughter of Amos Coffin Lunt Sr. and sister to Israel B. Lunt and Amos Coffin Lunt Jr., taught some children at kitchen tables and in family living rooms. Israel insisted that his children receive an education. He dedicated a room in his house to teaching his children and other family members, including nieces and nephews and his much younger half brothers and sisters.

Though classes were not held daily, Israel, Hannah and Amos Sr., took turns teaching reading and writing. Israel — the wealthiest Long Island resident — occasionally hired tutors from the mainland.

The results are evident. While some island children grew up barely educated, others became skilled readers and writers. Such skill is seen in the poetry penned by Rhoda Lunt, the letters written by Israel's other daughters such as Amanda, and the general success of children such as John R. and Albion K.P.

Israel's children were not the only ones who received an education. His brothers and sisters were educated, while cousins, such as Bartholomew Russell Lunt, George B. and Hiram A. Lunt, emerged as island leaders in the 19th Century.

Elsewhere, Hannah, followed by Rhoda, taught the Rich children, and likely the Rice children, in the cluster of homes built in the fields of Richs Head. John Rich was a prominent islander of the era, but few of the adults living on "The Head" could write, requiring teachers to come from the main village on the harbor. Both women walked two miles over wooded paths from Lunt Harbor to Richs Head to teach classes in family houses. No schoolhouse was ever built on Richs Head, but the settlement lasted for about 80 years.

Hannah also established the island's first library — the Long Island Seamans Library — in the late 1830s. The library loaned books to island residents and visiting fishermen.

## An Island School

Despite this private education, Israel, Hannah and other islanders realized a successful community needed a school. The issue arose again and again. The island was incorporated, along with several island neighbors, as Long Island Plantation in 1840. This gave the island the ability to raise taxes and make self-governing decisions. It paved the way for such issues as building a school.

Amos Coffin Lunt Sr. wrote (Maine Historical Society collections, Cyrus K. Lunt papers): *Friday, March 26th, 1841 — Hannah B. Lunt & Israel B. Lunt Esqr was here talking again about building a School House.*

Finally, they acted.

In 1842, Israel, Hannah, John Rich and others met at Joseph D. Lunt's house to lay the groundwork for one of the most crucial communal decisions of the island's young life.

Amos Coffin Lunt Sr. wrote:

*Friday April 1, 1842 — Simeon Milliken Esqr and Capt Isaac Ober came onto this Long Island as a committee appointed to regulate matters respecting building a School House on this island. Part of the male inhabitants met at the dwelling house of Joseph D. Lunt and acted on the following proposals, 1st choose Hannah B. Lunt for first committee & John Rich second committee & Israel B. Lunt Esqr, third committee and likewise proposed on two places to set the School House & then left it to the committee to say on whether of the places it should be built on.*

Amos donated part of his field — a spot between the houses owned in 1999 by Daniel and Tina Lunt and Ellsworth T. "Derry" Rundlett III — to build the school. The first schoolhouse, completed in 1842, also served as church and general meeting house. It was crucial to community development.

Early school years were irregular and short, usually lasting only a few weeks. The Outer Long Island school, like most rural schools, remained ungraded until the 20th century. One persistent problem was the lack of steady, professional teachers. For years, island residents or missionaries led the sporadic classes.

In its earliest days, the island operated two distinct school districts, one at Lunt Harbor for the main population and one at Richs Head for the three to five families who lived there. The official two-district system lasted until 1856, although classes continued at Richs Head for several more years. In 1860, 20 people lived in three households on The Head, including eight children 16 years old or younger. The heads of the three households were: William and Eleanor (Rice) Rich, Thomas and Mary Rice and Jacob and Dorcas Rice.

Despite a dedicated building, the school as a community force struggled for many reasons, including lack of compulsory education in Maine and lack of financial support from the state, not even 40 years old itself. Indeed, across Maine school duration varied from year to year, depending on both money and teachers.

The status of the island school is first detailed in state records (Maine Superintendent of Commons Schools, *Annual Report 1856*) for the year 1856. Outer Long Island operated the two districts previously mentioned and reported one "not in good repair" schoolhouse valued at $400. The schoolhouse was the original building built only 13 years earlier.

The town raised $55.90 to support its school, which had 75 potential students between the ages of 4 and 21. Average attendance during an eight-week summer session was 35. During a 12-week winter session average attendance was 42. The male teacher was paid $20 per month and received $8 toward his board. The female teacher received $2 per week as pay and an additional $1 per week for board.

Throughout this era, teachers taught per term, thus requiring the island to find two or three teachers each year. Teachers boarded with various island residents until the Parsonage was built in 1904. The Parsonage remained the primary residence for school teachers and ministers into the 1980s.

In 1857, Outer Long Island — temporarily incorporated as the town of Islandport — operated summer and winter sessions that lasted a combined 22 weeks. Of 80 potential "scholars" on the island, only 40 regularly attended classes, a 50 percent attendance rate. While certainly not stellar, it beat the Hancock County average of 47 percent. These attendance figures are good for comparison and general statements but are somewhat misleading. The rate includes young men and women up to age 21, who clearly were not all going to attend school. Many older teens were not only working but were married and raising children.

Also in 1857, the island paid its one male teacher $25 per month and its one female teacher $1.50 per week. This male-female pay disparity lessened over the years, but lasted into the 1900s. The amount spent per pupil in 1857 was $1.13.

In 1858, a whopping 115 "scholars" lived in town — a 53 percent increase in just two years. Summer attendance averaged 50 students and winter attendance 40 students, producing an average attendance rate of 39 percent. The island attendance rate generally remained in the 40 to 50 percent range for years.

By the late 1860s, the school had apparently deteriorated.

A scathing 1869 report written by an unnamed school committee member — and relative newcomer to the island — painted a bleak, though undoubtedly exaggerated picture of the island school and the island itself to hammer home the writer's point (Maine Superintendent of Common Schools, *Annual Report 1869*, 66-67). Note the political message in the last paragraph. He seems mistaken about the age of the schoolhouse:

> As a member of the so-called Superintending School Committee of this plantation, I have the honor to make the following report of the schools and scholars of this Island.
>
> 1st, School Houses. There is one house built about twelve years ago for a church, which has been used as a school-house, but is now unfit for religious or educational purposes until it is repaired and refitted.
>
> 2nd, Schools. During my residence of three years, there have been two (2) spasmodic attempts at a school, the first subsided in a fortnight, and the other ran through a period of three months. The expense was met with the State fund which had accumulated several years. The benefits derived did not equal the expense, owing to the dilapidated condition of the house, the inclemency of the weather, and the inexperience of the teachers.
>
> 3d, Scholars. There are about forty (40) children of all ages and sizes who are embraced in the above term, but there is not one among the whole whose qualifications would secure him a desk in any other than a Primary School, while many, yes, most of them are utterly

ignorant of the rudiments of learning. This sad state of affairs is the result of the general poverty which prevails among the parents of the said children, rendering them incapable of supporting a school, and causing them to require the services of their children as soon as they are old enough to earn something towards their support.

There is good material among the children here for scholars, provided they had the advantages which other children enjoy, and if a school could be established, I believe an average attendance of twenty-five scholars could be had.

The State fund is wholly inadequate, and the people can do little, if anything, towards a school, and as the law makes no provisions for such a case, I see no way of redeeming the children, and through them the people, from the poverty and ignorance into which the latter have fallen, and the former are fast growing, unless the humane and charitable take the matter in hand, and by well-directed effort bring light out of darkness, knowledge out of ignorance.

Without religious or educational privileges, with nothing to civilize, humanize or refine, it is no cause of wonder to me that there are but four republicans on this island. If you think I draw too strong on my imagination, please send a trusty agent here, and if he does not say as did one of old, "The half has not been told me," I will immediately resign my position as junior member of the Superintending School Committee.

While harsh, such a tone was common in Maine. Individual towns railed against inadequate emphasis on education and its effect on children.

An 1870 school report (Maine Superintendent of Common Schools, *Annual Report 1870*, 47) on Tremont, which always maintained connections to Long Island, had this to say: "We find that 426, or about 55 percent, of the scholars in town, either do not attend school at all or are so irregular in their attendance as to practically deprive them of any benefit of our schools. Many of them are young men loafing about doing nothing, no benefit to themselves or the community."

In 1872, the average attendance rate on Outer Long Island stood at 40 percent, 11 percentage points below the Hancock County average. The school operated a summer session of six weeks and a winter session of eight weeks. This means in the early 1870s, island students attended school for

14 weeks a year, compared to a Hancock County average of 18 weeks (State law in 1999 requires children to attend school for 36 weeks per year.)

The island's second school-house was built in the 1870s. It sat on the hill at the head of Lunt Harbor, above where the Frenchboro Historical Society sits in 1999. That school, which replaced the original 1842 schoolhouse, lasted until 1907. However, this small red school quickly fell into disrepair. In one instance before the close of the century pupils brought paper from home to decorate the area around their desks and hopefully brighten the build-ing. The schoolhouse was even-tually sold for $25 and used for firewood.

In 1875, Maine began passing laws to boost education. These laws made parents of chil-

*Courtesy of Frenchboro Historical Society*

*Long Island Congregational Church, early 1900s. The roof of the second schoolhouse is visible above hill to right of church.*

dren between 9 and 15 responsible for their child's attendance and required children to attend school for at least 12 weeks per year. Parents faced a possible $5 fine for truancy. Still, the average attendance of the Outer Long Island school's 68 potential scholars dropped to 34 percent. The compulsory law, which was increasingly strengthened over the years, initially did little to lift attendance rates locally or statewide. However, the island's school year did increase to 22 weeks (eight summer, 14 winter) in 1875, longer than the county average of 20 weeks. In tandem with that increase, the cost of operating the school rose to $230. Pay for male teach-ers dropped to $19.09, plus room and board of $3 per week. The island did not hire a female teacher that year.

Ten years later in 1885, the island school operated for eight weeks in summer and twelve in the winter. At a school district meeting on April 13, 1885 the following business was conducted:

1. Moderator, Calvin C. Lunt
2. District Clerk, William Van Norden
3. Voted that the summer school shall commence the first Monday in June and the winter school shall commence the first Monday in December.
4. Voted that the summer school shall keep two months and the winter school shall keep three months.
5. Voted that there shall be 5 cords of wood for the winter school.
6. H.W. Lunt furnishes the winter wood for $2.50 per cord.
7. Voted that a female teach the summer school and a male teach the winter school.
8. James T. Davis bid to board the summer teacher for $1.75 per week.
9. William J. Teel bid to board the winter teacher for $2.25 per week.
10. Voted that the sum of $2.00 be paid for cleaning the schoolhouse.

A meeting six years later on April 17th, 1891 details several changes.

1. Chose Calvin C. Lunt moderator and was sworn by clerk.
2. Chose W.A. Van Norden, clerk.
3. Voted that there shall be three terms of school during the year.
4. Voted that the two summer terms shall keep six weeks each and the winter term three months.
5. Voted that the term of school shall commence as follows, first term to commence the first Monday in June, the second the first Monday in September and the winter term the first Monday of December.
6. Voted that the summer terms of school be taught by a man.
7. Voted that there shall be 5 cords of wood for school purposes.
8. H.W. Lunt furnishes the wood for $2.75 per cord.
9. Voted that the winter term be taught by a man.
10. William M. Teel boards winter teacher for $3.25 per week.
11. Voted that if the first teacher cannot teach both terms of school, the agent shall employ a female for the second term.
12. Voted that the School agent secure a boarding place for the female teacher.
13. Voted that $2 be paid for cleaning school house.

Again, the problem plaguing the island throughout its first century remained finding and paying teachers. Finally, in the late 1880s, a possible solution arrived hand-in-hand with the church.

Rev. Jonathan Edwards Adams, the influential secretary of the Maine Missionary Society and a leader in Congregationalism, visited the island in October 1888 at the behest of islanders and Sunday school missionary Capt. George W. Lane. Adams, though visiting to decide what assistance he could offer to spark a religious revival, attacked the school problem as well. That fall he wrote (*The Christian Mirror*, Nov. 3, 1888):

"My mind turned to their school. There are forty or more scholars, who get about three months of summer and three months of winter teaching. The winter teacher comes from abroad. They pay twenty-five dollars a month and board. A thought and a question comes in a breath — why not let us send your teacher, a Christian man, and a half preacher, perhaps better, you paying the twenty-five dollars and board? Why not? they say. And so it stands the one who shall undertake this mission is to be envied for his rare opportunity to do good, and to get a rich experience in self-sacrifice, and a genuine Christian ministry."

*Courtesy of Frenchboro Historical Society*

*Pupils standing outside of the old red schoolhouse in the late 1800s. The school was located near where the Frenchboro Historical Society sits in the 1990s.*

The first man to answer Adam's call turned out to be another stroke of luck for Outer Long Island — Alexander P. MacDonald. MacDonald, a sophomore at Bowdoin College, taught school and spurred a religious revival that saw a Congregational Church organized and the island's first dedicated chapel built within three years (see Chapter Six). MacDonald continued his relationship with Outer Long Island, its church and its school after forming the Maine Sea Coast Missionary Society in 1905.

Despite MacDonald's presence, the school, held in a deteriorating building, continued to struggle.

The school operated for 24 weeks in 1890 with an average attendance rate of 44 percent. In 1895, average attendance was 60 percent with a 17-week school year. In 1900, with a 20-week school year, average attendance was 45 percent (compared with the county average of 53 percent).

*Courtesy of Frenchboro Historical Society*

*Frenchboro Elementary School, 1910s. Back row: Marie McLaughlin (left), George Perkins, Ray Teel, Alice Ross, Gertrude Lunt, Evie Lunt, Rena Birch.*
*Front Row: Lincoln Lunt, Everett Dalzell, Guy Lunt, Clifton Lunt, Etta Lunt, Lydia Thurlow, Silvia Lunt.*

Despite all these issues, change was in the air. In 1907, islanders built a third schoolhouse, a solid, reliable, almost grand building for the time, era and resources. That school still stands at the middle of a scenic trinity of white buildings at the head of Lunt Harbor. As the new school opened, not only was an unsettled education era ending, but just over the horizon awaited increased state mandates, a graded-school system, declining enrollment, the arrival of Sigma Kappa sorority workers, and finally the steadying 24-year run of school teacher Gladys Muir.

## Black Island and its School

For roughly 20 years around the turn of the 19th century, Long Island Plantation operated a full-fledged school on Black Island, which had experienced a temporary population burst in large part because of a granite quarry that opened there. The Black Island School probably started around 1888 and ended around 1914.

During this time, Long Island Plantation regularly paid Black Island teachers, paid their room and board, bought supplies and rented a school building. This activity came after nearly eighty years of island habitation.

Benjamin Dawes originally settled Black Island sometime between 1810 and 1820. Dawes raised his family there, although many relatives and descendants moved to Outer Long Island and married people living there. At least five of Benjamin's granddaughters married Long Islanders (McLane, *Blue Hill Bay*, 119).

Migration from Black Island, Placentia and other area islands to Outer Long Island was an interesting phenomenon during the 1800s. This movement represented a migration of families from smaller, less populated and less convenient islands to the larger and more developed Outer Long Island. After all, Outer Long Island had a school, stores, a larger population and more amenities than its smaller neighbors did. Ironically, a similar situation occurred in the 1900s with people moving away from Outer Long Island to the more developed mainland.

In 1860, the population of Black Island had dwindled to only the Joseph Dawes family. In 1870, only three people, Joseph, his wife Mary and Susan Hodgdon lived there. However, by 1880, the population had jumped to 15, including the family of David Nice.

Soon a granite quarry opened — operating for several years as the Black Island Granite Co. — luring workers and boosting the population to more than 50 people by the early 1890s. More people meant more children.

In 1893, plantation residents raised $50 to support a school on Black Island. The plantation's contribution, combined with $56.12 from the state, gave the Black Island School a total operating fund of $106.12.

What little is known about the school can be gleaned mostly from plantation expense records.

In 1897, the plantation rented a room or perhaps a small quarry building from Mr. Couch, manager of the Black Island quarries. Couch had previously managed a quarry on the Long Island near Blue Hill. He lived in a house on the island's northeasterly tip (McLane, 123).

In 1898, the plantation voted to hold school for eight weeks on Black Island, starting the first week in June.

In 1905, the Plantation paid Alice Sprague $25 to teach for five weeks on Black Island and then paid Laura Turner $24 to teach for eight weeks. Mrs. Moulden was paid $22 to board the teacher for eight weeks and Levi Moulden was paid $2 to cut wood and build fires at the school.

Other payments made to support the Black Island school included:
- March 6, 1906, $45 for Black Island scholars board.
- Aug. 6, 1906, $24 to Alice M. Sprague for teaching.
- Nov. 11, 1906, $20 to Sumner Morrill for teacher's board and $4 for school wood.
- March 2, 1907, $30 for two children to board at Gott Island.
- June 5, 1907, $25 to rent schoolhouse on Black Island.
- Oct. 27, 1907, $15 to Lizzie Hall, for partial payment of fall term teaching.
- May 5, 1908, Holsey Moore, board for two children at Gott Island, $28.50
- March 13, 1909, David Nice, board for scholars at Black Island, $12.00.
- Sept. 22, 1910, $25 to rent schoolhouse on Black Island.
- July 22, 1915, $20 to Berlin A. Gott for boarding Morrill boy for 10 weeks.

While the population on Black Island surged from 15 to as many as 75 between 1880 and 1900, it had collapsed again to less than 10 by 1910 after the quarries closed. The school did not last much longer, closing probably around 1914.

The Nice family left Black Island in the 1920s leaving only twin brothers, Henry and George Hersey, as year-round residents. Henry died in the 1930s and poor health soon forced George to leave as well (McLane, 130-131).

Their departure ended the life of Black Island as a year-round community, following Pond Island, Opechee (Calf) Island and Placentia Island as once-inhabited plantation islands.

## Calf Island

Other than the school on Black Island there is no record of Long Island Plantation raising educational funds for its other inhabited islands. What education existed on those tiny family islands during the 1800s is largely unknown. If adults provided education, it was likely through private efforts. Such was the case on Calf or Opechee Island.

Benjamin Cole Jr. moved his family to Calf Island, off Swans Island, in the 1840s. Cole hired private tutors to teach four of his children in his house. In 1857, he appealed to the state for help. He said he received no aid from the state or the plantation and that Outer Long Island was too far to take his children to attend school. He sought and received $10 from the state to help pay for his children's teachers.

# Chapter Eight

# 19th Century Civic Life

The first two decades on Outer Long Island, although mostly politically and legally unstructured, were guided by Israel B. Lunt. The families, not bound by any real organized government — nor even a church or school until 1842 — clearly took cues from Israel. He not only ran the major business but owned the entire island in 1835. He became a driving force behind building a school, starting a Baptist Church and guiding other community issues.

Beyond Israel's influence, few other details are known about the island's structure during the pioneer era. In 1834, Outer Long Island technically became part of Swans Island Plantation, which included most of the original Burnt Coat Group purchased by Col. James Swan.

Organized government came to Outer Long Island itself in 1840. A group of men met at Israel's house that October and carved a new Plantation from a group of islands that stretched from Great Duck Island to Harbor Island near Sedgwick. Following are the official minutes of that island meeting as preserved at the Maine State Archives.

By virtue of a warrant issued to Nathaniel Allen by Pelatiah Leach one of the County Commissioners of Hancock County the qualified inhabitants of the hear after named islands, say Long Island lying easterly of Swans Island and Duck Island easterly of Long Island, Black Island and Placentia Island lying south of Mt. Desert, Pond

Island, Calf Island and Black Island lying north of Swans Island and Harbor Island near Sedgwick were notified to meet at the house of Israel B. Lunt on said Long Island on the twenty fourth day of October at one of the clock in the afternoon. Accordingly at said time and place the aforesaid inhabitants met and organized into a plantation by the name of Long Island by choosing a moderator and a clerk and three assessors for said plantation.
Given under our hands this twenty fourth day of October in the year of our Lord one thousand eight hundred and forty."
Israel B. Lunt, Nathaniel Allen, Abner Lunt Jr., Assessors of Long Island Plantation.
Amos C. Lunt, Clerk.

Allen, who lived on Pond Island, may be the only non-Long Island resident ever to hold a top plantation office. The Legislature approved the new plantation, which included numerous uninhabited islands such as Sheep and Ram. Several of the original Long Island Plantation islands were eventually set off to other townships, including Calf and Western Black which were given to Swans Island in 1901.

Amos Coffin Lunt Sr. served as town clerk, probably until or nearly until his death in 1851.

The next plantation meeting for which a record has been found took place Friday, April 1, 1842. The island's male inhabitants were called to meet at the home of Joseph D. Lunt to form a school building committee. While only males were called, Rehoboth Hannah Lunt was chosen first committee member, a testament to her early influence. It is unlikely any other woman served in a top town position for decades. Ratification of the 19th Amendment giving women the right to vote was still 78 years away. At that 1842 meeting, John Rich was chosen second committee member and Israel B. Lunt, third committee. Amos C. Lunt Sr. was elected clerk.

Not everyone was pleased with the new plantation status. Inhabitants of some outlying islands petitioned the state in 1842 seeking release from Long Island Plantation. Lead petitioner Edward Carter and nine other men signed the petition seeking inclusion in Hog Island Plantation:

The undersigned inhabitants of the Plantation of Long Island in the County of Hancock beg leave respectfully to represent and inform your honorable body that they are greatly discommoded and inconvenienced in being united to said Plantation, some of us living on the islands herein after named, having to row our boats fifteen and sixteen miles to attend the Plantation meetings, which are uniformly held on Long Island, and not infrequently against head winds and a strong tide and sometimes too at a very inclement season of the year. Between some of the islands and Long Island there is a very strong tide and in rough weather a very high sea. We would further state that we were included in the Long Island Plantation at its organization, contrary to our wishes or knowledge. Your petitioners therefore respectfully request that Black Island, east of Placentia, Placentia Island, Calf Island, Black Island near Calf Island, John's Island and Harbor Island near Naskeag Point may be set off from Long Island Plantation and annexed to the Plantation of Hog Island in said County. And as in duty bound will ever pray.

Edward Carter

John B. Carter

William Foster

Moses (Pomroy?)

Shadrick Herrick

John Ross

John Smith

Thomas Ross

David Bridges

Moses Bridges

From other accounts, it appears Edward Carter and John B. Carter lived on Harbor Island off Sedgwick, Shadrick Jones lived on Johns Island off Opechee and John Ross and Moses Bridges lived on Opechee. Johns Island must have belonged to Long Island Plantation at the time, given its inclusion in the above petition. However, it was named in neither the article of formation approved by Long Island Plantation nor in an official letter confirming the plantation's islands in 1858.

It also appears no signers of the pro-Hog Island Plantation petition lived on (Western) Black Island, Placentia Island or Pond Island, even though those islands were listed. Indeed, those islands maintained close ties to Outer Long Island.

The earliest record found of an annual plantation meeting was for one held Monday, March 6, 1848.

*Courtesy of Southwest Harbor Public Library/Photo by George A. Neal/W.H. Ballard Collection*

*Lunt Harbor, 1800s.*

Elected at that meeting were: Israel B. Lunt, moderator; Amos C. Lunt Sr., plantation clerk; Israel B. Lunt, first assessor; Abner Lunt, 2nd assessor; William D. Lunt, 3rd assessor; John Rich, constable; Francis Pomroy, collector of taxes; Abner Lunt, Tythingman; Thomas Rice, Tythingman; Jacob Lunt 2nd, school agent; Israel B. Lunt and two others as superintending school committee. The plantation also voted to pay Amos C. Lunt Sr. $5.50 for recording town records from the plantation's formation.

The plantation took its first stab at becoming an official town in 1856 when Bartholomew Russell Lunt Sr. and a group of islanders petitioned the state to organize the town of Seaport. That petition was accepted by the legislature, but not acted upon.

Islanders returned the next year seeking township under a different name, Islandport. On Feb. 11, 1857, the state legislature passed an act incorporating the town of Islandport. For unknown reasons, possibly the extra cost of running a town versus a plantation, the legislature repealed the act on March 27, 1858, ending the life of Islandport in about one year. The islands reverted to plantation status and remained so until 1979 when they were incorporated as the town of Frenchboro.

The name Frenchboro has no ties to any island landmark or event. Rather it is derived from the last name of E. Webster French, a Tremont lawyer who helped the island obtain a post office in the early 1890s. From that point, the name Frenchboro slowly emerged as the better known name for the village on Long Island. The individual islands are all still known by their original names, including Long Island.

Plantation status gave islanders greater self-governance and the ability to raise taxes. Taxes were needed to run not only the affairs of Outer Long Island but the plantation's other inhabited islands as well.

The new body politic also enacted local statutes. These statutes help shed some light on island life. Within the sparse and clipped language of town records — including annual meeting minutes and treasurer's reports — emerge details of a growing community trying to take care of its growing responsibilities.

Rather than a narrative, the following pages include some of the ordinances enacted, the names of people elected and the business transacted as recorded in town books, state records, Amos C. Lunt's diary and the Maine Register.

Monday, September 12th, 1842
I (Amos Coffin Lunt Sr.) went to a plantation meeting to I.B. Lunts in the afternoon; there was 12 of us that cast our votes. There was 10 votes for Edward Robinson for governor and two for John Fairfield and each candidate on the Whig party had ten votes and each candidate on the Democratic party had two votes each.

I, Amos C. Lunt, clerk of the Plantation of Long Islands, do herby certify, to whom it may concern, that intentions of marriage, between William D. Lunt of the Plantation of Long Islands and Mary Elizabeth Allen of Sedgwick, have been published by me at three religious meetings and on three different public days, and posted up in a public place and in a house of worship on Long Island 14 days prior to the date hereof as the law requires.
Given under my hand the 14th day of December in the year of our Lord 1847.

Thursday, December 16th A.D. 1847
Israel B. Lunt come to me and requested me to record a bill of sale that Mr. William Stanly of Swans Isle had given him of two steers

about three years old, dark colour with some white spots on them. That the said William Stanly had sold him, the said, Israel B. Lunt Esqr. and that the said Israel B. Lunt Esqr. had released them to Thomas Rice and that he the said Thomas Rice, together with George W. Twist, was to keep them one year and then to return the said steers or oxen to him again at the years end of 1848 or pay the sum of the obligation specified in the said obligation given by the said Thomas Rice and George W. Twist.
Amos C. Lunt, Plantation Clerk

Long Island, March 5, 1877
Meeting called to order by the first assessor George B. Lunt
1.  George B. Lunt, moderator and sworn by Z.P. Lunt
2.  Bartholomew R. Lunt, clerk, sworn; Byron C. Wilson, clerk pro tem and sworn by moderator
3.  George B. Lunt, first assessor and sworn
    Bartholomew R. Lunt, second assessor and sworn
    Noel B. Lunt, third assessor and sworn
    Heard the treasurer's report, money in the treasury of $127.81, and voted to accept it.
4.  Zaphnath P. Lunt, treasurer
5.  James T. Davis, plantation agent
6.  Bartholomew R. Lunt, superintendent School Committee
7.  Zaphnath P. Lunt, school agent
8.  Hezekiah Davis, first constable
    George Butler, second constable
    Albion Butler, third constable
9.  Albion Butler, collector of taxes
10. Israel Lunt and James H. Lunt, tythingmen
11. James H. Lunt, fence viewer
12. Voted to raise $108.00 in support of schools
13. Voted to work one day on roads or pay $1

Agreeable to a notice to notify and warn the male inhabitants to meet at the clerks office on the 2nd day of April 1877.
Said inhabitants did meet and gave in their votes as follows:
•   1st, voted Hezekiah Davis and George Butler and Albion Butler out of office of constables and collector of taxes as they was not eligible to said offices and could not procure their bonds.

- 2nd, chose Levi T. Davis, first constable and collector of taxes. Chose B. R. Lunt Jr., second constable and that their last year's bonds and sureties be approved and endorsed and accepted. 3rd, voted to set the fifteenth day of May to destroy all dogs unlicensed and going about at large contrary to amendment of the 30th chapter of the revised statutes of the state of Maine and that there shall be a notice to that effect posted up in the store of Joseph D. Lunt.

April 2, 1879
At a special town meeting of the legal voters of the Plantation of Long Island said voters did meet and voted as follows:

- Article 1: Voted that each taxpayer bring in his valuation both real and personal and polls.
- Article 2: Voted to raise twenty-five dollars to pay the assessors for taking the valuation and assessment of each Island belonging to said Plantation of Long Island.
- Article 3: Voted that all dog owners shall pay a tax of $1.00 per head for every male dog and $2.00 per head for every female dog. They should not run at large but shall be in the immediate care of said owner or keeper. Anyone can lawfully kill a dangerous or mischievous dog wandering away from owners or keepers premises. Anyone bringing a dog in said Plantation shall pay a five dollars fine and cost.

Bartholomew R. Lunt, clerk.

Certificate of License Long Island Plantation
April 8, 1879
To whom it may concern:
This certifies that we the undersigned Board of Assessors have this eighth day of April, A.D. 1879 appointed George R. Rich as our Liquore Agent to sell pure spirituous and intoxicating liquores for said Long Island Plantation for one year. A bond of six hundred dollars was posted as surety.

Liquors can be sold expressly for medicinal, mechanical and manufacturing purposes.

Said Agent shall keep a true and just account of all Liquors by him purchased from whom purchased and cost of purchase. Also, an account of liquore sold, to whom sold and price of sale.

Said Agent George R. Rich is hereby prohibited from selling any intoxicating liquor to any drunkard or any persons making improper use of said liquors.

Agent George R. Rich shall not sell any less than one half pint nor over one gallon of pure unadulterated liquors at one time and to one person.

This instrument shall be to prove that George R. Rich is appointed to said Agency under said restrictions or forfeit and pay fifty dollars for each offense.

Assessors: George B. Lunt, Levi T. Davis, B.R. Lunt.

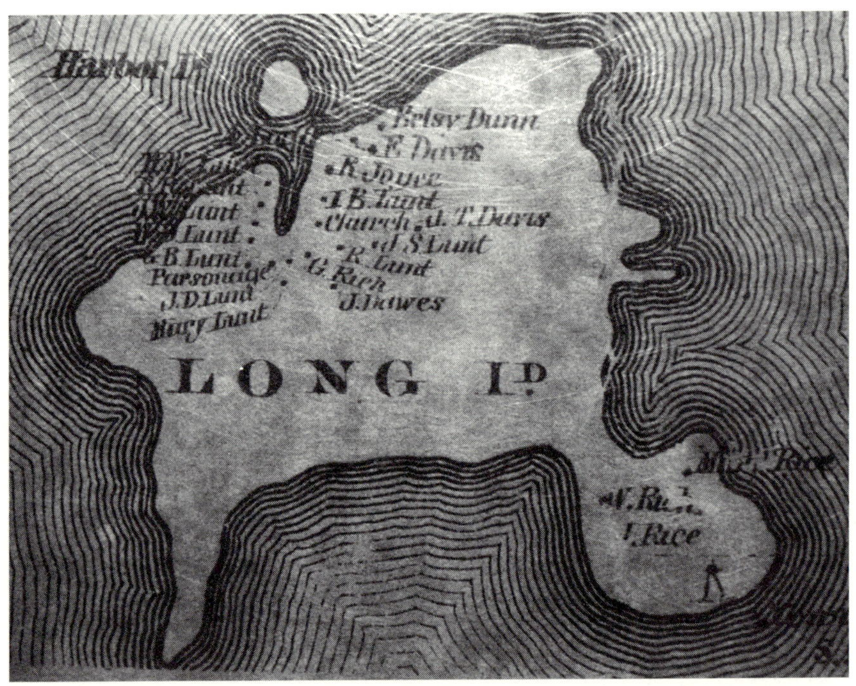


*Map of Long Island homesteads by H.F. Walling in 1860. Several homesteads are missing. The homesteads counter-clockwise from left are: Hezekiah W. Lunt Sr., Bartholomew R. Lunt Sr., Joseph W. Lunt, William D. Lunt, George B. Lunt, Parsonage, Joseph D. Lunt, Mary Lunt, Jonathan Dawes, Gilbert Rich, Richard Lunt, Joshua S. Lunt, James T. Davis, Church, Israel B. Lunt, Reuben Joyce, Ezra Davis and Betsy Dunn (Davis?). The homesteads on Richs Head are: Jacob Rice, William Rich and Mary Rice. Homesteads not named are: Capt. William Davis, Israel Lunt, Henry Murphy, George Butler, Amos C. Lunt Jr., Mary Davis*

Long Island Plantation, March 1, 1886
- Voted that each voter pay $1.00 for the repairs of the roads.
- Voted that Hiram A. Lunt collect the money for the roads for the present year.
- Voted that each man that pays $1.00 for repairs of roads have the privilege of working one day and draw his dollar back.

Long Island Plantation, April 5, 1886
- Voted that we raise 45 cents per head for vaccinations for the inhabitants.

School District meeting, May 5, 1886
- Voted that the schoolhouse be plastered overhead and patch the walls and paper the walls.

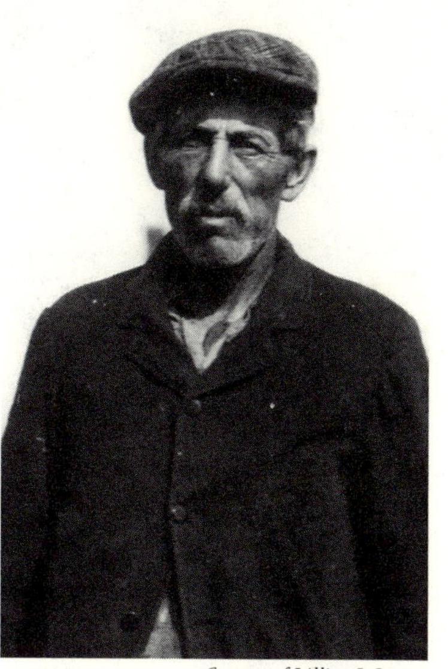

*Courtesy of Lillian J. Lunt*

*Hiram A. "Hite" Lunt Sr. (1862 - 1919).*

Plantation meeting, March 5, 1888
- Voted that any person caught hauling Lobster traps on Sunday shall be fined $15.
- Voted that any person found taking the young out of bird's nests shall be fined $5.
- Voted that any female from 15 years old to 70 years old found or heard quarreling, brawling or molesting any person on the public road or bypaths or fields shall be arrested by the constable and taken before the trial justice and fined $5.00 and costs.

Maine Register — 1890
Post Office: Tremont & Swans Island
Assessors: William A. Van Norden, H.A. Lunt, Calvin C. Lunt
Clerk and Treasurer: William A. Van Norden
Collector: Hiram A. Lunt
Constables: William S. Rich, Thomas N. Osier
School Committee: William S. Lunt, Calvin C. Lunt, Hiram A. Lunt
Clergyman: Vacant, Bap.
Justice: Bartholomew R. Lunt, Feb. 2, 1887, trial.

Merchants: Peter Powers, C.B. Vinal, general stores; Charles N. Gray, confectionery
Manufacturer: William Davis, boats

Plantation Meeting, March 2, 1891
- Voted that any man found hauling lobster traps on the Sabbath day should be fined $5.00.

Plantation Meeting, March 4, 1895
- Voted that the assessors post a notice naming each person owing a tax from 1887 up to April 1, 1895 to be paid within 30 days. If not, to be given to a sheriff for collection.

Long Island Plantation, March 1, 1897
- Voted that the collector collect all back taxes on or before the 1st day of July 1897 or sell the property for the same or jail all who refuse to pay a toll tax.
- Voted that the Plantation prohibit all out of town people from digging clams in Long Island Plantation.

*Courtesy of Frenchboro Historical Society*

*West side, late 1800s. Houses are: Nathan F. Osier (left), Hezekiah W. Lunt Sr. and Hezekiah W. "Will" Lunt Jr.*

# Chapter Nine

# 19th Century Work

For islanders in the 19th century, life itself was work as they struggled to carve a community from a rocky outpost. And it was work — harvesting island timber and fishing nearby grounds — that drew the first settlers and transient residents to Outer Long Island.

Along the tree-covered banks of what became Lunt Harbor, pioneers (see Chapter Three) such as John Perkins, William Post, Asa Smith, Jacob Lunt and William Pomroy staked claims to island land during the first two decades of the 1800s. The spruce, maple and birch they sought to harvest remained an important export through mid-century and made a brief but spectacular reappearance in the 1940s.

While trees were abundant, the thin and rocky island soil could not support any significant farms like those found on nearby islands. However, nearly everyone scratched at the earth to plant potatoes and vegetables, and many tended oxen, cows, sheep and pigs as well.

And, of course, they fished.

## The Golden Age

Despite an economic dependence on lobsters throughout much of the 20th century, traditional fisheries dominated the island economy during the 1800s. Fishing voyages took Long Islanders far from home and into the Gulf of St. Lawrence and other Canadian waters or into the ports of Boston, New York and the West Indies.

These Outer Long Island fishermen took part in a golden age of fishing in Hancock County. Wayne M. O'Leary, *Maine Sea Fisheries: The Rise and Fall of Native Industry, 1830 to 1890*, called Hancock County the most important coastal county in the history of the Maine offshore sea fisheries. In the pre-Civil War era close to half the state's cod and mackerel fishing tonnage called Hancock County home. At the same time, Maine dominated the nation's fishing industry.

To play their part in this dominance, Long Island men captained fishing schooners or worked on schooners owned either by fellow islanders or by men from other islands and coastal villages.

For example, Joseph Davis and Andrew P. Lunt agreed in March 1839 to fish with Capt. Edward Rogers on the *Palm* of Newburyport, Massachusetts. Joseph hired on for $20 per month and 16-year-old Andrew for $11. In preparation, Andrew, probably making his first offshore fishing voyage, paid $6.55 for a striped frock (long coat), calico shirt, comb, trousers, white plate and mug. Perhaps as part of an agreement with Amos Sr. for his young son's employment, Capt. Rogers gave Amos and his wife, Priscilla, some beans and six pounds of salt beef.

Also in 1839, Ezra Davis, William Davis and George Twist spent weeks fishing for herring off the Magdalen Islands in Canada. In January 1842, John Walls and Samuel Rice fished with Capt. Bunker of Cranberry Island.

During 1848, Amos received letters from his sons Andrew and Joshua Sylvester and his grandson Charles H. while they were stopped at a port in New York. The next month, Joshua sent word while stopped in East Jacksonville, Florida.

Men also worked local waters, which teemed with cod, "soule" (sole, a flatfish) and halibut. Often these early local fishermen were either poorer fishermen or those considered too old or too young to handle long and rigorous fishing trips that lasted for weeks. Local fishermen used rowboats or small sailing sloops and fished from the decks using hand-lines.

For them, fish were plentiful, although not overly lucrative. The upside for these men was that inshore fishing provided a more stable and predictable life, more attuned to the rhythms and lifestyle of modern-day lobster fishing than the offshore fisheries.

One afternoon in June of 1839, James T. Davis caught 216 cod and haddock between Money Ledge and Western Sister Island. He sold his catch for $3.56. Later that week, Davis sold another day's catch — 159 pounds of cod and 90 pounds of soule — to Israel B. Lunt for $2.04. This was an era when four ounces of tea cost 10 cents, two cod fishing lines cost $1 and two barrels of flour cost $9.

Fish were split, washed, heavily salted and laid on "flakes" to dry before being shipped to market. Flakes were wooden racks laid on wharves or along the shore. Dried fish, which lasted for months, was a critical and booming export for most of the 1800s. Dried codfish remains a popular food on the island, where for years a common meal consisted of dried cod, baked potatoes and stewed tomatoes.

Other island exports — mainly cordwood, kilnwood and beach stones — also remained a key part of the economy through mid-century. During this era, captains beached their schooners at island coves, points and harbors. They filled their holds with cordwood, used for heat, or kilnwood, used to fire kilns for the lime industry at such places as Thomaston and Rockland.

On various days in December 1840: Eben Walls, Andrew P. Lunt, John Walls and Cyrus K. Lunt loaded the *Native* with wood in Lunt Harbor; James and Joseph Davis loaded the *Mary-Ann* in Richs Cove (Eastern or Western Cove) and Yellow Head; James T. Davis and Cyrus loaded hay at the Sister Islands; and Eben and Andrew loaded the *Native* with kilnwood at Southern Cove.

At the same time, the smooth, ocean-polished rocks found at such places as Eastern Beach and Eastern Cove were loaded into schooners and shipped to Boston and other ports to fill a growing need for cobblestones to build city streets.

Locally, many men also worked for Israel B. Lunt, working on his wharf, operating his fishing boats or transporting his goods. At various times, captains such as Abner and John Pomroy, John Rich, Stillman Bridges, Abner Lunt and Amos Coffin Lunt Jr. all carried fish, wood and paving stones for Israel.

Basically, it was Israel's business — sometimes called I.B.L. & Co. — that established the island as a fishing port and fueled the overall economy.

During a three-decade period from the 1820s to the 1850s, Israel was sole or co-owner of at least 16 schooners.

A handful of other islanders also owned schooners large enough to register, and some co-owned vessels with Israel. During this era, many vessels had multiple owners. One person might own a half-share, and two others, a quarter-share each. Fishing profits were divided according to the various shares after the crew and other expenses were paid. It was essentially an era of cooperative ownership and fishing.

Schooners owned by Israel B. and others (Penobscot Marine Museum, Applebee papers) included: (Size: tonnage — length x width x draft)

*Native*, Bucksport
| | |
|---|---|
| Size: | 29 tons — 41.5 x 12.8 x 6.4 |
| Place built, year: | Eden (Bar Harbor), 1818 |
| Masters: | James Clark, '24 |
| Owners: | Franklin Spofford & Israel B. Lunt, Bucksport, 1824 |

*Arcade*, Swans Island
| | |
|---|---|
| Size: | 125 tons — 79.1 x 22.5 x 8.1 |
| Place built, year: | Swans Island, 1827 |
| Master: | Israel B. Lunt, 1827 |
| Owners: | Israel B. Lunt, sole, Swans Island, 1827 |

*Mary*, Long Island
| | |
|---|---|
| Size: | 25 tons — 48.4 x 12.4 x 6.3 |
| Place built, year: | Gloucester, Mass., 1804 |
| Masters: | Abner Lunt Jr., 1829 |
| Owners: | Israel B. Lunt, Long Island, 1829 |

*Napoleon*, Long Island
| | |
|---|---|
| Size: | 88 tons — 66.6 x 20.0 x 7.5 |
| Built: | Mount Desert, 1836 |
| Masters: | John Pomroy, 1836 |
| Owners: | Israel B. Lunt, sole, Long Island, 1836 |

*Walker,* Long Island
| | |
|---|---|
| Size: | 49 tons — 50.8 x 14.5 x 7.1 |
| Built: | Gloucester, Mass., 1827 |
| Master: | Abner Pomroy, 1844 |
| Owners: | Abner Pomroy, Israel B. Lunt, Joseph Davis, 1844 |

*Leo*, Long Island
Size:                40 tons — 52.7 x 14.2 x 6.1
Built:               Sullivan, Maine, 1819
Masters:             Joseph D. Lunt, 1845
Owners:              Joseph D. Lunt & Israel B. Lunt, Long Island, 1845

Other island men worked on shore in support of fishing.

Cyrus Lunt, Israel's younger brother, kept a log (Maine Historical Society collection, Cyrus K. Lunt papers) that details some of the local work available and how much it paid in the 1840s. The following list shows random days from the summer of 1847 when Cyrus was 31 years old. Cyrus died the following spring.

| | | |
|---|---|---|
| May 17th — | washing & carrying out 3 & 1/2 hogshead[1] of fish onto the flakes with Rollin and Baron Stow Lunt at 12 1/2 cts pr. hogshead, Rollin & Stow to have one-half | 23 cents |
| May 19th — | salting 2 hogshead of fish | 25 cents |
| June 5th — | carrying out six hogshead of fish onto the flakes with Rollin & Capt. Rueben Freeman's boy | 50 cents |
| June 17th — | carrying out fish with Rollin Lunt, then carrying in dry fish off the flakes into the store chamber | 42 cents |
| June 21 & 22 — | carrying 25 empty barrels from the barn down to the brook & filling them with water | 75 cents |
| July 2 & 3 — | getting fish on board Schooner Mary-Ann | $1.25 |
| July 6 — | one days work at the fishhouse and filling water barrels to carry to Mt. Desert Rock | 75 cents |
| July 8 — | carrying three men to Mount Desert Rock with James Davis | $3.00 |
| July 10 — | helping dress Mrs. Davis' fish in p.m. | 17 cents |
| Aug. 28 — | Carrying Elder C.P. St. Clair off to Duck Island with I.B. Lunt Esq. and Roland H.N. Lunt | 50 cents |
| Sept. 3 — | carrying out and salting fish | 33 cents |

---

[1] A hogshead is a unit of measure equal to about 17 bushels.

Cyrus also recorded expenditures made at Israel's store in 1847:

| | |
|---|---:|
| May 20th — 1/2 lb. hard bread | 4 cents |
| June 5th — 1 hoe, 33 cts, & 2 lbs. dry apple | 47 cents |
| June 16th — 5 & 1/2 lbs. of veal 4 & 1/2 cents per lb. | 25 cents |
| July 1st — 1 milk pan, 17 cts | 17 cents |
| July 3rd — 8 lbs. & 3/4 of salt beef, 9 cts, pr. lb. | 78.5 cts |
| July 5th — 1 lb. of powder | 10 cents |
| July 10th — 1 jackknife, 33 cts, & 6 sheets paper | 39 cents |
| July 27th — 2 & 1/2 quarter yards of cloth at 20 cents pr. yard | 52.5 cts |
| Sept. 9th — 1 butter pot | 9 cents |
| Sept. 15th — 1 bowl, 10 cts, & 2 candles, 3 cts | 13 cents |
| Sept. 18th — 1 lb. of molasses | 17 cents |

For women, work was always local.

Some early families produced as many as 17 children, while 10 or more children was not uncommon. Daily work for many women involved raising families, caring for the household, working small gardens and tending farm animals.

Some women earned outside income serving meals to fishing boat captains, providing the captains with a night's lodging, or washing and mending their clothes. Many times they bartered work for meat, cloth or other goods instead of cash.

A small number of women, sometimes working with young sons, did fish. One such woman was Rebecca Davis, mother of James T. Davis. With James, she fished for cod, haddock and other fish during the mid-1800s.

It is probable, given the dearth of non-fishing work and the era's social norms, that most women who actually went fishing were widows, never married or divorced. Many women also probably worked mending nets, stacking fish on flakes and so forth.

In any event, enough local "fisherwomen" worked on the island in 1878 that Samuel Wasson (*A Survey of Hancock County, Maine,* 39) wrote, "At Lunt's Long Island, women are seen almost daily rowing 'cross or open handed' on their way to the fishing grounds. Many of them are 'high-line' fisher men."

## *Decline of Offshore Fisheries*

The height of the island's role as provider of fishermen to the traditional fishing industry and its zenith as a commercial port was undoubtedly the 1840s and 1850s. These were the decades preceding Israel's death, and before outside forces, including the Civil War, dramatically changed life on the Maine coast.

Israel's death in 1861 removed a powerful island force and unfortunately coincided with negative outside forces to exacerbate the damage to a Long Island economy that was never considered thriving to begin with.

O'Leary examined these macro forces in *Maine Sea Fisheries*. Two of the most damaging changes were inflation and the end of government fishing subsidies.

Inflation ignited by the cost of fighting the Civil War hurt fishermen. The cost of 25 articles commonly used in fishing rose 141 percent between 1860 and 1864, while the price of salt, indispensable to the industry, rose 175 to 194 percent (O'Leary, 141). Adding to the increased fishing costs, O'Leary said, were higher tariffs imposed on imported goods and skyrocketing marine insurance.

The government threw a second devastating punch in 1866 when it repealed the fishing-bounty. That law, crucial to small fishermen, had provided government subsidies to owners of cod-fishing vessels and their crews since the late 1700s. The repeal ended three-quarters of a century of public support for fisheries and ushered in a long period of official neglect, O'Leary said. Places like Outer Long Island were hit the hardest.

> "The loss of the fishing bounty was most harmful to the small operator with limited capital, the same individual likely hit hardest by inflation. Penobscot and Wiscasset districts, home to innumerable independent owner-fisherman and economically marginal enterprises, bore the brunt of the dislocations caused in Maine by the loss of the bounty (O'Leary, 157)."

As a result of these changes, vessel ownership and fishing operations, once a fairly co-operative venture, became concentrated in fewer and fewer hands. It also meant the industry's most active areas moved from such places as Hancock County to more industrialized and wealthier ports such as Portland.

Smaller fishermen, fishermen with older vessels and those based at the more remote ports felt the effects most acutely. Certainly that described most of the Long Island fleet.

Beyond these factors numerous other issues affected the greater Maine fisheries and helped render offshore fishing ports like Lunt Harbor unnecessary. They included:

- Tariffs. New tariffs imposed on many goods needed by fishermen, including salt, iron and manila cordage, dramatically increased the cost of equipping a cod-fishing schooner.
- Technology. Until mid-century, fish were caught from the decks of schooners using hand-lines. New methods and technology such as dory hand-lining, multi-hook trawls and fishing nets required more capital outlay and thus excluded many smaller fishermen.
- Changing habits. The popularity of salted codfish that helped Israel establish his business gave way to a taste for both fresh fish and beef. The nation's growing rail system transported beef from the mid-west into eastern ports. And Maine's distant location and limited rail hampered its ability to ship fresh fish to key markets. Maine was suddenly isolated and Massachusetts emerged as the more dominant fisheries state.

The effect was swift and devastating.

"In 1861, Maine was the most important sea-fishing state in the Union," O'Leary said. (Judd, 392). "Five years later, its fisheries were in decline, and within a generation, they had become insignificant in national terms."

As these factors crashed together in the years following the Civil War, more and more Long Islanders, along with men from other islands, abandoned offshore fishing and stayed closer to home. Traditional fishing didn't die — Outer Long Island remained a fishing port to some extent into the early 1900s — but dramatic change was underway and unstoppable.

Indeed, as the 1800s dissolved and the old ways of fishing faded, Long Island became a village struggling to find its bearings and one searching for a new means of economic survival.

## *The Rise of Lobster Fishing*

Fortunately, the island's heaven-sent savior was already crawling around on the ocean bottom: lobsters.

While lobsters were caught starting in the early 1800s, the lobster fishing industry didn't truly begin developing as a statewide force until the 1860s and 1870s. The first lobster pound was built in Vinalhaven in 1875. In general, lobster fishing proved a more affordable fishery to enter, allowing men to work as sole proprietors. Lobstering was the opposite of the offshore fishing business, requiring less capital to start and allowing one man to work for himself in a small boat close to home.

According to George Brown Goode (*The Fisheries and Fishery Industries of the United States, Vol. 2, 1887*), lobster fishing as a business started in Western Maine and reached Penobscot Bay in 1848 or 1850. At the time, lobsters sold for about 2 cents per pound.

In 1855, Swans Island, the closest port to Outer Long Island, had 10 men considered lobster fishermen, but all 10 soon abandoned the business. About five years later, lobster fishing started again; this time eight to 10 men set 30 to 40 traps each (Goode, 702).

The rise of lobster fishing marked a rather abrupt change in image for the formerly dismissed crustacean. For years, lobsters were ground for garden fertilizer or used as bait to catch cod, hake, haddock, sea perch and other more valuable fish. In some cases, crushed lobsters were scattered on the water to attract mackerel.

In the early 1800s, lobsters were so plentiful they were considered nuisance fish. Fishermen initially caught lobsters using nets and gaffs. Lobsters sometimes annoyed fishermen by seizing bait on hooks or becoming entangled in fishing lines.

The earliest lobster traps were so-called hoop traps. The hoop trap consisted of a metal ring and an attached netting that laid flat on the ocean bottom. The bait was suspended over the middle of the ring. When the lobster crawled into the hoop to get the bait, the trap was hauled, thus pulling the netting into a bag and bringing lobsters to the surface. Hoop traps, hauled every 10 to 30 minutes, required near constant tending, thus limiting the distance a fisherman could travel and the number of traps he could fish.

Lobster fishing remained a seasonal, secondary fishery for most coastal villages into the late 1800s and sometimes even later. In many regions, men fished for lobsters only when unable to fish for more profitable stocks, usually in the spring and summer. As lobster fishing increased, one factor drove demand before the rise of tourism — lobster canneries.

The canning of lobster meat started in the early 1800s after entrepreneurs pioneered the use of hermetically sealed tin cans to preserve the meat. This invention eliminated the spoilage problems associated with shipping live lobsters. Lobsters were boiled, cracked and picked by crews of mostly women, and then the meat was placed in tin cans. Once the method was perfected, the number of lobster canneries grew fairly rapidly. Most canneries also canned other fresh goods, such as corn and fish.

The canning industry quickly spread up and down the coast of Maine and may have peaked sometime in the 1870s, according to Kenneth R. Martin and Nathan R. Lipfert (*Lobstering and The Maine Coast*). Among the most dominant operators of the era were Burnham & Morrill and Portland Packing Co., both of Portland.

By 1880, 23 lobster canneries operated along the coast of Maine, including one in Southwest Harbor. Canneries had also operated on Isle au Haut and Swans Island for a short period of time.

Before 1879, lobster-canning season in Maine generally ran from April to July or August and then September to November or December. After 1879, state law set the legal canning season from April 1 to August 1. Given their reliance on the canning industry, most lobster fishermen followed a similar season.

For example, in the Castine fishing district, which included Outer Long Island, 2.97 million lobsters were caught by fishermen in 1880 and 2.1 million or 71 percent of them were sold to canneries (Goode, 771).

However, the lobster industry soon began to worry about the obvious depletion of the lobster stock, a shortage that forced some fishermen to

*Courtesy of Frenchboro Historical Society*

*Island fishing vessels, 1907. The sloop (center) belonged to Eugene Van Norden. Trailing sloop is a dory and a peapod (above). At right is an early powerboat.*

abandon the business in the 1880s and helped trigger a steady stream of conservation laws.

Concern was certainly justified.

On Swans Island, anecdotal evidence cited by Goode suggests that a fisherman in the 1850s or 1860s might catch 200 to 300 lobsters from about 40 traps. The average weight of those lobsters was 3 to 3.5 pounds. By 1879, Swans Island reported that its fishermen averaged 40 traps and caught about 75 lobsters with an average weight of about two pounds. To those involved in the industry, the decline in both the catch and the average size of lobsters was obvious. The major cause of the problem was the canneries themselves, which were indiscriminate in the lobsters they used. As the average size of the lobsters caught decreased, the canneries simply used more and more small lobsters to fill their needs, thus devastating the future.

"By the early eighties, one-pound cans were commonly being crammed with the meat of however many half-pound lobsters it took to pack them; some said the number went as high as thirty per can." (Martin, 43).

Ultimately, conservation measures killed the lobster canning industry in Maine by 1900. Lobster canneries moved to Canada. In Maine, former lobster canneries turned to other fish, such as sardines.

## *Local Fishing*

In the Castine District, which included Outer Long Island, Swans Island and Deer Isle, 311 men engaged in lobster fishing in 1880. That year, those 311 men fished a combined 28,050 traps and caught nearly three million pounds of lobsters collectively valued at $52,839 (Goode, 755). That means in 1880, the average lobsterman fished about 90 traps and caught about $170 worth of lobsters during the season.

On Swans Island, about 74 men fished for lobsters, although more than 50 of them were seasonal lobstermen who set traps in spring and early summer only, according to Goode. Swans Island fishermen averaged about 100 traps each and typically owned two boats, one for lobster fishing and one for catching bait. They set traps close to shore on eelgrass. Some traps were set in such shallow water they were uncovered at low tide.

On Outer Long Island, eight of the island's 41 fishermen went lobster fishing in 1880. Those eight men fished an average of 50 traps each from April to August and earned about $75 a year.

The local or inshore fishermen during this era used mostly dories, peapods and sloops to haul their traps.

Dories, usually rowed standing up, later became widely used in the seining industry (a method of trapping fish in coves using nets) and remained a common sight on harbor banks for decades. Peapods were smaller doubled-ended rowboats that could be rowed standing up or sitting down. The now famous sailing sloops typically featured a square stern and at least one sail.

Lobstermen sold their catches to so-called smackmen, men who roamed the coast in smacks buying lobsters and carrying them back to mainland dealers. A smack was a vessel with a deep well that could hold thousands of pounds of lobsters bought from hundreds of fishermen. Lunt Harbor was visited by dry smacks running to Southwest Harbor and Deer Island, and wet smacks running to Portland and Boston. A wet smack carried lobsters in holds filled with seawater, while a dry smack did not have that ability. As a result, a wet smack could carry lobsters for a longer period of time than a dry smack, but it moved more slowly because of the added weight.

With eight lobstermen in 1880, the lobster industry remained relatively small on Outer Long Island, and for decades island fishermen chased a variety of species along with lobsters to make ends meet. However, lobster fishing had established a permanent foothold and continued to grow in importance.

*Courtesy of Frenchboro Historical Society*

*The Long Island fishing fleet, 1800s. Notice house along Northeast Point shore.*

## *By Sea, but also by Land*

Most soil on Outer Long Island is not only thin, but also rocky. Such poor soil kept farming from emerging as a major economic presence, although clearly farms still played an important role in island life.

The island's largest farmers were Israel B. Lunt and his wife, Nancy, on Lunt Harbor, and the Rich and Rice families on Richs Head.

In the 1840s, Israel and other settlers planted acres of potatoes on a large tract of land they called "Green Sword," which ran from Israel's house on the east side diagonally up the hill toward the current ballfield. He even planted potatoes on Crow Island to sell at his store.

According to the 1860 U.S. Agricultural Census, Israel and Nancy cultivated 50 acres of improved farmland and owned 750 wooded acres valued collectively at more than $600. On the farm, the family owned five cows, four working oxen, four other cattle and two pigs. They also picked 100 bushels of Irish potatoes, churned 400 pounds of butter and cut 10 tons of hay.

Also in 1860, William and Eleanor (Rice) Rich cultivated 50 acres of land on Richs Head valued at $800. On their farm were two cows, two oxen, three other cattle and 20 sheep. They sheared 25 pounds of wool, picked 50 bushels of potatoes, churned 150 pounds of butter and cut nine tons of hay.

The island's third largest farmer in 1860 was Thomas Rice, who lived on Richs Head with his wife, Mary. The Rice family worked 40 acres valued at $350. They had three cows, three oxen and 20 sheep. They sheared 30 pounds of wool, churned 100 pounds of butter and cut seven tons of hay.

By 1870, Rich operated a smaller but more productive farm. His 24 developed and 40 wooded acres were valued at $1,500. He owned three cows, two oxen and 40 sheep. He produced 120 pounds of wool, harvested 10 bushels of potatoes, churned 250 pounds of butter and cut 14 tons of hay. He also sold $75 worth of animals for slaughter. When ready to shear his sheep, Rich would herd them to a small point on the northeastern side of the Head and trap them against the shoreline. This small point facing Great Duck Island is still called the "Sheep Yard."

That year, Nancy P. Lunt, now widowed from Israel, owned 12 acres of developed land and 800 acres of wooded land valued at $4,000. She owned two cows, two oxen and two sheep. Her farm produced seven pounds of wool, 30 bushels of potatoes, 175 pounds of butter and eight tons of hay.

Of the other islanders in 1870, Bartholomew Russell Lunt cultivated 20 bushels of potatoes and sheared 15 pounds of wool from six sheep; Robert Ross picked 40 bushels of potatoes and made 50 pounds of butter; George B. Lunt grew 40 bushels of potatoes; and Joseph D. Lunt — who lived next to the present-day church — had 13 sheep from which he sheared 90 pounds of wool. Joseph also churned 125 pounds of butter.

The other islands of Long Island Plantation supported larger farming operations. In 1860, these farmers included Nathaniel Allen on Pond Island, Benjamin Cole Jr. on Calf (Opechee) Island, Charles Mitchell on Placentia Island and Joseph Dawes on Black Island.

Cole had 240 acres valued at $1,500. He farmed 80 acres and tended 48 sheep, churned 400 pounds of butter, sheared 196 pounds of wool, cut six bushels of wheat and 20 tons of hay and harvested 150 bushels of potatoes and 40 pounds of barley.

Mitchell had 180 acres, improved 100 of it and kept five cows and 40 sheep. He sheared 160 pounds of wool and harvested eight bushels of wheat, 100 bushels of potatoes, 22 tons of hay. He churned 300 pounds of butter.

On Black Island, Dawes owned 180 acres and farmed 80 with a total value of $1,000. He had five cows, two cattle, 13 sheep; and he sheared 39 pounds of wool. He also grew 20 bushels of potatoes, churned 200 pounds of butter and cut 22 tons of hay.

Allen ran an even bigger operation on Pond Island. He owned 207 acres, valued at

*Courtesy of Frenchboro Historical Society*

*Minnie (Cross) and Joseph W. Lunt Jr. (1865 - 1922)*

$2,000, and farmed 130 acres. He owned 12 cows, 10 cattle, two oxen and 60 sheep. He harvested 180 pounds of wool, 200 bushels of potatoes and 75 pounds of barley; churned 700 pounds of butter; made 400 pounds of cheese and cut 30 tons of hay.

While many Long Island families maintained small gardens and owned a handful of animals well into the 1900s, any significant farming was finished by the turn of the century.

## Miscellaneous Work

Fishing and early exporting were always the island's economic staples. However, some residents earned money through several other methods.

From the time Israel opened his store in the 1820s through the 1970s, the island hosted two, sometimes three general stores without interruption. The island's last long-running store closed in the 1980s. While a couple of stores have opened for short periods since then, no island store exists in 1999.

The better known stores included those operated by Joseph W. Lunt Jr. on Western Point, William Sanford Lunt on the east side, and Jennie

*Courtesy of Frenchboro Historical Society*

*East side, 1800s. House at left belonged to William Sanford Lunt. House at top center belong to Alphonso "Fon" Lunt, who later added a second story. Wharf (center) belonged at time to either Jake Siegal or Joe Dondis.*

Mitchell, near the church. Other stores of the era were owned by Levi T. Davis, H.E.S. "Kai" Lunt, Sylvester Morse, Charles and Asenath Wallace, Jake Siegal and Joe Dondis.

The only person ever listed as an island physician was Zaphnath P. Lunt in 1877, but it is unlikely he possessed formal training. Bartholomew Russell Lunt was the island's trial justice and Justice of the Peace (see Chapter Four) for many years. "Judge" Lunt also billed himself as an auctioneer in 1880.

Nineteenth-century island boat builders included William Davis in the 1870s and later his son, Leaman. The 1900 Maine Register lists three small boat builders on the island: Sylvester Morse, Walter M. Robinson and Leman Bros.

## *End of an Era*

Also, starting with Israel B. Lunt's business in the 1820s, large fish wharves operated on Long Island uninterrupted for nearly a century. But by the early 1900s, with the industry in decline, their days were clearly numbered.

Still, at the turn of the century two major fish wharves operated from Lunt Harbor.

Everett Edward Dalzell Sr., known almost interchangeably as Edward Everett Dalzell, helped operate one of the island's major fish wharves at the turn of the century. Eastern Fish Co. operated wharves on Swans Island and

*Courtesy of Frenchboro Historical Society*

*West side, mid-to-late 1800s. Large houses are: H.E.S "Kai" Lunt (left), Joseph W. Lunt, Hiram A. Lunt Sr. and Leaman T. Davis. Schooner is docked at the Capt. William Davis/Leam Davis wharf.*

*The Dalzell wharf extended in Lunt Harbor around the turn of the century. Note ice house at right of church. E.E. Dalzell built the ice house (on land leased from George C. Lunt) to support his fish buying business.*

Long Island. In 1906, Herbert W. Joyce of Swans Island served as company president, while Dalzell served as treasurer. Dalzell's wharf was located between the houses owned in 1999 by Ellsworth T. "Derry" Rundlett III and Duncan and Gretchen Bond.

Probably to support an expansion, Eastern Fish took out a mortgage in August of 1906 with Charles C. Burrill of Ellsworth. It turned out to be bad timing. Roughly two years later, Burrill served a foreclosure notice on the company and Eastern Fish closed. Parts of the Dalzell wharf were later removed and used by local fishermen for their own fishhouses.

The era's largest island fish wharf, located on the same site as the original Israel B. Lunt wharf, was operated by Clarence E. McIntire. The McIntire wharf, owned in 1999 by Ben S. Davis Jr., included the largest structure ever built on the island. The building, with its jutting ramps and floats, dominated the harbor. However, McIntire's business, buffeted by the winds of change, ultimately met the same fate as Eastern Fish.

McIntire started his business in the 1880s. He quickly accumulated much of the island property once owned by Israel. After a few years, the business became the Frenchboro Land and Fisheries Co. Frenchboro Land and Fisheries, part of a larger operation based in Belfast, was officially incorporated in 1909 and billed as "successors to Clarence E. McIntire," although McIntire still served as president.

Several islanders worked for McIntire either on the wharf or as captains. By 1915, Frenchboro Land and Fisheries apparently could no longer pay its mortgage and was shut down by the Waldo Trust Co.

*Courtesy of Vivian D. Lunt*

*The McIntire fish wharf, probably in the late 1800s.*

How long the company struggled is unknown. Certainly times were changing. The company may have struggled from the start, but more likely it simply grew too much and misread the shifting economy. After all, the 1895 to 1915 era represented a time when powerboats began replacing sailing vessels, and shipping methods continued to improve, rendering full-service offshore ports less important for fishermen and mainland businesses.

A hint of McIntire's problems is found in town records. In probably a rare action for the era, plantation voters exempted the company's wharf from taxes in March 1911. It appears even from the minimal language found in town records that the decision generated heated debate. The next year, voters indefinitely postponed an article seeking to rebate some back taxes to the company. Later in that same meeting, the town voted, "that the property which was exempted from taxation last year shall be taxed this year, and the matter dropped."

Three years later the business closed. Even at foreclosure, the company's assets remained impressive.

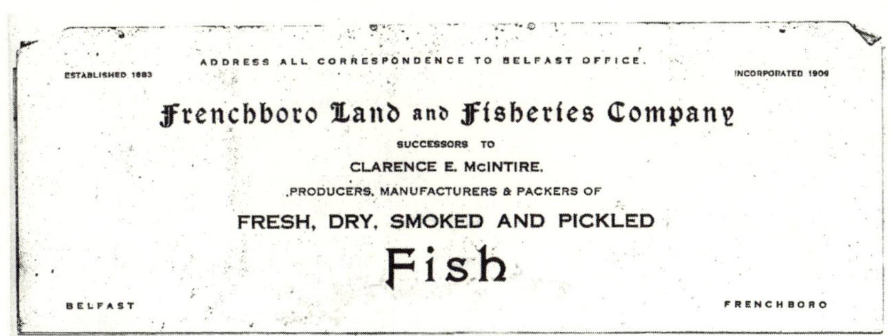



*Courtesy of Frenchboro Historical Society*

*Letterhead of Frenchboro Land and Fisheries Co.*

The company's holdings at Frenchboro included: two 1,200-pound Howe platform scales, two 600-pound scales, 40 oil barrels, 86 liver barrels, 225 hogshead for salting fish, one 14.5 horsepower stationary engine, one 27-foot seine boat and equipment, three splitting tables, six fish forks, 50 hogshead of salt, 30 herring horses, 19,500 herring sticks, 47 fish boxes, 26 gill nets, anchors, 47 wire hake flakes, 29 fish flakes, 24 hogshead salted fish with approximately 24,000 pounds of fish, 32 6x6 timbers, two 25-foot power boats, 25 500-pound fish boxes, lumber, one 26-foot power boat, one 24-foot power boat, one engine and other items such as rope, nets, fishing lines, etc.

*Courtesy of Frenchboro Historical Society*

*Walter Robinson (left), Charles Lunt and Clarence McIntire inside a building on the McIntire wharf around the turn of the century.*

Islanders who operated boats for McIntire when his business closed included: Wilson Carter, Bert Perkins, Harry Lunt and Tom Higgins. But as the McIntire closed, island fishermen continued to struggle to make ends meet.

The failure of McIntire's firm was only the latest blow to an island plunging ever deeper into economic depression.

*Courtesy of Lillian J. Lunt*

*View of east side from near the Osier house, early 1900s. Large structure is Clarence E. McIntire wharf. Camp in foreground belonged to Calvin B. "Cade" Lunt. The white fence surrounded the cemetery near the Osier house.*

*Chapter Ten*
# Sorrows & Tragedies

Pioneer life has never been easy. Sickness and death were frequent island visitors. Each cemetery tells a story. Small markers remember those who died as children or as young adults, while fieldstones often mark graves of the poor. And scattered across the Long Island hillsides are dozens of unmarked graves, their locations long forgotten.

Many of the island's elderly and sick died at home, nursed and comforted by husbands, wives or children — no hospital, ambulance or other professional care existed. Others hunkered down in their island homes until death was at hand, then perhaps left for a short time until they returned for burial in their native soil.

Marjorie (Dalzell) Giamo remembers the feeling as a child even in the 1920s when someone left because of illness.

"In the past when anyone needed to go to the hospital, the *Sunbeam* would come to transport them," she said. "They did my mother. She had to go to the hospital, I was probably 10 or 11 years old, and I remember them coming. I was crying. I knew people left the island and you just didn't see them again.

"They just didn't go to the doctor period, didn't believe in doctors, didn't believe in hospitals, they had babies at home. They brought the bodies back here and had the funerals."

Valeria (Lunt) Davis, the mother of nine children, died of cancer at 48 in 1944. Like many island ill, she spent months largely confined to her bed. She lived on the old Davis wharf on the west side. Her oldest daughter, Vivian, helped care for her, learning to inject pain relief into her mother's arm, which was soon riddled with prick marks.

"I gave her shots of morphine for months," said Vivian, who was 29 when her mother died. "She was in such pain that she couldn't hardly stand it. That was a way to relieve the pain for a few minutes."

Her death was also somewhat typical of an earlier era.

"I used to go down to the house every night to take care of her and see what needed to be done," Vivian said. "Nora (Lunt) lived across the road here, and she would go down with me each night. On the night she (Valeria) died, Nora

*Courtesy of Vivian D. Lunt*

*Valeria Davis and family, about 1920.*
*Back row: Vivian (left), Valeria and Lawrence.*
*Front row: Elmer and Vincent.*

and I were playing cards in the kitchen. Momma was in the bedroom just off the kitchen and I heard a groan. Daddy was sitting on the couch. I said, 'Daddy, go see if Momma wants something.' He went in, and she was gone. Someone went around and got Lillian who was living across the harbor. Word got around the island and then people came to stay with us, stay with the family for awhile."

## Dying Young

In the 1800s and early 1900s, children were acutely susceptible to illness. Nearly every family buried one or more of its children.

Women gave birth with the aid of family and midwives, but not doctors. Stillborn deaths visited the island like a plague. Into the 1900s, it seems rarely did an island woman not lose at least one baby during childbirth, and often lost two or more.

Doctors, such as there were during this era, usually lived on Mount Desert Island or Swans Island and came by sail or rowboat, weather permitting. With no telephones, no telegraph nor any other type of communication, islanders could not contact doctors in advance to ask even the simplest questions.

Amos Coffin Lunt Sr. buried his 22-month-old daughter Mary in the bitter cold of February 1827, writing that her death *"cut us deeply."*

In May 1839, old Mr. Rich came for Cyrus K. Lunt. Cyrus trudged to Richs Head to dig a springtime grave so John and Jane (Lunt) Rich could bury their 11-day-old son.

Five-year-old Charles P. St. Clair Rich was buried in the frozen ground on the northwest side of the harbor in January 1848. Jacob Lunt 2nd preached at the funeral and spoke from Job when he asked, "Why died I not from the womb? Why did I not give up the ghost when I came out of the belly?"

But such was life. Cyrus himself died three months later at the tender age of 31. His father, Amos Sr., wrote: *"Cyrus King Lunt died on Long Island, Monday morning a little after daylight, April the 17th, 1848. Aged 31 years, eight months and 25 days. Buried on Long Island, April 18th, Tuesday p.m."*

Five of Amos' 17 children died in their 30s or younger.

Similar sorrows, though specific details are lost to time, are found in most family histories.

Bartholomew Russell and Asenath (Allen) Lunt had 12 children between 1833 and 1851, and five died young. A sixth, youngest son Bartholomew Jr., died in his 30s.

Between 1892 and 1915, James H. and Elizabeth "Lizzie" (Lunt) Thurlow lost five of 16 children, including three who were born dead. John R. and Flora Eveline Lunt lost five of their 15 children between 1905 and 1930. Hiram A. and Mary Susan Lunt's first three children all died before their 10th birthdays. And of Alphonso L. and Sadie L. (McKusick) Lunt's four children born between 1900 and 1914, two were stillborn and one died at 18.

Overall, between 1900 and 1920, on an island with fewer than 200 residents, at least 30 children were either stillborn or died before their 10th birthday. The cause of many island deaths is unknown. In some cases diets were poor and medical attention scarce. Pre-natal care was unheard of and complications at birth proved disastrous for the baby and some-times the mother. Israel B. Lunt's 18-year-old daughter Amanda died during childbirth in 1851.

Other islanders died in their 20s, 30s and 40s. Some died accidentally, such as 18-year-old Wilson Carter who died of an alcohol overdose in 1913, and 13-year-old LaForest Rich, who accidentally shot himself in 1884. But who knows why 16-year-old Roseanna (Pomroy) Downes died 12 days after her marriage to George Downes?

Toward the end of the 1800s and early 1900s, polio — listed in town records as infantile paralysis — and pneumonia proved deadly to young and old alike. Polio took Ruby M. Thurlow at 5 and Edna G. Lunt at 4, both in 1916. Pneumonia killed six children in one 17-year span.

Alvina Lunt lost her one-month-old daughter to pneumonia in 1905; eight-year-old Mary Lunt, daughter of Amos and Betsy Lunt, died of scarlet fever in 1895; Grant and Lena (Higgins) Lunt lost an unnamed one-month-old baby to a ruptured navel in 1903; Eight-year-old Roy Thurlow, son of James H. and Lizzie (Lunt) Thurlow, died of pneumonia in 1917; and one-year-old Carrie Elliot, daughter of Orrin and Bessie (Roberts) Elliot, died in 1915.

Child deaths didn't end after the first two decades of the 20th century. In the 1920s, 20 deaths were recorded on Long Island, and seven of the deceased were younger than 15.

Among the island's unmarked and nearly forgotten graves are those of two young girls buried just off the Lincoln Road above the ferry pier. The two girls died after drinking poisoned well water. Legend claims a mentally disturbed island resident poisoned the water.

Three-year-old Phillis Lunt, son of Atwood and Angeline Lunt, also died after drinking contaminated well water.

Starting in 1930 as transportation, medicine and diets improved, the death rate among the young dropped dramatically.

One notable exception was Rita Hughes, who lived with Eugene and Vera Van Norden. Rita, 19, died at home of tuberculosis in 1937.

## *The Sea*

One of the great single tragedies of the 19th century occurred in October of 1851 in the waters off Canada.

The *Henry Clay*, captained by 25-year-old John Walls of Long Island, was among the schooners caught by the infamous "Yankee Gale" in the Bay of Chaleur. The northerly gale struck the coast of Prince Edward Island without warning on the night of October 3, 1851. While estimates vary, the storm may have killed more than 300 New England fisherman and wrecked more than 100 vessels. Among those who died was Capt. Walls, widower of Amanda S. Lunt.

Also lost were 16-year-old Edward P. Lunt, Israel B. Lunt's son, and Joshua Trask, 44, of Swans Island. Trask at one time also lived on Long Island. A gravestone for Capt. Walls and Edward Lunt rests in an old island cemetery, although the actual bodies were probably not returned. Newspapers reported that because of the carnage, mass graves were dug on Canadian beaches to bury the fishermen who washed ashore. The tombstone reads:

> *No village bell shall toll for them*
> *Its mournful solemn dirge.*
> *The winds shall chant a requiem*
> *For them beneath the surge.*

Details of the disaster trickled into Maine for days, and only slowly did the magnitude become known. Newspapers and family members relied on letters and returning sailors to bring reports. The loss of the *Henry Clay* did not appear in the *Eastern Argus* of Portland until Oct. 27. But on Oct. 14, the Portland newspaper, which carried daily dispatches from Canada, provided this report:

Halifax, Oct. 11 — We are enabled to give you the following additional particulars relative to marine disasters in the Gulf of St. Lawrence, and along the coast of Prince Edward Island. The whole shore is strewed with the wrecks of vessels, and the bodies of their crews. The Charlottetown coroners have gone to the village of Cavendish, to inquire into the deaths of twelve persons, whose bodies had been washed ashore at that place.

"The body of a man, with a boy lashed to his back, came ashore at Pestico, not recognized. There is reason to believe that over 100 bodies have floated to the beach since the storm. ...

"In Gloucester, Newburyport, and other seaports, the greatest excitement prevails, and the families of those who are on board the various vessels are in a state of suspense, which is truly agonizing, fearful as they are that the next hour will bring them sad tidings of fathers, husbands, and brothers, who found a watery grave."

That was likely the scene on Outer Long Island as relatives awaited word of Walls, Lunt and Trask.

Being a fishing village, many local deaths certainly occurred on the ocean. But most 19th-century island sea tragedies have been forgotten. Census records of the 1800s list numerous young widows, some of whose husbands were likely lost at sea.

It is recorded that Pearl Rice, 44, drowned in 1939.

Carrie Brewer, granddaughter of Capt. William Davis, grew up on Outer Long Island. In an interview with *The Bar Harbor Times* in 1938, Brewer related some local 19th century tragedies. She said her father, Capt. James Long, was fishing off Mount Desert Rock, likely in the 1880s, when his vessel capsized in a squall. His body washed up at Rum Cove off Black Island about three weeks later. He was identified only by his sock.

Brewer said two other 19th century wrecks near the island also caused deaths. In the late 1800s, the *Para*, disabled in a fierce winter gale, crashed onto Southwest Point. The entire crew died, but the beaten hull lay on the beach for many years.

The *Elizabeth Orchard* was returning from the Grand Banks loaded with fish when it crashed on a nearby ledge. It was a bitter winter night, and the captain and his crew sought refuge in the rigging. Every one of them was frozen to death, Brewer said.

## Unexpected and Tragic

Maria (Lunt) Teel, wife of William M. Teel, died of severe burns after a paint can that was heating on the stove caught fire. Maria tried to put it out but somehow fanned the flames, and the entire house caught fire. Lizzie Ross nursed her in an apartment above a fishhouse, but Maria lived only a few more weeks. She left three boys.

On April 14, 1948, carbon monoxide killed two Southwest Harbor fishermen as they slept aboard their boat while it was tied up at the pier. When the two men, Warren D. Stanley, 27, and Ralph L. Ramsdell, 29, went to bed down in the bow they lighted a small stove for warmth. That night, the gas killed them while they slept.

Llewelyn "Hud" Lunt died in the winter of 1958. He was just outside the harbor hauling traps in his skiff and outboard on Nov. 28 when he collapsed and died. He was 62. The skiff, Hud's body inside, washed ashore on the northern end of Harbor Island. He was found by Clarence Lunt and Vincent Davis near the edge of dark. They towed the skiff into the harbor like a floating casket.

*The William M. Teel family, 1890s. Clinton (left), William Sr., Sawtelle, William Jr., and Maria (Lunt) Teel.*

Such sudden deaths were not uncommon.

Hiram Albert "Doonie Hum" Lunt Jr. died on the road between Sanford L. "Dick" Lunt's house and Millie (Davis) Hunton's house in 1966. Young Kevin Holland found Lincoln Lunt dead in his camp at the head of the cove in 1973. Everett Edward "Ebbit" Dalzell Jr. died on the road above the pier in 1968. Joseph Warren "Innie" Lunt sat down on the church steps to rest and died in 1954. And Kenneth Gardiner Lunt lay down to rest and died in 1961.

The worst island tragedy of the 20th century occurred March 1, 1971 when Bennie S. Davis Sr., 66, and Clyde V. Onyett, 62, drowned in the frigid winter water just off the ferry pier.

Bennie and Clyde were driving down the pier hill in an old truck to meet the mail boat. The pier hill leads to a metal ferry ramp that includes a steel apron at the end. The apron is raised to an angle by steel cables when not in use. On either side of the ramp are two paved wings for parking.

As the two men drove toward the pier, the truck's throttle stuck open. Cars were parked beside the ramp, but Bennie chose to steer down the middle as he sped down the hill. He apparently hoped the apron and its steel cables would stop the truck.

Paul "Rusty" Crossman, on the pier waiting for the mail, helplessly witnessed the tragic event.

John R. Lunt Jr. and Robert Lunt remember Lillian Lunt speeding by Robert's house on the high road, yelling, "They've gone off the pier! They've gone off the pier!"

The island reacted immediately, but there was nothing to do.

In one of the most heartbreaking and gut-wrenching tasks of the century, island fishermen hooked the submerged vehicle with an anchor and dragged it up the harbor using a lobster boat. Then using a block and tackle attached to a tree, the truck was pulled ashore so the bodies could be removed. Fishermen lugged the bodies across the flats to a waiting Coast Guard boat.

Ben Davis was an island leader and fisherman who traced his 19th-century island roots to both Capt. William Davis and Israel B. Lunt.

Clyde, originally a summer minister, had moved to the island only recently with his wife, Mildred. Mildred remained as the island's school-teacher for several years following Clyde's death.

The ferry pier is dedicated in their names.

# Hauling By Hand

## Part II

*Chapter Eleven*

# An Island at War

## Soldiers and Fishermen

It is difficult to sit in the stillness of Lunt Harbor and imagine 19th-century island fishermen and farmers leaving homes and families for the bloody battlefields of the Civil War. Or to imagine them fighting across South Pacific islands during World War II.

What must an island man, who spent his youthful days fishing for cod on Blue Hill Bay, have thought when he first saw thousands of Union soldiers shivering in the muddy trenches before Petersburg, Virginia? Or as he watched fellow soldiers die on such battlefields as Deep Run or Bermuda Hundred? What went through the mind of a gangly young lobsterman storming a South Pacific beach even as Japanese guns littered the sand with the bodies of his comrades?

Islanders who fought in the Civil War never fully recovered from their wounds and illnesses. How World War II veterans were affected, I don't really know. Unquestionably, they were changed. How could they not be?

World War II was the first war from which I knew veterans and a war that remained etched into the American psyche even into my generation.

Sixteen people with ties to Long Island, including some lifelong residents, served in the war. On the home front, some islanders moved away to work in shipyards while those who remained rang the church bell at 6

Photo by Dean L. Lunt

*Rod Forsgren (left) and Vincent A. Davis, 1980s.*

p.m. each night for four years to honor their soldiers. Each soldier carried a prayer book given him by Gladys Muir and the Sunday school children.

The veterans I knew best were my great-uncles, Clarence L. Lunt and Vincent A. Davis. I knew them while growing up in the 1970s and while a teenager in the 1980s. By then they were older men, or at least they seemed that way to a young boy. I rarely connected the war I saw in history books and movies with the lobstermen that I saw every day. I simply considered these guys colorful old fishermen who taught me to swear, chewed on cigars, watched soap operas, told tall tales and observed life in the slow, unhurried way of another era.

Clarence and Vincent were fixtures of my early island childhood. For years it seemed that Vincent and Clarence (and non-veteran Cecil E. Lunt) were sentinels stationed on the Lunt & Lunt dock — always watching. It is only a slight exaggeration to say that every time I landed at the family wharf on a summer day, they were there, sitting on a bench against the building or kicked back on an old lobster crate.

Many nights around dusk they wandered down past our house toward Lookout Point to sit on the ledges or to rest beside the old duck-shooting blind. It was long an island tradition.

My most enduring image of Clarence — grandson of a Civil War soldier and great-great-great-grandson of a Revolutionary War soldier — is this: black hip boots rolled down, a partly-chewed, half-smoked Phillies

178

cigar, gray cotton baseball cap with a long black bill, green cotton pants and scruffy whiskers. He walked with a slow, slightly bent gait that seemed more like a slow roll.

He and Vincent knew at least something about my activities. They knew about Little League games, Mount Desert Island high school, American Legion baseball, Syracuse University, some of my girlfriends and a few other personal matters. And I knew something about them. But never too much. It was the way.

Clarence was not the stereotypical island bachelor of the 1940s and 1950s who never strayed far from island shores. He actually lived in Tremont, owned a fine fiberglass boat, helped run a seining operation, had two children and served as a selectmen. But it seemed he was always on the island.

The last time I remember seeing Clarence was in a parking lot in Bass Harbor overlooking the Maine State Ferry pier on a hot summer afternoon in 1988, the year I graduated from college. He sat in his car. I leaned through the window. We told a few jokes, briefly discussed my plans. But, as usual, it was nothing too deep or personal. Just daily banter about baseball, family, fishing, gossip and nostalgia. That was our connection.

*Clarence L. Lunt, 1969.*

Vincent said he knew when I was on the island because he could hear a ball bouncing on pavement. He constantly tried to roust me from his apple trees — "Hey, get the hell out of that tree! — while I clung low on the branches. My baseball idol in the 1970s was Boston Red Sox catcher Carlton Fisk. Vincent told me almost daily that Bob Montgomery was better: "That damn Fisk couldn't hit the broadside of a barn."

The summer I helped run a take-out restaurant he came down to the wharf every day after *The Guiding Light* signed off and ordered the same

*Courtesy of Ella V. Lunt*

*Kenneth Gardiner Lunt (left) Catherine Lunt and Clarence Lunt, 1940s.*

thing: Three grilled hotdogs and a Coke. He called me "Da-Dean-dos" or "Boy" and he called most young women "Girl."

Vincent, a lifelong bachelor, was a legendary drinker, but he gave up alcohol sometime in the 1970s for health reasons. He was sober from the time I remember or would really know the difference.

"Vince" had no running water in his two-room cabin, which overlooked both the harbor and the run-down Alec Davis homestead and wharf where he grew up. He lugged water from my parent's house in gallon plastic milk jugs or in an uncovered red plastic pail that smelled like cigar smoke. He usually filled the jugs at our outside faucet, but when the faucet didn't work we filled them at the kitchen sink. I don't remember him coming past the front door. He usually waited on the lawn or stood just inside the doorway.

As he grew older, we often filled the jugs and left them at the foot of our long stairs. Sometimes we lugged them to his door stoop just up the road a few paces. I never went past his front door, either.

Vincent was the last great island storyteller, with a keen memory and the unrushed time to talk. He knew more stories about Long Island and its people than anyone in the past half century. I heard many of those stories — some true, some embellished — many a late afternoon at the wharf or while sitting by the workshop fire on a chilled December day. Unfortunately, I have forgotten nearly all of them.

In the war, Vincent served on a cable-laying ship in the Atlantic. He remained in the service from Jan. 18, 1941 to Dec. 16, 1945 and was promoted to staff sergeant, the highest rank attained by an island soldier. While he operated under constant threat of submarine attack, he never saw any serious combat and remained a war buff until his death. He often talked about the heroes and the war.

It was Clarence who saw the war in its uncensored brutality.

Twenty-year-old Clarence was inducted Feb. 11, 1943 and served with Company F of the 594th Engineer Boat and Shore Regiment. The lifelong fisherman drove an amphibious assault vehicle in the South Pacific while the U.S. Army fought through the Marianas Islands, the Bismarck Archipelago, New Britain, New Guinea and the Philippines on its way to Japan.

He saw the beaches run red with blood.

On one of the Marianas Islands in tall grass, Clarence engaged in hand-to-hand combat. During one fight, an

*Courtesy of Frenchboro Historical Society*

*Vincent A. Davis, 1940s.*

enemy soldier tore into Clarence's side with a bayonet. Wounded and bleeding, Clarence kept fighting, using his own bayonet to kill his Japanese opponent. Clarence powdered and bandaged his wound but remained pinned down by snipers for nearly three days until reinforcements came.

He received a Purple Heart.

By the time the war ended, he also received: an Asiatic Pacific Theater Campaign Ribbon with Bronze Service Arrowhead; an American Theater Campaign Ribbon; a Philippine Liberation Ribbon with one bronze service star; a good conduct medal; and a Victory Medal.

Not that I heard him say much about this. Nor did many of his closest friends.

"If people started talking about the war he would get up and leave," said John R. Lunt Jr., his youngest brother.

More than once, Clarence said, "I was there, that was enough."

He refused to collect his war pension.

Clarence died of a heart attack in June of 1989 at the age of 66. That was nearly seven years before Vincent died in 1996 at the age of 82.

Vincent was confined to a nursing home in Bar Harbor for his final days. But at times near the end, as he sat on the edge of the bed, he often imagined he was down at the wharf.

Just sitting and watching and talking.

*Courtesy of Frenchboro Historical Society*

*Clarence L. Lunt, 1940s.*

# The Civil War: 1861 to 1865

Nearly 140 years after Confederate guns fired on Fort Sumter, the Civil War remains the defining event of this nation. It still fascinates us, inspires us and gnaws at us. The war reunited a country and abolished the unconscionable institution of slavery, finally freeing all men who, as President Abraham Lincoln pointed out on the fields of Gettysburg, were created equal. It was also the bloodiest, deadliest war in United States history. More American men died in the grassy fields of such places as Pennsylvania and Virginia than died in all of the nation's other wars combined. Overall, more than 620,000 men were killed and about 470,000 were wounded in the war (Long, *Civil War Day by Day*, 711).

Farmers, fishermen, laborers and immigrants died not only in battle but also from diseases, infections and other ailments contracted in the field or in the notoriously unsanitary hospitals. At the time, no one knew how disease spread. Drinking water was unknowingly contaminated. Bacteria and germs spread like wind-whipped brushfires.

In addition, soldiers were sometimes malnourished and exhausted from inadequate food supplies, forced marches through unfamiliar territory and climates and, of course, battle.

More than three-fifths of all Civil War deaths were attributed to diseases such as chronic diarrhea, typhoid, malaria, pneumonia, consumption and smallpox. Many survivors bore the scars of battle and the pain of disease until they died, sometimes with little apparent sympathy from a government they helped save.

Overall, about 18,000 Maine men were killed or wounded during the war. Of the nearly 9,400 that died, more than 60 percent died from disease (Jordan, *Maine in the Civil War*, 72). In the 11th Maine Infantry, which included many of the soldiers from Long Island, more than 125 men were killed or mortally wounded in battle, while more than 220 men, about 64 percent of all deaths, died from diseases (Maxfield, *Story of One Regiment*, Appendix). In total, about 770 men in the 11th Maine were either killed in battle, wounded or died from disease.

Into such conditions came fishermen from the islands of Maine. They traveled hundreds and hundreds of miles into harsh and unfamiliar territory to valiantly fight a war over great issues, but ones that touched their daily lives in only the most tangential ways. And some clearly resisted.

Islanders George R. Rich and Abraham Rice initially wrote that they were unable to fight because they were the sole supporters of their elderly parents. They both, as pointed out in a letter written to the Adjutant General by George B. Lunt, had voted for a Democrat (read anti-Lincoln) in the most recent election and opposed the war. Their claims were suspect, he said. George Rich would later be forcibly sent into service.

But, while some motives were questionable, most island soldiers did have families to support. The only way to earn money on Outer Long Island in 1864 was through the sweat of hard labor. Take away that ability and you strike a blow at a man's life and his family. Take away several healthy young men from a small island village and you damage that village's ability to support itself.

When a government notice came to the island in 1862 seeking seven men to fight, George B. Lunt and Richard H. Lunt sought help themselves. All abled-bodied men, they wrote back, were "gone to sea" leaving only "cripples and old men."

"We have no enrolled militia in this place and we are unacquainted with the business," they wrote. They asked for help and pointed out that men from Long Island had gone to fight in the war but had enrolled from other places.

The debate was short-lived. Ultimately, at least 12 men with direct ties to Long Island — including seven long-time residents — fought in the Civil War. Two of those 12 died.

Five of the soldiers were either born or raised on the island or lived on the island for many years but did not spend most of their adult lives there:

William T. Lunt, born April 5, 1842, was the eldest son of Abner Lunt Jr. and Abigail R. Tinker. He was born either on Outer Long Island or Placentia Island but grew up on Outer Long Island. He lived in Ellsworth when he volunteered Feb. 16, 1863. He served with the 1st Maine Heavy Artillery, Co. C. He was killed outside Petersburg, Virginia on June 18, 1864.

On the day William was killed, the 1st Maine suffered the most losses of any single regiment in any one action of the war; 632 of its 900 men were either killed or wounded during one hopeless charge (Boatner, *Civil War Dictionary,* 503). William is buried in a Virginia fortification dubbed Fort Hell. He never married, but was supporting his mother and ailing stepfather when he died.

James H. Lunt, born Oct. 15, 1843, was William's brother. He served in the 11th Maine Regiment, Co. H from Oct. 28, 1864 until June 12, 1865. He lived on Long Island before the war, and returned there for at least several years in the 1870s. He married Hannah Walls.

Jacob Lunt (III) Jr., born Nov. 6, 1836, was the third son of Jacob Lunt 2nd and Sally Allen. He served in the 31st Maine Regiment, Co. D from February 1864 to July 1865. He was born and raised on Outer Long Island but moved to Mount Desert in the 1850s. Jacob was wounded in the left side at Spotsylvania on May 12, 1864. He sought a disability pension at age 37 because of his wounds and illnesses. He lived in Mount Desert in the 1870s but owned neither land nor home. At the time he worked "for anyone who saw fit to hire him." He married Elizabeth Robertson. He died March 31, 1913.

Henry L. Lunt, born April 18, 1838, was the fourth son of Jacob Lunt 2nd and Sally Allen. He was likely born on Outer Long Island and lived there for some time. He served in the 1st Maine Heavy Artillery. He enlisted Feb. 16, 1863 from Ellsworth and was discharged Sept. 11, 1865. He was wounded at Petersburg on June 19, 1864 and again at Farmville, Virginia on April 6, 1865. He also suffered from typhoid fever and chronic diarrhea. He had married Mary G. Lunt at Mount Desert on April 10, 1861.

Brothers Jacob III and Henry L. were first cousins to James H. and William T. All four were great-grandsons of Abner Lunt and Jane Dawes, one of the first Lunt families on Outer Long Island.

Daniel Stow Lunt, sometimes known as Baron, was the youngest son of Amos Coffin and Priscilla (Butler) Lunt. He was born and raised on Outer Long Island. As a 24-year-old he enlisted in the 8th Regiment Co. G at Ellsworth and enrolled at Augusta on Sept. 7, 1861. He served part of his time in South Carolina and participated in the captures of Forts William and Beauregard and the siege of Fort Pulaski. He became sick in South Carolina and was eventually shipped to New York where he was discharged in January of 1863 because of illness.

He never made it home. By the time he reached Boston he was taken directly to a local physician's house, unable to walk or stand. There he remained bedridden, too weak to even sit up, until his death on Feb. 5. Baron had first married Mary A. Dawes, and later Lydia J. Leach in 1858. He had one daughter, Flora Ella Lunt, born Jan 21, 1860.

The Union armies initially consisted solely of volunteers. Eventually, states paid bounties to encourage volunteers. But as the war dragged on and casualty lists grew horrifically longer, the United States resorted to the first-ever draft in 1863.

In general, some people opposed not only the draft, but also stipulations allowing a drafted man to avoid service by either paying a commutation fee or hiring a substitute. At one point, both cost about $300. Eventually, the cost of hiring a substitute increased, because paying commutation saved a man from only one draft call, while hiring a substitute saved him from the entire war.

The draft rules unquestionably favored the wealthy, giving rise to the complaint that this was a rich man's war and a poor man's fight.

Of all the men drafted nationally for the Union army, 86,724 paid a commutation to avoid service, 42,581 non-drafted men hired substitutes, 75,429 drafted men hired substitutes and 52,068 drafted men actually served (Boatner, 858). On top of that, some drafted men just didn't report.

In Maine, more than 5,350 men — both drafted and non-drafted — hired substitutes (*Annual Report of the Adjutant General of the State of Maine, 1866*, 362). Another 2,000 paid commutation. Overall, about 70,000 men from Maine went to war.

There is no record of a resident of Long Island, which was a mostly poor island, hiring a substitute. However, at least three prominent captains who lived in Tremont at the time, but who were born and raised on the island, did. They were: Albion K.P. Lunt, John R. Lunt, and Roland H. Lunt. They were not unique. The list of men hiring substitutes as the war dragged into 1864 included the most prominent family names in Tremont, Swans Island, Cranberry Island, Deer Isle and most other coastal towns.

A look at several island towns illustrates the practical effect of the draft in 1864. The following statistics do not reflect volunteers who filled town quotas nor the non-drafted men who hired substitutes.

On Swans Island, 44 men were drafted in 1864, but none actually served. Instead, 10 hired substitutes, 24 were exempted for physical disabilities, two were over age and seven failed to report (Adjutant General, 1864/65, 721).

In the district that encompassed Outer Long Island, Marshall Island and Harbor Island, 12 men were drafted in 1864. Four actually served, three were exempted for physical disabilities, one was "illegally drafted" and four failed to report (Adjutant General, 1864/65, 721).

On Deer Isle, 198 men were drafted in 1864, but only two actually served. Instead, 49 hired substitutes, 51 had physical disabilities, 13 reported and deserted and 77 failed to report. Of the 49 substitutes hired, 32 were from foreign countries. Only four substitutes were actually from Deer Isle (Adjutant General, 1864/65, 718).

Those entering the service in 1864 also witnessed growing resistance and outrageous propaganda by anti-war forces. Some Long Island men entered the service through Belfast. The local newspaper there was *The Republican Journal*. Despite the name, the *Journal* was in fact an anti-war, anti-Lincoln, Democrat newspaper. When the *Journal* announced a draft call in the summer of 1864, it also ran an article (*The Republican Journal*, July 22, p. 2) under the headline "More Victims for the Slaughter Called for." That article included this sentence; "Lincoln appears to act as though the American people were but cattle in the shambles to be slaughtered for his pleasure." In later editions the *Journal* called the draft "Lincoln's lottery of death."

On Nov. 4, the week four men from Long Island were drafted, the *Journal* ran a column on page four that originally appeared in a Wisconsin newspaper. That verse in part read, "Bow down your grey heads, mothers, for your loved and petted sons go forth never more to return. Steady your tottering limbs, old men, for the pride and support of your declining years is being marched to the Valley of Death."

## William Davis and the 11th Maine

With all that turmoil swirling along the coast, men from Long Island went to war, most as part of the 11th Maine Infantry Regiment.

The 11th Maine was organized at Augusta and mustered Nov. 12, 1861. At various times, the regiment was part of the Army of the Potomac, the Dept. of North Carolina and the Dept. of the South. In 1865, the regiment was part of a reorganized Army of the James. It belonged to the 3rd Brigade, 1st Division, 24th Army Corps.

Islanders in the regiment, their age, company and year they entered, were:

William Davis, 24, Company B, 1862
George "Colver" Colliver Lunt, 25, Company E, 1864

Hezekiah W. Lunt, 31, Company E, 1864

Joseph Warren Lunt, 35, Company D, 1864

George R. Rich, 35, Company A, 1864

Also, William S. Rich, probably about 16, joined the 61st Massachusetts Infantry Volunteers, Company G, in 1864.

Samuel Rich, 42, joined the 9th Maine on April 5, 1865, only days before the surrender of Gen. Robert E. Lee. He did not see action and was mustered out May 10, 1865.

Twenty-four-year-old William Davis was the first Long Islander to enter the war. During the 1800s, several men named William Davis lived on Long Island. The veteran William Davis, born Dec. 28, 1837, was likely the son of Ezra and Rebecca Davis and a brother to Levi, Joseph and Hezekiah Davis. He was not the man commonly known as Capt. William Davis, an island boatbuilder. The veteran William Davis married Emeline Dawes of Black Island on Nov. 18, 1857 and the couple lived near Whale Beach.

Although William returned to Long Island, he also lived in Blue Hill and Grand Manan, New Brunswick. As an elderly man he moved to Surry, where he is buried in Hillside Cemetery.

When William volunteered from Outer Long Island he already had a one-year-old daughter, Charlotte "Lottie" Davis. After William returned from the war, he and Emeline had more children, including John G. and Addie M.

William, brown-haired, blue-eyed, and 5 foot, 9 inches tall, volunteered for a three-year term at Blue Hill on Aug. 5, 1862. He likely joined his regiment at Yorktown and marched into North Carolina, South Carolina and Florida.

In 1863, he saw action in South Carolina at St. Helena Island, Beaufort, Morris Island and Charleston. In May 1864, the 11th Maine moved to a new front outside Petersburg and Richmond, Virginia.

During the Petersburg Campaign, Davis saw action at Bermuda Hundred, Port Walthall, City Point, Fort Darling, Drury's Bluff, Deep Bottom, New Market Heights and Strawberry Plains.

The Petersburg Campaign lasted from May 1864 to April 1865 as Union forces lay siege to Petersburg and the Confederate army led by Gen. Robert E. Lee. The 11th Maine and Davis took one break in November to help protect New York City from rioters during the reelection of President Abraham Lincoln.

Despite considerable battle action, William remained unscathed and relatively healthy until early 1864. Then while at Charleston, he started to suffer from the onset of chronic diarrhea, a problem that lingered for years. He reported to the hospital in both March and April.

Chronic diarrhea and dysentery, among the worst causes of mortality in the army, killed more than 44,500 Federal soldiers during the war, (Long, 712).

After moving on to Virginia, Davis was wounded in the left side at Bermuda Hundred, a front outside of Petersburg, on May 17, 1864.

At Bermuda Hundred, the 11th Maine was rousted shortly after midnight because of nearby Confederate movements. In the skirmish, six companies of the 11th Maine moved through dense woods lighted only by the moon. When met by a Confederate musket volley:

> "Our men threw themselves on the ground or behind trees, and opened an answering fire. For an hour fierce fire was exchanged by the opposing lines and at close range, the dark woods echoing to the crack of rifles, and the yells of combatants whose positions could only be conjectured by the lighting up of the wood by intermittent rifle flashes" (Maxfield, 189).

During the skirmish, two 11th Maine soldiers were killed and 24 were wounded, including William Davis. Davis later was wounded in the left arm on Aug. 16 at Deep Run.

> "Almost immediately we were subjected to the most severe fire we were ever under. No mere skirmish line this, but an outlying line of battle. The wood fairly rang with the screeching of the bullets." (Maxfield, 244). During that fight, 13 soldiers of the 11th Maine were killed, 81 wounded, and six taken prisoner. William Davis, who served for another year, forever suffered from his wounds and illnesses. Davis signed a statement (Civil War Pension Records, William Davis) in 1887 detailing his health problems:

> "While engaged in the battle of Deep Run, I received aforesaid wound in left arm on Aug. (16), 1864. While at Charleston, S.C., I contracted aforesaid chronic diarrhea caused by exposure, hardships and privations incident to army life. In 1864, while on James River in Va., I contracted aforesaid disease of eyes, caused in same manner as above-mentioned chronic diarrhea. I have suffered continuously since discharge from aforesaid diseases and now claim a pension on same.

In 1889, he was considered "three-fourths" disabled.

"I have known William Davis for forty years and before he went to the war he was a well man and ever since he come home from the army he has been sick and has not been able to work not more than half of his time with chronic diarrhea, loss of eyesight and wound in hollow of left arm which grows worse as he grows old," said George "Colver" Lunt in an 1891 affidavit witnessed by Thomas N. Osier and Hortense B. Van Norden (Civil War Pension Records, William Davis). "He is a near neighbor of mine so I have a chance to know about him."

By 1892, a doctor described William Davis' left arm as roughly one-half the size of the right arm and said "lack of strength is apparent."

William received a disabled veteran's pension of $2 per month starting in 1893, six years after he first applied. The pension was retroactive to 1887. His monthly pension topped out at $30 per month in 1912.

## *Petersburg*

The battles outside Petersburg where William Davis was wounded were part of an overall Union strategy to defeat Lee.

In 1864, President Abraham Lincoln placed Grant in charge of all Federal forces, establishing crucial coordination and skill at the top of the military chain. It was Grant who sent Gen. William Tecumseh Sherman storming into the south, and it was Grant who decided the sole target of the Army of the Potomac — and later the Army of the James as well — was Lee.

Throughout 1864, the Army of the Potomac fought Lee at every turn in Virginia from the Battle of the Wilderness to Spotsylvania Court House to Cold Harbor. Jacob Lunt III was wounded at Spotsylvania. Unlike his predecessors, Grant pressed the attack after each battle rather than retreat and reorganize. It was an effective but often costly strategy.

In June 1864, Grant ordered two hopeless frontal assaults against the fortified city of Petersburg. He hoped to capture Petersburg and then march on to Richmond, the Confederate capital. Instead, he was repelled both times and suffered heavy losses. William T. Lunt was killed during an assault on June 18th.

Finally, realizing such direct assault was impossible, Grant settled on a siege strategy. He placed Gen. Lee and Petersburg in a withering vise-like grip that would last nine months and feature frequent skirmishes. The siege of Petersburg lasted into the spring of 1865. During the siege, William Davis was joined by his Long Island neighbors and relatives.

Three Lunt cousins — George "Colver" Lunt (William Davis' brother-in-law), Hezekiah W. Lunt, Joseph W. Lunt — and George R. Rich were all drafted Oct. 27 or 28, 1864, about two months after the battles at Deep Run. The Lunts were among 201 new recruits who replenished the 11th Maine at Chaffin's (sometimes called Chapin's) Farm, Virginia in December 1864. Chaffin's Farm was the winter camp of the 11th Maine and part of a Union line – mirrored by a Confederate line — that at one point stretched about 50 miles from near Richmond to south of Petersburg.

William Davis was already at Chaffin's Farm. George R. Rich would arrive in January.

In Company D of the Eleventh Regiment Maine Infantry, Albert Maxfield and Robert Brady Jr. wrote (p. 56), "The winter of 1864-5 was passed by our men in the rude huts they erected of logs, boards and canvas, getting height by digging a few feet into the ground, sealing and flooring the sunken portion. These huts were heated by sheet iron stoves."

The Virginia winter was unusually cold.

"The duties of the winter were the usual military ones of drill, fatigue, guard and picket, supplemented by the carrying out of an order to have the troops in line of battle every morning from shortly before daybreak until sunrise, that they might rush to the parapets and repel any attempted surprise by the enemy, who were doubtless standing in a shivering line behind their works as we were behind ours, both lines with an identical fear (Maxfield and Brady, 56)."

At Chaffin's Farm in February of 1865, George C. Lunt, often known as "Colver," fell on ice while carrying wood for the company cook. He suffered a rupture and a hernia and was treated at various hospitals during the next five months. He received an honorable discharge in June 1865.

"Colver" Lunt, born Dec. 28, 1839, was the fourth child of Miriam and George B. Lunt. He married Harriet "Hat" Davis, daughter of Ezra and Rebecca Davis, on March 13, 1867. They had at least six children including, Angeline, Edwin L., Daniel R., Alvina, Jasper, and Mary E.

*Courtesy of Lillian J. Lunt*

*Harriet "Hat" (Davis) and George C. "Colver" Lunt, 1920s.*

Mary died young. "Col" lived on the west side near the head of the harbor, just south of the house owned in 1999 by Myron and Sarah Lenfestey.

Colver, 5 foot, 8 inches tall with black hair and hazel eyes, reported for duty Nov. 11, 1864. He arrived in Portland on Nov. 28 and at Gallop's Island in Boston Harbor on Dec. 7, 1864. He shipped from Boston on Dec. 23, arriving in Virginia on Dec. 28, his 25th birthday. While waiting at Gallop's, Colver suffered frostbite in his left foot, a problem that plagued him for years. Levi T. Davis (Civil War Pension Records, Colver Lunt) later said:

"I know the said Colver Lunt ever since his discharge, by being ship mates with him and living near him for years; I have known him every year since his discharge, at Plantation Long Island. He has been troubled with these diseases by injury of left foot and rheumatism, by times in arms and legs, also rupture in right side, becoming more disabled every year. I should say that he is unable one-half of the time to perform hard labor. Said Colver Lunt's habits are good."

After six years of trying, Colver received a veteran's pension of $8 per month starting in 1894, retroactive to 1888.

Colver died April 29, 1924 at the age of 85. He is buried on the west side in the cemetery beside the Osier house. Harriet, buried beside her husband, died Dec. 31, 1935 at the age of 84.

## The Appomattox Campaign

Spring in Virginia brought warmer weather and the climactic campaign of the Civil War: Appomattox. The spring action included the storming of Petersburg, the capture of Richmond and the final pursuit of General Lee.

On the eve of the Appomattox Campaign, the Civil War was essentially being fought in two primary theaters.

In South Carolina and Georgia, Gen. Sherman continued to overwhelm the Confederates. He had already captured Atlanta. After reaching the sea at Savannah in February 1865, he turned back north, his army a relentless force roaring through South Carolina and Georgia toward North Carolina. The primary Confederate force in the region was Joe E. Johnston's Army of Tennessee. Johnston was helpless to stop Sherman's powerful army.

At the same time, Lee's Army of Northern Virginia, the main fighting force of the Confederacy, remained trapped in Virginia by Grant. By this time, Lee was outnumbered and suffering. His only option was to slip past Grant, and join Johnston in North Carolina to create a single unified force.

In late March, after the roads dried, Lee struck part of the Union line. He hoped he could force the Union line to contract, thus allowing him to escape around one end and head south. On March 25, Confederate forces attacked a union fortification known as Fort Steadman and temporarily seized control. The victory didn't last. The Confederates were quickly ousted and Grant seized control.

Days later, Grant sent Phil Sheridan's cavalry to a critical railroad junction called Five Forks where Sheridan severed Lee's southern rail connection and blocked his southern route. Any escape route now would have to start by first going west. The next day Grant assaulted Petersburg, driving the confederates into full retreat across the Virginia countryside.

## Long Islanders and the pursuit of Gen. Lee

Marching, fighting and serving as eyewitnesses to the dramatic final days were William Davis, Hezekiah W. Lunt, Joseph Warren Lunt, George R. Rich and William S. Rich. As part of the 11th Maine and the 61st Massachusetts, they fought the battles of March and April and raced Lee to Appomattox.

The 11th Maine's role began March 27 when they moved across the James and Appomattox Rivers toward a place called Hatcher's Run.

"The march of Ord's force on the night of March 27th and the day of the 28th was a forced one, and was made over roads that were in terrible condition. The night was a dark one, with rain. The soft roads, cut up by artillery wheels and wagon trains, stretched here and there into wide morasses of knee-deep mire, into which we would plunge unexpectedly, to wallow through as best we could (Maxfield, 309)."

On March 31st and April 1, they fought at Hatcher's Run, where two 11th Maine soldiers were killed, 19 were wounded and 16 were taken prisoner. On April 2, the division helped assault and capture Forts Gregg and Baldwin, the last footholds Lee had on the Petersburg's front. During those three days of fighting, eight 11th Maine soldiers were killed and another 41 wounded and 16 taken prisoner.

On April 3, the Army of the James started its role in the dogged pursuit of Lee, a foot race under often-brutal conditions with little sleep or food. Then on the morning of April 8th, the 11th Maine marched from a spot near Farmville, Virginia, accompanied by Grant.

> "It was a question of legs and endurance now. On and on our men plodded, none falling until worn out. All were too tired even to raise a cheer in passing General Grant as he was sitting on a roadside log resting himself while enjoying a quiet smoke.
> "As the day passed we found ourselves on the track of Sheridan; prisoners, guns and trains of wagons captured by his vigorous advance, lined the roadside, encouraging our tired men to put forth every exertion. Darkness found us still pressing on, and it was not until after midnight that we halted for a few hours rest (Maxfield, 326)."

It was a short nap. Shortly after 3 a.m., the regiment started again. Near daybreak, the men reached a field serving as Sheridan's headquarters. The soldiers, tired and hungry, drank coffee and ate slices of raw bacon found on a captured supply train.

It was now the morning of April 9, near Appomattox. The men would soon drop the frugal meals and march quickly; Lee was trying to force a passage. Indeed, it was Lee's last desperate attempt to break through the lines of Union cavalry blocking his army's avenue of escape. The Confederates initially pushed back the Union cavalry but were then confronted by the surging blue mass of the Army of the James.

> "The struggle was short and sharp, and within a few minutes the last Confederate onset of the war was turned into a rapid retreat. Beyond

the woods we were driving the retreating confederates through was a wide ox-bow-shaped field, beyond which again, the roofs of the hamlet of Appomattox Court House could be seen (Maxfield, 327)."

The fight that last day at Clover Hill ended when a mounted Union officer yelled, "Halt boys! Halt! Lee has surrendered, and the war is over." Suddenly, the men of the 11th Maine and its four Outer Long Island soldiers found themselves in peace at Appomattox Court House.

And so on Palm Sunday, April 9, 1865, Robert E. Lee surrendered his Army of Northern Virginia to Ulysses S. Grant. Confederate troops further south held out for a short time, but in reality the war was over. The Confederacy was dead.

A formal surrender came three days later when John B. Gordon led 20,000 Confederate soldiers to Union lines to stack arms and surrender battle flags. Grant picked Major General Joshua Lawrence Chamberlain of Maine to accept the surrender.

The stately and eloquent Chamberlain, already a hero for his defense of Little Round Top at Gettysburg, later wrote, "On our part not a sound of trumpet more, nor roll of drum; not a cheer, nor word, nor whisper or vain-glorying, nor motion of man ... but an awed stillness rather, and breath-holding, as if it were the passing of the dead."

## Long Island Men and the Aftermath of War: Troubled Lives

While the Civil War was over, it could never be forgotten on Outer Long Island, Maine.

Among those at Appomattox was 31-year-old Hezekiah Wills Lunt, 5 foot, 6 inches tall, with blue eyes and brown hair. Hezekiah, born July 26, 1833, was the eldest son of Bartholomew Russell and Asenath (Allen) Lunt. He married Lydia M. Dawes of Black Island on Nov. 21, 1858. The couple had 12 children (see Chapter Four), including two, Adelbert W. "Del" and Cora H., before Hezekiah went to war.

While in Virginia, Hezekiah completed the marches, fought the battles and suffered the hardships without incident. His luck changed after Lee's surrender. Following the final battle, he developed "overheated blood" and open leg sores.

From April to June, Hezekiah was in three hospitals: Fly Hospital Ward 7 at Point of Rocks, Maryland; Paterson Park Hospital, Baltimore,

Maryland; and Hicks U.S. General Hospital, Baltimore, Maryland.

"He was in the hospital at Point of Rocks, Virginia soon after the surrender of Lee in 1865, for I was sent to that hospital and found Lunt there, unable to walk," said George R. Rich (Civil War Pension Records, H.W. Lunt). "From his knees down to his feet was covered with ulcers or boils. He claimed he also had rheumatism, and he had very sore eyes. I know Lunt well as we were raised together. I remember the above dis-tinctly. I left him in the hospital."

Hezekiah was honorably discharged June 21, 1865. But, as with so many others, he never fully recovered from his ailments despite living into his 80s.

"He was in three different hospitals and was discharged and sent home and has been suffering from the above troubles ever since," wrote George "Colver" Lunt in an 1894 affidavit (Civil War Pension Records, H.W. Lunt). "The rheumatism has been growing worse gradually over time and a greater part of the time he is helpless."

Hezekiah lived a few years in Blue Hill and Grand Manan after the war, but returned to his home on Outer Long Island in the 1880s.

*Courtesy of Frenchboro Historical Society*
*Hezekiah W. and Lydia (Dawes) Lunt, 1880s*

He applied for a veteran's disability pension in 1890. Although poor and ailing, he was initially rejected, and, like all local soldiers, forced to produce documentation, including affidavits from island residents, doctors and the military. Not an easy task at the time.

"Said Lunt is very poor, but a deserving, temperate man," wrote William S. Rich in 1892 (Civil War Pension Records, H. W. Lunt).

In October 1894, four years after his first application, Hezekiah was approved for a $6 per month pension. His pension increased after further applications and relaxed pension laws.

Hezekiah died January 29, 1914.

For more than 80 years, he rested in an unmarked grave on an island hillside, near the site of his former house on the west side. The grave, among perhaps dozens of unmarked graves on the hill, is beside the Butler Road and behind the Osier house. In 1999, an official Civil War military stone was placed in the field to commemorate Hezekiah's service. Lydia, known to succeeding generations as Gram Liddy, died Sept. 15, 1917 and is buried beside him.

### George R. Rich

George R. Rich was in his mid-30s when drafted Oct. 28, 1864. He married Lucy B. Lunt, daughter of Joseph D. and Rehoboth Hannah Lunt, on June 4, 1861. He had one daughter, Zerelda, and another child on the way when drafted. Zerelda died while George was in the service. She was 2. George and Lucy also had Joseph F. Rich, born March 21, 1865, and Lester P. Rich. George R. Rich was likely the son of William Rich and Eleanor Rice.

The prospect of war apparently did not appeal to George.

After being called in 1863 and then drafted in 1864, he fled the island to avoid service. He boarded a brig for New York, but his freedom didn't last. He was arrested in Rockland December 22, 1864 while returning home and fined $30 for desertion. He then shipped out to join the 11th Maine, Co. A on January 6, 1865.

Full-fledged desertion was a major problem during the war. Overall, more than 200,000 Union soldiers deserted (Boatner, 858). In 1864, more than 7,300 men deserted each month (Long, 714). During the war, about 125 men deserted from the 11th Maine in the field (Adjutant General, 1866, 291).

Ultimately, George served without incident following his arrest, and was honorably discharged in November 1865. He returned to Long Island Plantation after the war but later moved to Boothbay Harbor with his wife. Lucy B. Lucy's parents and her brother, Zaphnath, also moved to Boothbay Harbor. George died there June 11, 1901 and is buried in that town.

On the final day at Appomattox, George Rich was wounded by shrapnel in the right testicle, right thigh and right knee. The wounds left him partially disabled, but still able to work some. He applied for a disability pension in 1876 but was not approved for 13 years.

After George's death, his widow, Lucy, applied for a widow's pension. She, like other widows, needed considerable documentation to qualify before receiving any assistance.

Some affidavits provided were similar to these.

Albert H. Kenniston, an undertaker in Boothbay Harbor in 1901, wrote (Civil War Pension Records, George R. Rich):

> "I furnished the casket for the above named soldier, Geo. R. Rich; attended his burial in person, soon after his death which occurred on the eleventh day of June last, and I saw the casket covered in the cemetery at Boothbay. I also testify that I have known the soldier many years, and know that he and Lucy B. Rich lived together, in this town as man and wife, and were so regarded by the citizens and neighbors. I also know that Mrs. Lucy B. Rich has not remarried since the death of her husband, as being a neighbor, it would be almost impossible that the ceremony could take place without my knowledge. I also believe that she has neither property or income. She is known to be in indigent circumstances."

Lucy also described her plight (Civil War Records, George R. Rich), "I am suffering from rheumatism, and indigestion, and with disease of the feet so I am unable to work, save a very little," she said. "I am wholly dependent, and there is no one legally bound to support me. I only have the clothes which I wear and no other property of any kind."

Lucy died July 18, 1918.

## William Samuel Rich

William Samuel Rich, born March 17, 1848, was the son of William Rich and Eleanor Rice. He volunteered Nov. 22, 1864, when only 16 years old. William apparently lied about his age when he volunteered, claiming he was 22. He received a bounty of $100. He joined the 61st Massachusetts Infantry, Co. G. and was discharged July 12, 1865. The 5-foot, 8-inch, brown-haired, blue-eyed William married Abbie E. Davis on April 1, 1869. William and Abbie maintained a 19th-century showplace home on the road to the old Gilman Field. They had one daughter, Nellie E. (Robinson) born January 26, 1873. William was likely the brother of George R. Rich.

It is unknown why Rich volunteered in Massachusetts, although his ancestors did come from that state. When Rich joined the 61st Massachusetts, it was an independent brigade in the 9th Army Corps and part of the Army of the Potomac.

From the time William joined his regiment in January 1865 until March 28, 1865, he was stationed at City Point, Virginia, erecting fortifications and performing basic picket duty. His regiment was ordered to Petersburg on March 28 and participated in the assault on that city and in the pursuit of Lee.

Throughout the winter, Rich was hospitalized several times for health problems, including diarrhea and measles, but was sent back to the field

Courtesy of Frenchboro Historical Society

*The Abbie (Davis) and William S. Rich house, late 1800s. The house was located on the path to the old Gilman Field.*

each time. In May, his problems grew worse and he was sent to Augur General Hospital in Washington D.C., so weak he had to be carried. While at Augur, he was diagnosed with typhoid fever. He attributed his problems to "poor diet, exposure and hardship." He was sent home July 12.

"On the 27th of August 1865, immediately after his return from the service, I was called to see the claimant who was on the way to his island home and found him greatly emaciated and feeble and nearly incapable of assisting himself in the commonest personal necessary acts and suffering from the affects of an abscess or great irritation of the right lung, complicated with diarrhea which has since assumed a chronic form and necessitates frequent active treatment," wrote Dr. William A. Spear of Tremont (Civil War Pension Records, William S. Rich).

After returning to Long Island, he remained confined to his house for the better part of two years. Despite persistent problems, William Rich was rejected for a pension in 1885. Six years later, he finally received $6 per month plus $2 per month retroactive to 1885.

William died August 16, 1908. He was 60.

He is buried in the cemetery beside the Osier house.

His wife, Abbie, lived in New Harbor, Maine after his death, but is buried next to her husband on Long Island.

## Joseph Warren Lunt

While "Colver" Lunt, Hezekiah Lunt, George Rich, William Davis, William Rich and others were all partially disabled, most devastated by his experience and nearly abandoned by his government was Joseph Warren Lunt.

*Courtesy of Frenchboro Historical Society*

*Joseph Warren Lunt Sr. (1828 - 1891) in Civil War uniform, 1860s.*

Like Hezekiah, Joseph was the patriarch of a large family. As such, his inability to work full-time and his early death unquestionably impacted both his family and the island.

Joseph, born April 28, 1828, was the second born of Amos Coffin Jr. and Eliza (Pomroy) Lunt. Joseph, often known as Warren, married Alice A. Twist on March 6, 1859. Joseph and Alice had nine children and built a homestead that still stands, although in sad disrepair, on the west side near the house owned in 1999 by Joseph's grandson, Sanford L. "Dick" Lunt.

Joseph, 36, had three children — Atwood L., Hiram A. and Joseph Warren Jr. — when drafted. He was drafted at Belfast, Maine on Oct. 28, 1864. He and Alice later had: Lizzie B. (Ross), Grant H., Maria L. (Teel), Nelson P., John R., and Cora A. Lunt.

The 5-foot, 6-inch, black-haired, blue-eyed Joseph was a member of the 11th Maine, Co. D until his discharge Nov. 4, 1865 at Fortress Monroe, Virginia.

Like his fellow islanders, Joseph took part in the final pursuit of Lee's army. He remained with the regiment when it occupied Richmond after the surrender.

However, two months after the surrender, he was hospitalized with jaundice, liver ailments and other problems caused apparently by the climate, exposure and fatigue. One doctor later added malaria to the list.

He was treated in a camp hospital for several days, but when problems worsened, went to Lee Hospital in Richmond, Virginia, and later to a hospital near Fortress Monroe where he remained until his discharge.

In 1883, Joseph, with help from Tremont lawyer, E. Webster French,[1] filed for pension benefits citing partial disability at the age of 55. It took two years.

Joseph's problems were debilitating. During the early 1880s, he suffered from sharp pains that started in his abdomen and shot through his spine and into his head causing "sick headaches" that sometimes lasted three to four days.

Despite all this, an examining surgeon for the U.S. government initially said he could not specifically tie Joseph's ailments to the war. It was a battle, and a government defense, that disabled and ailing soldiers would wage against the government in other wars to follow.

In contrast to the government's doctor, Dr. Spear, the Tremont physician, said:

> "I know he was at the time of his enlistment an able bodied and
> robust man and free from all disease and that after his discharge and
> return home I was called to prescribe for him and I readily detected
> his case to be malaria causing congestion of the liver and kidneys,
> that the relief afforded by treatment was only temporary and that I

---

[1]French was the first lawyer on the backside of Mount Desert Island and the same man for whom the Long Island post office and village of Frenchboro were eventually named.

have frequently prescribed since, certainly as often as every two months. … I further believe him to be incurable and liable to acute disease of the kidney, that may prove fatal (Civil War Pension Records, J.W. Lunt)."

William J. Teel of Long Island signed an affidavit attesting to Joseph's condition. Teel was asked for more proof of his claims in a letter from John C. Black, a commissioner with the Department of Interior's Pension Office. In March 1885, Teel replied that Joseph Warren Lunt was often confined to bed. Teel said, "He is surely a sick man and not able to work more than one-fourth of the time and then only light work. I hope he may get his pension he needs it very much (Civil War Pension Records, J. W. Lunt)."

In 1885, Joseph received a monthly pension of $4 for disease of the liver, retroactive to his first application in 1883.

In March 1889 some of Dr. Spear's fears came true. Joseph was stricken by a shock and left nearly paralyzed, needing assistance for almost every daily activity. Dr. Spear, appearing before trial justice Bartholomew R. Lunt, again asserted that Joseph's condition was caused by "the sequence of the disease contracted while in the service of the United States."

Joseph obtained a pension increase to $8 per month in October 1889. In the last years of Joseph's life he still had three children younger than 16 living with him, John R., Nelson P. and Cora A.

If the years following his time in the service were tough, the final three years of his life were hellish.

Alice (Civil War Pension Records, J.W. Lunt) said, "He kept going down, but kept about until about three years before he died when he broke down entirely and didn't do a thing after that. The older boys helped in the heavier work in fishing and his garden work or he could not have made a living. … He was not a man to complain and here everybody works while they can."

Later, his son, Hiram, said:

"He failed up for about a year and there he took spells or shocks. I always saw them when he was sitting in his chair. His whole body would tremble and shake and he would roll his eyes and twist his face and would be unconscious and would draw his breath with a noise like a person choking to death (Civil War Pension Records, J.W. Lunt)."

*Alice (Twist) Lunt (1841 - 1907).*

The family occasionally sent for the doctor, but, as one doctor testified, "they only came when they felt it was a case of life and death."

So for the most part, Joseph dealt with his illness. His family, mainly Alice, tended to him with little professional help or medicine. It simply was common practice on the island that people died at home, no matter how sick or how old. During winter it was frequently impossible to cross the ocean in 19th-century sloops and other sailing boats.

During his final months, Joseph was helpless. He slipped into a coma the week before his death. He died Jan. 18, 1891. He was 62. He is buried in the family cemetery overlooking his former house on the west side.

His lengthy sickness and inability to work undoubtedly took a toll on the family. Alice, a forceful woman of nearly 300 pounds, according to one estimate, said she tore up most of her bedclothes for cloth to tend him. His death left her with nothing but a house, a lot and a cow, collectively worth about $175.

In the years following his death, the federal government continued to investigate whether Joseph's disability and death were "sufficiently" related to the Civil War to continue paying Alice her small widow's pension. It is likely Alice did not receive assistance for some period of time.

According to pension records, Joseph's last check issued in December 1890, was withheld because of his death. Alice immediately applied for its release, but was unsuccessful for two years.

And still the case lingered. Joseph died in 1891, yet five years later a government agent, Samuel Irvine, visited the island to investigate. He interviewed several islanders and deposed doctors who treated Joseph.

Ultimately, Irvine concluded (Civil War Pension Records, J.W. Lunt) thusly, "I believe the claimant is sincere in her claim. There has been no attempt at deceit in the case; but the question of whether these "shocks" were due to disease contracted in army service is too much of a medical one for me to answer."

In the end, Alice received her pension. She died June 18, 1907.

In retrospect, it seems the government put its veterans and their widows through unnecessary suffering and anxiety. All were surely disabled in part by the war. And it is hard to believe any doubt existed whether Joseph, and later Alice, were entitled to the relatively small pension.

Alice certainly faced unnecessary anxiety so soon after losing her husband. On 19th century Long Island there was virtually no way for a single woman to earn money. And in the grand scheme, all these men did help end slavery and preserve a nation.

After the war, Hezekiah W. Lunt said this (Lunt, V., *History of Long Island Plantation*, 270) about his fellow veteran Joseph: "Never in my life have I seen a man as brave as Joseph Warren Lunt. He was in the thick of every fight and was not scared of the devil. He would run into the thickest of the battle. He got a bullit in his leg and kept on fighting. A daredevil – never saw a man like him in my life."

# World War I: 1917-1918

World War I began July 28, 1914 when Austria declared war against Serbia. Soon, nearly all the nations of Europe were involved in a war that raised 65 million men for various armies and navies. Ultimately, eight million men died and another 21 million were wounded before fighting ceased.

The United States remained neutral for nearly three years. Then in 1917, Germany launched an unrestricted submarine campaign. Germany said it would sink any vessel — even those belonging to neutral parties — without warning when found near the coast of Allied countries.

U.S. President Woodrow Wilson declared war April 6, 1917.

Before the war ended on Nov. 11, 1918, 126,000 American soldiers were either killed in action or died from disease. More than 204,000 were wounded.

One Long Island soldier, Frank S. Rich, died during this era, but his death occurred before the war started.

Rich, the son of Martin Hall Rich and Charlotte "Lizzie" Davis, was serving aboard the U.S.S. Nebraska when an overhead spar broke loose and killed him on July 12, 1912.

A memorial stone in the Israel B. Lunt cemetery marks his grave. The stone reads: "Gone but not forgotten. Killed in the performance of his duty July 17, 1912. Age 20 years and 1 month. Erected by his shipmates U.S.S. Nebraska."

Three others served during wartime. They were:

### Hollis P. Dalzell

Hollis, born on Long Island Jan. 30, 1898, was the fourth child of Everett Edward and Linnie D. (Rice) Dalzell.

Hollis, 19, enlisted in the army at Portland on Oct. 18, 1917. He served with Co. A 56 Regiment Pion Infantry until his honorable discharge on July 2, 1919. He was overseas in Germany or France from Sept. 4, 1918 until June 25, 1919. In France, he took part in the Meuse-Argonne offensive. It is believed he was exposed to mustard gas during the war, which forever affected him.

He left the island in the 1920s or 1930s.

*Courtesy of Frenchboro Historical Society*

*Hollis P. Dalzell (b. 1898).*

### Clinton B. Teel

Clinton, born on Long Island, May 11, 1888, was the oldest child of William M. and Maria L. (Lunt) Teel. His mother died in 1904 from burns suffered during a house fire.

Clinton, 29, enlisted from Vinalhaven and was inducted in Rockland on Oct. 2, 1917. He served in Battery D of the 303 Field Artillery until his

*Clinton B. Teel (1888 - 1963).*

honorable discharge on May 1, 1919. He was promoted to private first class on March 15, 1918. He served overseas from July 16, 1918 to April 26, 1919. In France, he also was involved in the Meuse-Argonne offensive.

Clinton married Elva V. Dalzell of Lubec on Aug. 10, 1907. He died Dec. 7, 1963 at 75. Though he lived in Vinalhaven, he is buried in the Joseph Warren Lunt cemetery on Long Island.

Both Clinton Teel and Hollis Dalzell took part in the Meuse-Argonne offensive. The Meuse-Argonne is a region of France between Verdun and Vouziers that extends 25 miles west from the Meuse River to the Aisne River. The Battle of Meuse-Argonne lasted 47 days from Sept. 26 to Nov. 11. The offensive included 29 American combat divisions and 1.2 million American men. It was part of a general engagement that pressed against the entire German line from Verdun to the English Channel. When the offensive was over, Germany surrendered.

## Joseph W. "Innie" Lunt III

Joseph, born Jan. 15, 1893, was the third son of Atwood L. and Angeline Lunt. Joseph was the grandson of Civil War veteran Joseph Warren Lunt and is buried in the family cemetery.

"Innie" enrolled in the U.S. Navy April 26, 1917. He served on several ships, including: *USS Wissahickon* from April 27 to May 10, 1917; *USS Admiral* from May 10, 1917 to Sept. 30, 1917; and *USS Halcyon* from Dec. 8, 1917 to May 1, 1918. He also spent time on land including a stint at the Naval Hospital in Chelsea, Massachusetts from May 1, 1918 to Nov. 11, 1918.

Following the war, he remained in the service, regularly sending home service checks to support his parents and siblings who lived beyond the head of the cove.

Innie is considered the island's early 20th century island poet. His commanding officer submitted several of his poems to magazines, and they were published anonymously. Innie remained a lifelong bachelor and lived in a small camp on the path to Gooseberry Point.

On Aug. 17, 1954 he felt a pain while walking home from Leonard "Nardy" Lunt's store. He sat down on the church steps and died. He was 61.

*Courtesy of Frenchboro Historical Society*
*Joseph W. "Innie" Lunt (1893 - 1954).*

# World War II: 1941-1945

The United States entered World War II on December 7, 1941 after Japan launched a surprise attack on Pearl Harbor, killing more than 2,300 people and destroying a large portion of this nation's fleet. The war ended nearly four years later in two stages. In May of 1945, Germany officially surrendered, ending the conflict in Europe. In August of 1945, Japan surrendered.

In all, more than 362,500 American soldiers died during those four years. World War II became a galvanizing event for the nation and a generation. The United States emerged from the war a world power, and a generation emerged to guide the country for the next five decades.

In all, 16 men with ties to Long Island — 15 percent of the island population at that time— served in World War II. At least five men saw combat in the South Pacific and Europe. Amazingly, all survived.

## The Soldiers

***Elmer C. Davis*** — Elmer, born Feb. 4, 1917, was the third child of Alexander P. and Valeria M. (Lunt) Davis. He was one of three Davis

*Courtesy of Frenchboro Historical Society*
*Elmer C. Davis (1917 - 1969).*

brothers who served in the war. He worked as a cook in Bar Harbor during high school and later as a chef at a Boston hotel. He served with the 302nd Engineers Combat Batallion and left the service as a Technician Fourth Grade. He saw action in the South Pacific, including many of the same campaigns as Clarence Lunt. His medals included: Good conduct medal; Asiatic-Pacific Campaign Ribbon; Philippine Liberation Ribbon and one service star; Service Star for Mandated Islands Campaign; Service Star for participation in Southern Philippines Campaign; Service Star for participation in Ryukyu Campaign. He married Vera Linscott. He died Oct. 24, 1969 at 52. He is buried at Frenchboro.

***Clarence Lunt*** — Clarence, born July 29, 1922, was the 11th child of John R. and Flora Eveline Lunt. He married Elsie V. Reed on Oct. 21, 1946. In addition to the severe action he saw on the islands of the South Pacific (see prologue), Clarence also landed in Japan as part of an occupational force following VJ Day. On at least one occasion, he transported Gen. Douglas MacArthur and his wife off the Philippines. He left the service as a Technician Fifth Grade. He died July 13, 1989. He is buried at Frenchboro.

***Ronald E. Mitchell*** — Ronald, born Aug. 1, 1921, was the son of Charles and Jennie (Rice) Mitchell. He joined the service Feb. 22, 1943 and served with the 483rd Anti-Aircraft division. He participated in the invasions of Anguar and Iwo Jima. He was present on Iwo Jima when Marines raised the American flag, an act that became a famous symbol of World War II. His name is etched on the Iwo Jima memorial in Cape

Coral, Florida. He remained on Iwo Jima until November 1945. He was discharged as a corporal on Jan. 1, 1946. He married Marion Coolidge in 1947. He now lives in Florida.

***Kenneth Gardiner Lunt*** — Gardiner, born Aug. 13, 1911, was the 13th child of William Sanford and Edna F. (Rich) Lunt. He was a member of the Military Police, 51st M.P. Co., and was stationed in Italy. He never married and lived most of his life on the island. Gardiner came in from hauling lobster traps on June 8, 1961, lay down to rest while his brother Guy cooked lunch. He never got up. He suffered a heart attack and died. He was 49. He is buried in the Clifton Lunt cemetery.

***Lawrence H. Davis*** — Lawrence, born Sept. 21, 1919, was the fourth child of Alexander P. and Valeria M. (Lunt) Davis. He enlisted in the U.S. Army in February 1941 and was discharged in October 1945. He spent most of his time as a cook in the South Pacific and left as a Tec 5. He once told his sister Vivian that the trouble with standing watch in New Guinea was that "you never knew when you would get a bullet in the back." According to an often-told war story, Lawrence, a rugged man with a quick temper, was leading a donkey at an army camp one day. When they came to a tree, the stubborn donkey wanted to go on one side and Lawrence on the other. Lawrence punched the donkey in the head. Lawrence broke his hand, but knocked the donkey cold. He married Pauline M. (Lunt) Bergeron and later Rosemund Berry. He lived in Southwest Harbor and died in 1987. He has a memorial stone at Frenchboro.

***Ralph Stanley*** — Ralph, born Feb. 4, 1917, was the son of Lester and Helen E. (Borland) Stanley of Swans Island. He married Lilla F. Lunt on July 1, 1941 and moved to Frenchboro. He served in the U.S. Navy from March 16, 1945 until his honorable discharge in April 1946 as a Seaman Second Class. He served on the *USS Rixey* and

*Courtesy of Frenchboro Historical Society*
*Hugh Stanley*

209

received the World War II Victory Medal, the American Theatre Medal and the Asiatic-Pacific Medal. While on a South Pacific island he stepped in a Japanese booby trap and broke his leg. He died of leukemia on Oct. 4, 1956 while living on Bartlett Island as a caretaker. He was 39. He is buried at Frenchboro.

***Hugh Stanley*** — Hugh, Ralph Stanley's brother, was also born on Swans Island. He married Marguerite H. Lunt on Aug. 28, 1943. He died in the 1980s. He is buried in Southwest Harbor.

***Lewis Nickerson*** — Lewis, born Nov. 27, 1912, was the eldest child of Jephtha Nickerson and Ellen F. Lunt. He served on destroyers in the U.S. Navy from 1941 to 1944. He was based in Norfolk, VA and left the service a First Class Petty Officer. He married Mary Simmons. He lived in Rockland after the war. He died Feb. 16, 1994.

***Ernest B. Nickerson*** — Ernest, born Sept. 17, 1915, was the third child of Jephtha and Ellen F. Nickerson. He was the twin brother of Esther Nickerson. He was inducted in the U.S. Navy on Feb. 9, 1942 and served nearly four years. He was discharged Dec. 31, 1945 as a Boatswain's Mate First Class. He was stationed in Boston, Portland and Rhode Island. He received the America area medal, Good Conduct medal and the World War II Victory medal. He married Margaret Lois Gordon. He died April 23, 1984. He is buried in Rockland.

***Frank W. Dalzell*** — Frank, born March 20, 1922, was the third child of Milton S. "Robbins" Dalzell and Vera M. Ross. He entered the service as a Seabee (a U.S. Navy construction battalion) in 1941. He later transferred and spent three years in charge of a floating dry dock in the South Pacific. The floating drydock was used to repair damaged war ships. His last stop was New Guinea before returning to the United States. He left the service as a Boatswain Mate, 1st Class. He was released Jan. 30, 1946. He died April 27, 1966. He is buried in Golden Gate National Cemetery in California.

***Vernon E. Dalzell*** — Vernon, born April 18, 1920, was the eldest child of Everett E. "Ebbit" and Lula B. (Lunt) Dalzell. Vernon was with the 322nd Engineer Battalion of the 3rd Army in Germany under General George Patton. He also served in Japan with the 8th Army under General Douglas MacArthur. He married Lernice J. (Martis) Murphy of Tremont on Jan. 4, 1954. Vernon died Feb. 22, 1991. He was 70. He is buried at the Veterans Cemetery in Augusta.

***Erland "Manny" Dalzell*** — "Manny," born June 16, 1925, was Vernon's brother, served with the U.S. Army and spent the war on U.S. soil. He married Betty Cary in 1974. He died May 3, 1985. He was 59. He is buried at Frenchboro.

***Malcolm W. Lunt*** — Malcolm, born Aug. 26, 1924, was the oldest child of Clifton M. and Ella V. Lunt. He joined the U.S. Navy and served most of his time in Massachusetts. He married Shirley B. Maddocks on March 27, 1946. He died June 27, 1991. He was 66.

***Thomas B. Lunt Jr.*** — Tommy, born Nov. 17, 1920, was the oldest child of Thomas B. Sr. and Helen (Dalzell) Lunt. He enlisted in the U.S. Navy in July of 1942 and was honorably discharged in January 1946. He served on a tugboat and spent time in both Guam and Alaska. He received the World War II Victory Medal, the American Theater Medal, the Asiatic Pacific Theater Medal and the Good Conduct Medal. He married Priscilla Howard. He died July 3, 1996. He was 75.

***John K. Mitchell*** — John, born Feb. 22, 1924, was the son of Charles and Jennie M. (Rice) Mitchell. He trained at Fort Bragg and was stationed as a member of the Military Police in Colorado. After the war he helped return prisoners of war to Italy. He married Madeliene M. Dee of Fort Kent on Sept. 28, 1949. He died June 4, 1993. He is buried in Southwest Harbor.

***Vincent A. Davis*** — Vincent, born Nov. 2, 1913, was the oldest child of Alexander P. Davis and Valeria M. Lunt. Vince, the third Davis brother in the war, served during the entire war, entering the service Jan. 18, 1941 and being discharged Dec. 16, 1945. By the time he left he had attained the rank of staff sergeant. He was a quartermaster on the *USCS Joseph Henry*, a cable ship that laid submarine communications cable along the Atlantic Coast. He died Feb. 20, 1996. He is buried in the Joseph W. Lunt cemetery.

# Vietnam War

The United States became involved in the conflict between North Vietnam and South Vietnam in the mid-1950s when the U.S. sent military advisors to help train South Vietnamese troops. Involvement was escalated in the 1960s by Presidents Kennedy, Johnson and Nixon. The U.S. pulled its last ground troops out of Vietnam in March of 1973. South Vietnam fell two years later.

***Randall Sawyer*** — Randy, born Sept. 17, 1944, is the son of Harvey and Charlotte (Turner) Sawyer. He served in the U.S. Army with the 103rd Engineer Co. from September 1963 to Sept. 1966. That included 13 months in Korea and nine months in combat in Vietnam. His tour in Vietnam included stops near Ben-Cat, Vung-Tou (Cape-St. Jacques), Long Bien and Bien Hoa. He married Barbara Ann Lunt on Jan. 27, 1969. They have two children, Corey and Christopher. He lives on Long Island.

***Ralph D. Reynolds*** — Ralph, born Jan. 30, 1948, was the son of Rosco Reynolds and Rebecca Reed. Ralph joined the U.S. Navy in 1966 and was discharged at Marietta, Washington in May 1970. He was stationed in Puerto Rico for part of his tour, but also spent time aboard the *U.S.S. Jamestown* off the coast of Vietnam. He married Carmen Vizecorrando. They have two children, John and Mark, and live in Puerto Rico.

## Other Long Island Servicemen

Other island men who have served in the U.S. Armed Forces include:
- Paul L. "Rusty" Crossman, son of Lillian J. Davis and Raymond D. Crossman.
- Kenneth A. Davis, son of Harold and Dorothy Davis.
- Richard E. "Sam" Davis, son of Alexander P. Davis and Valeria M. Lunt.
- Basil Dempsey Lunt, son of Thomas B. Lunt and Helen E. Dalzell.
- Carroll W. Lunt, son of Wallace L. Lunt and Lenora L. Higgins.
- Clifton M. Lunt, son of Nelson P. Lunt and Alvina E. Lunt.
- Robert A. Lunt, son of Wallace L. Lunt and Lenora L. Higgins.
- Donald K. Osier, son of Willard K. Osier and Genevieve McKown

*Chapter Twelve*
# 20th Century Church & School

## One-Room School

Not until junior high school did I realize that attending a tiny one-room school was THAT different. I certainly didn't know that the number of one-room schools in Maine had dropped from more than 600 at mid-century to less than 50 by 1972 to maybe a dozen today.

Comfortably buffered from the mainland by eight miles of Atlantic Ocean, I couldn't imagine such things as eating lunch in a cafeteria instead of dashing home, riding a bus instead of walking, using lockers or waiting for a bell to change class. I clearly remember thinking that having your daily life controlled by a bell was an absurd way to live. I guess being unique made us cocky.

Our small white schoolhouse, built in 1907, sat just above the Congregational Church and just below the parsonage. The oiled wooden floors emitted an unmistakable odor that rolled across the room like a gentle wave. The ever-present chalk dust left you perpetually on the edge of a sneeze. The windows rattled during winter storms and spring winds. I don't believe the building was insulated until the mid-1970s. The discolored water was undrinkable. The on-again, off-again inside bathroom meant that we sometimes trudged to the outhouse.

Still, school life was relatively structured, in an unstructured sort of way. We started class at 8:30 a.m. (I was often dashing across the flats at

8:29) and walked home for lunch at 11:30. I usually left my house again around noon to deliver outgoing mail before the afternoon session began at 12:30. Carrying mail to Norma Teel's post office was a regular chore for island children. I carried mail for my parents and my grandmother, who usually put hers in a yellow Country Kitchen bread bag, knotted at the top for extra protection. School ended at 3 p.m.

We took a 15-minute to 30-minute recess each morning and after-

Photo by Pamela Pierce

*Amy A. Bergeron, Dean L. Lunt, and Tim W. Bergeron, early 1970s.*

noon. We played kickball, tag, hide and seek and so forth — when there were enough kids. During winter we slid down the "school hill" on Flexible Flyer runner sleds, sometimes making it around the cove to Herman Lunt's house. Or we sped down the hill between the Clifton Lunt cemetery and the church on either plastic sleds or flattened cardboard boxes that we waxed with candles or crayons for extra speed. My teacher from kindergarten through second grade was Mildred Onyett.

I left the Frenchboro Elementary School in the spring of my seventh grade year, at the age of 12, for one simple reason: I was the Frenchboro Elementary School. It was just me. It was time to move on.

The island had already closed the actual schoolhouse during that winter of 1979, believing it wasteful to heat the old building for just me and my teacher, Arin Teel.

Three other pupils started that school year with me, but two brothers, John and Mark Reynolds, moved to Puerto Rico. The fourth, five-year-old Corey Sawyer, spent much of the year in the hospital. He returned to the island later that spring.

So there in the dead of an island winter, Arin and I sat at her dining room table each day conducting school from about 8 a.m. to maybe 1 p.m. We listened to Peter, Paul and Mary, cooked pizza, studied tools, analyzed weather patterns and even published a magazine. But by the first blush of spring, I was simply marking time.

So, I left for Mount Desert Island where during the school year we lived in the village of Bernard, near where my mother was raised.

My eighth-grade class at Tremont Elementary School was still barely more than 20. Although island kids always fight some stereotypes when they first come ashore to school, I do not remember struggling to make any major adjustments. I don't think I was initially as aggressive or forward as I might have been — and I remain far more comfortable in small groups. But I already knew a few kids from my Little League team, was among the top students academically, and was a good athlete. One dilemma was trying to figure out junior high school girls. I failed.

Looking back on my island school, I was relatively lucky. On an island, your entire academic foundation is built by a single person: the teacher. Perhaps in no other setting do the educational careers of students hinge so intimately on the enthusiasm, competence and dedication of one person, who is often young and also facing a whole new experience.

With that said, my teachers during the four-year stretch from third to sixth grade — Marcia and Mike Giberson — rank among my better teachers.

I can't say, specifically, why.

Perhaps it was just a strange intersection of time and personalities. They certainly helped instill or at least nurture an appreciation for learning, most notably reading. Yet Frenchboro was not some educational backwater. Generally, the students in school during those years were well behaved, somewhat academically inclined, and had parents who supported education.

Had we been a larger, more rambunctious group, would they have been so successful? I don't know. Would they have failed? No. They had energy and ideas and that took them a long way.

Fundamentally, the Gibersons represented an era of change.

In one dramatic shift, the school went from decades of Mr. and Mrs. to Marcia and Mike, from the Mission-influenced teacher-preacher to the 1970s liberal. We moved from Dick and Jane to *The Hobbit*, from Sing Along with Mitch to Jackson Browne, from iambic pentameter to haiku and from rows to groups.

Photo courtesy of Vivian D. Lunt

*Marcia, Aaron, Mike and Izaak Giberson, 1979.*

Where Gladys Muir represented much-needed structure and stability in the 1930s, Marcia and Mike represented a sort of deconstruction in the 1970s. We watched films on reproduction and were fascinated with what could be seen and found in *The Whole Earth Catalog*. We learned about pregnancy while Marcia was pregnant with her first child, Isaak.

Marcia was the actual "teacher." She taught the younger students, who in 1974 included myself and fellow third grader Tim Bergeron, who later attended Tremont as well. Mike, the teacher's aide, initially taught eighth graders Michael Holland and Anthony Brown. After Tony and Mike graduated, Mike Giberson taught Tim and me, essentially becoming our personal instructor for three years. The three of us often sat clustered on one side of the room while the remaining pupils, including Amy and Dale Bergeron and

Mark and John Reynolds, sat on the other side. During the 1977-1978 school year there were six of us.

Something worked.

From my original island class of two, Tim graduated as salutatorian of Mount Desert Island High School in 1984 and earned his degree from Washington University in St. Louis. I performed well academically, lettered in three sports, and earned a dual degree in business and journalism from Syracuse University.

My first memory of Marcia and Mike as an eight-year-old was not encouraging. In the summer of 1974, I was coming into Bass Harbor aboard one lobster boat, and they were sitting on the stern of another lobster boat pulling away from the town float.

Mike had a beard and ponytail — not your standard male fashion accessory on Long Island. To me, the couple, only in their early 20s, looked like hippies. And I guess, in a land of Johnny Cash, church suppers and bobbing for apples, they were hippies, as cliched as that sounds. They certainly were more liberal than any of us were or ever will be.

My first sighting of a Grateful Dead album was in their living room (although, I still hate Garcia and company). We tie-dyed shirts and dried apples on cheesecloth and string. Marcia and Mike were our first honest-to-gosh vegetarians and they yammered on about recycling and other causes. Marcia was the first woman I remember who breastfed her baby. We weren't quite sure what to make of that, either.

They drove an old green Saab in a world of pick-up trucks and wagons. We called it a "slob" or some such derogatory name that seemed really funny to us.

Outside the classroom, we traveled as a school. We loaded into a Maine Sea Coast Missionary Society van and visited Boston, journeyed to the Olympic village in Montreal and camped in the mountains of western Maine.

On one trip they got mad at us after they picked up a hitchhiker and we moved to the back of the van not speaking to him. They chided us for being rude, but they could only push us so far. We just stared at each other while staying at what we felt was a run-down house in Dresden, which I recall as being overrun with cats. And we despised our week at the Bryant Pond Conservation Camp. Tim and I, as eight-year-olds, preferred to call it a concentration camp.

Certainly, town politics and arguments came and went as school progressed. They always do. And not everything changed, nor should it

*School Christmas show, 1973. Steve Day (left), Kevin Holland, Dean Lunt, Michael Holland, Daniel Lunt, Anthony Brown, Tim Bergeron, David W. Lunt and Charlie Day.*

have. I was too young to remember the debates, but ultimately, although certainly frustrating for those involved, the town and the teachers struck some balance. Mike cut his ponytail.

One important tradition was Christmas. While the era of the teacher-preacher vanished, the school Christmas tree — with our arts and crafts decorations — and annual play at the church remained a community staple. There is no better way for new teachers to enter a small community's good graces than by staging a Christmas show.

As I said, building a solid reading foundation proved a critical step. It struck me while researching this book that few people remembered many details of their school life except for one thing: many recalled a teacher or an adult reading to them.

We certainly read. Afternoons we sat clustered in a little corner set aside for a small library and read or listened.

I don't remember all the books, but they included *The Hobbit, Lord of the Rings, The Martian Chronicles, Catcher in the Rye,* and *Lord of the Flies.* Although I am not really a science fiction fan, the impact of J.R.R. Tolkien's books was immeasurable. I was fascinated. For years after reading about Frodo, Mordor, Khazad-Dum and the One Ring, I spent Halloween nights as a "Black Rider" roaming the island roads.

Thinking back, it stuns me to think that Marcia, 24, and Mike, 23, were essentially kids themselves, fresh from school and just winging it. I have never really talked to them about the whole experience. Mike did tell me once he was basically a chapter ahead of us when teaching math. He wasn't surprised my verbal SAT scores were higher than my math scores.

And then, life changes.

Marcia and Mike left in the spring of 1978 after my sixth-grade year. They returned briefly after a one-year hiatus.

They divorced soon after leaving the island again. Mike never taught again and Marcia never returned to a public schoolroom. He co-owns and runs a diner in Gardiner. Marcia, now a social worker, has remarried, lives in Northeast Harbor. She still owns a house in Frenchboro.

I have not seen either of them more than a half dozen times combined in the past two decades. In fact, I don't think I saw Mike for 17 years after the end of my sixth-grade year.

The other principals also changed. Pam and Wayne Bergeron moved off the island in 1978, soon divorced and have remarried. Tim lives in Missouri, Amy lives in Bass Harbor, and Dale lives in Bangor. The Reynolds family still lives in Puerto Rico.

Meanwhile, school enrollment has risen and fallen, and teachers, both good and bad, have come and gone for the past two decades.

But the school soldiers on. The one-room heart of a community.

———◆◆◆———

# Religion, School and a New Century

The Congregational Church of Long Island continued along steadily after it was founded by Alexander P. MacDonald in the summer of 1889. Regular attendance at worship numbered in the 40s, and the Maine Missionary Society continued to support the church and wage its unflagging war against alcohol.

In 1904, islanders built a church parsonage for $1,100, finally eliminating the need for islanders to board each minister and schoolteacher.

James T. Davis transferred the parsonage lot to the Congregational Church from his deathbed in 1891. At the time, James was the last living trustee of the old Baptist Church. Ministers and schoolteachers used the parsonage, located above the church, as their primary island residence into the 1980s.

While the island's 1890s Congregational Church was somewhat more liberal than the old 1840s Baptist Church, it could still be harsh on members who had drifted away. In the era's church notes on baptisms, the clerk noted members who, it felt, were seeking acceptance after they had admitted such problems as "backsliding" or having been "convicted of sin."

During this era, a committee of three interviewed each candidate for membership to discuss their faith. The committee reported back to the membership, which then voted to accept or reject the applicant. It appears everyone was accepted. However, acceptance did not bring a lifelong entitlement. Some islanders were actually expelled from church fellowship by vote, while others asked to be removed, at least temporarily.

*Courtesy of Frenchboro Historical Society*

*Islanders and visitors outside the Long Island Congregational Church, early 1890s.*

In once instance, Henry Whitfield "Whit" Lunt asked the church to remove his name from fellowship and said that when "he could live a Godly life he would come back again." Despite that request, he remained a church member.

In 1891, the church sought to mediate a dispute between two feuding members. After a full discussion by the membership, "The trouble was then settled between Sister Alice Lunt and Sister Agnes Davis."

At another meeting, the membership discussed the "matter of" one wayward member and "decided that it was the duty of the church to investigate the questionable proceedings." The church appointed a committee of three women, Katie (Dawes) Lunt, Agnes (Joyce) Davis and Hortense (Lunt) Van Norden "to call on" the woman and "bring her back to the church by words of encouragement and Christian fellowship."

That didn't happen. Committee Chairwoman Hortense Van Norden reported a week later that the woman rebuffed the committee. As a result, the membership decided that because she did not come to church, had abandoned her family and husband for another man, had "turned a cold shoulder to all, and ridiculed the church and all of the members" that it could not "fellowship such works by a member." She was unanimously voted out of the church.

During that early church era, a handful of other members withdrew their fellowship "for the lives they were leading," but later sought and were restored to "proper fellowship."

## Long Island Elementary School

Meanwhile, the school struggled. Despite longer school years and more regular classes, it still suffered for lack of money and teachers. And by the late 1800s, it operated in an inadequate schoolhouse.

As envisioned by Rev. Jonathan Edwards Adams of the Maine Missionary Society in 1888, school and church life remained entwined, with one person often serving as both pastor and teacher. The Maine Missionary Society reemphasized its desire to nurture the connection in 1909:

> "Another plan carried out during the winter, which is not new but
> has not been much employed of late, was the arrangement made
> with the School Committee on Frenchboro, Outer Long Island,

*Frenchboro Elementary School, about 1913. Back row: Winnie Lunt (left), Helen Dalzell, Flora Davis, Elva Lunt, Edith Thurlow, Granville Dalzell, Mrs. Eaton.*
*Second row: Marie Lunt, Mildred Dalzell, Ethel Lunt, Evelyn Osier, Gladys Lunt, H. Lunt, Willard Osier, Orrin Lunt, Otis Lunt, Earl Thurlow, Clinton Dalzell.*
*Front row: Alma Lunt, Lilla Lunt, Ben Davis, Kathleen Lunt, Virginia Lunt, Ella Lunt. Note that the boys are all barefooted.*

whereby the selection of teachers for the winter term was made with special reference to his conducting a religious service on Sunday and helping in other ways the work of the church. The plan worked smoothly and well, the town and churches each paying a sum agreed upon for the work done." (Maine Missionary Society, *Annual Report 1909*, 690)

However, by the turn of the century, the Missionary Society itself struggled to support its rural churches. Into this breach stepped an old island friend: Alexander MacDonald.

The 39-year-old MacDonald, the same dynamic minister who oversaw the birth of the island's Congregational Church (see Chapter Six) and helped erect the "fisherman's chapel," created the Maine Sea Coast Missionary Society in 1905. During the ensuing 17 years until his death in 1922, he emerged as a powerful presence and guiding influence on Long

Island, other islands and small coastal villages. His far-flung parish included Crowley Island, Head Harbor Island, Muscongus Isle and Criehaven. Even after his death — he died of a heart attack aboard the first *Sunbeam* — the Mission remained an important presence. It sponsored dental clinics, brought Christmas gifts and clothing, transported and tended to the sick, supplied teachers and nurses and provided a market for island-made goods such as quilts. In the 1920s, the Mission regularly brought boxes of used clothing that it sold for pennies after realizing islanders were reluctant to accept outright charity.

Its educational influence extended beyond the island's small elementary school as well. Many island students who were able to attend high school in the 1920s and 1930s did so in part because of scholarship money provided by the Mission. Roughly half of the $600 that Vivian (Davis) Lunt paid to attend Kents Hill High School in the 1930s came from the Mission.

The mission's influence in the overall community began to diminish in the 1950s and 1960s as the island became less and less isolated and the economy improved after World War II. However, the Mission still provides full-time ministers in July and August and holds monthly church services during other months.

## Alexander P. MacDonald and the Maine Sea Coast Mission

In the beginning there was simply MacDonald and an idea.

MacDonald, a man of Scottish ancestry, was born on Prince Edward Island and grew up in the seaside community of Bath. He started the Long Island church in 1889, helped build the chapel in 1890, graduated from Bowdoin College in 1891 and received a degree from Andover Theological Seminary in 1894. He was ordained Oct. 24, 1894.

After graduation he spent time at churches in North Dakota and Washington state, but returned to the Maine coast in 1899 to supply a church in Wiscasset. He moved to Mount Desert Island in 1901 to tend churches at Seal Harbor and Otter Creek.

Throughout his travels, he apparently never forgot the ministerial roots set during his early days on Long Island.

According to one story (Mitchell, 11), the idea for starting the Sea Coast Mission came to Alexander while he and his brother stood atop Green Mountain, later renamed Cadillac. The pair, both ministers, gazed out over the glorious expanse of sea and islands that spread out across the

Courtesy of Frenchboro Historical Society

*Sunbeam III entering Lunt Harbor, 1940s.*

bays as far as the eye could see. Alexander slapped his brother on the back and cried, "Angus, what a parish!"

The Maine Sea Coast Missionary Society was born.

The Mission operated from Bar Harbor, the summer playground of business tycoons and wealthy denizens of the industrialized Northeast who vacationed there in elegant "cottages" and massive summer hotels. From the beginning, the Mission sought financial support from Mount Desert Island's well-heeled and philanthropic-minded visitors.

At the time, Angus supplied a wealthy seaside congregation. According to another story, Angus asked Alexander to take the pulpit one Sunday morning shortly after Alexander started the Mission. Alexander delivered an impassioned sermon and heartfelt plea for the islands and coastal towns. So inspired, Alexander Mackay-Smith, an Episcopal minister from Philadelphia and summer resident of Seal Harbor, donated his private yacht to the cause. The renamed *Morning Star* replaced the original small sloop *Hope*. The *Morning Star* was replaced in 1912 by the first of five vessels to be called *Sunbeam*.

MacDonald, a large fiery man, usually settled disputes with diplomacy but did not oppose force when necessary.

According to another tale, he stopped in the middle of a sermon being delivered at a quarryman's boarding house on Head Harbor Island to confront an agitator. He told the man, "Brother, I think the Lord would like it better if you did your praying outside." He proceeded to throw the man through the window (Mitchell, 12).

Mitchell, in *Anchor to Windward*, described MacDonald:

"He was a man who, once he had an idea, pursued it as relentlessly as the Hound of Heaven pursued Francis Thompson. He was a pioneer type, a huge-fisted man of enormous energy and driving power, who, when he saw anything needed to be done, set to work doing it. If an island needed a road, a school, or a church, Alexander MacDonald started to build it with his own hands. He dressed in rough clothes and beat the bounds of his far-flung parish in the small Mission launch."

From the beginning, the Maine Sea Coast Mission was based on a broad interpretation of spirituality and not confined by individual denominations.

Indeed, the Mission was founded by an ordained Congregationalist minister but employed other Protestant denominations including Baptist, Methodist and Universalist ministers. Mission preachers, officially authorized by the Interdenominational Commission of Maine, had full church authority in any church represented by the commission.

The Mission's official creed, *"The Christian Brotherhood of the Sea-coast of Maine,"* started:

"Whereas, the scattered communities of the Sea-coast are too small in numbers to permit the organization of separate churches, and Whereas, fellowship in Christian life is a source of strength and comfort: Therefore, We, the undersigned, agree to unite in a Christian Brotherhood, with the name above given."

Technically, for more than a decade after the Sea Coast Mission started, the Long Island church officially remained under the auspices of the old Maine Missionary Society (MMS). However, the Sea Coast Mission was emerging as the more vibrant force, frequently visiting Long Island.

This encroachment did not go unnoticed by the MMS, which immediately felt the financial pinch.

In 1905, the Sea Coast Mission's first year, six coastal churches —

which had collectively donated $183.84 to the MMS in 1904 — gave nothing. Three other churches that had previously donated $60.13 gave only $10.20. All nine churches were suddenly under MacDonald's influence. In 1905, the MMS reminded its churches to whom they owed both allegiance and money.

> "It is possible that the advent of the Sea Coast Missionary Society is not responsible for this in some cases but in others it is, and while cordially wishing God speed to this and to all good work the Secretary cannot refrain from expressing the conviction that the first and paramount duty of every church which has been fostered and built up by the Maine Missionary Society is to the Society which has helped it in its time of need (Maine Missionary Society, 1905, 114)."

However, the Maine Missionary Society and its descendant organizations could not stem the tide. In 1919, the Congregational Home Missionary Society surrendered care of the Long Island church to MacDonald's organization 30 years after MacDonald helped the old MMS organize the island church.

After assuming control, the Sea Coast Mission decided Long Island had been neglected. MacDonald sent Katherine B. Haskel to address the problems.

The Congregational Church was set to emerge as an island force.

## *The Women of Sigma Kappa*

Soon after MacDonald took control, additional help came from a seemingly unlikely source — the Sigma Kappa sorority. This college sorority, in connection with the Sea Coast Mission, helped bring an important new outlook and culture to the island, especially for the women and children who lived in a unquestionably male-dominated era and region.

In the May 1913 edition of *The Triangle,* the monthly publication of Sigma Kappa, Rev. Hannah Jewett Powell, assistant missionary for the Sea Coast Mission and a 1893 graduate of Colby College, detailed the Mission's island goals. Powell, a former teacher and the first woman to serve on the Mission staff, called out to her sister sorority members (*The Triangle,* 1913, 197):

> "Would the Sigma sisters minister with their presence? Would they share gifts of teaching, of music, of housewifery? (Oh, for a permanent coast teacher of domestic science.) Would they spread the

graces of womankind, the beauty and laughter and light for which the young so naturally crave? Would they do it, not for a day but for a whole summer, or - for a life?"

The plan took time to develop. Powell and Myrtice D. Cheney, chairwoman of the national philanthropy work, emerged as the key forces pushing the alliance. At a meeting in 1917, the sorority's Grand Council adopted the Sea Coast Mission as its national philanthropy, in part to honor the five Colby College students who founded Sigma Kappa. The sorority's annual convention endorsed the action in 1918. This decision not only created a $100 annual scholarship for an island girl, but also set the stage for sorority representatives to work on the islands.

The sorority's stated goal was to hire a "Domestic Science Social Worker who will labor for the educational advancement of the women and children of the isolated spots of the Maine Coast." Sigma Kappa members also began knitting and sewing clothes and collecting goods for needy island families.

The first Sigma Kappa-backed worker, Lucy Allen King of Worcester, Massachusetts, arrived on Long Island in the fall of 1920. King had six years experience teaching music and had spent four years as a secretary at Syracuse University. She attended numerous classes and performed community-oriented volunteer work prior to arriving on Long Island. How much this work prepared her for mission work is unknown. After all, she was a young woman nurtured in academia who suddenly found herself alone on a remote Maine island.

Her early letters from Frenchboro reveal her amazement at such things as how well a five-year-old boy could swing an axe and her frustration in trying to get island men to gather wood for the school. She initially seemed overwhelmed.

But by that fall, King started Sunday school and church services, developed community activities and, since the island could not find a teacher, organized the school.

In October of 1920, Allen wrote to Cheney describing her activities (*The Triangle*, March 1921, 208):

*Frenchboro, Me., Oct. 26, 1920*

*My dear Miss Cheney:*
*"Thus far there has been no opportunity for much loneliness. There is such a lot to do, I am just hoping I may do what you wish done.*

*Sewing Circle, between 1910 - 1920. Back row: Annie Teel (left), Alice (Ross) Howard, Lizzie B. (Lunt) Ross, Vera Van Norden, Minnie Lunt, Sophronia "Toni" Teel.*
*Front Row: Elva Teel, Vera (Ross) Dalzell, Mary "Mame" (Bridges) Osier, Lizzie M. (Lunt) Thurlow.*

*Sunday I attended the Sunday school, and taught a class of primary age. Eleven boys and girls, all built on springs. It is entirely a boys' and girls' school, the only adults present being the teachers. The attendance numbered twenty-eight.*

*There were but eleven at the Junior service in the afternoon, and forty at the evening service.*

*Yesterday morning we opened school for some classes until a teacher comes or I am transferred. Before eight the twenty scholars were at the door ready for classes called at nine. The groups are divided as follows: 4 in Grade I; 3 in II; 3 in III; 3 in IV; 2 in VI; 3 in VII; 2 in VIII.*

*After recess we served hot potato soup and crackers both yesterday and today. Following the early dismissal yesterday afternoon grades VII and VIII came to the house for a cooking lesson. They set the table, made cocoa, served and drank it; cleared the table and washed the dishes according to rule. The girls put into practice to-day the serving at school lunch time.*

*Mr. MacDonald said it was unnecessary to start the school as I was not called upon to do it. However, it seemed to me they needed such discipline a lot. If my program is not in accordance with your plans, please let me know.*

*I visited the girls' Lend a Hand Club this afternoon. Last night the parish house was open until eight for reading, games, and "sings." They behaved very well, were not as rough as on the first night. I would that they did as well outside as they do inside the parish house.*

*Oh! There is so much to be done to raise the standard! I'd like to be very, very wise.*

*Tomorrow night there will be a praise service and on Friday a social and "Ice cream and cake." I should have said ice cream and cake social.*

*There is no wood as yet for the school house, but Izora is doing well agitating the wood question. We used church wood yesterday to take the chill from the school house; but it smoked a blue gray cloud all morning. I found it was not the fault of my building for "it allus does ut when the wund uz sou'west." I'm just hoping the sou'westers come Saturdays.*

*Ever sincerely,*

*Lucy A. King*

By November, with no teacher in sight, the superintendent of schools asked King to teach school for the entire term. She agreed.

King also taught music, cooking, ran community gatherings, organized women's clubs and called on homes of island families, some of whom were very poor. Many of the activities and organizations she started were firsts for the island. Her requests to the Mission included such essentials as bedding and clothes.

In a November 17 letter, King wrote to Cheney (*The Triangle*, March 1921, 213):

*"Oh, can you think how joyous I was on Sunday to see the Sunbeam? Almost four weeks I had been here and never a word from them. I really did not mind but I knew my ecstasy was unreasonable simply because I was wound up to the bursting point. I did not "burst" but it was great relief to talk with Mr. MacDonald. He was really very fine and said as far as he noted all was going well. That helped.*

*He held the service on Sunday evening. There was a great number out.*

*Sunday school and Junior meetings were also well attended. Monday the Sunbeam left to get wood for the school. On the return they left as soon as possible as it looked like a storm. The storm came and has raged ever since.*

*I called on Mrs. John Lunt after school tonight. I took some of the yarn you sent to make the children some mittens. Cecil is the only one who has them at present. Lilla and Alma do the best in cooking class and they practice more at home than the other girls. Oh, I hope I may reach the right point with them all. They need so much that they never dream of.*

*Even in the blow and driving rain tonight there were fifteen beside myself at praise service. They wanted to sing afterwards so it was rather a long session, not late, however.*

*It is much easier to work with the children in home economics at present for the older ones stand a little aloof in that respect. I am just hoping and trusting all will come out right.*

*Always sincerely,*

*L.A. King.*

*P.S. There are some really funny things that happen. I'd love to show them at times. The expressions are unique. Vincent had the toothache and did not come to school one morning. He was able to play out "as soon as school began because it knocked off aching." Cecil stayed after school to whistle to me and before he finished we both felt like crying. He did but you never saw a better boy than he since that night.*

Finally, King offered a wrap-up of the island's holiday festivities in 1920 (*The Triangle*, March 21, 214):

*December 31, 1920*

*Dear Miss Cheney:*

*I am wishing you a happy New Year, for 1921 will march in very soon.*

*The last of our holiday celebrations is now island history. We had a New Year's party tonight but because we are on an island we made our own time and rang the bells a little early and it did just as well. We introduced tonight a comb orchestra which gave several selections during the evening. Santa Claus appeared for us singing "Old Black Joe" and did splendidly. The girls delighted in the flag drill and motion songs.*

*Father Time walked in and gave a few suggestions for utilizing the New Year's time and then introduced Lady New Year who appeared very attractively decorated with Christmas tree tinsel. She prophesied a prosperous year; brought in turn her four seasons to convince all what might be done in Spring, Summer, Autumn and Winter. The Circle ladies served ice cream, cake and coffee and everyone wished of course all a happy New Year; and we plodded through the snow — well pleased I hope. I for one was not unhappy.*

*The girls who dressed the dolls would have been pleased to have seen one girl where I called this week, loving her blue silk gowned child — adjusting her blue silk hat after each affectionate kiss she bestowed upon her. The fact that the doll baby really closed her eyes when she was in horizontal position rather interfered with long naps for the little mother evidently liked to see her waken.*

*Marjorie loves her black Dinah. She brought her to the Circle meeting when she came with her mother yesterday. All the children love their dolls.*

*The Christmas eve entertainment and tree was a success. I heard a number say it was a "good" Christmas for them. Did I tell you that Almena said at the church hugging her doll to her "Now I have my doll — and I want to go home and go to bed." Before she went to bed she hung her stocking by my stove, because the door was larger than the others. When I tucked her in she informed me that she should "turn out" early in the morning for she wanted to see what Santa Claus "hove" in her stocking.*

*She carefully pinned a Christmas tag on it that there might be no mistake.*

*Tonight at the New Year's party we were to raise money to pay for the new hymn books so I decided to put on sale some of the things my sister sent me from Rochester. I am convinced that the plan of selling the articles of clothing is far better than giving. Already I find a different spirit. Four people came to the house yesterday to know if I had something they could use.*

*Courtesy of Frenchboro Historical Society*

*School clinic, 1940s. Ben Davis Jr. (left) Richard "Sam" Davis, Nurse, Elmer Lunt, Donald Osier, W. Kenneth Osier, Donna Howard, David Lunt.*

*There is a tendency to remind each other unkindly of that which is given them; but when they purchase even at the smallest silver piece — it changes the attitude. Unfortunately I let the overcoat requested go yesterday for a quarter, but the man needed it. It would be better for me to say "unfortunately I have not another overcoat." If you Ladies' Circle wish to send more clothing I will say that everything thus far has been used and we could use more.*

*I need all the helpful thought waves that come this way.*

*As ever,*

*Lucy A. King*

Following King, other Sigma Kappa and Mission-supported women worked on Long Island, including Caroline W. Peasley, Miriam B. Adams and Alice "Ma" Peasley. The Sea Coast Mission also helped supply a Red Cross nurse for several winters, whose duties included teaching hygiene and preparing hot school lunches. One of the better remembered nurses was Mildred Wye.

Courtesy of Frenchboro Historical Society

*First Aid Class, 1930. Back row: Marguerite Lunt (left), Rita Hughes, Miss Douglas, Marjorie Dalzell and Genevieve McKown.*
*Front row: Verna B. Mitchell, Naomi Stanley, Mable Lunt and Thurza Lunt.*

*Courtesy of Lillian J. Lunt*

*Frenchboro School, 1934. Edna Lunt (left), Orville Mitchell, Norma Lunt, Priscilla Howard, Erland "Manny" Dalzell, Lillian J. Davis, Pauline Lunt, Malcolm Lunt, John Mitchell, Rosemary Dalzell, Clarence Lunt, Ronald Mitchell, Catherine Lunt, Thomas Lunt Jr., Frank Dalzell, Jessie Mitchell, Mable Lunt, Lawrence Davis, Vernon Dalzell.*

*Courtesy of Lillian J. Lunt*

*Frenchboro School, 1939 - 40. Rosetta Davis (left), Louise Dalzell, Edna Lunt, Norma Lunt, Orville Mitchell, Priscilla Howard, Erland Dalzell, Lillian J. Davis, Pauline Lunt, Hilda Lunt, Ruby Davis, John Lunt Jr., Dempsey Lunt.*

One of Wye's first memories of Long Island was her January night trip from Swans Island in Clarence Howard's open boat, with only a canvas windbreaker for shelter. The winter weather was freezing, but the boat stifling hot from the engine. A light placed in the front window by Aunt Rose welcomed her to Lunt Harbor. Aunt Rose (Murphy) Lunt lived on the hill just above where Lunt & Lunt is now located. Rose often welcomed harbor visitors from her perch.

*Courtesy of Vivian D. Lunt*

*Graduating Class, 1928. Marguerite Lunt (left), Vincent Davis, Nora Higgins, Lewis Nickerson, Annie Lunt.*

Mitchell provided excerpts from Wye's handwritten journal in *Anchor to Windward*:

January 8, 1940: "We started in with hot lunches for the school today serving cocoa and white bread-and-butter sandwiches. At 9:45 I left the house and was met by one of the children. I can't carry very much as I walk along with my kettle this year, as it is very full to care for eighteen youngsters. We also gave out cod-liver oil tablets, each one being equivalent to three teaspoonfuls of the fluid form. They are a bright orange color, and really quite attractive looking (Mitchell, 176)."

Louisa Rae Pullen, another Sea Coast Mission/Sigma Kappa worker, taught school from 1930 to 1932. She continued the music lessons, cooking classes and community activities started by her predecessors.

Pullen wrote an article (*The Triangle*, June 1931, 199) called "Why bury Oneself on an Island?"

"If one proves himself friendly, simple in his talk, easy to meet and willing to mingle with them as one of the community, he finds soon he has been accepted and taken into the inside life of the little settlement, but woe-betide the worker of such poor judgment that he tried to 'high-hat' them. His doom is sealed and his wisest course is to move on.

*Frenchboro School, 1956. Back row: Earlene Lunt (left), Rosalie Stanley, Marilyn Crossman, Paul "Rusty" Crossman, Wayne Bergeron.*
*Middle Row: W. Kenneth Osier, Ralph Reynolds, Gladys Muir, Jean Stanley.*
*Front Row: Joan Mitchell, Russell Hooper, Sharon Stanley, Billy Teel, Barbara Lunt.*

Life on an island is just like life anywhere else. There are poor people and people in comfortable circumstances; idle people and busy people; cultured people and unlettered ones; people with fine ideals and people whose ideals and morals are very low."

During the first half of the 20th century, island residents also taught school. Resident teachers included Silvia Lunt in 1922, Gertrude Lunt in 1923 and Willard Osier in 1925. Alice (Ross) Howard, who also taught

*Graduation Day, 1957. Rosalie Stanley (left), Earlene Lunt, Wayne Bergeron, and Marilyn Crossman.*

on Eagle Island and Swans Island, taught school on Long Island from 1926 to 1930.

An important church figure of the era was Sophronia Sumner Teel. "Toni" was the daughter of William J. and Rhoda (Lunt) Teel. She inherited the Israel B. Lunt homestead. Sophronia, a quiet, private person, was the longtime church clerk, Sunday school superintendent and an unofficial island historian. Vivian Lunt used Toni as a primary source for her first history of Long Island Plantation.

A tribute was written after Toni's death in 1959. Part of it follows:

"She died as she had lived; bravely, simply, never asking help for herself, but always with a deep concern for the welfare of her friends and neighbors. She dearly loved the Church; from the day of her early youth and throughout her entire life she gave to it her loyal, faithful service. The value of such service can not be measured. It is known only to God.

She had a keen interest in books and reading. Her remarkable memory of people and places was an inspiration. To spend a half hour with her in her little kitchen, talking over the work of the church, recalling incidents of the past and planning work for the future was always a pleasure."

During the second half of the 20th century two island sisters have dominated church life: Vivian (Davis) Lunt and Lillian (Davis) Lunt. The two women ran Sunday school and guided the church and its activities for upwards of four decades, serving in various positions including trustee, president, treasurer and superintendent of Sunday school. Both stepped down from official roles in 1999. Rebecca (Reed) Lunt was also active in the church for most of those years. She served as church secretary, taught Sunday school and often played the piano during Sunday services.

The trio's most visible work included the annual church sale at the Parish House each November, lighting the annual Christmas tree and overseeing the annual Lobster Dinner. In the summer of 1999, Vivian, Lillian and Rebecca were recognized and honored for their dedication to the church.

One of their mentors was Gladys Muir, who worked for the Sea Coast Missionary Society. For more than two decades, Muir guided the school, the church and various community groups.

Muir followed Louisa Rae Pullen to Frenchboro in 1932 and didn't leave until 1956, an unprecedented run of 24 years. During her stay she served as the school teacher, full-time pastor and Sunday school teacher. Deeply religious, she opposed almost any activity on the Sabbath and believed in morning prayers at school.

Muir was a dedicated teacher and a stern disciplinarian not opposed to slapping a ruler across the palms of disruptive students, making them stand in a corner or write on the chalk board. She was loved by some students and disliked by others, but her influence was unmistakable. She brought stability to the school and church and nurtured community involvement from the

Courtesy of Frenchboro Historical Society

*Graduation Day, 1944. Hilda Lunt (left), John R. Lunt Jr. and Ruby Davis.*

"Women's club" to Memorial Day flag ceremonies. Muir's school plays for Christmas, Easter, Thanksgiving and other holidays became valued parts of island life.

Mitchell described the school in the winter of 1940:

"Although the Frenchboro school is a one-room affair, it is not the little-old-red-schoolhouse type of building, but a square, spacious, well-lighted structure. Outside the door was a sturdy, homemade sled used for hauling wood to feed the school stove, but the stove was not going because it was Saturday. On the walls inside were pictures of Washington and Roosevelt, and exhibitions of the pupils' work. From this work you could tell at once that here was a school of the most up-to-date kind. Even knot-tying is taught and there is

Courtesy of Vivian D. Lunt

*Frenchboro School, 1940s. Back row: Mrs. Gladys Muir (left), Richard "Sam" Davis. Middle row: Bennie S. Davis Jr., Carroll W. Lunt.*
*Front row: W. Kenneth Osier, Donna Howard, Donald Osier, David L. Lunt, Elmer Lunt, Robert A. Lunt.*

a rhythm band. On one of the blackboards was a notice about banking day. Each child has a porcelain-frog bank. Part of the money which the school receives for books is used to pay for the batteries for the radio over which are received the broadcasts of the American School of the Air. In contrast with the little-old-red-schoolhouse type of equipment, I noticed that there was a water cooler instead of a pail for drinking water. (Mitchell, 175)"

In the 1950s and 1960s, Muir was followed by other mission workers/school teachers including Helen Perkins, Blanche Beal, James Truxes and finally Arthur Cramer.

Cramer, who taught for three years, was the last person to both teach and preach and the island's last resident minister. The mission's role was changing and evolving as Long Island became less isolated and the more basic social services offered in the 1920s and 1930s became unnecessary.

Cramer's departure in 1969 marked the official end of the direct connection between the school and the Mission more than 120 years after Baptists taught islanders to read using the Bible, and more than 80 years after the fiery Alexander P. MacDonald brought the Congregational church to Long Island.

## Foster Children: Saving Kids, School and Island

While Gladys Muir provided a steadying presence for the island school, her tenure was marked by a continued decline in school enrollment. Many islanders left to serve in World War II and others left to work at shipyards or other industries in Southern and Central Maine. Many island men during this era remained bachelors or childless. Others just left for a more convenient life. The total population dropped from 119 in 1940 to 57 in 1960.

And by 1964, the school faced crisis. Barbara A. Lunt and Cheryl Hooper were the only students in the spring of 1964. That fall, only Hooper and kindergarten student David W. Lunt were slated to attend. The state threatened to withhold aid, a direct threat to both school and community. As Ben S. Davis Sr. would later say, "A town is a sad place to live without a school and the sound of happy children."

The islanders looked to solve the problem. So in 1964, they devised a unique plan and then proceeded to overcome skepticism and obstacles to succeed. They decided to become foster parents en masse and open their homes to more than a dozen foster children.

*Photo by Sandra Lunt*

*Frenchboro School, 1965. Cheryl Hooper and David W. Lunt.*

The plan was to provide good homes to needy children while saving the island's school at the same time. A string of islanders trooped to the child welfare office in Ellsworth to make their case.

They needed to convince Charles King, the man who headed the local welfare office. King initially said the island's size, distance, lack of transportation and lack of telephones among other things greatly discouraged him. Eventually, he relented to pressure and agreed to visit Long Island so he could "discuss intelligently the reasons why the Division of Child Welfare would regretfully be unable to license any foster homes in Frenchboro" (*The Ellsworth American*, May 10, 1967).

Instead, his visit proved a revelation. He did not find the backward island slum he imagined. He immediately changed his mind.

He met islanders, discussed licensing procedures and began wondering where to find appropriate children. He knew he needed children in need of long-term placement, both to benefit the children and the island. He succeeded.

*Photo by Pamela Pierce*

*Michael Holland (left), Anthony Brown (background), Kevin Holland, Phoebe Leach and Timothy Bergeron, 1968.*

The first children arrived in the summer of 1964. Two sisters from Surry, 11-year-old Phoebe and nine-year-old Lilly Leach, moved in with Cecil and Lillian Lunt. Cecil, 49, and Lillian, 39, were also the parents of Barbara A. Lunt, who had just graduated from the island elementary school and was heading for high school at Higgins Classical Institute in Charleston.

Phoebe and Lilly had lived with their grandmother in "abject squalor," according to King in *The Ellsworth American*. Their grandmother approached the state for help.

The two girls, King wrote, were withdrawn and underweight. But

*Photo by Sandra Lunt*

*Back row (left): Billy Holland, Bobby Holland, Phoebe Leach. Middle row: Anthony Brown, Lilly Leach, Kevin Holland, David W. Lunt, Daniel Lunt. Front row: Kevin Lunt, Ralph Lunt, Joan Holland, Michael Holland and Theresa Holland, 1966.*

they were placed together and never suffered any serious adjustment problems.

"When the girls first came, they were scared to death," Lillian said. "They would go upstairs and if they dropped something I would go upstairs to see what happened and they would be hiding under the bed. They thought they were going to get beaten."

Indeed, they grew up in a household where they were frequently yelled at and sometimes hit for the smallest of infractions. After going to bed at night, they were not even allowed to use the bathroom. Phoebe said they were indeed uncertain when they arrived in Frenchboro.

"It was totally different than anything we had seen before," Phoebe said. "My life was school and my grandmother's. It was very scary. It was very hard and I think my reaction was, 'where the heck are we going?' We had never met Lillian or Cecil. We had never met anyone on the island. We didn't know anybody.

"I don't think we left the yard for three weeks or so, we weren't used to that. But finally we realized we could go and not get yelled at or hit when we came back. It was then a lot of fun growing up down there. Mom taught me how to swim. Mom taught me how to ride a bike. When the grass died on the hill, we went sliding on cardboard boxes."

More importantly, they felt at home. "We weren't used to calling someone Mom or Dad," Phoebe said. "It was nice."

The two girls started classes that fall. Also arriving that fall was four-year-old Anthony "Tony" Brown, who lived with Dick and Vivian Lunt.

©*Peter Ralston, 1999*

*Frenchboro School, 1988. Back row: Kerry Hartman. Middle row: Travis Lunt (left), Luke Higgins, Wayne Crossman.*
*Front row: Jacob Betts, Carrie Betts, Zachary Lunt, Samantha Betts.*

On the mainland, Anthony had already been in two foster homes, but remained withdrawn and barely able to speak. However, within a few months of arriving on Long Island, he "really blossomed," according to a social worker, becoming more verbal and showing emotion. His main fear, according to King, was that he might be taken away again to another home. Tony, who remains an island landowner, lived on the island through elementary school and returned for several years as an adult.

That January, eight brothers and sisters taken from a poor home in Washington County where the family had been living on potatoes and were peeling wood off their house to burn for heat. They were all brought to Frenchboro in the dead of winter and placed in five different homes.

The youngest brother was Michael, 4, who spent nine years in the island school and lived with Cecil and Lillian Lunt. He lived on the island for five years as an adult following a three-year stint in the army.

Ultimately, 15 foster children came to an island with a population of only about 60. Not all went smoothly. Some children did not adjust and were removed shortly. But most stayed at least through eighth grade, and some lived on the island as adults.

Phoebe returned to Long Island in the late 70s for about two years. She married Richard "Dickie" Horton there in 1978.

"I wanted to get married out there," Phoebe said. "Dickie and I talked about it. I wanted one of the ministers from my childhood out there to do it, so I called up Jim Miller (a summer minister) and he and Janet and the three kids flew up from Pennsylvania. With Barbara and Randy (Sawyer) standing up with us, we got married two days after Christmas in a snow storm at Gooseberry Point."

The foster children story brought a national spotlight to the island. *The Saturday Evening Post* dubbed Long Island, "The Island that Borrows Children." It said, "The young people were all leaving, the school was nearly empty. Then the tiny Maine community used Yankee ingenuity to renew itself."

The local newspapers came, *The Boston Globe* came and the *Christian Science Monitor* came. Even Charles Kuralt stopped by to film an *"On the Road"* segment. Kuralt's opening was eloquent: "Frenchboro is bleached by the sun and weathered by time. From a distance it appears old, which it is — even dying, which it would be — except for one thing and that is the children."

In the 1980s and 1990s, the school has remained open, although the enrollment has fluctuated. The longest serving teacher during the era has been Marie LaRosee who taught for three and one-half years in the 1980s.

For the first time in 20 years, the school's enrollment dropped again to one pupil, Mariner Beal, during part of the 1998-1999 school year. His teacher that year was Cathy Kozaryn.

In the fall of 1999, the school has two full-time pupils, Mariner and Joey Charpentier, and a third, Kodi Carl, who attends school during the fall and spring with the latest schoolteacher, Rebecca Smart. However, the most encouraging news for the island school is that four pre-school children between the ages of 1 and 4 are waiting to attend. They are Lance Bishop, Jessica Charpentier, Audrey Beal and Elijah Wiggins.

*Photo by Arthur Pollock/Boston Herald*

*Schoolteacher Cathy Kozaryn and Mariner Beal, 1998.*

## *Island Memories*

"Mrs. Muir, she taught the boys different things. Like my brother Orville, there was no one in his class, so he would go in with the other girls and she taught him to embroider and to sew and things like that and even today he does all the patching in his house. She would also have Innie come in and teach all the girls how to tie all these square knots, and bowline knots and different knots. She never said 'boys do this' and 'girls do this.'" Verna "Bunny" (Mitchell) Dobson, born 1919.

"I used to be janitor up at the school. I used to carry water for the school because they didn't have any water up there then. I carried it in glass jugs from down to the spring. I got five cents a day when I first started. Later, I got I think a dollar a week for being janitor. I would go down to the spring for the water until it froze up and then I would go to Robbins and Vera's because they had a well in the cellar." Robert A. Lunt, born 1938

"If the wind was going to be Sou'west [some of the kids] would take the stovepipe apart and put a rag in there so it would smoke: No school! Then they would drive'a to Sou'west Point gunning." John R. Lunt Jr., born 1930

*Courtesy of Verna B. Dobson*

*Frenchboro School, 1932 - 1933. Rosemary Dalzell (left) Catherine Lunt, Clarence Lunt, Ronald Mitchell, Thomas Lunt Jr., Lawrence Davis, Frank Dalzell, Mable Lunt, Verna B. Mitchell, Malcolm Lunt, John Mitchell, Orville Mitchell, Lillian J. Davis, Erland Dalzell, Norma Lunt, Pauline Lunt.*

"I liked Helen Wade — she was from Massachusetts — the best. She was awfully nice to me. I didn't have any mother then. I used to go to school and stay in recess and she taught me how to knit and crochet and do tatting." Ella V. Lunt, born 1909

"I used to sing solos. I laugh about it now, me singing a solo. Of course, we didn't have any accompaniment or anything. I remember with Mrs. Pullen, we would have a musical program at school where we would recite things and sing songs sometimes together. I used to get out there and sing 'My Darling Nellie Gray.' I think about it now, I could hardly carry a tune, let alone sing songs." Marjorie (Dalzell) Giamo, born 1918

"I loved to go to school. The last four years of going to school Alice Howard was my teacher. Every Friday afternoon after recess she would read out of story books. That was the first time I ever heard Anne of Green Gables. I just thought that was the greatest thing. We would sit there with both ears wide open, listening."

Vivian (Davis) Lunt, born 1915

*Courtesy of Donna Hasal*

*Alice (Ross) Howard (1898 - 1969)*

# Chapter Thirteen

# 20th Century Economy

## Sanford L. "Dick" Lunt

To me, one man symbolizes work: Sanford L. "Dick" Lunt. My grandfather. I don't mean simply hard work; I know many hard workers. Nor a corporate workaholic, they're as common as field mice. No, Gramp Dick has defined a sun-up to sundown, seven-day-a-week, work as way-of-life existance for nearly nine decades.

He symbolizes a hardscrabble era and embodies the relentless tenacity required to rise from it. He was born poor and raised poor in a way almost unimaginable on the island today. The family rationed shoes and sometimes shared mittens to keep their hands warm. Thus, starting from boyhood, his everyday life became inextricably interwoven with work — the wharf, the boat, the traps, the land, the house and the town. No meaningful way or reason existed or exists to separate his daily work from his daily life. It is one.

Dick is a near legend now; 89 years old and still hauling lobster traps. Slower, less frequently, but still grinding away regardless of the effort required for even the most basic fishing tasks.

In a much broader sense, Dick is a true Downeast Yankee. He is amongst a band of men and women who recast a region and a way of life through sheer effort and perseverance during a seemingly endless economic depression, and then came to define it. In that vein, Dick brings all the glorious ideals and bedrock ethics, and the sometimes maddening traits that make them so intriguing, define their identity and have earned them respect from even their enemies: they are generous, ambitious, cautious, tireless, honest, community-minded, stubborn, slightly eccentric, single-minded, cantankerous and willing to carry a grudge to the very end of time. They don't readily heed advice and, while family blood runs thick, are not overtly affectionate or emotional. Dick is a man who doesn't ask for help much, but who might complain if no one pitches in. Yet he rarely would make helping convenient.

He carries with him an older generation's sense of value and ethics. When he took care of a small island property for a summer couple, he hired teenagers to work around the house and yard for a few bucks. But if work didn't meet his expectations — which it rarely did — he redid it himself, for free. No matter how long or how hard he worked, he didn't want to "overcharge." It just wouldn't seem right.

He is a man who adheres to ritual. It is no exaggeration to say he has eaten Kellogg's Corn Flakes before the crack of dawn most every morning for the last 60 years. Why? There was simply no good reason to change. That says as much as anything.

Sanford L. Lunt was born May 30, 1910, the oldest son of Flora E. and John R. Lunt. His following 89 years is a case study in the evolution of Maine fishing, and a virtual history of the island's 20th century. He is 20 years the elder of any other island man and has lived for nearly half the island's existence as a year-round community. In the eyes of many long-time summer visitors and older mainland folk, Dick Lunt is Frenchboro.

By the age of 10, he helped support a growing family for his sick father. He ran errands, hauled wood, fished for lobster, gathered berries, and tended animals. His parents eventually raised 10 children, not including five who either died at birth or as toddlers.

He bought his first lobster boat at 12 and quit school following eighth grade to work full-time. He served as the captain for a summer family on Swans Island at 16 and even delivered milk one summer for a mid-coast dairy farm. He hauled miles of hake trawls by hand, set seine to catch herring, built his own boat, worked with his younger brothers, and started his own business. As a young man he fished to earn enough money to strike out on his own.

Still, for all his righteous independence, he has not succeeded alone. He married Vivian May Davis on Nov. 21, 1936 before a Notary Public in Southwest Harbor. He was 26. She was 21. For the 63 years since he has worked the sea, she has run the household. Little has changed.

The couple started small. He and Vivian lived off the land, adhering to a meager budget. They have never incurred a debt.

The year they married, Dick paid $100 cash for a house, a 12 x 16 building with a kitchen on the first floor and one bedroom on the second. That's it. He added to it slowly, and only when needed.

By 1938, he was able to save $300 to buy materials and an engine for a new 36-foot boat. He built it nights and off -days over the course of a year.

In 1944, at 34, he bought his first car, a second-hand Chevrolet. He bought his first new car, a Hudson, in 1948. Both times he paid cash.

In 1951, he started S.L. Lunt Lobsters, the forebear of

*Courtesy of Vivian D. Lunt*

*Sanford L. "Dick" Lunt launching the David & Vivian, January 1939.*

Lunt & Lunt, with nothing but a set of scales and a few lobster crates. He bought lobsters from other fishermen from his boat until he built his own lobster pound and began the methodical, relentless building of his wharf.

Carroll W. Lunt, a Bass Harbor fisherman who grew up on Long Island, calls Dick the hardest-working man he has ever known. In the 1950s, Dick, no longer a poor man, signed bank papers so Carroll could buy his first outboard motor. He has co-signed many such papers from the 1950s through the 1990s, helping fishermen get a start.

Did Dick possess a great business mind? No, I don't think so. He was a commonsense, relentless worker. His son, David, has expanded the lobster business over the past two decades. Was he a financial wizard? Again, no.

No disrespect to my grandfather, but Vivian handled the family money, what there was. He kept a wad of cash in his wallet; Vivian started to stash every spare cent in U.S. Savings Bonds at the first opportunity in the 1940s. She kept a meticulous budget, putting cash in individual budget envelopes for groceries or gasoline and spending no more.

Indeed, Gram Vivian is a good ol' Yankee herself: thriftiness held as religion. There is no waste in the Vivian and Dick Lunt household.

"You never forget the Depression," she says often, usually when I am complaining about her not replacing some decades-old chair that has duct tape covering a rip in the leather or vinyl. The tape, of course, covered by an afghan. For appearance sake, you know.

Vivian has always operated on needs, not wants. And she hasn't needed much. Like Dick, change is not high on her priority list. Vivian has been as focused and has worked as hard as Dick. She helped run the church for decades and built the Frenchboro Historical Society with her sister, Lillian, focused on her high school education, controlled the company finances, oversaw the household and vowed to never be poor again.

"It seemed as if I was always right on the ragged edge of nothing," she said. "I was so poor growing up that I never wanted to be that way again; that was my goal. Momma had a big family. Daddy did carry the mail, but with so many kids it took a lot just to feed everyone. So, I wanted to save every nickel and get to the point where I could be independent and live comfortable."

They have succeeded. But my grandfather is still driven by a sense that work remains. While some men moved to the mainland as they aged, closer to stores, closer to doctors, closer to everything, 89-year-old Sanford has grown an ever more reluctant traveler. He simply does not like leaving Frenchboro. I suspect he has many reasons.

Mostly, I believe that after a nine-decade partnership with Long Island and as the sixth generation of Lunts to work from the same shores, Long Island is a part of his very soul.

And vice versa.

[Sanford L. "Dick" Lunt died Oct. 18, 1999. He was 89.]

# The 20th Century

In the early 20th century, the United States was changing and so was Long Island. On the mainland, people flocked to factories and cities as the industrial revolution gripped America, forever changing the way people worked and lived. The mechanization of the nation also played a role in the fate of fishing and Frenchboro.

As the new century dawned, portions of Long Island's fishing industry continued an unalterable decline. The majestic fishing schooners that once graced Lunt Harbor with their sloping lines and unfurled sails were rapidly becoming a memory. The decline in traditional offshore fisheries caused by overfishing, improved shipping methods, and the internal combustion engine all conspired to cause the eventual failure and collapse of Long Island's last large fish firms — Frenchboro Land and Fisheries Co. and Eastern Fish Co. Both failed by 1920. Never again would a successful island firm cater to a fishing fleet based beyond Lunt Harbor.

The closing of Frenchboro Land and Fisheries Co. also meant the fish wharf tracing its roots to Israel B. Lunt's original business now sat dormant.

Continuing to supplant such fish as cod, mackerel and hake were lobsters, an increasingly vital industry slowly becoming the island's economic backbone. However, it was not a smooth transition. Lobster fishing — as a business that could reliably support island families — developed in fits and starts throughout the crunch of depression-era America.

The island's lobster catch remained low and the price depressed through much of the century's first 50 years. At one point "poverty crate" became the unofficial nickname for a lobster trap.

As a result, island men still pursued other types of fish such as hake, haddock and herring to supplement lobster fishing. They used methods ranging from hooks to trawls to nets. It can be argued that herring, not lobsters, actually brought the island out of its long depression and primed the economy in the 1940s.

## *Economic Depression*

The early 20th century ushered in, and in some cases continued an era of relative island poverty. This occurred in part because the island lacked

*Samuel Rice (1864 - 1935).*

*West side, 1920s. Houses are: Hiram A. "Hite" Lunt Sr. (left), Leaman T. Davis, Nathan F. Osier, Hezekiah W. Lunt Sr., Hezekiah W. "Will" Lunt Jr. and L. Glendon Lunt. The boat in the harbor was owned by James H. Thurlow.*

an economic staple, in part because the world had changed and in part because large families pushed the population toward 200.

Certainly Frenchboro lacked any type of economic diversity. Unlike some other Maine islands and coastal towns, Long Island remained almost exclusively reliant on fishing. Tourists, who might have brought outside money to the island, were unheard of and largely unwelcome. Although actual hostility was exaggerated, there is no question the coast's budding yacht crowd was at times wary of Long Island. It didn't help that one survey book of Maine islands in 1891 said Long Island was "conspicuous for the semi-civilized nature of its inhabitants (Drake, *The Pine-Tree Coast*, 288)."

Furthermore, no wealthy summer residents or "rusticators" built homes on the island. Such people could have provided income through caretaking jobs and unleashed the general largesse that came with big money during that era. Likewise, neither summer cottages nor summer hotels were ever built on Long Island.

On the other hand, lack of tourists and wealthy summer residents also meant Long Island didn't see such problems as overdevelopment, harbor-side displacement of its working residents or the imposition of will that comes hand-in-hand with wealth. Even today, the island has only three

*Courtesy of Lillian J. Lunt*

*Hezekiah "Kai" Davis standing in the door of his camp around 1910.*

relatively pricey summer estates. As a result, islanders are still largely able to guide the island's destiny and its character.

In any event, as a result of all those factors, the Long Island economy in the early 20th century was largely self-contained and troubled.

Basically, Long Island was on its own.

For various reasons, some residents "called on the town" off and on for the first 30 years or so of the century. Calling on the town meant the plantation provided some food staples and covered certain bills. The plantation was in turn reimbursed by the state. Some elderly widows relied on such assistance for food and clothing.

Poverty — as contrasted with simply being poor — was not pervasive, but was certainly not uncommon. The island conditions helped spur continued alcohol abuse in some quarters, contributed to health problems, and forced young children to work.

Being poor was commonplace. In some homes, even such basic items as shoes and mittens were rationed or shared. During the later 1800s and early 1900s, Angeline and Atwood Lunt were trying raise more than a dozen children in a small house along today's Bennie June Road. One of the younger children was Otis Lunt.

"(Atwood) used to take the shoes in the spring and put them in a crocus sack bag and leave them hanging so that the kids went barefoot all summer," said Russell Lunt, Otis Lunt's son. "Then in the fall after the first frost, he would get the sack down, dump the shoes on the floor and then the kids  would go for them and take whichever pair fit. That was their shoes for the winter, come spring, they would put them up again."

Such conditions on Long Island did not go unnoticed by the state. For whatever reasons, and legends vary, at least three times during the early 1900s, state officials removed either elderly residents or children from island homes. They took some to foster homes and some to a state poor farm. Some of these islanders eventually returned, but others did not.

At some point between 1917 and 1919, officials took four young children, including Otis, from Atwood and Angeline, who had given birth to 15 children.

Among the children taken was Tina or Tena, born in 1911. Tena Wilkinson later told her granddaughter, Pamela Savoy, "I would rather have stayed on the island with nothing to eat than be taken away from my mother and father."

Tena said that after the children were taken to the mid-coast area, Angeline found out where they were staying and took them back to the island. The state, however, retook them.

One sister, June (originally named Flora), was adopted and eventually moved to the mid-west. Sixty-seven years after they were separated, June and Tena tracked each other down for a long-belated reunion.

Meanwhile, on Long Island, two of Tena's older siblings, tipped off about the state workers, managed to avoid relocation. In one case, officials met and asked Llewellyn Lunt, known as "Hud," his name. He said "Hud." They asked him where they might find Llewellyn. He said, "I think he is over that way," and then fled.

Hud hid in trees near Big Beach while state officials unsuccessfully searched for him. Hud often told how he clung to the top of a big spruce tree while the officials walked below. They finally gave up.

Courtesy of Frenchboro Historical Society
*Martin Hall Rich (1852 - 1925).*

His brother Grover fled to Black Island for a couple of days. He hid in a large pipe left from the island's old granite quarry. A Black Island woman supplied him with food and water while he hid.

A third brother, Joseph W. "Innie" Lunt III, 17, lied about his age and entered the U.S. Navy in 1917. He sent checks home to help support his parents and siblings.

Even young Otis made things difficult for state workers. Otis told Russell that state officials came three times before they caught him. Each time a "strange boat" entered Lunt Harbor, he ran. Eventually, Otis was taken to a farm, from which he ran away after one year to another farm. He stayed on the second farm until he was 15. Then he ran away again, lied about his age and joined the U.S. Army. Otis returned to Long Island throughout his life and fished several summers as an adult. His grandson, Billy, still owns a cabin on the island, near the former site of Atwood and Angeline's old house.

Then in the early 1920s, children from the Grant "Nuckie" Lunt family were also removed and taken to a poor farm. Grant had died a few years earlier leaving Lena Martha "Matt" (Higgins) to raise the children alone. Matt also spent some years in a state home.

Several elderly men, including Martin Hall Rich, George Butler and Hezekiah "Kai" Davis, were also removed from their island camps on Lunt Harbor and taken away.

Martin returned after Leonard "Nardy" Lunt and Irving "Pean" Lunt, his grandchildren, and other relatives pledged financial support. Although the town helped support other residents, those controversial removals were probably the only

*Courtesy of Frenchboro Historical Society*

*George Butler digging clams in Lunt Harbor, 1920s.*

such actions taken on Long Island during the 1900s.

Amidst all the converging economic and social circumstances, islanders scrambled to earn a living. Children worked, and, for the most part, extended family members, often poor themselves, opened their doors when needed.

"I done all kind of jobs when I was a kid, anything to make a cent or two," said Dick Lunt, born in 1910. "I would go in the woods, haul out wood on a hauling sled — all I could haul — and sell it to Charles Wallace for sometimes 15 cents, sometimes 25 cents. I dug clams and sold them, would get mussels if anyone wanted some and sell them. I would run errands for five cents. I was the only one in them days who could make any money (for the family). My father was sick.

"Everybody pitched in. Alma [his oldest sister] cooked like the devil. Of course, we had to pick blueberries and raspberries and cranberries and everything else and put them down in jars so we could eat in the winter."

Added sister Mable (Lunt) Hall, "Alma could get a meal together with nothing. She could have the biggest kind of supper out of nothing. How she did it, I'll never know."

Some people, such as Rosanna (Murphy) Lunt, a long-time widow who lived on the hill above what is now the Lunt & Lunt wharf, sold eggs and milk from their own animals and helped families with housework, sometimes for $1 a day. "Aunt Rose" regularly helped John and Flora E. Lunt wash clothes and clean the house. She also washed floors and dishes for Vera and Milton "Robbins" Dalzell, sometimes in exchange for supper.

Eventually, some men supplemented incomes serving as captains for summer residents on other islands, while some women spent summers working in mainland hotels, restaurants and other businesses. Sisters Lilla and Alma Lunt worked on Swans Island as housekeepers and cooks for the Munsell family, while their brother, Dick, worked as the family's captain.

Robbins Dalzell left the island each summer throughout the late 1920s and the entire 1930s. He took his boat, *Laura*, and worked out of various ports including Islesboro, Cranberry Island and Northeast Harbor. In Winter Harbor, he was based at the Grindstone Inn.

## *The sputtering start of King Lobster*

In 1899, Hancock County was the state's dominant supplier of clams, eels, flounder, codfish and scallops and a major player in the ground fish, salmon and smelt industries. The county trailed only Knox County in catching lobsters. In 1900, it was number one.

But even then, the lobster catch fluctuated statewide. State and federal officials already feared an industry collapse as the total catch fell under the crush of overfishing and the absence of any meaningful regulations.

Throughout the latter 1800s, the industry tried to police itself by enacting conservation measures such as closed seasons, minimum and maximum lobster size restrictions and restocking. Many measures proved either ineffective or were widely ignored by fishermen. The state did effectively shut down lobster canning, a thriving 19th century business that ravaged the smaller lobster population.

The state also tried lobster management. In 1899, 36.9 million fry lobsters were dumped into Maine waters, including 200,000 off Long Island, in an attempt to restock the species.

That year in Hancock County, 503 boats, including 30 on Long Island, caught 1.76 million lobsters with a total value of $229,068 (Public Documents of Maine, 1901, 26). That calculates to about 13 cents per pound.

Statewide, decline was obvious. In 1900, 3,100 fisherman caught 14.2 million pounds. By 1919, the total catch had dropped nearly 60 percent to 5.8 million pounds, and by 1924 it had fallen still further to 5.51 million pounds (Martin, 77).

On Long Island during this era, Alphonso "Fon" Lunt, son of Israel B. Lunt Jr. and Isora Rich, was one of the wealthier and larger fishermen. In September of 1904, Fon usually caught between 13 and 43 pounds per day selling them for 10 to 15 cents per pound. In September of 1911, his daily catches were usually in the 40 to 60 pound range. His total fishing and lobstering income from the fall 1910 to the fall 1911 was $1,450.

The general island economy remained poor enough in the early 1900s that fishermen used small lobsters, or shorts, along with legally-sized lobsters, or counters, as currency in a barter system for food and other supplies. Some island fishermen carried their shorts to Ellsworth and surrounding towns to exchange with farmers for potatoes and other vegetables into the 1930s. In this way, islanders helped stock a winter supply of food when money was scarce.

Islanders would run their boats up the Union River to Ellsworth and tossed weighted bags of lobsters overboard. The bags were collected by locals who then supplied the lobstermen with food and other goods.

To a lesser degree, similar activity continued along the coast into the 1950s when some fishermen still carried bushel baskets of short lobsters into Aroostook County to peddle or exchange for vegetables.

Exchanging short lobsters for food was only a small part of the industry's short lobster problem during the early 1900s.

Out-of-state lobster smacks — vessels used by dealers to temporarily store and transport lobsters — sailed into Maine waters to buy short lobsters and sell them in other states. Some in-state smacks and dealers followed suit to stay in business. Both operators helped maintain a short lobster market, which in turn prompted fishermen, who needed money, to keep and sell them. The government admitted that such problems were difficult to solve.

"Coincidentally, with the first law relating to the regulation of taking lobsters, limiting the sale to a given length, began a campaign along the coast of Maine to discover the greater number and variety of ways and means to evade the law with the least liability of detection ... The lobster is fast approaching extinction, already on the danger line, yet they will not learn from the many object lessons of the past generation" (Maine Public Documents, 1918, 32).

The number of lobsters caught and their value declined again following World War I. And when the Great Depression hit in 1929, the price of lobsters collapsed. The average statewide price per pound in 1919 was about 25 cents. It rose to 32 cents in the mid-1920s, but during the 1930s prices sometimes fell to as low as 10 cents on Long Island and lobsters remained scarce.

When John R. Lunt Jr. and Orville Mitchell started to fish as kids in the late 1930s and early 1940s, lobsters remained difficult to find.

"I first started (lobster fishing) in 1941, I was 11 years old, with a skiff and oars," said John Lunt. "I had a 14-foot or a 16-foot punt. She belonged to Willard Osier. Orville and I went fishing in her in the summer and before school. We had 20 to 25 traps and some days we would get one lobster for maybe 20 cents. There were not a big lot of lobsters in those days."

However, the statewide lobster catch did start to recover in the 1940s. In 1940, 3,707 fishermen caught 7.54 million pounds (Martin, 77). Although an increase from 1919, it was still a far cry from the more than 25 million pounds caught in 1889.

On Long Island itself, the economy also improved in the post-World War II years, although lobster prices recovered slowly, occasionally dipping below 20 cents per pound into the 1950s.

One summer in the early 1940s, Dick Lunt and Ben S. Davis Sr. caught and stored

*Courtesy of Frenchboro Historical Society*

*John R. Lunt Jr. (left), Orville Mitchell, Louise Dalzell, Betty Dalzell, 1930s.*

some 3,000 pounds of lobsters. They had trouble selling them for what they considered a reasonable price. The two finally convinced George Lunt, who owned Lunt's Lobster Pound restaurant in Trenton, to buy the entire lot for 12 cents per pound. He didn't want them all at once, forcing Dick and Bennie to deliver them over the course of a few weeks.

During the 1920s and 1930s, only the largest Frenchboro fishermen set close to 100 traps, and everyone fished within a mile or two of the island. By the 1940s and 1950s, larger lobstermen fished into the 200-trap range and then pushed up into the 300-trap range by the late 1950s.

Everyone worked to make a living, but occasional feuds and lobster theft occurred in the early part of the century. While intra-island lobster feuds never reached the destructive level seen at some islands and fishing villages even today, squabbles existed.

According to legend, one small offshoot of the Lunt family controlled a stretch of the island's coastline from Northeast Point to Eastern Cove and vigilantly protected those grounds from interlopers. Any fisherman who set lobster traps in that area usually lost them all by sun-up the next day. Dick Lunt said as a teenager he could safely set traps from Whale Beach to Northeast Point, but if he went one trap beyond the point, he lost it.

"There was a lot of bad actors around in them days," he said. "You didn't want to mess with them."

Legend also has it that when the same family needed new warps for their traps, they could be seen loading up a boat to go hand-lining for codfish. But when they returned a few hours later, especially if it was a foggy day, they tossed out coils of rope instead of cod.

Several cases that involved charges of hauling another fisherman's lobster traps — not cutting off the buoys — did end up in court early in the century. In some cases, it was cousin versus cousin. Occasionally, squabbles have also erupted between Long Island fishermen and non-island fishermen over territorial grounds as well.

In general, the lobster fishing industry continues to run in cycles, affected by any number of issues from storms to competing industries to the success or failure of natural predators. Catches rise and fall within each decade. After swings up and down from the 1960s through the 1980s, the lobster industry roared back in the mid-1990s producing catches not seen on Long Island in three generations. On some days during the fall of 1997 the island's largest fishermen sometimes sold more than 1,000 pounds per day. Statewide, fishermen caught a record 46.9 million pounds worth $138 million. In 1998, lobsters fell from that peak but remained plentiful. Statewide, lobstermen caught 45.5 million pounds of lobsters, a decrease of only about 3 percent.

The island's large lobstermen in 1999 fish upwards of 800 traps. During the course of the fall, average catches can hit the 300 to 600-pound or more range. The average price per pound in October of 1999 was $3.30. These lobsters are caught even as scientists and lobstermen again debate conservation measures and the potential collapse of the lobster stock.

## Catching Lobsters

While powerboats appeared early in the century, many boats on Long Island remained fairly primitive into the 1920s. Peapods, dories, rowboats and sloops remained active in the island fleet even as the internal combustion engine stormed onto the scene. In fact, some adult fishermen continued to row around the island hauling their traps by hand into the 1950s when outboard motors became affordable.

"There was still a lot of skiff fishermen in the 1940s," said David L. Lunt. "Both younger guys and older guys. Wallace and Doonie, Hud and Lincoln and Innie, all those guys used skiffs. A lot of them used to row right around the island to haul."

Courtesy of Verna B. Dobson

*Charles L. Wallace standing in a typical early powerboat in inner part of Lunt Harbor, 1920s.*

During an early era, fishermen might row or sail a couple of miles or so each way to haul traps, which numbered maybe 50 or 70 for the island's largest fishermen. Rowboats and small sloops made lobstering during winter months difficult, if not impossible. Those fishermen who kept traps in the water during the winter might only haul two or three times the entire season.

Courtesy of Frenchboro Historical Society
*Shirley Lunt rowing to set lobster traps, 1940s.*

While some people continued to row, the gasoline engine dominated by the 1920s, dramatically changing the industry. The first such boat on Long Island was owned by Walter Robinson, a carpenter, coffin maker and boat builder.

"He had the first boat with an engine," said Marjorie (Dalzell) Giamo. "My mother {Vera Dalzell} said everyone was afraid of it. So they would have him cast off from the wharf before he started the engine up because they thought the thing would blow up. It was a putt-putt boat that barely moved."

"Fon" Lunt bought an engine for his boat in 1915, but it was probably not his first one.

Early powerboats were small and narrow with a low profile. The engines, typically one-cylinder or "one-lungers," sat in the center or stern of an open boat often exposed to the elements. The boat's shelter, if any, was a low canvas spray hood.

Dick Lunt's first boat was a double-ender in 1922. It was 18 feet long and six feet wide with a one-cylinder engine and a canvas hood. The boat cost him $100. He was 12 years old and fished fewer than 50 traps.

For decades, lobstermen hauled traps by hand. However, with even the crudest engine came mechanized haulers, and hauling by hand soon became the province of skiff fishermen. In the 1990s, even skiff fishermen began installing hydraulic winches.

Early trap haulers worked by transferring some of the engine's power from the drive shaft to a winch. Fishermen manually shifted the belt onto the hauling winch at each trap. In later years, the belt remained connected both to the drive shaft and the winch; thus the winch continued to spin between traps. It was disconnected only during long runs.

On very early haulers, the belt was connected to the flywheel of the engine and to a horizontal shaft with a winch head attached to one end. The trap's warp ran up over the side of the boat and over a snatch block, essentially an open-ended pulley. The rope was then wrapped around the winch head, which spun vertically like a car tire. The winch head didn't necessarily pull the trap by itself, but greatly aided the lobstermen.

"They were a help, but they were still a lot of work," Dick Lunt said. "If the tide was running you still had to do a lot of hauling by hand. And in them days we still used glass bottles for toggles and sometimes they would swing around and smash on the boat."

In other instances, the winch head sat on a shaft that stood vertically; thus it spun horizontally like a top. In this case, the warp was pulled up over the side of the boat across a roller placed on the boat rail and then wrapped around the winch.

Various types of haulers existed over the years until hydraulic-driven winches, the type still used in 1999, exploded onto the scene in the 1960s.

Powerboats and mechanized winches allowed fishermen to set more traps and fish them in deeper water. They also greatly extended the lobster season, allowing lobstermen to fish longer into the fall and start earlier in the spring.

## *Making Traps the Hard Way*

Despite technological advances during the century's first 50 years, there remained two key factors limiting the number of traps a lobsterman could fish: trap construction and maintenance. Both were time consuming tasks.

Before the era of wire traps, wharves were regularly stacked high with wooden traps drying out or waiting for repairs. Those traps, occasionally filled with rotting crabs, leftover bait, sea urchins and dead starfish, helped give fish wharves their distinctive smell.

The time-consuming construction encompassed every aspect of lobster fishing — from building traps, to repairing traps, to knitting mesh heads and bait pockets, to treating rope and carving wooden buoys. Local fishermen hauled most of the necessary materials from island woods.

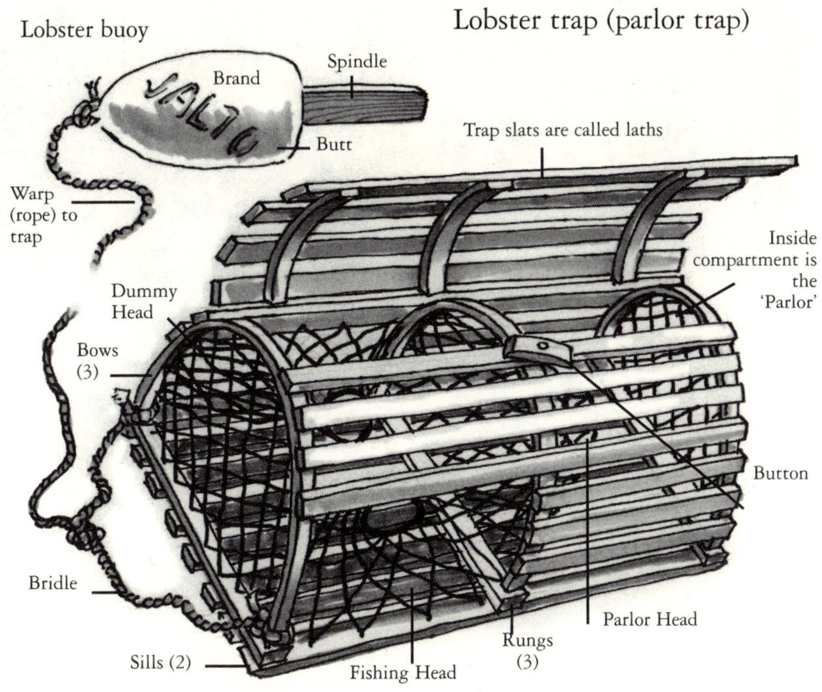


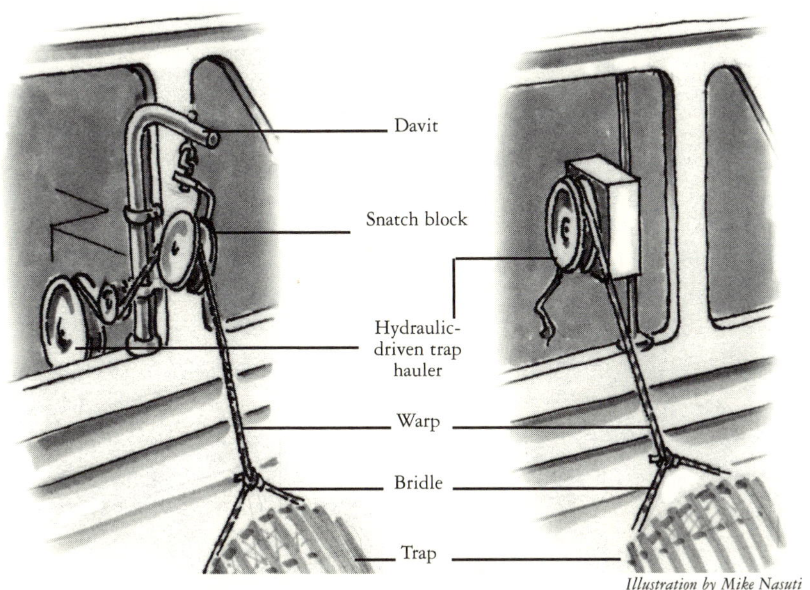


*Illustration by Mike Nasuti*

*Inner Lunt Harbor, early 1900s. Houses along ridge are: Hiram A. Lunt (left), Thomas B. Lunt, Leaman T. Davis, Nathan F. Osier, Hezekiah W. Lunt Jr., Rosanna Lunt.*

Island buoys, dried and repainted regularly, were generally made of fir until the 1950s, when cedar became more popular. Cedar, not a native wood on Long Island, came from other islands such as Bartlett Island in upper Blue Hill Bay.

To make a buoy, trees or limbs six to 12 inches in diameter were peeled, cut to length and carved. Some fisherman carved tapers into round buoys to create the traditional buoy shape. Others split larger trees and used semi-round buoys with one flat side. Shapes varied depending on available material, patience and personal preferences. The shapes ranged from short and squat, to long and narrow, to rectangular. Once carved, a staple or ring was driven into the end of each buoy so the rope could be attached.

In the 1950s, Dick Lunt bought his first turning lathe, a two-horsepower machine discarded by a metal shop. He set it up in the fishhouse he shared with his brother, Cecil E. Lunt. The family turned hundreds of buoys on that electric lathe for themselves and others.

For toggles — a float used between the buoy and the trap to keep the rope off the ocean bottom — fishermen often used water or beer bottles of various sizes. Fishermen often used two-quart bottles, which are more buoyant than one-quart bottles, in deeper water.

Yet another chore was making and mending trap "heads" and bait pockets. Heads are the mesh netting made of twine that is stretched across the ends of traps and forms the entrance to a trap on the side. Inside each trap, a mesh, funnel-shaped netting allows the lobster to move from the compartment with the bait to a second compartment called a "parlor." It is in the parlor that the lobster is trapped.

Some lobstermen nailed laths across the ends of each trap instead of netting, but they still needed the mesh heads on the side. A "bait pocket" is a mesh bag filled with bait, usually dead herring, to lure lobsters inside the trap.

A common sight in island homes during the first 75 years of the 20th century was a man or woman sitting in the kitchen with a string attached to the kitchen doorknob, pulling wooden needles and cotton twine around a "mash board" — a wooden block similar in shape to a harmonica — to make heads or pockets. Islanders sometimes held knitting bees at which eight or 10 people might gather at a house for ice cream and cake and to knit heads.

The chief problem with early twine was durability; cotton simply did not last in the ocean. It was treated, repaired, retreated and frequently replaced. Untreated heads lasted only a few months. Even when treated with hot coal tar, heads were changed or repaired every six months or so, usually at the same time that traps were taken up to dry and repair.

To treat heads, fishermen dipped them in hot coal tar before stringing them into traps. Stringing a head involved threading twine through the heads' end loops and wrapping it around the trap bow. When stringing heads men slathered their hands with lard to prevent tar from seeping into pores and to keep the heads from sticking to their hands.

Cotton bait pockets were dipped in coal tar for similar reasons. However, melted wax replaced tar as the treatment of choice for bait pockets.

The cotton rope used for warps was also treated. Properly coating rope usually required two men. One man used a notched stick to submerge the rope in a kettle or pot of heated coal tar. Another man, who wore wool mittens, used one hand to grip the rope at the edge of the pot. With the other hand he pulled the rope, thus pulling it through the other mitten-covered hand. The mitten removed the excess tar, let it drip back into the pot, and helped coat the rope. Like heads, cotton warps were retreated every five or six months and replaced every two years or so.

In the 1940s, pre-treated hemp, marlin and other more durable natural fibers replaced cotton. And by the 1950s and 1960s, even longer lasting synthetic materials such as nylon began to dominate. Synthetics, another advancement spurred by World War II, lasted longer and handled easier.

## Wooden Traps

In addition to the accessories, the hand-built wooden traps also required constant care.

Fishermen stacked wooden traps, usually made of spruce, onto their wharves to dry and repair two to three times per year. Fishermen often handled smaller jobs, like repairing a broken lath, while hauling. They typically kept a hammer, nails and laths on the boat for such quick jobs.

"You had to work on them all the time to keep them up," said Dick Lunt. "The laths were always breaking up and you had to patch them on the boat. It would be cold and you'd be wearing mittens and you would have to take the mittens off to patch the wet trap and then you would try to get warm again. And you couldn't leave them out a year or they would just fall apart."

More durable oak laths, purchased on the mainland, came on the scene in the 1940s and 1950s. The one disadvantage is that oak split more easily when pierced by a nail. Thus even oak laths were patched on the boat using the softer spruce laths. Some fishermen initially resisted oak, believing oak "soured" and didn't fish as well as spruce traps.

While fishermen typically used purchased, uniform-length laths to build traps, the other materials came almost exclusively from island trees. Those parts are: sills (the bottom runners of a trap), bows (which give the trap a half-round shape), rungs (which connect the two sills) and cleats (which are used to make the door).

"To make my first 50 traps when I started going on my own, in my own boat, I hauled everything out of the woods except for the laths," said John R. Lunt Jr., who started seriously lobster fishing in the 1940s.

To make those wooden traps, islanders cut fresh spruce limbs about one inch in diameter that could easily bend into half-round bows. One end of the green limb was pushed into a hand-bored hole in a trap sill. The limb was then bent so the other end was placed in a hole in the other sill. Each trap had three bows. Laths were nailed across the spruce bows.

To make a sill, fishermen cut trees or limbs of the approximate right diameter. They placed the limb in a vise to hold one end tight. Fisherman then cut down the limb or tree to the proper size — four or five inches in diameter — and squared it using a drawknife that they pulled toward them.

Outside of a shop used by Leonard "Nardy" Lunt, Irving "Pean" Lunt and other sons of William Sanford Lunt, shavings from trap sills and buoys sometimes stood six to seven feet high.

Most Long Island fishermen preferred the half-round wooden traps to square traps largely part because they were easier to make and in part because they didn't move as easily on the ocean bottom. However, all wooden traps moved, especially during storms, and were "stove-up" on the ocean floor, smashed on rocky beaches and ledges or snarled together in a tangle of traps, ropes and buoys.

"In them days there wasn't many traps going and there wasn't much money and any storm that come up, you might lose the works and have to go in the woods and start building all over again," said Dick Lunt.

Of course, small storms sometimes proved beneficial to small or young fishermen.

"I started when I was 10 (1948) with just a few traps around the harbor. The first year I had a rowboat and the next year I had a little air-cooled Lawson outboard that I put on it. I started out with maybe 25 traps right around the harbor," said David L. Lunt. "We used to go around the shore and pick up traps that people didn't want to bother with and patch those up. We also had some traps that the bigger fishermen didn't want and had discarded. We would patch those up too. The traps were good enough to fish inside and for us to haul by hand, but they weren't good enough to haul in boats. They wouldn't hold up.

"We also picked up old buoys and stuff around the shore. We used rope people had discarded and couldn't haul with the winch heads anymore. That is just about what everyone started out with — everyone my age."

Unfortunately, storms, which came with little warning were not always small. Back-to-back hurricanes in the early 1950s, devastated some fishermen. Following those hurricanes, so few traps remained in the water that fishing, for those able to haul, was extraordinary.

Together, brothers Dick Lunt and John R. Lunt Jr. were able to repair and bait up maybe 150 traps after the hurricanes. The first day out in John's boat, despite still-nasty weather, the brothers caught more than 1,200 pounds. Similar hauls followed.

While wooden trap design remained similar over the years, changes did occur. Early traps had mesh, funnel-like entrances at both ends of the trap and none on the side. Eventually, this was considered less effective because fishermen felt lobsters could more easily crawl out.

That trap was initially replaced by two styles: the scoot trap and the parlor trap. A scoot trap still had a mesh entrance in one end, and a parlor head in the middle, but the other end was closed.

Eventually, all styles gave way to the parlor trap. With a parlor trap, lobsters crawl to get bait through either of the two side openings. Once inside, lobsters crawl through a second, funnel-shaped mesh opening into a parlor compart-ment.

The greatest change in lobster traps during the past half-century has been the advent of wire.

Wire traps began to appear in Frenchboro in the late 1970s and achieved almost total dominance in the 1980s. Wire traps, which are square, provide numerous advantages.

*Photo by Ben S. Davis Jr.*

*Ben S. Davis Sr. hauling traps in the "Bennie Jr," 1960s. Ben built the boat himself, in his brother Grandville's boatshop, and launched it in 1944.*

They do not require as much repair, they do not require drying, they do not drift as easily, and are easier to stack.

They are also costly. In 1999, outfitting a single pair of traps — the most common fishing configuration in Blue Hill Bay — can cost from $85 to $100, including about $80 for two traps, $5 for rope, $5 for the buoy and toggle and $2 for bait pockets.

## The Modern Lobster Boat

The change to a modern lobster boat design on Long Island started in the 1930s when boats with smooth, sloping lines, a square stern and full pilot houses began to appear.

Perhaps the island's first large modern-style boat was a 42-footer owned by Clarence Howard. Howard, who originally came from Eagle Island, moved to Frenchboro after he met and married Alice Ross, a schoolteacher. Alice met Clarence while on Eagle Island, but she also taught school on Swans Island and Long Island.

Some older-style boats and a few with a more modern design were built on Long Island. The Davis family, which included several talented boat builders, were the most active in the trade.

Leaman T. "Leam" Davis, who died in 1938, built boats in his shop on the harbor's west side near the wharf owned in 1999 by Robert Roxby. He followed in the footsteps of his father, Capt. William Davis. Leam Davis once built an 18-foot boat on Mount Desert Rock, located about 15 miles from Long Island. Leam's son, Grandville "Sim" Davis, who became a well-

©*Peter Ralston, 1999*

*Warren "Pard" Higgins unloading lobsters from Old Habits onto Lunt & Lunt's lobster car, 1989.*

known boat builder in Bass Harbor, got his start while growing up on the island, likely under the tutelage of his father. Two of Leam's other sons, Elmer S. "Goog" Davis and Ben S. Davis Sr., also built boats.

In 1938, Dick Lunt, with some help from Goog, built his lobster boat from scratch in Leam Davis' boat shop. That year, Dick saved $300 to buy lumber and an engine. He hauled the wood down from Belfast in Clarence Howard's boat and then spent days and nights, when not fishing, building his boat. He launched the 36-foot-long, 10-foot-wide *David & Vivian* in January 1939, after nearly a year of construction. The *David & Vivian*, the second largest in the harbor at the time, plied local waters for more than 40 years.

Over the years, the average lobster boat grew larger and more powerful, but saw few dramatic changes until the 1970s when fiberglass boats arrived. Fiberglass boats are more durable and require less upkeep. The first based on Long Island was a 30-foot Repco owned by Russell Lunt in 1970. In 1975, Russell bought the 37-foot *Marty*.

During the later 1970s and early 1980s, the era of fiberglass boats emerged rapidly. Clarence Lunt bought the harbor's third fiberglass boat, the 36-foot *BR,* in the summer of 1977.

Also starting in 1977, four hulls were purchased and finished at the Lunt & Lunt wharf. They were: *Starburst*, a 36-foot Stanley hull for David W. Lunt in 1977; *Sandi*, a 33-foot Young Brothers hull for David L. Lunt in 1978; *Tina Marie*, a 31-foot Flye Point hull for Daniel L. Lunt in 1980; and *Old Habits*, a 31-foot Flye Point hull for Warren "Pard" Higgins in 1982.

The oldest classic wooden boat that remains active in Lunt Harbor is the 34-foot *Rebecca Jane*, owned by John R. Lunt Jr. It was launched in 1963.

The largest boat in Lunt Harbor today is David W. Lunt's second *Starburst*, launched in October 1989. It is 45 feet long and 15 feet wide, with a 324-horsepower Caterpillar engine. It cruises at about 13.5 knots.

Other large boats in the island's 1999 lobster fleet include: Daniel L. Lunt's 42-foot *Zachary Nathaniel*; Wyatt Beal's 37-foot *Lorena Fay*; Lewis Bishop's 38-foot *Provider*, Chuck Carl's 43-foot *Sea Walker*, and Chris Sawyer's 40-foot *Renegade*. The *Lorena Fay* is probably the island's fastest running boat, cruising at a brisk 18 to 20 knots.

## *Technology*

Numerous technological advancements have worked their way into the consumer market to make fishing easier.

In the early 1950s, the depth recorder, which provided a printout of ocean depths, helped fishermen find reefs, ledges and other lobster grounds. It also detected large schools of fish for seining.

Also in the 1950s came the ship-to-shore radio, a large, heavy, bulky machine that sent over-the-air signals. These machines also allowed boat operators to contact a marine operator in Boston, who could then patch calls into telephone lines. The 50- to 150-watt radios used by some Long Island boats could blast up and down the coast.

The ship-to-shore quickly became antiquated and the airwaves cluttered with noise from too many users. It gave way to the citizen's band (CB) radio in the 1960s and 1970s. CBs, smaller and less powerful, also became cluttered with static and gave way in the 1980s to the very high frequency (VHF) radio. VHF has more limited range but provides a much clearer signal.

In the 1970s and 1980s, radar became widely available, allowing boats to move easily and safely through thick fog. Until then, the compass reigned supreme.

Fishermen found traps and harbors using compasses and marks and tracking their running time in the fog. A foggy boat ride to Bass Harbor required captains to follow certain compass points and hit various marks. Since each boat had a unique cruising speed, each captain needed to track his individual running time between marks. Still, many a foggy ride saw passengers stationed on the bow peering into the thick fog trying to spot obstacles or land.

Depending on tides and other factors, Dick Lunt, in the *David & Vivian*, ran about five minutes at about 45 degrees to Crow Island Head; ran 12 to 14 minutes at 15 to 17 degrees to Rum Cove Point on Black Island; ran about six minutes at 45 degrees to the can buoy (off Gott Island) and then 12 to 14 minutes at 14 degrees to the old cold storage wharf just this side of the Bass Harbor ferry terminal.

When a captain was forced to run in from offshore with no set marks, a foggy boat ride could be doubly tricky. In the 1930s, Dick and Cecil Lunt might set hake trawls more than three miles offshore. Sometimes the fog rolled in.

"We were running in one day with Cecil," Dick Lunt said. "It was calm, and the boat — it was one of them open boats — was right full of fish. I was on bow peering in the fog and looking down to watch the water. All of a sudden I looked down and saw the bottom. I yelled 'Back up, back up,' and he come back on her hard. It was Johns Island ledge. We had to run back about 10 minutes and bring her down south to find Southwest Point Ledge before we could come in."

Today, the electronic revolution continues.

Radar systems, Loran systems, high-tech fish finders and other navigational devices are all common in today's boats.

## Other Businesses

The rise of lobster fishing spawned another small business: the lobster dealer. Local lobster dealers serve as middlemen between fishermen and larger regional dealers. Typically, a lobster dealer also offers other necessary services such as fuel, bait and basic supplies.

Leam Davis operated one of the first island businesses dedicated to buying lobsters. Leam moored his lobster car off the west side, near the wharf now owned by Lunt & Lunt Lobster Co. Leam sold his lobsters to Portland-based Willard & Daggett, which regularly collected lobsters in a dry well smack.

Frank W. "Scotty" Ross was another large lobster and fish dealer. He also sold fishing supplies and provided loans to fishermen. He operated on a wharf on the east side now used by Ross Giamo, his great-grandson. However, Frank's wharf was inaccessible during many tides so he moored his lobster car in the outer harbor. Frank died in 1948.

*Courtesy of Frenchboro Historical Society*
*Frank W. Ross (1870 - 1948)*

*The McLoon lobster smack leaving Lunt Harbor, 1972.*

Leonard A. "Nardy" Lunt, who also operated a general store, started Leonard A. Lunt Lobster Co. in 1928 and ran it until he died in 1964. Nardy bought lobsters from a smack moored in the outer harbor and sold his lobsters to A.C. McLoon of Rockland. Nardy's smack, *Adele McLoon*, was owned by McLoon and contained a wet well to store lobsters until another McLoon smack came to collect them.

Following Nardy's death, Lunt & Lunt and its predecessor, S.L. Lunt Lobsters, became the principal island lobster business and remains so today.

Lunt & Lunt is now the longest-running business in the island's history. Dick Lunt, Nardy's nephew, started S.L. Lunt in 1951. During that first summer, 41-year-old Dick bought lobsters from his boat. He stored them in floating wooden crates that he strung along a rope tied to a mooring. He kept a set of scales aboard his boat to weigh lobsters. He built a lobster car that fall and continued to expand his business.

That first summer, Dick paid fishermen 17 cents per pound and sold them to Morris Rich in Bass Harbor for 18 cents.

Dick's son, David L. Lunt, now runs Lunt & Lunt and has been a principal in the company since about 1958. Dick's wife, Vivian (Davis) Lunt, controlled the company's finances for more than 40 years.

For a few years in the 1950s, Vivian also worked on the lobster car. Each morning she rowed to the car and spent the day buying lobsters from fishermen. Skiff fisherman usually started to sell their catch at about 9 a.m. while larger fishermen started to sell by mid- to late-afternoon. Vivian, who rowed back in for lunch, passed the idle time crocheting squares for tablecloths.

Vivian's sister, Lillian (Davis) Lunt, who married Dick's brother, Cecil, also bought lobsters in the 1950s. She supplemented that income by making coffee and cakes and pastries to sell to fishermen.

Robert A. Lunt and Carroll W. Lunt, two brothers, also worked for Dick in the 1950s.

"I bought lobsters for Dick the whole time I was in high school," said Robert Lunt, whom Dick also helped get started as a lobsterman. "I bought them on the lobster car off the harbor for one cent on a pound. I think I also got one cent for every gallon of fuel I sold. I also used to go with him in an old island scow to get rocks. We used to go over to Harbor Island almost every morning when the tide was right, and we would load that scow up with rocks. We would tow it back over to fill in the [Lunt & Lunt] abutment down there."

Following Nardy's death, Dick began selling his lobsters to McLoon, whose white smack remained a common sight in Lunt Harbor into the 1970s.

In 1999, Lunt & Lunt sells its lobsters to City Fish of Sorrento, Maine. Lobsters are now shipped in crates to Bass Harbor and loaded into trucks.

## Haking

While lobstering has been the island's most consistent industry for decades, supplementary fishing endeavors such as haking and seining have taken place during the past 50 years.

Haking or tub trawling, was an important, although not especially lucrative, business prior to the 1940s.

"You didn't get much out of it really," Dick Lunt said. "Just enough to live on."

Hake were caught using fish trawls that were usually set three to five miles off the backshore of Long Island. Upwards of 50 to 60 boats, including six or so from Frenchboro, fished at any one time in the area. Haking season typically ran during May, June and July. One tub contained a trawl with about 800 hooks. A fishing trawl is a length of rope with hooks set at regular intervals. A typical trawl, which usually had eight sections of rope spliced together, was about 400 fathoms or 3,000 feet long. Dick Lunt and other Long Island hakers typically set eight to 10 trawls. Dick left at about 2:00 or 3:00 a.m. to set his trawls, a process that took about two hours or so. A short time later, they ran back to the begin-

*Courtesy of Lillian J. Lunt/Photo by Frank Mancuso*
*Cecil E. Lunt (1914 - 1992) baiting a halibut fishing trawl. An old hake trawl had more hooks, closer together, than a halibut trawl.*

ning and began hauling the trawls. It took several hours to haul back what amounted to roughly five to seven miles of line with 8,600 to 10,000 hooks.

"It was hard work, and if it was rough you would get chop (rough seas) breaking on your back sometimes," said Dick Lunt. "It took maybe five hours to haul them all back by hand. If you got a lot of cusk, which puffed up with air quickly while on the hook, you could look out a half mile or so and see them flipping on top of the water."

Dick sometimes fished with his brothers Cecil or Clarence Lunt or with Clarence Howard. Dick and Cecil's largest hauls were in the 5,000-pound range. They sold their fish for two to three cents per pound. Five thousand pounds at three cents per pound amounts to about $150 before expenses for a 12-15 hour day. Dick and Cecil split that two ways.

In the early years, Dick and Cecil loaded fish into the 26- to 30-foot open boats common to the era. The only shelter was a small spray hood.

Among the largest single catches on Long Island was one by Herman Anderson, who came in from Mount Desert Rock one afternoon with about 10,000 pounds. He had about 5,000 pounds of hake and 5,000 pounds of cod, with no cod weighing less than 50 pounds, according to Dick. Herman Anderson, who married Emily "Bud" Thurlow, was later injured in a heartbreaking fishing accident. While he was fishing in the waters between Long Island and Mount Desert Rock, Herman's leg became caught in a fishing winch. In order to save his life, he was forced to cut off his own leg between the knee and the thigh with either an axe or a knife. Another fishermen found Herman's boat circling pilotless as Herman lay on the platform, and he towed it into Southwest Harbor.

Over the years, island fishermen sold fish either to local wharves such as the one run by Clarence McIntire; or to boats from Southwest Harbor or Bass Harbor; or they ran into Southwest Harbor to sell.

"The haking routine was this," said Ben Davis Jr., whose father went haking. "Around midnight they would leave the island to go off outside and set the trawls. My father used to run eight tubs — I think that is about five miles. They would set that, and then by daylight they would run back to the first end and start hauling. They'd haul until they hauled it all back and got whatever they got for fish. They would come in here and drop off the trawls so the baiters could rebait them for the next day, and then they would strike out for Southwest Harbor to sell the fish."

Fishermen rarely baited hooks themselves given the time constraints.

"You would find anyone who wanted to bait them and drop off the tubs. We paid 50 cents and later a $1 per tub. In them days, a lot of people needed that money," said Dick Lunt.

Island women, who rarely fished, often baited the hake lines. Baiters placed herring on each of the 800 hooks per tub and coiled the trawl so it could easily be set.

"Some of the men used to bait trawls, but mainly it was the women. My mother and a lot of the women at the time used to bait for several different people who went fishing; like my father, Ebbit (Dalzell) and Tommy Lunt and even Herman Lunt," said Ben Davis Jr.

As a young girl in the 1920s, Vivian Lunt used to baby-sit her sister Lillian while their mother, Valeria Davis, baited trawls.

"In my mother's generation, a lot of women baited trawls," said

*Hauling seine, 1940s or 50s. Ralph Stanley (left), Clarence Lunt, George Francis and Sanford L. "Dick" Lunt.*

Vivian. "I even baited a few. Ebbit used the wharf that used to be Clarence Howard's. We used to bait down there, Nora {Lunt} and I and a few others. That was before we had two cents to put over our eyes. I didn't like to do it and I was slow, but I did in the beginning because it was a way to make money. No matter how careful you were you would get one of those hooks in the end of your finger and oh, the hook was just like poison. As soon as Dick started seining and making a little money, I gave that business up."

## Seining

Indeed, in the late 1930s and early 1940s, seining for herring emerged as an important fishing industry into the early 1960s. Seining played a crucial role in bringing the island out of it decades-long depression.

"When Dick got on to seining with Clarence Howard, he was able to make a little money," said Vivian Lunt. "They got in down to Marshalls Island and the herring were so thick you could almost walk on them. He was lucky with seining. He could not have made that kind of money anywhere else, doing anything else." After he started seining in 1939, Dick Lunt never set another hake trawl.

During its height in the 1940s and 1950s, islanders shut off — trapped — fish in coves as far away as Marshall Island, North Haven and Vinalhaven. Seiners during that era included: Dick Lunt, Cecil Lunt, Clarence Howard, Ben Davis Sr., Ben Davis Jr., Tommy Lunt Jr., Willard Osier, Charlie Hooper and Ralph Stanley. Some island fishermen also worked with the Quinns of Eagle Island.

The various seining outfits also shut off such places as Western, Southern and Eastern Cove on Long Island, Popplestone, Sand and Bauxham Cove on Marshall Island, and Toothaker, Irish Point Cove and Fine Sand Beach on Swans Island.

Perhaps the largest single catch came at Marshall Island in the 1950s when after seven days and nights the crew had taken out roughly 100,000 bushels of herring, according to Dick.

Seining season ran from May to November. It wasn't always easy to find the fish.

During daylight hours, herring usually remain dispersed in deeper water, but as darkness falls they move to the surface to feed and then run toward coves. Fishermen generally went looking for fish near dark. As darkness fell, the boats would sail along slowly and watch for the fish to "fire the water." They also searched using spotter planes to detect them from above, or used "fathometers" to detect them underwater. Sometimes they just watched and listened.

"They would come to the surface, and especially if it was calm, you could see and hear a flipping of the fish breaking the surface of the water," said Ben Davis Jr. "If there was a big body of them, they would give off an oil which you could smell."

Once the fish were found and had swum into a cove, the seining operation started. In seining, a net, or running twine, is set from one side of a cove to the other from the "net boat." Lead weights keep the twine down, while cork on the top line keeps it from sinking. During the 1950s, the deepest running twine used was typically 10 fathoms or 60 feet. The running twine was sometimes tied to trees on either side of the coves.

Outside of the running twine, a pocket seine is set. The pocket, which also touches the ocean bottom, is usually 80 to 100 fathoms long but is run in a square with one side touching the running twine. The "holding net" is laced to the running twine as it is let out of the dory.

After the pocket is set, the section where the running twine and the pocket twine touch is sunk so the trapped fish can swim into the pocket. This usually happens near daylight when fish try to leave the cove.

When enough fish have swum into the pocket, the lines are refloated. It can be a touchy business. If too many fish swim into the pocket at one time, they can smother each other.

Also inside the pocket is the seine boat, usually a dory, loaded with yet another mesh net called the "purse seine." The purse seine is used to actually gather the fish.

The purse seine, similar to a volleyball net with a loose middle, is set around the fish. The purse seine has rings on the bottom and a drawstring. When the drawstring is pulled, it gathers the bottom of the netting like a purse and sweeps the fish toward the larger boat.

Once an amount of fish is pulled in, the fish are scooped out using dip nets or a mechanical scoop. Eventually, the fish were pumped directly into a large sardine carrier. That process of pumping fish also removed fish scales. These scales were then gathered and sold to cosmetic companies as "Pearlessence." The removal process is repeated until all fish are funneled from the cove into the pocket into the purse seine and finally into a boat.

The seining boom died in the 1960s and has enjoyed only sporadic revivals on Long Island, most notably in the late 1970s when Clarence Lunt operated a small outfit.

Over the years, a handful of other fishing industries have also come and gone, or remain only a fraction of their former size. These endeavors include scallop dragging, clamming, shrimping, gill netting, hand-lining for codfish and setting halibut trawls.

Most fisheries were relatively short-lived, cyclical and at best supplementary. Because of severe overfishing and other problems, none ever could sustain an entire community.

*Photo by Pamela Pierce*

*Unloading fish, 1964. Cecil E. Lunt (left) and Clarence Lunt.*

Indeed, without the rise and sustainability of lobsters, Long Island certainly would have met the same fate as the quarrying islands and the farming islands that died long ago, which now sit as vacant island relics or as the summer playgrounds and exclusive preserves of the rich.

## Island Memories

"I started fishing as soon as I was big enough. I started with my father [Wallace Lunt]; I just sat in the bow of the skiff to make it row a little easier. That is all he ever had was a skiff. He did get an outboard the last few years.

"When I was about 11 or 12, I found an old skiff down there. I patched it up. It still leaked bad, but I put in laths and timbers and stuff and set a few traps out.

"When I got out of the service in December of '55, Doonie sold me a skiff; he had two. He sold it to me for $100 and he threw in, like 20 traps and buoys and stuff. He was helping me get started really. Then Dick said, 'If you want to fish for me, I'll help you get started.' He went over to the bank before me and talked to them. Then I went over and I said 'Dick Lunt said I could get money here to get me a motor,' and they said 'If he said you could have money for a motor, you can have it.' And that is when I got started, really.

"I went lobstering with Cecil, Dick, Clarence and John over the years while growing up and then when I stayed there and worked later. I can remember, especially Cecil, would give me $5 on each hundred pounds he got. He

*Courtesy Vivian D. Lunt*

*Robert A. Lunt (boy, left), Vincent A. Davis, Wallace L. Lunt and Elmer Lunt, 1940s.*

always had that Republican pocketbook, I called it, with the two snaps. One side had change. He always paid me every night. I would go up to Lillian's to play cards and have ice cream and get paid. He would get 200 or 300 pounds on a really good day. We would go out the west'ard until noontime, come in, get lunch and then go to the east'ard."

Carroll W. Lunt, born 1933

"I used to do wash all day on an scrub board for a dollar and then I would wash floors for a dollar. I used to paint Cliff's boats, paint his punts, paint his buoys and paint his trawl tubs. I used to bait his trawls too, and God, I used to work down there on the wharf cold enough to freeze the hair off your head. I wouldn't give in; I stayed right there.

"I used to bait trawls — hake trawls — for Bennie Davis and Robbins Dalzell too. I got paid 50 cents per tub. There used to be eight lines of twine and hooks in a tub.

"I tell you, I have worked. It has not been all a pleasurable life. It has been rugged, but I don't regret a day of it, not one day. I feel proud of myself for what I did." — Ella V. Lunt, born 1908.

"When I got home from my freshman year in high school, my dad had built the punt that I still have. And that first year we rowed in it. My mother, the dog and me used to row out and tend some of my father's traps.

By the time the season was well under way, I had about 40 traps out. Then when I got

*Courtesy Ella V. Lunt*

*Malcolm Lunt (left) and Ella V. Lunt, 1926.*

home from school the second year, my father had put an inboard engine in the punt. It had a four-cylinder Arnold in the center of the boat. I used that for the next three years. Then after my senior year in high school, they already had fish over at Marshalls Island when I came home; so I just caught a ride over with one of the carriers from Underwoods."

— Ben Davis Jr., born 1935

286

*Chapter Fourteen*
# 20th Century Milestones

## An Island Personality and Heritage

The major events in the life of a village — formation, first church, first school — are relatively easy to chronicle. The subtleties prove more elusive. Every region, sometimes every town, has language, customs and rhythms that help define it although over the decades many differences have been erased, in part by television and in part by increased mobility.

I spent 12 years, living throughout New England and attending college in upstate New York, and any distinctly Maine accent I once had has been largely obliterated although I still speak too quickly, and occasionally a colloquialism or two sneaks out.

However, much from Frenchboro's past remains either in my memory or in actual practice. Some sayings and customs are unique to Frenchboro, some to islands, some to the coast, some to Maine, some to New England and some to an English heritage. How else to explain the Lunt family's addiction to vinegar? Cider vinegar, of course, preferably Heinz, not some yuppiefied balsamic offshoot.

In this vein, I asked a lot of questions while writing this book. Not only of other people, but also of myself. Like what really matters? What everyday events, what sayings, what customs really matter in the course of a life or an island?

Photo by Pamela Pierce

*Summer Picnic at the Salt Ponds, 1970.*

And what effect did this have on me and other islanders?

Does it matter that I spent a childhood building rafts out of logs, driftwood, and Styrofoam buoys to float in the Salt Ponds?

That I pretended seagrass was lobsters and beach rocks tied to string and a stick were lobster traps?

Does it matter that Uncle Cecil whittled propellers from trap laths for airplanes and windmills?

That I think dried codfish and goose grass greens are two of the best foods on the planet? And that dried fish, baked potato and stewed tomatoes make a fine supper?

That I picked dandelion greens at Syracuse University and cooked them with salt pork to prove to my New Jersey and Massachusetts friends that they weren't just weeds?

That my grandmother goes "tipping" for spruce boughs and "greening" for dandelions?

And that when she finishes she usually has a "mess a greens" that are "some good?"

That I know "Oh, sugar" is a swear word?

That I started lobster fishing at 8 using my dad's beaten-up wooden traps and the leaky 13-foot skiff he had first passed down to my brother?

That I translated Gramp Dick's colloquialisms and accent for high school and college girlfriends?

That I ate Ella Lunt's homemade popcorn balls and bobbed for apples in an old metal tub every Halloween?

That Gram Vivian constantly yelled at us to "get off the church lawn?"

That Tony, Kurt, Jimmy and I spent most summer nights sleeping under the stars at "The Head" and the Salt Ponds and the Grove and Whale Beach?

And we brought pepperoni sticks, Pop Tarts and Suzie Qs to complement a bag or two of green apples?

That I was once the only student in my K-8 island school?

That my grandmother saved Country Kitchen bread bags, and actually used them as mailbags or storage bags for picnic lunches?

That we sang Christmas carols in school and put-up an honest-to-gosh Christmas tree right next to the blackboard?

*Photo by Pamela Pierce*

*Halloween at the Parish House, 1972. Back row: Steve Day (left), David W. Lunt, Dale Bergeron, Sandra Lunt, Paul "Rusty" Crossman and Rebecca Lunt.*
*Front Row: Tim Bergeron, Kevin Lunt, Karen Lunt, Ralph Lunt, Dean Lunt, Bobbi Jo Lunt.*

That my grandfather eats fish spawns for meals and actually wants the gizzard, neck and heart at Thanksgiving?

That old fishermen taught me industrial-strength swear words at 5?

That my grandfather says "bom-by" for later and "nigh on" for near?

That to open Christmas presents was to "pick the tree" and that we bought "fancy work" at the annual church fair?

That I roamed the island countryside at 4 or 5 years old?

That I know a sea urchin is really a "whore's egg?"

That I dug clams with a clam hoe, not a clam rake, and put them in clam hod or a clam roller, not a clam basket?

That I've patiently listened to wealthy people in quarter-million-dollar yachts and rowing thousand-dollar dinghies complain how they paid 10 cents less per pound for lobsters at the next island over?

That I know what birds and dumplings are? And I don't eat them?

That my 91-year-old great great Aunt Ella always wishes she had "a mess a fish heads" to eat whenever I see her?

That I know fishermen aren't all wizened old sages?

And that I know old fishermen aren't all backward, country bumpkins either?

That my mother lugged water in pails when her first two children were infants?

Photo by Sandra Lunt

*Dean L. Lunt (left), Daniel L. Lunt and David W. Lunt at a Pond Island picnic, around 1969.*

That I still ask questions such as "Where are you going to?" and "Where did you get that at?"

That burning grass is a glorious spring ritual?

That we celebrated the Fourth of July on other islands with steamed clams and watermelon?

That we celebrated May Day and decorated the cut-off bottoms of milk cartons for baskets?

That I have played cribbage and rummy at my grandmother's kitchen table? And Uno and Mille Bourne and Hearts with great aunt Lillian?

That I have been rousted from island apple trees?

That I know what "good weather clouds" look like?

That I know when it is "colder than a witch's tit?"

That my grandparents grew up "poor as church mice?"

That I have watched the bow plunge under heavy seas and felt the boat shudder when it bottomed out?

That I have been lost in fog on the open ocean?

That I have made "bailers" for my skiff out of Clorox bottles?

That I knew "Gotts Island blue" paint was jinxed?

That I know what "a Jonah" is?

That I know fishermen use bait pockets, not bait bags; that you fish lobster traps, not lobster pots; that you eat "Scollops," not Scallops; and that it is Mount "Dessert," not Mount Desert?

That I know Maine extends beyond Greater Portland?

That I know Amazin' Grace is the most popular island church hymn of all time? And it sounds just fine even with 12 people singing off key?

That I know dulse from kelp and have roamed the shore looking for it? And then have chased white-tailed deer from the clothesline when they tried to steal some?

That it can be a long walk "over the hill a piece?"

That an island is sometimes a lonely place in the dead of February?

That I used skiffs, punts and rowboats, not dinghies and tenders?

That I know when it is "blowin' a gale" or what damage a "raking" wind can cause? And that a big storm is a "christa?"

That hot dogs — Jordan's red hot dogs — taste best when stuck on the end of whittled alder branches and cooked over burning driftwood?

That I have eaten rice and raisins as a meal? (Not often.)

That I know how cold it can be going to the bathroom over a hole cut in the wharf when the winds of December are blowing?

That you need to really want spruce gum to make it through the first 20 minutes of chewing?

That traps get "stove up" in storms?

That to reduce in numbers is to "limb 'em up?"

That I know when someone is "numma than a pounded thumb?"

Or that a poor hunter or baseball player can't "hit the broadside of a barn?" Or even "hit a bull in the ass with a barn shovel," for that matter?

That virtually any four-letter vulgarity can be combined with the word "head" and applied to a person?

That some people are just "crazier than a shithouse rat?"

That I put vinegar on ham shoulder, corn beef, beef stew, French fries and steamed clams? And that is just to start?

That I understand legitimate debate exists whether Saltines or Royal Lunch is the proper cracker for a meal of crackers and milk?

And that my grandmother still eats crackers — Royal Lunch — and milk every week?

That some people simply deserve a "kick in the ass with a frozen boot?"

And that sometimes, when the road is "glare ice," you might just "fall ass over teakettles?"

That you should always be wary of "state men" or "men from the state?"

Especially if they are from that "damn LURC" or the "damn DEP?"

That a true fathom is the distance between two outstretched arms?

That you patch lobster traps, you don't repair or fix them?

That on an island you can always count on an afternoon breeze to cool off a hot summer day?

That most places are either to the East'ard or the West'ard?

That you "shock" scallops, you don't shuck them?

That a legal-sized lobster is a "counter?"

That a lobster with no claws is a "pistol?"

That Ken Curtis was the state's best governor because he actually visited Frenchboro?

That I have gotten warm sitting on the engine box next to a glowing red, tinfoil-wrapped exhaust pipe inside the pilothouse? And then stepped into the cold to escape the stifling heat?

That when tired, I have gone to my grandmother's to "sit a spell?"

Does all this make me a better person? No.

Singularly, most of this is trivial. Sometimes it is stereotyped, or pegged as "quaint." But what it all means singularly is irrelevant.

Collectively, it is a heritage.

And that is important.

◆

*Lunt & Lunt Lobster Co. wharf, 1980s. The BR is docked at the wharf and the Starburst is running along Western Point.*

# The Milestones

In the sweeping 200-year history of Long Island, islanders' most crucial attributes have been perseverance, dedication and character.

Often, islanders lacked the basic amenities already enjoyed by mainland residents for years, if not decades. And while not necessarily missed, each advancement did change life immeasurably, often for the better — or at least for the easier. Many improvements have proven important for long-term island survival.

## *From Island Outpost to Town*

In 1840, roughly two decades after permanent settlement, Long Island and several nearby islands were organized into Long Island Plantation, thus establishing the political structure that lasted for 139 years. For a one-year span — 1857 to 1858 — the islands were officially incorporated as the town of Islandport. Initial township status was likely abandoned because it was more costly to residents.

In the late 1970s, the islands permanently became a town, largely to escape oversight by the Land-use Regulation Commission, better known as LURC. LURC is a state agency that guides and controls development in the unorganized territories and plantations. Islanders basically did not want LURC dictating what to build or where. Although it is more expensive to operate as a town, such status created increased self-control and greater self-government.

The original post office was named Frenchboro in honor of E. Webster French in the 1890s, and the village quickly adopted the name as well. Over the years, Frenchboro has sometimes been incorrectly used as both the name of the village and of the island itself.

In fact, the town of Frenchboro in 1999 encompasses Long Island, Harbor Island, Crow Island, Eastern and Western Sister Islands, the two Green Islands, Drum Island, Little and Great Duck Island, Black Island, Placentia Island, Pond Island and Mount Desert Rock.

At one time, Long, Great Duck, Black, Placentia and Pond were all inhabited. Today, Long Island is the only island with a year-round community. Three other islands have at least one summerhouse, while Great Duck and Mount Desert Rock have automated lighthouses.

## U.S. Postal Service

For about 70 years after settlement, no island post office existed. Mail, carried by residents or visitors, came irregularly from Tremont or Swans Island via rowboats, sloops and schooners.

Even as the island became an organized plantation in 1840, and saw its population soar past 150 by mid-decade, an actual post office remained years away.

Specific details about the post office's formation are not known. It is likely that islanders felt a community need and formally petitioned the federal government. An interested Tremont lawyer, E. Webster French, aided their efforts. French ultimately gave the post office, the village and later the town its name.

By 1883, French lived in Bass Harbor as the first practicing lawyer on the western side of Mount Desert Island, according to Nellie C. Thornton in *Traditions and Records of Southwest Harbor and Somesville.* During the ensuing years he developed ties to Long Island either via sailing, or simply because islanders occasionally needed his services. In the early 1880s, French helped Joseph Warren Lunt obtain a Civil War disability pension.

At some point, French agreed to help islanders maneuver through the legal and regulatory maze necessary to establish a post office with apparently one condition: name the post office after him. The islanders obviously obliged his request. When the post office opened in the early 1890s, it carried the name Frenchboro.

The first island postmaster was Sylvester Morse. However, mail service remained irregular, arriving only a few times each week and less frequently during winter. Outgoing mail went to Swans Island and then to Rockland via steamship.

Early mail carriers included: Henry Whitfield "Whit" Lunt, Walter Robinson, Clinton B. Teel, Charles Lunt, Glendon Lunt, James H. Thurlow, Alexander P. "Alec" Davis, Milton "Robbins" Dalzell and Willard K. Osier.

Postmasters and postmistresses have included: Morse, Sophronia "Toni" Teel, William Van Norden, Franklin E. Gilman, Eugene Van Norden, Vera (Kelley) Van Norden, Raymond Teel and Norma (Lunt) Teel. The longest serving postmasters were Eugene Van Norden from 1929 to 1953 and Norma Teel from 1972 to 1997. Lorena (Lenfestey) Beal was named postmistress in the summer of 1998.

*Courtesy of Marjorie D. Giamo*

*Vera and Eugene Van Norden, 1950s*

Because the post office has always been located either in a resident's house or combined with a general store, it has relocated depending on the postmaster or postmistress.

Morse kept the first post office in the building now owned by Ben Davis Jr. for about three years. He then moved it to the wharf owned in 1999 by Marjorie (Dalzell) Giamo. He used the top of the building as his house and the bottom as a post office and store.

The post office was also located next to the William and Hortense (Lunt) Van Norden home. The building, later owned by Eugene and Vera Van Norden, is now owned by Harold and Evelyn Burr.

Frank Gilman kept the post office in his house, a workshop owned by William Sanford Lunt, and a building at the foot of Brook Hill. Frank served as postmaster between William Van Norden and his son Eugene.

Norma Teel kept the post office in her house, the old Israel B. Lunt homestead, from 1972 to 1997. Lorena Beal keeps the post office at her house.

Over the years, the post office has served as an important community gathering spot, while the mail service has provided somewhat regular, although often roundabout, transportation.

Mail service also emerged as a way for islanders to import goods — especially with the early-20th-century rise of mail order catalogs such as Sears and Montgomery Ward. Vivian Lunt remembers purchasing nearly everything from clothing to kitchen stoves via catalogs during the 1930s and 1940s. Before World War II, large items came from Rockland via steamship to Swans Island and then to Frenchboro via mail boat.

Verna "Bunny" (Mitchell) Dobson said many goods and supplies, including fruits and vegetables, sold in her mother's (Jen Mitchell) store, arrived via mail boat.

Mail service finally began a daily schedule in the 1920s, only increasing the post office's role as a central gathering place while the daily mail was sorted and handed out.

During World War II, steamboat service from Rockland was discontinued. Frenchboro's mail then came from Rockland to Stonington via Barter's Express, then to Swans Island and Frenchboro on private boats.

The mail route changed again in 1952 when the mail contract was awarded to the passenger ferry *SeaWind*. The *SeaWind* provided a direct mail route from Bass Harbor to Frenchboro. The route changed again in 1961 when the *SeaWind* was discontinued. Mail service again took a Bass Harbor to Swans Island to Frenchboro route via the Maine State Ferry Service and a private contractor.

In 1999, Paul Joy of Swans Island delivers the mail from Swans Island.

## *Electricity*

Electricity finally came to Long Island on March 19, 1956 after an underwater power cable was laid from Duck Cove on Swans Island to Lunt Harbor.

Before that electrical cable, only a handful of islanders enjoyed any type of electricity and then only by using a large and work-intensive system of batteries and generators.

Indeed, island life revolved around candles, kerosene lamps, wood stoves and hand-dug wells long after many mainlanders enjoyed indoor plumbing, refrigerators and television.

At the schoolhouse, a janitor, often a student, lit wood fires each morning before school to warm the building. Sometimes when the wind came from the Southwest, or when mischief-inclined students blocked a stove pipe, smoke rolled back into the school forcing the teacher to either cancel school or suffer through an uncomfortable few hours.

At the church, a janitor lit fires in the basement long before scheduled services, while kerosene lamps hung from the chapel ceiling for night programs. Local residents cut and split wood for both institutions.

"I was janitor as soon as I got big enough. I kept the fire going in the morning," said Carroll W. Lunt. "I had to be there early enough to take care of it. We had a woodstove out in the middle with a big frame around it. In the winter, I got there probably an hour and a half before school started. Even then when school first started everyone was standing around the stove trying to get warm. You had to start the fire, split the wood and cut it. There was a woodshed out back of the schoolhouse, we fixed the wood right there."

Local power arrived for a few residents in the late 1940s. In 1947, Sanford L. "Dick" Lunt and Cecil E. Lunt built a battery-operated personal power plant on the wharf below the Joseph Warren Lunt homestead. Their power plant consisted of 56 two-volt batteries and a gas-powered generator that ran five or six hours per day to charge those batteries. Cables carried the current from the wharf to the old homestead and then up to houses owned by Dick and Cecil.

Any appliance operating on that system, whether tools or lights or radios, had to be converted to DC power. The power supply was insufficient to operate water pumps or other devices. The last person to bed each night walked to the wharf and turned off the plant.

During the same era, Willard K. Osier owned a 32-volt generator that also supplied DC power, while Clarence Howard owned one that supplied his house and that of Vera and Milton Dalzell. The Van Nordens also owned a small generator.

Ben Davis Sr. operated a small generator that supplied him with AC power, meaning he did not need to convert his appliances to DC. Lillian and Ben Davis ran a washer and spin dryer and small appliances such as a coffee maker on the system. However, the charge was relatively short-lived, so the Davises walked out on the wharf to start the generator when they needed power and out again to turn it off.

By this time, the mainland and neighboring Swans Island enjoyed increasingly important electrical power. Soon, plans were under way to supply this staple of modern life to Frenchboro. In 1953, islanders met with Nelson White, president of the Swans Island Electric Co-Op, and a federal representative, to discuss running an underwater cable from Swans Island to Lunt Harbor.

Most island families became co-op members. After three years of delays, a $40,000 loan financed the project, and workers began clearing trees and land, setting poles and stringing wire.

The project was completed in 1956, and the first lights were turned on March 18. Raymond Teel, who lived on Western Point, was the first person to have electricity in his house that Sunday. The next day, electricity circled the island. The lights were officially dedicated July 12.

## Running Water

Even into the early 1960s, some houses had no running water.

One concern of state welfare officials when they were first considering whether to place foster children on the island in 1964 was the lack of inside rest rooms at the school.

Some houses still had an outhouse or used a "slop pail" for a toilet, a situation not uncommon in many rural mainland towns. Slop pails were dumped into the harbor. Even after inside plumbing arrived in the 1960s, some houses essentially ran straight pipes into the harbor instead of building septic systems, and some houses still used slop pails. Meanwhile, men at their

*Photo by Sandra Lunt*

*David L. Lunt hauling water from the well during the winter of 1959. He used the axe to break away the ice.*

wharf workshops simply cut holes in the floor and built a small box for a toilet. They nailed on a toilet seat for added comfort. Houses built over the harbor utilized the same type of system.

Water was another story.

For years the so-called "Wes well," named after Wesley Lunt, was a primary well on the west side. It was located on the harbor side of the road just up from where John and Rebecca Lunt's house now sits. During winter, islanders carried an axe to chop out ice to access the water beneath. Various other wells were dug for water, although some were used only for washing and not drinking. The wells often went dry during the summer.

On the east side, the main well was "the spring," located below Marjorie Giamo's house. Actually, many islanders used that natural spring at one time or another even into the 1980s. Islanders buried a tiled reservoir in the ground there to collect water. Marjorie's parents also had a well in their basement which typically did not freeze up during the winter.

A well dug in the 1950s above Lillian and Cecil Lunt's house supplied water to three houses down the hill. They used a pipe and gravity to run water down the hill and into their houses. With no electricity, there were still no pumps.

When David L. and Sandra Lunt were married in 1958, most people still lugged water. Many island families kept a bowl and ladle in the kitchen, and people dipped out a glassful when they wanted a drink.

Sandra, even with a new house and two infants by 1960, lugged water from a hand-dug well on the west side. With the arrival of electricity and then ferry service in the 1960s, many families quickly had artesian wells drilled.

## Town Roads

For decades, roads on Long Island were essentially footpaths that circled the harbor in much the same location as the paved road does today. The paths were wide enough to accommodate animals and carts. Other paths ran from the main harbor to the backshores, including Richs Head and other major coves and points.

No road existed around the head of the cove, which was basically a swamp area. Instead, a wooden bridge ran from near the house owned in 1999 by Myron and Sarah Lenfestey across to the church.

A shorter wooden bridge, not replaced until 1948, spanned the brook just below Marjorie Giamo's house at the foot of Brook Hill.

In the 1800s, islanders levied a $1 tax on all male residents to maintain the roads. Any male could avoid the tax by working on the roads for one day each year.

Toward the end of the 19th century, the island grew more serious about its road system. In 1883, George R. Rich, the Civil War veteran, was elected the first road surveyor. In 1884, the town raised $40 to cover road costs.

In 1885, William J. Teel was elected surveyor. The town raised an additional $10 for Teel to lay out plantation roads. To cover expenses, the per-male road tax was raised to $2.

As the 1900s rolled along, roads continued to improve. When the Great Depression throttled the nation, Maine provided money for so-called state aid roads using local labor. Construction of the one-mile island road started in 1934 and took six years to complete.

Building the road required slow, often grueling labor with no aid from heavy construction equipment. Essentially, islanders used a pick and shovel to cross sand, rock and ledge. In places, they blasted ledge with dynamite. It was painstaking labor. For example, the stretch of road from the house owned by in 1999 by James and Susan Miller past the David L. Lunt house was mostly ledge.

Construction required three-man teams. One man held a long rod that served as a drill bit with four cutting edges. While he held the rod, two other men took turns hitting it with a sledgehammer. After each blow the man holding the rod rotated it a quarter turn. Each day, using that method, the men bored 6 to 10 holes deep enough for dynamite.

In 1938, a road was built around the head of Lunt Harbor, replacing the old dam. With the new road in place, islanders tore down the bridge near the church. Clarence Howard used the top to plank his wharf. Posts from the old bridge are still visible at low tide.

In 1948, the town built a branch road to Everett E. "Ebbit" Dalzell's house, owned in 1999 by Richard Hamblen Jr.

In 1964, the "high road" was completed. That road ran up Schoolhouse Hill, looped parallel to the lower road, and reconnected with the main road near Marjorie Giamo's house. It encompassed the spur road built in 1948.

Over the years other road construction has included: a turnaround near Western Point; a road to the Salt Ponds in 1969 (now restored to a private

*The old bridge across from the Frenchboro Congregational Church prior to 1937. House at left belonged to Charles and Asenath Wallace, house at right beloned to H.E.S. "Kai" Lunt.*

path); and a road to Gooseberry Point built by Ben Davis Jr. in 1965.

The island's other roads, including those to Eastern Beach, Beaver Pond, Southwest Point and Richs Head, are old logging roads built during the 1930s and 1940s.

## Ferry Service

For decades, private boats or the circuitous mail route provided the only transportation to Frenchboro. As a result, a trip to the mainland meant going from Frenchboro to Swans Island on a private mail boat and then riding the steamboat to Rockland.

By mid-century, residents wanted regular and more convenient ferry service. The town already owned land and a rudimentary pier courtesy of Thomas Proctor, who donated property for such a purpose in 1939.

The pulpwood company of Mattattal and Allen, which pulped the island, donated logs for an improved pier, including a float and bridge, built in June 1941. That pier was faced with granite and resurfaced in 1954, enlarged again in 1958 and finally outfitted for a ramp in 1961.

During the era, islanders used a town-owned scow to transport cars or other heavy equipment to the island. The scow, towed by a boat, took a couple of hours to cross the bay. Islanders beached the scow and drove cars off at low tide. Other islands sometimes rented Frenchboro's scow for similar purposes.

The island's first passenger service began in 1950 when Bay Ferry Corp. was founded and shares of stock sold. The *SeaWind*, a 50-foot passenger ferry with an enclosed cabin, operated daily until July 1, 1960. It ran from Swans Island's Burnt Coat Harbor (sometimes called Old Harbor) to Lunt Harbor, then to Bass Harbor.

With the demise of the *SeaWind*, the island again faced life without regular ferry service. As an emergency measure, the state provided temporary service via the *Kiboko* for six months in October of 1960. Charles B. Hooper served as captain and Paul L. "Rusty" Crossman as first mate.

*Courtesy of Frenchboro Historical Society*
*The SeaWind provided daily passenger ferry service to Frenchboro from 1950 to 1960.*

*The William S. Silsby, 1961. In the early days of ferry service, the ferry was forced to make side landings because of the rudimentary pier. Note the double track ramp.*

However, islanders wanted better service. The Maine State Ferry Service already provided passenger and auto service to Swans Island via the *William S. Silsby*. The *Silsby* had essentially put the *SeaWind* out of business because the *SeaWind* simply could not survive financially running one daily round-trip to Long Island. The islanders wanted the new ferry to provide a trip, but Swans Island balked at giving up any of its runs.

A group of islanders began agitating the state for improved service. The group met on April 7, 1960 to decide a course of action and soon hired a lawyer to lobby Augusta. Islanders raised about $850 to cover initial attorney fees. The plan worked.

On Nov. 1, 1960, Leonard "Nardy" Lunt wrote this entry into his journal: *"Leonard Lunt, Bennie Davis, Dick Lunt, David L. Lunt, Willard Osier, Ray Teel, Gardiner Lunt, Philip Whitney and Bob Clough went to Augusta to appear before the governor and council and when we returned we had a ferry boat."*

On Oct. 12, 1961, the *William S. Silsby* made its first run to Frenchboro carrying both cars and passengers. On its initial runs the ferry made a long and inconvenient run from Bass Harbor to Mackerel Cove on Swans Island and then to Frenchboro, before returning to Bass Harbor. However, the ferry soon switched to a direct run from Bass Harbor to Frenchboro two days a week. These twice-weekly morning arrivals and departures became a major island gathering time.

The early pier and ramp system at Frenchboro, though vastly

improved from its passenger-only days, remained difficult for several years. Its inadequacy forced the first ferry to make side landings and prevented cars from disembarking at low tide. Thus the ferry schedule varied week to week depending on the tides. The side landings also required cars to maneuver on deck before driving up over the side on the ramp, which was basically two metal tracks.

The state rebuilt the pier in 1969 to accommodate bow landings and facilitate more regular service. Gov. Kenneth Curtis officially dedicated the new pier Aug. 15, 1970.

With that change, the ferry began regular runs on Thursday and Friday from September to June and on Wednesday and Thursday during July and August.

Over the years, the state has upgraded the pier to improve safety and ease of use, although trips are still occasionally, and sometimes controversially, cancelled because of weather conditions. The captain makes the decision. In the mid-1990s, a third trip was added to Frenchboro on Sunday afternoons.

In 1997, a seasonal passenger ferry, the *R.L. Gott*, began round-trip service on Fridays.

## *Harbor Dredging*

For centuries, Lunt Harbor provided boaters and fishermen with safe and sheltered anchorage, but the harbor also drained to a fraction of its size at low tide. Essentially, the inner harbor drained to a mere stream that ran from the head of the cove past the head of Ben Davis' wharf. Typically only two to three feet of water remained off the Lunt & Lunt wharf.

In 1970, the federal government authorized a harbor improvement project. The project, based on a federal survey of the harbor, provided a five-acre, 10-foot deep anchorage in the outer harbor and a six-foot deep, 75-foot wide channel to the inner harbor where another 1.5 acres provided a six-foot anchorage.

The dredging contract was awarded to Prock Marine of Rockland, which started work in 1975 and finished in 1976. Harbor dredging also provided round-the-clock access to the bait shed and to what is now the town float, and added a handful of full-time moorings.

## Telephones

For decades, back fences and personal visits served as the only means of island communication. By the 1950s, some boats installed ship-to-shore radios, and in the 1970s, CB radios became common. But dedicated, reliable off-island communication remained a dream.

David L. Lunt built the island's first rudimentary telephone system in the mid-1950s when he connected about 10 houses on the west side using an old cable that formerly connected Bartlett Island to Mount Desert Island. He ran the cable either buried under the flats, along the ground or in the air from house to house and installed crank telephones that also came from Bartlett Island. The system was basically one large party line. Each house answered calls based on the number of rings. For example, three long rings would signal one house, while two short and two long rings would signal another. That system lasted until 1973.

The roots of a more modern system were set in 1970 when Jeffrey Webber of Providence, Rhode Island arrived on Long Island to research building his own telephone company. Webber, an elementary school teacher, had been a telephone buff since the day his father brought home some old telephone equipment when Jeff was a young boy. The Rhode Island native eventually moved to Maine to teach elementary school.

In the summer of 1971, Webber met with island residents to gauge interest. Fourteen people immediately signed up for service and nine more signed up shortly thereafter.

Jeff negotiated with the heirs of Nardy Lunt for a building to house his company and himself. He rebuilt old telephone equipment such as switches and telephones and battery plants to create the necessary infrastructure. He strung telephone wire from one end of town to the other, mainly along existing electricity poles.

On the last day of August 1973, Webber threw a switch, bringing true intra-island telephone service to 20 island residents and officially giving birth to his Island Telephone Co.

In August 1974, the 23 subscribers of Island Telephone Co., all located within a one-mile stretch, made 3,336 telephone calls to each other. At no time during the first 13 months did monthly calls fall below 2,000.

However, islanders still could not call the mainland. They continued to rely on CB radio, an increasingly unreliable and static-filled medium, to communicate with the mainland.

With little cooperation from New England Telephone Co. concerning the air connections, with an underwater cable too costly and unreliable, and with other expensive options unrealistic, it took time to find and develop the right approach. Eventually, Jeff decided to transmit signals from a small microwave tower on Long Island to a tower in Bass Harbor, thus connecting the island to the world's telephone network.

Jeff faced endless regulations and a blizzard of paperwork from the Federal Communications Commission, the state Public Utilities Commission, the Department of Environmental Protection and the Land-use Regulations Commission (LURC).

He also faced opposition from some Bass Harbor residents who were either scared of the potential tower because of alleged health concerns, or simply didn't like how it looked.

Through these struggles an engineer from another of Maine's independent telephone companies told him: "You'll never get a telephone on Frenchboro." Ironically, even the Rural Electrification Agency, which expanded in 1949 to bring telephone service to the nation's rural areas, termed Jeff's company too small to qualify for a loan.

However, Jeff did receive help from other independent telephone companies and colleagues. They helped find equipment and string wire; and rebuild switchboards, switchhouses and trunks; and meet the endless requirements from Bell.

In late November 1983, the system was ready for testing and the first experimental calls were made. For a short time, islanders received occasional off-island telephone calls as Webber ironed out technical problems.

Finally, on Dec. 22, 1983 the switches were flipped and Frenchboro had telephone service: one more piece of isolation eliminated.

In 1985, Sen. William Cohen presented Webber with a national service award for his efforts on Long Island. Webber, who went on to establish off-island telephone service on Isle au Haut in 1988, eventually sold his telephone companies.

Frenchboro telephone service is now provided by Chicago-based TDS Inc.

### *Homestead Project*

Roughly 20 years after Frenchboro garnered national attention for its efforts to reenergize its one-room school with 15 foster children, town leadership initiated a plan that brought an even brighter spotlight: the Frenchboro

Homestead Project. The Homestead Project was one of the most important steps undertaken by islanders this century to sustain the community.

From 1940 to 1980, the island population fell from 119 to 43 and residents continued to age. Unlike mainland towns, an island has no natural flow of people who might live in town and work at nearby jobs. A person must specifically seek to move to island.

Islanders have always realized this problem. So continuing to pursue unique and groundbreaking ways to address the small and fluctuating population base, islanders devised a plan to entice new residents by providing low-cost land and three-bedroom Cape Cod-style houses set back in a spruce forest.

However, the plan did not constitute a land giveaway. It included safeguards and commitments. The selection process included a detailed application that required potential residents to visit the island and discuss any special qualities they offered Frenchboro. Islanders sought to not only boost population and school enrollment but also to diversify the economy by attracting at least some people who supported themselves by a means other than lobster fishing.

Once details of the plan became public, media requests flooded the island. Television cameras from CBS and other news organizations arrived on the scene and newspapers from *The New York Times* to *The Bangor Daily News* to *The Star* magazine came to tell the tale — as did magazines such as *Yankee*, *DownEast* and *Country Living*.

The various articles ranged from straight news to feature stories to amateur attempts at analyzing the psyche of a small island town. At times the stories were sensational. *The Star* ran its story under the headline: "Come Live With Us On Fantasy Island."

After the compelling and romantic story was told — low-cost land on a remote but beautiful Maine island — Frenchboro received inquiries from across the globe: letters rolled in from California; telephone calls came from Yugoslavia. Daniel Blaszczuk, grant administrator, received 80 telephone calls within hours of *The Star* story hitting the newsstands. He then received 57 letters in one day based on the same article.

Overall, the Frenchboro Future Development Corp. (FFDC) received more than 3,000 inquiries in the first few months. Some letter writers understood reality; some did not. Some wannabe islanders even planned to commute to mainland jobs.

"This one schoolteacher said she really wanted to live in Frenchboro but wanted photographs of all the eligible bachelors sent to her first. She said she wasn't too fussy. We only have three bachelors, and one of them is 74 years old. I don't think we even sent her an application," Tina (LeMoine) Lunt told *The Hartford Courant* in 1987.

At one point, the project even spurred a man to write an original stage play set on a thinly veiled fictional Maine island. The Belfast Players performed the play. Unfortunately, the script was not only hopelessly amateurish, but also highly insulting to native islanders.

All this attention came after the program was under way.

Several years before the crush of applications and media attention, the multi-faceted homesteading project was conceived in broad terms by James Haskell, community development director, and David L. Lunt, an island selectman. Jim Hatch was soon hired as the FFDC secretary and still administers the program.

Haskell and Lunt, who knew such a project was necessary to create long-term island viability, convinced David Rockefeller's daughter, Margaret "Peggy" Dulany, to donate more than 30 acres of land to the FFDC. The Dulany land was located essentially along a wooded ridge above the harbor on the island's east side. At one time, some of the island's most beautiful homes sat in this general area, but they either burned or were torn down over the years, leaving the area mostly a spruce forest.

Using that land and its value as financial leverage, the town won a $366,830 Community Development Block Grant (CDBG) from the state. Forty-four cities and towns had applied for a share of $4.5 million available and 12 applicants were approved. The previous year, the state had rejected the island's original application seeking nearly $1 million in funds for a more sweeping island project.

The block grant, awarded in May 1985, was part of a 10-year development strategy that included funds to develop seven house lots, build a community center and upgrade some existing houses. The funding paid for roads, septic systems and wells for the new houses. The master plan also included five undeveloped lots for outright sale. The nonprofit FFDC administered the grant.

In addition to the CDBG, the FFDC received a low-interest loan from the Maine State Housing Authority to help build six houses. A seventh new house was set aside for the island schoolteacher. In addition, David L.

Lunt spurred a fundraising drive that raised another $250,000.

In exchange for using CDBG and Maine Housing funds, the FFDC set aside some houses for lower-income residents.

Initial applicants completed a detailed multi-page application that included college-style essays on why the applicant wanted to move to Frenchboro, what they could contribute to the town and how they would make a living. In short order, the FFDC narrowed the field to 18 hopefuls including a weaver, a glass blower, a computer-based data processing company, two fishermen and a writer. The final group came from a purposely diverse background. Their home states included: Maine, Connecticut, Massachusetts, New York, Colorado, California and Ohio.

From that group, 12 finalists visited the island for personal interviews over two weekends in May 1987. The groups stayed with island families and were treated to such small town basics as lunch on the church lawn.

That month, the new residents were chosen and invited to move to Frenchboro in 1988 after the houses were built.

One couple from Jonesport, Wyatt and Lorena Beal, already intrigued by island life after visiting Grand Manan, read about Frenchboro and the Homestead Project in the newspaper. By coincidence, they soon ran into Rebecca Lunt wearing a Frenchboro shirt in an Ellsworth fast food restaurant and discussed the island with her. They soon visited the island.

Explaining her reasons shortly before moving onto the island, Lorena told *The Hartford Courant,* "We just fell in love with Frenchboro."

Wyatt and Lorena soon moved to the island and rented a house while awaiting construction of their new home. However, they grew anxious during original

Courtesy of Lorena Beal

*Wyatt and Lorena (Lenfestey) Beal, 1987.*

construction delays and wanted to settle, so they bought a house on the harbor and pulled out of the program. They still live on the island with their two children, Mariner and Audrey. Lorena's parents and her brother now live on Long Island as well.

However, other would-be residents were neither as aggressive nor as anxious. Even after the effort expended by themselves and the town, most of the originals pulled out before they moved to the island or houses were even started.

Only the two lobstermen, Walter Pietrowski of Connecticut and Steve Beote of Massachusetts, remained from the original group and actually moved to Frenchboro.

The FFDC selected new homesteaders by the summer of 1988, but largely abandoned its plans to diversify the economy: all the replacements were fishermen. As a result it was crucial that island fishermen prove willing to share the fishing grounds to help the community.

"The island was a lot more open to bringing in outsiders than many places," said James Hatch. "That is absolutely the most unique aspect about the Frenchboro program: they realized they needed to bring in outsiders and gave up the bottom to help the community."

Finally, in December 1988, at the very onset of winter, three families rolled off the ferry and into their new houses. In all, five new families initially came to the island. The sixth, Jon and Debbie Crossman, already lived on the island.

The original deal, financial options and contingencies were complicated. Basically, the new residents lived in brand-new three-bedroom Capes on roughly 1.5-acre lots for about $375 per month. The two upstairs bedrooms were unfinished. The new residents provided a deposit of about $5,000 and agreed to a certain amount of so-called sweat equity, which was basically work on the house and property.

Homesteaders who remained three years could buy the house at a below-market rate ranging from about $40,000 to about $70,000 depending on income and other factors. At least some rent money could be applied toward the purchase price. The rest helped fund the program itself, including property tax payments and general upkeep.

"This was the first time such a program had been done. There were no guidelines," said David L. Lunt. "All the things we did were just things that we thought needed to be done to properly run the program and make it work."

To dissuade land speculation, couples who decided to sell their house had to first offer the property back to the FFDC.

Although some of the original six families remained longer than three years, none actually bought their house. And each one eventually left. They have been replaced once or twice over.

The original people, and some other homesteaders who followed, left for various reasons. Some simply didn't enjoy island life, some couldn't handle it and others just didn't take the proper steps to adjust. Exacerbating problems was the unfortunate timing of a down lobster-catch cycle, which helped depress incomes and cause some financial hardships.

Indeed, the program has hit some rough spots during the past 12 years. During that time, some homesteaders fell far behind on rent, and at times houses stood empty, reducing income and forcing the FFDC to rene-gotiate terms with a sometimes-reluctant Maine State Housing Authority. The MSHA even threatened foreclosure in the early 1990s.

The program has also changed and adapted it rules to meet the shift-ing circumstances. For example, the FFDC eliminated the three-year waiting period to purchase a home. Meanwhile, rent has increased only about $10 per month in 12 years.

The FFDC retains the right of first refusal on any resale, in part because some houses must remain open to lower-income individuals, but also to ensure they remain year-round residences and dissuade real estate speculators.

Despite problems, the groundbreaking program has unquestionably succeeded overall and provided the island with a much brighter future. Two houses have been sold, occupancy is usually high and four additional houses have been built on the five once-vacant lots. The three school pupils and four other pre-schoolers are tied to the program. The general concept has been adopted and modified by Isle au Haut and Cliff Island.

In 1999, 25 island residents are directly tied to the Homestead Project, representing more than half the current population. They include:

Lorena and Wyatt Beal. The Beals, originally of Jonesport, have two young children, Mariner and Audrey, and still live in the house they orig-inally purchased. Lorena became the island postmistress in 1998 and chairs the School Committee. Wyatt is one of the harbor's top lobstermen. Lorena's parents, Myron and Sarah Lenfestey, and Lorena's brother, Mike, have also moved to Long Island. For part of the 1998-1999 school year, Mariner was the only island pupil.

Christopher Sawyer. Christopher, a direct descendent of the island's founding fathers, is a single lobstermen. His parents also live on the island. Chris, who was born on the island in 1975, returned to the island as an adult in 1997 after growing up mostly in Tremont.

Tim and April (Davis) Wiggins. April, also a descendant of the island's founders, was born on the island. Her grandparents, John and Rebecca (Reed) Lunt also live there. April and Tim welcomed their first child, Elijah, in 1999. Tim and April have purchased their house. Tim is a fisherman and April has held town offices.

Marissa and Roman "Ski" Rozenski. The couple moved from Dennysville, Maine in 1997. Marissa is head of the town library and involved in other community activities. Roman is one of the island's larger fishermen. They have purchased their house.

David Lewis. David is a single fisherman from Dover, Maine. He has served on the School Committee. He has two children who spend some time on the island. David's brother Linus also spends time on the island.

Two of the six houses are vacant, but interviews of potential residents are ongoing.

Joann Albano and Jeff Hilliard orginally moved to the island to live in one of the homestead houses in 1997 from Vermont. The couple now rent another island home on the harbor. Jeff is an island fisherman.

Four of the five original undeveloped lots have also been developed. These are owned by:

Lewis and Rachel Bishop. The Bishops moved from Addison and originally lived in one of the homestead houses, but purchased a lot and built their own house in 1998. They live on the island year-round with their son, Lance. Rachel is the town clerk and Lewis is a top fisherman.

Kathy and Charles "Chuck" Carl. The Carls are from Columbia Falls, Maine and live on the island during

*Photo by Dean L. Lunt*

*Lance Bishop, 1996.*

most of the year. He is a fisherman. Kathy was the island's schoolteacher for two years. They built a house in 1997. They have one son, Kodi, who lives with them. Another son, Charles Carl Jr., also lives on the island.

Paul and Kay Charpentier from Connecticut built a house and have recently purchased the former Israel B. Lunt homestead from Norma Teel. They have two young grandchildren, Joey and Jessica, who live with them. Joey attends the island school. They are retired and plan to open a Bed & Breakfast on the island. A son, Andy, also lives on the island.

Richard and Joan Daignault, of New Hampshire, have spent summers on the island. They have now sold their mainland house and plan to live there year round. They are retired.

314

*Chapter Fifteen*
# Voices of the 20th Century

## The Characters

The achievers, the builders, and the community leaders all play crucial roles in a town's development, forming its muscle and its spine. But the soul of a village is also defined by its sometimes-eccentric parts.

These residents, perhaps just outside the mainstream, may not always affect a community's future and often leave little tangible legacy save for fading memories, but they remain an important part of history by giving a village its distinctive flavor. Many, especially those who lived during the 1800s and early 1900s, have already been lost to time. My life overlaps with few of these men and women, although I knew many characters. Certainly, times were changing when I came along.

I do remember Lincoln Lunt, an old man who died in June of 1973 at the age of 74. Kevin Holland, a grammar school pupil at the time, found Lincoln dead one afternoon in his house at the head of the harbor. Lincoln's house, a one-room shack really, was filled with magazines and comic books piled wall-to-wall like a thick paper carpet.

Lincoln's house was actually the "L" from an old island house. The L was torn off and floated down the harbor for Lincoln, who at one time also lived in an boat pulled onto the harbor banks.

*Lincoln Lunt (left) and Robert A. Lunt, late 1960s, standing outside the house of Flora Eveline "Mammie" Lunt.*

By the time I can remember him, he sometimes abandoned his old cot and slept with a blanket and pillow in a shallow indentation atop the magazines themselves. Actually, that was his winter home.

He summered in an old blue car pulled to the edge of small spruce and apple trees near his house. The front end stuck out so he could watch the road through the windshield.

I don't remember, nor have I ever heard any stories about him causing problems. As a younger man, he often stayed long into the night at Vera Dalzell's house listening to the radio. He might eat dinner at Mammie's or buy some bread and ham at Almy's store. He walked to Dick and Vivian Lunt's house every few days for a gallon or two of kerosene to fire his small stove used to both heat the room and cook meals. He kept a few lobster traps in the outer harbor that he rowed to tend. Lincoln belonged to a different era; a different world, really. But he was a part of the island. He belonged.

Still, after dark, with no streetlights near Lincoln's house, island kids sprinted past his camp. After his death, the old shack seemed extra spooky and we ran a little faster.

I never knew Ed Lunt. Growing up in the 1920s, my grandmother and other kids of her generation were scared to death of him. Ed was referred to as "a little slow," and island kids sometimes teased him into a rage. It wasn't difficult. At times, he emerged from his house on the west side when he saw someone coming and just started to yell. Or he might fire a shotgun in the air to make his point. To this day when someone becomes a little irrational or flashes a quick temper, it might be known as an "Ed Lunt spell."

Charlie Rice rowed the eight miles between Bass Harbor and Frenchboro for years. Any time day or night, he might "borrow" a skiff and set off rowing. Unlike the wine-sipping Lincoln, Charlie drank. Sometimes when a group of island men sat around drinking, they would send some kids to Nardy's store for bricks of ice cream. Charlie sat and whittled out spoons while he waited.

For decades, various single men and some women lived in one-room shacks or alone in houses scattered around the harbor. All had different reasons and circumstances. In those days, not everyone left as illness set in. But few had any money while healthy, let alone saved any for old age. They just grew older and poorer.

They stayed because Frenchboro was home and the living was relatively easy. Sometimes family land came down through generations to them, or they bought a piece for short money — island land wasn't worth much back then. Often relatives just let people live in old camps, if necessary. They were family after all.

These men functioned in a place where you could survive with little money and minimal help. You had few, if any, bills and lived off the land. Someone usually looked out for you in an emergency anyway, or offered a bed and a free meal in a pinch.

One of the most intriguing, and certainly better-remembered island bachelors of the 20th century was Hiram Albert Lunt Jr., universally known as "Doonie Hum."

Doonie, 61, died in the spring of 1966, a month before I was born. He collapsed of a heart attack in the road near Sanford L. "Dick" Lunt's house. In truth, he drank himself to death.

Doonie was my great great uncle. His house, essentially a one-room, tarpaper shack, sat on the hill just north of the Butler Road nestled amongst the alders not far from my house. It looked down on the harbor and out over the baitshed. He slept on a bunk built into the wall. I didn't know Doonie, of course, but I knew that house. I have written numerous short stories based on that rundown shack and what might have transpired there.

*Courtesy of Frenchboro Historical Society*

*Hiram A. "Doonie Hum" Lunt Jr. (1904 - 1966)*

Among other things, Doonie, known at times to "run his mouth," spun tall tales. He occasionally roamed the streets drunk. Or got into an occasional fight or carried out a little family "dirty work" when he was a younger man. But usually when on a bender he holed up in his house or crashed with a few drinking buddies. They were not difficult to find.

"Some of the old guys always had a pint of liquor in a flat bottle in their back pocket. And Doonie Hum always wore a big overcoat," said Carroll W. Lunt, Doonie's nephew. "They always told a story about Doonie, with a bottle of liquor in his back pocket and under that coat, falling down one time. He laid there for a minute and said, "Jesus, I hope that is blood I feel running down my back."

Doonie Hum was born Oct. 2, 1904, the eleventh child of Hiram A. "Hite" and Mary Susan Lunt.

Raw-boned and famously rugged, he was known for his endurance, especially when digging holes or smashing rock. He supposedly could hammer or dig all day — "like a beaver." He dug numerous wells and outhouse pits for islanders. John R. Lunt Jr., tells this story:

"He came down the house one time; he was drunk, but was trying to straighten out and get over a bender. He was broke, didn't have a cent. He said, 'You want a ditch dug from that well to the house don't you?' I said 'yeah.' He said, 'You send over and get me a couple cases of beer so I can sober up, and I'll dig you a ditch.'

"He sobered up and got over his bender and he was feeling pretty good. So he came up one night and asked me where I wanted it dug. I showed him. Then I came in from traps one night just before dark, and he had it two-thirds dug. I was in the house, and every once in a while I would see a shovel full of sand fly out of that hole. So finally, I went over and looked down and said 'What are you doing?' He said, 'Diggin a trench for you.' I said, 'You haven't got to dig it down that far.' He said, "You have to dig down to the bottom of the well don't you?' God, he dug it down about 12 foot deep, right into the house. We had to push the fill back in."

Doonie, considered a good fisherman, could earn good money and hauled upwards of 200 heavy wooden traps by hand in a skiff every day.

When brothers Robert and Carroll Lunt worked at Dick Lunt's lobster pound as teenagers, they usually ran out to collect Doonie's lobsters at mid-day. The lobsters couldn't survive all day in his skiff, and he didn't have room for them, anyway.

Doonie might work months on end without touching a drop of liquor. Then one day, after he had salted away some cash, he would start to drink and might not stop for a month or so. While "on a drunk," he hired someone to tend his traps.

Carroll, who along with his brother, Robert, helped look after him for a few years, tells it this way:

"He wouldn't drink for months; then when he got some money in his pocket, right in the middle of the best fishing, he would get someone to tend his traps; then he would go get some liquor.

"He would drink for days, weeks, even a month straight. He would be drunk, although he wasn't much of problem. My mother — he was daddy's brother — she would cook some stuff and send me down with it. He wouldn't eat it, but he didn't want her to know it. Then he would send me to the store for checkerberry and vanilla and peppermint and stuff. I thought it was something to get him well; come to find out he was drinking it.

"It would take him days to get back on his feet, and he would be almost helpless. Then he would be well enough by fall to get himself five or six bags of potatoes, a couple bags of flour, a few pounds of beans and other stuff to store up for the winter."

Doonie even had a path named after him: The Doonie Hum Road. It ran from his camp to the backshore between the Salt Ponds and Lookout Point.

It is all grown over now and is hard to follow, if you can even find it. It has long been overshadowed by more important roads.

But if you are so inclined and you look hard enough, you'll remember.

# Voices

"If one proves himself friendly, simple in his talk, easy to meet and willing to mingle with them as one of the community, he soon finds he has been accepted and taken into the inside life of the little settlement, but woe-betide the worker of such poor judgment that he tries to "high-hat" them. His doom is sealed and his wisest course is to move on.

Life on an island is just like life anywhere else. There are poor people and people in comfortable circumstances; idle people and busy people; cultured people and unlettered ones; people with fine ideals and people whose ideals and morals are very low."

— Louisa Rae Pullen, 1931, field worker for Maine Sea Coast Mission

"The young men of the island have always been willing to help. They appear always at the right time to cut wood, bring water from the well, shovel a path to the well — rescue a drowned pail or axe, for several times the axe has slipped from inexperienced hands while chopping away the ice and gone to the bottom of our water supply. They often come with a portion of their fish catch which is always appreciated."

— Lucy Allen King, mission worker, 1921

*Courtesy of Frenchboro Historical Society*
*Rosanna (Murphy) "Aunt Rose" Lunt,*
*(1861 - 1945).*

"Aunt Rose is 78 years old today. The Sunshine Club girls prepared a party for her. Please tell Mrs. Young that the paper garlands and festoons that she sent a few days ago were used at this party and I think meant really the most to her, for she touched them lovingly and said: 'You girls hung them pretty roses up for me. Ain't' they pretty.' Then she noticed the paper butterflies and her quivering lips gave the words: 'I hope the butterflies and roses will be on my grave, for I love'em both.'"

— Gladys Muir, November 4, 1939, schoolteacher

"Money is very scarce at present. The seas have been very rough, traps have been lost, and the men have not been able to get out to their traps much this month, which means that few lobsters have been sold. I have learned that some of the men are now buying their clothes through some magazine ad of a Chicago concern that deals in second-hand clothing which has been scrupulously cleansed. The trousers cost $1.00 a pair and coats $1.50. Then there are work shirts too. While the majority are khaki-colored woolen, one man got a navy blue suit which looks very good indeed. I admire the men for wearing these clothes."
— Mildred Wye, January 1940, Red Cross nurse

"When the first ice appeared, the children talked incessantly of skating. I visited the 'pond.' The walk through the woods, bespangled with snow and ice was quite worthwhile, but the pond — a clearing in the woods, not more than forty by fifty feet — where water had settled and frozen rather unevenly was the skating ground. One pair of skates served for all; the children wearing them in turn and trying to balance on them while clinging tenaciously to assistants on either side. The real sport, 'skating' consisted of running and sliding across the little stretch of ice. This proved quite exhilarating."
— Lucy Allen King, mission worker, 1921

*Courtesy of Frenchboro Historical Society*

*Skating at The Meadow, 1940s. Clifton Lunt (left), Sanford "Dick" Lunt, Cecil E. Lunt, Raymond L. Teel and Leonard Higgins.*

"When we were kids we played up over the hill all the time. We liked going to Eastern Beach because you could get dulse, and on the way down there was a brook that run with water that was always ice cold. You could lay down on your stomach and drink that trickling stream until August when it dried up. We would go down and through the head of the field. Grammy's cow was always there and the family let Lizzie Ross put her cows up there too. When we went through we had to watch to make sure all the cows were lying down or were cows that we knew weren't ugly so we could get by them."
— June Elizabeth (Davis) Thompson, born 1919

"I bought lobsters for Dick. What I would do was I bought the lobsters, but I would also make cupcakes and coffee and sell it to fishermen when they came in to sell. There wasn't much money going at the time, and that helped. After Cecil and I were married I also used to bake cakes and go around in the truck selling them door to door."
— Lillian J. (Davis) Lunt, born 1925

"These fishermen all rise early but there is seldom need for haste. Fishing seems to carry an atmosphere all its own."
— Lucy Allen King, mission worker, 1921

*"Dear Sister {Ella V. Lunt},*
*Today being Sunday I will drop in and say a few words. Everything is going pretty good here. Got the package from Nardy and Pean alright. Also got a package from Annie, two cans of crabmeat, it tasted pretty good. I'm waiting now for that box of dried fish. The weather here is just the same plenty hot, it rained a little this morning. I suppose the boys are doing well this summer. Got a letter from Burge saying he was fishing in the old boat. I suppose she looks pretty good. Tell Nardy to let me know if he rec'd the last two money orders I sent in June and July."*
*Best Wishes, Gardiner*
*Aug. 6, 1944, somewhere in Italy*

*"Dear Son {Clifton Lunt},*
*Just a line letting you know I received your letter and tobaco and glad to get it. I was tickled over my Christmas present you sent me. I am going to send you a Christmas present and the kids (are too) if we can get them ready to send New*

*Courtesy of Verna B. Dobson*

*Jen (Rice) Mitchell (1890 - 1966) standing in a field outside the old Will Lunt house.*

*The Osier Family, 1906. Back row: Mary "Mame" (Bridges) Osier and Nathan F. Osier. Front row: Willard and Evelyn Osier.*

*Years. When I had the letter and you said you was going to send them something they danced and laughed for joy. You don't want to inlist nor go across to France neither one. What is Lincoln doing. Why he don't write home once in a while. You want to see that he pay his board every week. We have had only one letter since he left. Don't know whether he is dead or alive."*
*Happy New Year, Your father {Nelson Lunt}*
*Frenchboro, Me., December 30, 1918*


"We had one of the hand sleds and we used to go clear over to Big Beach Hill and Southwest Point to get wood. It would hold about a quarter of a cord. We cut spruce and birch. We sawed it with a hand saw and used an axe. We put it on those sleds, which were probably five -foot with steel runners, so it would go through the snow better. I had to get the wood for home and I had to saw it and split it and lug it in. Every Saturday we were over there, getting enough to last a week. We walked through the meadow, which was all ice, and there used to be a good beaten path over there. It was just me for my house, but there would be Wallace, Hud, Doonie Hum, and Tommy. We would all be over there getting wood; they were a lot older than I was. We would get one so far and go back and get another load. They had them piled up high and they would upset if someone wasn't helping tend it."
— John R. Lunt Jr., born 1930


"We used to go to Swans Island for the dances some nights. Pean would take a boat full of us over to one of the dance halls. One night we got started out, it came up a thunder storm and the boat stopped in the middle of the ocean between home and Swans Island. He finally got the boat started, but didn't it rain. It was just an open boat with, I think, a canvas spray hood.

Down there where Bennie Jr. lived, there was a dance hall in that old fishhouse. There was a beautiful dance hall up top. Hud Lunt, he could play a violin like everything. He played the violin and others played some other instruments. They used to have them, seems to me, every Saturday night."
— Mable (Lunt) Hall, born 1918

*My Dear Son {Clifton Lunt},*
*Just a few lines to let you know I am well and hope you are the same. Yes, I received the shirts all right and got the money. The ice has been quite thick down here. The snow is about 9 feet deep. I guess if you should step in the deepest you should never be seen again. We have only been out to our traps only twice all winter. Mrs. Haskell has come back again. Mr. McDonald brought her yesterday. I believe it is going to be awful sickly down here this spring. The slosh will be clean to your middle. Alma is awful sick. Her tempeture has been up to 101. McDonald tested her tempeture yesterday. She is better this morning then it was yesterday. It is awful sickly down here. Virginia Lunt is awful sick. Ella is sick too.*

*Hud and Edwin and Dib has been here. They have been here the whole evening, but they have just left from here. I have come home to stay now. I took my bed and walked over in the morning. I have been to work all day hauling wood and cutting wood and stowing wood.*

*With love, Nelson Lunt*
*Frenchboro, Me., March 4, 1920*

Courtesy of Frenchboro Historical Society

*Alvina (b. 1876) and Nelson P. Lunt (1875 - 1921).*

"When I was little, we just played around a lot. We played house and things like that and had a great time. We had an old barn down at the house and there were cracks in the barn. We used to put shingles in the cracks and put broken glass on it and make believe that was our cupboard. We didn't have many toys to amount to anything. Gosh, we were as poor as church mice."

— Vivian Davis Lunt, born 1915

"We didn't have a washing machine for the longest while. When David was in boarding school (in the 1950s), we still didn't have one. Out in the shed we had a little two-burner kerosene heater and we were still washing by hand.

"We had a boiler on that little stove to heat sheets and things and a tub and washboard to wash them. You heated your boiler on the stove and boiled pillowcases and white things; then you put them in the washtub and washed them."
— Vivian Davis Lunt, born 1915

*Photo by Dean L. Lunt*

*Vivian Davis Lunt, 1990s.*

"Innie would always chase your grandmother {Vivian Lunt} and my mother (Nora Lunt} to the post office, down to Van Norden's. They had soda pop and stuff down there. Innie would always write little rhymes, and he did pretty well, really. They used to drink Coke, your grandmother and my mother. And he would go down and get orange soda and wait for the mail to be picked over or something. They would always leave part of their soda, and he would drink all his. He would write a little song, he would say, 'Orange soda is good to the very last drop. Coca-Cola is only good from the center to the top. I drink all my orange, they leave half their Coke. I will have plenty of money, when they both go broke.'"
— Carroll W. Lunt, born 1933

"We had 155 traps between the two of us and we had pretty near 1,200 pounds. We went out and baited up; it was rougher than hell; nobody else was out. The traps were scarce. Of course, there was no warning about hurricanes in those days. We did well the first two or three times after that hurricane, no one else baited their traps up. That was a lot of lobsters for 155 traps."
— John R. Lunt Jr., born 1930

"Clarence Howard and I went down to the east'ard with a load of lobsters. When we got down to the east'erd there was bait, a load of herring, so we got 160 or 170 bushels of herring on her. It was quite choppy.

"He had a mast in the aft, the back end of her. He took that out and didn't cover the hole up. Every time the bow would go up in the air and the stern would go under, water would go down the hole. We got down there in the Western Way by Sou'west Harbor and were coming out through. Something gave him the idea, I don't know what, to go out and see what was going on. He got through and he hollered to me, 'Come out here with your knife quick!' We had a punt tied on the stern of her, bottom side up. The boat was full of water in aft. The punt was lashed down on deck and we had to cut the lines off to get the punt up.

*Courtesy of Donna Hasal*
*Clarence E. Howard (1899 - 1971).*

"The punt was 10 foot long and about four feet wide, or something like that. We got that out and went up bow in the steering shelter. I stood outside and he told me to hang on to the punt. I was small, I didn't have much strength and almost lost her. But anyway, he started to put her in gear hard, see if he couldn't drag her through and get over to Gotts Island. But when he put her in gear, she stalled. He started down forward. She was one of those boats that didn't have a starter; you had to crank her to start her. I hollered, 'Don't go down forward. Grab that kettle and let's get the punt.' He did, and we got in the punt and the boat went right down stern first.

"We had to row from there to Gotts Island. It was choppy. She was dipping down. I had to bail all the time steady while he rowed. We got to Gotts Island about 12 o'clock at night. First two houses we came to, we told them what happened but wouldn't let us in, 'No room,' they said, and shut the door on us. We came to Les Morrill's and he said 'Sure, come right in.'" — Sanford L. "Dick" Lunt, born 1910

*Courtesy of Frenchboro Historical Society*

*Everett Edward "Ebbit" Dalzell Jr. (1899 - 1968).*

*Courtesy of Frenchboro Historical Society*

*Hezekiah W. "Will" Lunt Jr., (b. 1871).*

*Courtesy of Verna B. Dobson*

*Ronald Mitchell feeding the family calf on Long Island, 1920s.*

*Courtesy of Marjorie D. Giamo*

*Milton "Robbins" Dalzell (1896 - 1952).*

*Courtesy of Frenchboro Historical Society*

*Frenchboro School, early 1980s. Back row: Alan Albers (left), Virginia Mitchell, Jennifer Mitchell, Warren P. Higgins Jr., Darcy Higgins.*
*Front Row: Lynn Smith, Christopher Sawyer, Steve Smith.*

*Courtesy of Lillian J. Lunt*

*Vernon E. Dalzell, 1940s.*

*Photo by Dean L. Lunt*

*Zachary D. Lunt, 1996.*

Courtesy of Frenchboro Historical Society
*Marjorie (Dalzell) Giamo, 1920s.*

"There wasn't any money you could speak of. Luckily people who lived out here didn't have mortgage on a house, didn't have to pay electricity bills, didn't have running water. You bought kerosene for lamps, you had your own cows, you got your own milk. You lived on cereal and you lived on fish, very little meat. Everyone had a flock of hens for eggs and you had a little vegetable garden; for the short season and the amount of ground space, that was suitable. You canned everything. I remember John Lunt and Bert Perkins planted potatoes all along the banking just past Cecil's wharf. That whole banking was all planted in tiers of potatoes. That is how people survived."

— Marjorie (Dalzell) Giamo, born 1918

"Looking for fish was part of the mystique, I guess, of going sardine fishing. You would go out night after night and lay in some cove, listen to the short-wave radio, and have supper and fiddle around waiting to see if there was any fish around.

"Of course, fish weren't going to come in until at least dusk or later. And I wanted to play baseball. So I would want to be in the ballfield in a ball game or a practice game or something. Then about four or four-thirty in the afternoon — this was in the summer time when it didn't get dark until almost nine o'clock — my father would be prowling around ready to go. It was only going to be a 15-minute ride down to Eastern Cove, but at four-thirty he was ready to go. So, if it was high water he would be in here in the harbor blasting his horn and waiting for me to come down from the ballfield to get going. He'd be in a complete lather to get down there and sit for hours."

— Ben Davis Jr., born in 1935

"I doubt, though, that I shall ever be native enough to eat dry fish with relish the way I've seen some of the children doing. They chew on it as if it were a piece of candy, and a very special kind at that."
— Mildred Wye, January 1940. Red Cross nurse

*Courtesy of Frenchboro Historical Society*

*Back row: James H. Thurlow (left), Elizabeth "Lizzie" (Lunt) and unknown baby, 1910s.*
*Middle row: Lydia M., Violet B., Thelma V., and James Earl.*
*Front row: Ruby and Roy.*

"In the summer we would go down to the shore; we were always barefooted. We got a pair of new shoes to start school with and we got a pair of shoes for Easter. That was it. We went barefoot if they wore out, or Grammy would retapt them or whatever had to be done. Grammy made our clothes, everything I ever wore, the slips, the underpants, the little dresses. She did it for years. When she was married she would do other people's sewing for enough materials to make one of her kids something. She even made Daddy's suit that he was married in."
— June (Davis) Thompson, born 1919

*Courtesy of Verna B. Dobson*

*Genevieve (McKown) Osier and Donald K. Osier sitting on the steps of Jen Mitchell's store, 1940.*

*Courtesy of Vivian D. Lunt*

*Grover C. Lunt (b. 1898) and Alice Winnifried Lunt (1903 - 1934).*

*Courtesy of Frenchboro Historical Society*

*Adelbert W. "Del" Lunt (1859 - 1908).*

*Benjamin S. "Dib" Lunt (left) (1890 - 1965) and Llewellyn "Hud" Lunt (1896 - 1958).*

*Charles R. "Tar" Mitchell (1884 - 1953).*

*Helen (Dalzell) Lunt (left), Valeria (Lunt) Davis and Jessie (Lunt) Perkins, 1920s. The two children are probably Thomas B. Lunt Jr. and Lawrence Davis.*

"[One of my boats] you had to tie the tubs to the side of her, because if you had a little bit of chop she would upset them. Dick was out with me hauling in her once. We were on the backside of Southwest Point. All at once we were picking up water on the belt going to the hauler. I looked down forward, and she was half full of water. I started pumping — she had one of those brass pumps on the side of her that you pumped by hand. I got her down a ways and saw that one of the planks had started off. He took his shirt off and caulked it from the inside. When we got in, we went in the woods and got the root of a tree that was already bent into a "U" and we put that in there. The piece in there was completely rotted, wouldn't even hold a nail."
— John R. Lunt Jr., born 1930

"We [Theda and June] were always together. We went berrying up in the woods. We had playhouses all over the place. Up on the piece of land past Momma's house, we had a playhouse there. There was a great tree with a swing and under it was rock and that rock was a playhouse. Every playhouse we kept, we would name it after a young man. I was probably six or seven. We had the Maynard Higgins house because we thought Maynard Higgins was nice looking. We had the Ray Teel house because Ray Teel had white teeth and when he smiled he was good looking. We would say, 'Let's go up to the Ray Teel house.' It was just an open house, and we didn't need to have dishes and things; we used leaves. If we found a big leaf, it would be a platter. We would crumple up daisies, and that would be sugar or whatever."
— June Elizabeth (Davis) Thompson, born 1919

"Nardy had [the boat], and I think his father had her before that. Clarence had her before me. It was the double ender that I gave to Lawrence when I got the new one.

"He hauled her up in Leam's dock down there, and after he took the pilothouse off, he shook her and she split right down the middle. One half went one way and one went the other. The only thing that held her together was the pilothouse, I guess."
— John R. Lunt Jr., born 1930

"Salt Ponds and Big Beach, they were our second homes. Back then, the Salt Ponds were still deep. We used to build rafts in there and paddle them all over. We hauled traps, which were just rope tied to a rock and stick for a buoy. We even got brave enough after awhile to sail them out of the pond at highwater, but we didn't go far. We always wanted to paddle them around the point and up in the harbor, but we knew we would get in big, big trouble for that.

"In the woods behind the ponds, we tied a big orange fish net up in the top of all these trees. It was tied maybe into 10 or 12 trees to keep all the ends and sides up. It was like a trampoline maybe 20 feet or more up in the air. We jumped off the very tops of the trees right into the net."
— Michael Holland, born 1961

*"Dear Friend {Clifton Lunt},*

*I thought I would drop you a few lines to let you know I am well and hope you are the same.*

*I am sorry that you have been sick, but it couldn't be helped. Lilla has had a doll come and she is putting her together and when she got it done she called it Little Income. That is what they call Shirl, and Leam Davis said he was going down to call Little Income and talk about the war. Well, Mr. Grant Lunt has cut his foot and can't walk on it.*

*They are going to take Mr. Nickerson away to the hospital. Well, Hud and Mother has just had a quarrel over spitting on the floor, but they are all right, just the same. Well, there is quite a crowd here, but they are all crazy. Mr. Herman Anderson house is up for sale the 1 of March. Lilla is making a dress for Little Income and it is red, white green and all colors of the rainbow."*
*With Love, Alma.*
*Feb. 23, 1920, Frenchboro, Me*

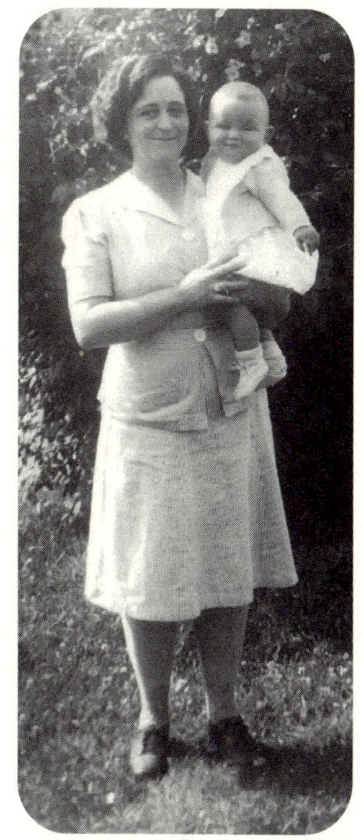

*Courtesy of Lillian J. Lunt*
*Alma and Earlene Lunt, 1943*

*Courtesy of Lillian J. Lunt*

*The Davis Family, about 1906. Flora (left), Grandville "Sim", Alexander, Millie, Elmer "Goog", Ben, Grace and Abby.*

*Courtesy of Lillian J. Lunt*

*Agnes F. (Joyce) Davis (left), Naomi B. Stanley (baby), Millie Davis and Flora (Davis) Stanley, 1919.*

*Courtesy of Frenchboro Historical Society*

*Lillian J. (Davis) Lunt and her dog, Patty, 1930s.*

*Courtesy of Sandra Lunt*

*William Morris Jr. and Bessie (Farley) Morris, 1940s.*

*Courtesy of Lillian J. Lunt*

*Mary "Mame" (Bridges) Osier and Leaman T. Davis, 1920s or 1930s.*

*Sliding on Almy's Hill, 1940s. Ruby Davis (left), Carroll W. Lunt, John R. Lunt Jr., and David L. Lunt, 1940s*

"The Wes well would freeze over and you had to break through it. We used to carry water in the winter and water the road after the snow was on there. It would freeze. We would carry water all the way from my house down past where John's house is. We could go around the head of the harbor and across that dam from my house. We just kept watering it at night; it was dirt road then."

— Carroll W. Lunt, born 1933

"Hud (Llewellyn Lunt) used to live in a camp up back of Mom's house, and I used to walk up there. He showed me how to put grass between your fingers and blow on it to make noise. He also kept all these lines of dulse hanging out up there, and we would always go get some of that."

— Barbara (Lunt) Sawyer, born 1949

"When we were six years or so we would borrow Robbins Dalzell's punt. I remember the first time because we got in and Theda said 'Come on, let's go rowing.' I said, 'Do you know how to row?' because I knew I didn't. She said, 'Of course I do.' We got in the punt and we went round and round. She didn't know how to row and she could only reach one oar."

— June (Davis) Thompson, born 1919

"I went to high school at Fryeburg Academy, and back in those days that was the other end of the earth. When I started going to high school we went in a taxi. My father hired Harvard Stanley to take my mother and I up there. We went from Bass Harbor to Fryeburg in a taxi. By Thanksgiving, when they came to pick me up, they came in their new '48 Buick. That was our first family car."
— Ben S. Davis Jr., born 1935


"Mom would pack us up a picnic lunch, and we would go to the Salt Ponds or wherever, just roam the island. We would go anywhere; it was fun and a great place to grow up as a kid."
— Phoebe (Leach) Horton, born 1953


"Emily Gilman was a midwife, and I was the last one she delivered. There were two women on the island who used to do that, and they used to fight over each job. I guess they took turns, and it was her turn to deliver me. They got $2."
— Verna "Bunny" (Mitchell) Dobson, born 1919


"We got our water down to the Wes well. It was a dug well. It used to freeze over in the winter and you had to break through it. We had to get it every day, and at my house in the winter, the water froze up every night right in the house, right by the window. You couldn't heat that house except right around the stove."
— Carroll W. Lunt, born 1933


"We ate duck and deer; we never ate a lot of fish, but we did eat lobster and crab and dried cod. That was mostly through the fall to spring. We ate well spring to fall. Through the summer, you could go anytime to the store in the good weather, but in the winter and fall you didn't go away as much. When the kids were little, I didn't go for months at a time. In the fall we would get a 50-pound bag of potatoes, and I would put up tomato pickles and vegetables, make jelly and we would freeze greens. The winter is when we ate off the land."
— Sandra (Morris) Lunt, born 1940

"Alec Davis was always good in the fog. I'll never forget one time I was coming home from school, and there was one boat going down. It was owned by a woodsman who had a boat but didn't really know anything about the water. It was foggy as could be. Alec was going with us, but he went to sleep down bow. About halfway down, Alec came right out of a sound sleep, come up, looked around, looked at this guy and said, 'you aren't going in the right direction.' The guy didn't have any compass or anything. Alec said, 'Turn the boat around and go this way.' They argued for a little while and finally the guy did what Alec told him, and we came right into the harbor. He knew enough about the water or the waves or something that he knew which way to go.

"My father was like that too. He would take John out lobstering, and John would go right around in circles and John would pull the same trap about three times. John would say, 'Dad, something's wrong.' He said, 'Yeah, you're going around in circles.'

"He wanted to prove a point."

— Verna "Bunny" (Mitchell) Dobson, born 1919

*Courtesy of Vivian D. Lunt*

*Lillian J. (Davis) Lunt (left) and Vivian (Davis) Lunt, 1940s.*

"I would go up the road when I was kid before dark, and I would wait for Rose Murphy to go home so I could go home with her. If she wasn't around I would start from that house of Millie's, and I would run until I got to my door. I wouldn't stop. Didn't I hate those old cemeteries."

— Lillian J. (Davis) Lunt, born 1925

*Courtesy of Lillian J. Lunt*

*Alexander P. Davis (1888 - 1968).*

Courtesy of Dean L. Lunt

*Michelle (left) and Dean Lunt, Susan and James Miller at Gooseberry Point, early 1990s.*

Photo by Dean L. Lunt

*Kurt Forsgren at Eastern Beach, 1990s.*

Photo by Dean L. Lunt

*Kristi L. Lunt, 1980s.*

*John Rodney Lunt Sr. (1876 - 1951)*

"My father would get up in the morning and then he would come around and say, 'Let's go girls,' and off we would go into the woods. We would go down to the Head to get raspberries, maybe 20 quarts of raspberries in those days. My mother would take them and can them for winter and she would stew them for sauce and made some jam. We also used to have to go pick dandelion greens. We had two crocks full of them in the basement. You would clean them, wash them, salt them and store them in those big crocks."
— Mable (Lunt) Hall, born 1918

*Courtesy of June E. Thompson*

*Theda Davis (left), Thelma Davis, June E. Davis and Violet (Thurlow) Davis, 1940s or 1950s.*

*Courtesy of Pamela Pierce*

*Amy Bergeron (baby), Pamela Bergeron and Timothy Bergeron, 1968.*

*Courtesy of Frenchboro Historical Society*

*Esther Nickerson, 1930.*

"We didn't go to Bass Harbor that much in the early days, that was just like going to the moon."
— Vivian Davis Lunt, born 1915

"It is surprising how a boy of five can manage an axe, saw and 'lug' wood. His loads correspond to those his elders "back" from the woods. All fuel is "backed." If a community team of horses or oxen was provided to do such work it would save much labor in severe weather, for the woodpile is so often neglected until the need of it is felt."
— Lucy Allen King, Mission Worker, 1921

"I used to go over there in the evening when I was as a kid, and Robbins wife (Vera Dalzell) was a very good reader and she used to read to him. I used to enjoy going over there and listening to her read books. I hadn't heard anyone read that good, you know? She would read the story and it just kept going and it flowed right out."
— Carroll W. Lunt, born 1933

"We had running water before we had an artesian well. Doonie Hum was going to dig a hole for an outhouse for Cecil up on the hill. Well, he dug — Doonie Hum was just like a beaver — the biggest kind of place over and when he got down there so far it kept filling up with water. It filled up with water and it never went dry. We used it for a well for Cecil's house, our house and Eva's house.

"With gravity feed right down to the house, we had water coming right in. It got kind of low in the summer time, so you had to be a little careful, but all the rest of the year it was no problem."
— Vivian Davis Lunt, born 1915

"I remember one winter everyone had the flu, the whole island had the flu, I think. Bert Perkins and John Lunt walked around the harbor to every house, every day to check on people, make sure they had food and water and wood. I was probably 8 years old and I'll never forget that. Their house was always open too with a bed or food for anyone who came along, and they didn't have that much to share."
— Marjorie (Dalzell) Giamo, born 1918

*Flora Eveline "Mammie" Lunt (1887 - 1984).*

"When my mother did wash, they used to say, 'Sears and Roebuck has got her washing out.' In the field, she had I don't know how many clothes-lines, and they would be loaded every other day. They called her Sears and Roebuck because she had such large washings out. Poor Old Rose used to come up and help my mother with her wash. She was a good soul. They had these big wash tubs and a couple of boilers on the stove. She would boil her white clothes, her sheets and things. My mother's whites were just as white as could be. Then they would wring them all out by hand and hang them out to dry." — Mable (Lunt) Hall, born 1918

"I used to go down where Nardy lived; Danny's got a house near there now. There was five brothers there and I would go down there after school and eat with them quite a lot, because we didn't have a heck of a lot back then. They all had nicknames: Pean, Guy, Birge, Dib and Nardy.

We picked cranberries down there a lot in the fall, and a big meal down at Nardy's was hot cranberry sauce, hot biscuits and strong cheese. One of the guys would cook and then another would cook; they had two or three cooks in the house. Nardy would say, 'I would rather clothe you for a year then feed you for a month.' Or 'Eat to fill yourself, but don't eat to kill yourself.' I don't know if he was trying to tell me not to eat so much or what."

— Carroll W. Lunt, born 1933

*Courtesy of Ella V. Lunt*

*Nardy's store, 1950s. Thomas B. Lunt Sr. (left), John Mitchell, Leonard "Nardy" Lunt, Richard "Sam" Davis, Guy Lunt and Vincent A. Davis.*

*Courtesy of Frenchboro Historical Society*

*Angeline Lunt (1868 - 1937).*

*Courtesy of Frenchboro Historical Society*

*Atwood Lunt (1860 - 1937).*

*Courtesy of Sandra Lunt*

*Flora Eveline "Mammie" Lunt (1887 - 1984).*

*Courtesy of Frenchboro Historical Society*

*Shirley W. Lunt (b. 1890).*

Courtesy of Frenchboro Historical Society

*Sabra (Lunt) Rice (1866 - 1943).*

"We used to pick berries and sell them to the trawlers that would come in the harbor. We used go up to the Dalzell's, the house that Dickie [Hamblen] has now, and the blackberry bushes were up over your head. We would pick them and take them off the harbor and sell them."

— Lillian J. (Davis) Lunt, born 1925

"I worked for Mrs. Muir weekends and nights for a dollar a week doing all her chores, and I worked for Vera Dalzell and Robbins [Dalzell] for $1.25 a week, and that included splitting wood and carrying it in and washing floors. We did all kinds of things.

"Mrs. Muir thought she was just helping me out; we didn't have very much. I used to take the money and go right down and get dry beans and molasses and flour and things from down to Gene Van Norden's so we would have that to eat."

— Robert A. Lunt, born 1938

"My father was always in a hurry. Everything had to be done that instant. It used to be a good source of entertainment for the fishing crew, having me and my father argue with each other. We would have these running arguments about how to do things. He was in a hurry to get it done, and I was like, 'Wait, let's think this over; how do we want to do it? Let's try to do it the easier way.'

"And he was, 'Oh gorry, we got to get going, Son.'"

— Bennie S. Davis Jr., born 1935

*Courtesy of Bennie S. Davis Jr.*

*Bennie S. Davis Jr. (left) and Bennie S. Davis Sr., 1940s.*

"Daddy (Cecil Lunt) used to dig clams and shell them for me. I would then take them and go peddle them door-to-door. I got enough money to buy my first bike that way. I also used to go with Dad handlining for cod just off the back of the Head; fishing was that good back then. Daddy always had a stove aboard the boat. We used to take hot dogs, stick them on forks and cook them over the flames for lunch."

— Barbara (Lunt) Sawyer, born 1949

Photo by Lillian J. Lunt
*Barbara and Cecil Lunt after cod fishing, 1960s.*

"Scotty Ross — Frank Ross his name was — sold gas and stuff down there where Clarence Howard had his dock. He bought lobsters on a car off the harbor. Anyway, if you went down there to get gas or something and the ballgame was on in the summer — he would give you the key. He wouldn't leave that game."

— Carroll W. Lunt, born 1933

"Almy used to make the best doughnuts, and I used to love just the dough. I would always stop by her house on the way to school and beg her for some doughnut dough. She would never sell me any dough. Finally, she would give me a doughnut and say, "Now get on your way."

— Barbara (Lunt) Sawyer, born 1949

"Them older guys, they were rugged. Wes Lunt and Kai Lunt, now they were powerful. They hauled them old 15-foot dories, filled with bait, and haul them right down the flats to the wharf. Each dory had 25 or 30 bushels of herring, 60 pounds to a bushel. Each one could just pull their dory down the flats at low tide to their wharves."
— Sanford L. "Dick" Lunt, born 1910


"We camped out all over: Northeast Point, down to The Head, up in the Grove. We never stayed around the harbor; we got out of the way. We had freedom."
— Michael Holland, born 1961

*Photo by Lillian J. Lunt*

*Anthony Brown (left) and Michael Holland, 1960s.*


"I still remember coming across and wanting to go home and being homesick and from that day until the day I die, no matter where I live, Frenchboro will be down home."
— June (Davis) Thompson, born 1919

*Bert Perkins (front), Myrtle Perkins (left) and Erland "Manny" Dalzell, 1920s.*

*Charles Rice (b. 1915), hauling firewood on a homemade sled.*

*Kevin Holland (left), Sanford L. "Dick" Lunt and Anthony W. Brown, 1960s.*

"We lugged water from down by Doonie's or from the Wes well up the road. Then we had the dug well just up the hill. When I came home from the hospital with Danny (1960), David had put a bathroom in." — Sandra Lunt, born 1940

"We cleaned out the well, put rocks around it, put in a pump with an electric motor and a switch. We dug a ditch down the hill and buried the hose. Then every time you wanted water you just had to flip the switch." — David L. Lunt, born 1938

*Photo by Dean L. Lunt*

*Back row: David L. Lunt (left), Sandra Lunt, Michelle A. Lunt, Dean L. Lunt*
*Front row: Vivian D. Lunt, Emily A. Lunt, Sanford L. "Dick" Lunt, 1996.*

358

*Chapter Sixteen:*
# Casting the Net

## Island Sports

I was obsessed with sports during childhood, especially baseball and football. Dallas Cowboy quarterback Roger Staubach and Boston Red Sox catcher Carlton Fisk were my two boyhood idols. The New York Yankees and the Pittsburgh Steelers embodied evil.

I loved the games, the competition. My only trouble? I was often alone. During the winter of 1978-1979, I was 12 years old and the only person under 20 on Long Island. For most of my childhood, I was one of the only "year-round" kids really interested in sports. Of course, that was not surprising when enrollment in the island's K-8 school never rose above six during my last five years, before finally dropping to just one — me.

Still I tried. When the ice finally gave up each spring and the ground dried to squishy, I took a home plate, a makeshift pitching rubber and my grandfather's 100-foot tape measure to the island ballfield. I set home plate in the batter's box and measured off where bases should go. (I would have killed for REAL white chalk). I measured the proper distances to the mound and set the distances down each power alley, which ended in spruce trees; a natural Green Monster, if you will. I mowed out baselines and foul lines through the thick dead grass. Let's just call it spring fever.

By the time I finished, you could see a baseball field, albeit one with a dirt road running across second base. Unfortunately, we rarely played a game there. Maybe an occasional undermanned softball game or two over the course of the 1970s.

I was not dissuaded. During the spring of my seventh grade year, I left Frenchboro to finish out junior high school in Tremont. I left in time to play baseball. I also played organized ball on the mainland each summer.

I played Little League for the KPs in Tremont, Pony League for the Dolphins on Mount Desert Island, and still later American Legion for the MDI Acadians. I was co-captain of my high school baseball team and captain of a club team at Syracuse.

For Little League and Pony League games, my father ran me across eight miles of ocean for each game or practice. With no telephones to communicate with the mainland, we guessed whether looming storm clouds meant a rainout or we tried to contact Allen Murphy on the CB radio. We always erred on the side of playing, sometimes making the trip in dense fog or choppy seas. We returned across Blue Hill Bay as darkness fell, eating ice cream cones from Hopkins store. I loved it.

But to play in all those leagues, I needed practice. And just marking out a baseball field didn't cut it. So, creativity was the key.

Options for solo baseball were essentially two: a rubber ball off the roof of my parent's house or batting rocks with a stick.

My house overlooked Lunt Harbor. It was built partly on ledge in the late 1950s, so fill was hauled in to make a small front lawn. About 20 to 30 feet from the house a stone wall holds the lawn in place. The edge drops off about six feet to a rocky, unkept area. A two-foot high wooded fence sits along the edge.

I spent hours there listening to Red Sox games or sports talk shows out of Boston on the old WMEX AM-1510 and WHDH AM-850.

And, of course, playing ball.

I faced the house with the fence at my back and tossed a rubber ball (I preferred the "Super Pinky," light and very bouncy) high into the air. It hit the roof and bounced back toward my field. I played the ball wherever it went (or was "hit"). Catching the ball was an out. If the ball hit the ground it was a single. If it hit the ground and bounced over the fence it was a ground rule double. If it went over the fence on the fly, it was a homerun. I played the wall carefully on long flies; it seemed a long way down to the splinter bushes.

It sounds simple, but I devised complex rules for the sake of reality.

Like many builders of old Maine houses, my parents built additions as needed: have a child, add a room. Our house had one original section — basically a one-story cape — and a smaller addition on the right that was set back, creating a little jog to the cellar door. On the left, the roofline ran perpendicular to the main house, as if it were a giant dormer.

If the ball hit the dormer section, the ball shot sideways into the driveway for a double, or possibly a triple if the imaginary runner dared test my arm. If the ball missed the roof and landed on the steps or in the cellarway, it was another double (although if it hit the ground directly, it was a foul ball).

The addition had only one small facing window far to the right, allowing me to fire the ball directly off the side for line drives, groundballs, bunts or throws to a base. For example, if a runner broke for third, I threw the ball off the wall and caught it like third baseman applying the tag. If the runner tried to steal or score from second on a hard single, again I fired the ball off the wall and caught it like the second basemen or catcher. There was virtually no situation I could not play out.

The underdog Boston Red Sox (or sometimes my upstart Maine team) won many a World Series during the early and mid-1970s, usually with a line-up that featured me batting third, just before Fisk.

Another baseball option was batting rocks.

I used several fields. A major stadium existed on the shore between the Lunt & Lunt wharf and the bait shed. It faced the Ben Davis wharf, which sat across a small channel of water at low and medium tides.

I used either an old trap lath (oak was the best choice), a broomstick, gaff handle or even a good piece of driftwood for a bat. My actual wooden baseball bats were too precious to damage with rocks, and, call me a purist, I didn't like the ding of rock on aluminum.

A rock batted up onto the top of the wharf was a homerun. A line shot into the facing crib work was usually a double (high off the wall). A shot down the lines (as defined by a mooring buoy on the left and the harbor ledge on the right) was also a double. Depending on tides, the outcropped ledge provided a short porch down the right field line, almost like Fenway's Pesky Pole. Pop flys were outs, ground balls were outs, three misses was a strike out and so forth.

For close plays, I threw rocks at specific targets, meaning a tree or a rock along the shore. I used all the proper motions and techniques, and hitting the target was an out.

Football was a similar story.

On some fall weekends my friend Kurt Forsgren came down from Old Town and we played catch. But for the most part, I walked the road that circles the harbor as an eight and nine-year-old boy throwing a football — or sometimes a lobster buoy for want of actual pigskin — high in the air and catching it. I threw it out away from me so I had to run to make the catch. I wasn't perfect, so I also spent time coaxing the ball back to shore after it rolled into the harbor. My teams called very few running plays.

The most involved football games occurred on my back lawn during the fall and winter. I tended to stick to the proper seasons.

My mother had a clothesline with a T-shaped pole at each end. For the sake of realism, I tied two poles — at first giant plastic Tinker Toys and later broken antenna pieces — on either side to make goal posts.

Facing the clothesline, I hiked the ball to myself, dropped back under pressure, scanned the field and picked out receivers. A big towel was an easy 3 or 4-yard gain, a washcloth in the last row might be a 50-yard pass. But danger lurked. The hand towel might be an interception. A jacket might be 10-yard pass completion, but should the ball stick in the hood, it was an interception. The left leg of a pair of pants might be 10-yard gain; the right side an incompletion.

For extra points and the inevitable game-winning field goals, I used my makeshift goal posts. I set the ball on a plastic T, clumped snow or a bunch of twigs, paced back (two steps back, two steps to the left) and tried to split the uprights.

Thankfully, a lot of silly penalties called back a few misses, giving me a second chance at three points.

And a childhood of gridiron glory.

———◆◆◆———

## *Rebecca Lunt's Frenchboro News*

In 1976, Rebecca (Reed) Lunt began providing readers of *The Bar Harbor Times* with a weekly down-home dose of news from Frenchboro. Her news has ranged from the historic (the first telephone calls), to the disastrous (Paul "Rusty" Crossman's house burning down), to hardships (frequent loss of electrical power). Beyond that, she has covered such events as births, deaths and community suppers and provided her famous list of those coming and going on the Maine State Ferry.

Rebecca tried to retire once in 1997, but after a few weeks she received enough calls and letters that she again started to write.

Courtesy of *The Bar Harbor Times*

*Rebecca J. Lunt, 1980s.*

Her very first column detailed an anniversary party thrown for her brother-in-law, Cecil Lunt, and his wife, Lillian (Davis) Lunt.

"On Lillian's and Cecil's 30th wedding anniversary someone said 'Why don't you do a write-up on the anniversary party and send it to the paper?' I said 'O.K., I'd just as soon.' And then before I got that all written, someone said 'Why don't you add a little news to it and see how that goes?' Well, everyone liked it," Rebecca said. "And I've kept on going."

Starting with that news item, Rebecca wrote for twenty-two more years and penned more than 1,100 columns. An illness finally forced her to give up the column in the fall of 1999.

The following is her first column from *The Bar Harbor Times* in September 1976:

"Mr. and Mrs. Cecil Lunt celebrated their 30th wedding anniversary at a surprise party given by their daughter & son-in-law, Mr. and Mrs. Randall Sawyer.

"They received many lovely gifts and a beautiful cake made and

363

decorated by their daughter. Refreshments were served buffet style and a good time was had by all.

"Those present were: Mr. and Mrs. Randy Sawyer and boys Corey and Christopher, also Mrs. Lunt's son Paul Crossman. Mr. and Mrs. Russell Lunt, Donald Lunt from Union, Mrs. Helen Lunt, Mrs. Mildred Onyett, Mrs. Marcia Giberson, Mrs. Carmen Reynolds, Mrs. and Mrs. Sanford Lunt and their grandson Dean Lunt, Mr. and Mrs. Rod Forsgren and son Kirt from Old Town and Mrs. Rebecca Lunt."

Since that column, regular readers of *The Bar Harbor Times* have in many ways come to know the residents of Long Island and their weekly trials and triumphs. Some people who have never set foot on the island nor even know any residents track who is sick, who is building a house and who has just moved on.

Following are snippets from her columns over the years:

January 17, 1980: "Fire! And that's just what it was the morning of January 6 at Frenchboro. John and Rebecca Lunt were sitting at the snack bar in their kitchen when they heard a voice on the CB say, "I've got a fire!" John knew the voice was Paul "Rusty" Crossman, and by the time Arin Teel and Sandra Lunt were on the CB hollering that Rusty's place was on fire, John had grabbed his hat and coat and was down in the cellar with the garage door up lugging Indian pumps outside, and trucks were coming from every direction. "They had to get chainsaws to cut down trees so the fire wouldn't get into the woods. Billy Teel went aboard his boat and called the Southwest Harbor Coast Guard through his VHF radio at 10:30 and they weren't long getting here. All the men turned out to help and even some of the women. David Lunt had his boat in at his wharf, so he took Randy Sawyer across to Rusty's place and he got onto the wharf and threw about 125 traps into the water and then the heat drove him and he returned to the boat.

"That's all they saved and Rusty lost everything else."

She described the evening of the first off-island telephone calls, made while new equipment was being tested, in her December 3, 1983 column:

"The Historical Society had their third annual meeting at the schoolhouse Friday evening. Before we started the meeting we were waiting for the news on Channel 2, as the children visited Gov. Brennan and it was to be shown that evening. While we were waiting the telephone rang and Alan Albers went to answer it.

"He came back and said, "It's for you, Rebecca, it's John." Well, what he told me was he had received the first telephone call from my friend Carole Vaughn in Norman, OK. And that she would call back at 8:00 so as to talk with me. (Which she did.) Jeff said, 'What a coincidence to be from Oklahoma – that's where I got the equipment from for the telephone.'

"In the meantime, before Carole called me back, I came home from the meeting and called my mother Mrs. Flora Reed in Bass Harbor, so she was the first to receive a call from here (except what Jeff had made in testing). Charlotte Sawyer was next with a call from her son and daughter-in-law Randy and Barbara Sawyer. Barbara had Charlotte call her sister Marilyn Brown in Ft. Lauderdale, Fl. So as to let her know she could call in. Marilyn called Barbara and then made a surprise call to her mother Lillian, and her Aunt Vivian Lunt, and brother Rusty. Alan Albers called his brother.

"Later Friday evening Lillian also had a call from her sister Rosetta Seavey in Bernard. Your correspondent had a call Monday morning from her niece Earlene Lunt who lives on the Bayside Road.

"I often wondered why those people on the quiz programs got so excited when they'd win. Well, I felt like that when our telephones began to jingle and we knew we could talk to people on the mainland. What a feeling!!!"

Mostly Rebecca's columns detailed more routine events.

July 16, 1981: "The Fourth of July found us engulfed in fog, so most of the island folks and visitors drove to the Eastern beach for a picnic. There were 45 in all at the beach.

"Mr. and Mrs. Randy Sawyer took their son Corey to the Pine Tree Camp for a week-and-a-half stay last Sunday.

"Clarence Lunt got towed to Bass Harbor Thursday afternoon by his son Cary Lunt as something was out of kilter with his engine. He got the parts that were needed and had John Lunt tow him back Saturday morning. We all gave him a razzing and told him he was just saving on his gas."

Dec. 20, 1984: "We've really been having bad luck in the past two weeks. We've had blowy weather and that causes the ferry to change her days of coming to Frenchboro.

"Davie, Debbie and Travis Lunt also came back on Thursday's ferry. Debbie is a mother to be, and she had been over to the doctors.

Watch for the news in February; that's when she's due.

"Danny and Tina Lunt are also expecting a new baby in their family come March, and Zachary says its 'O.K.' with him."

August 25, 1988: "Last Friday was the day and most of the women were right in the dough dish, making pies for the Lobster Festival.

"Lobster Festival day came and we crawled out of bed real early, the sun was coming up and all that fog went somewhere for the day. This was our 28th year and I can only remember once we had rain and I think that was the first year.

"We served over 600 people, who started arriving at 11 a.m. and the last ones went out the door about 3 p.m."

February 16, 1989: "Last Friday evening all the kids, and some of the parents, were on the hill by the schoolhouse, having a good time sliding.

"The community supper went over good, and for as cold as it was that evening, there were 30 who showed up.

"We had baked beans, hot biscuits and yeast bread, along with a chicken casserole, macaroni and cheese, goulash, coleslaw, broccoli-cheese casserole."

Feb. 11, 1993: "Early Thursday morning at 1:45 a.m., we lost our power. My husband, John, and also Dannie Lunt had been up during the night and heard draggers in the cable area, so they figured that was it. In dragging up the cable from Swans Island the end where it split was down near John's Island. They finally got both ends but had to buoy them for the night."

## *State Rep. Raymond L. Teel*

In the history of Frenchboro, only one person has ever sought, let alone won election for political office beyond the confines of Long Island Plantation or Frenchboro. In 1940, Raymond L. Teel was elected state representative for the district that then included Swans Island, Tremont, Mount Desert, Lamoine, Southwest Harbor and Cranberry Island.

Ray, son of William M. Teel and Maria (Lunt) Teel, was born Feb. 9, 1900. He worked as a fisherman for most of his life and served as island postmaster from 1962 to 1972.

During his one term in the legislature he served on the Sea and Shore Fisheries Committee.

The crux of his campaign was a political advertisement that he wrote and placed in local newspapers.

It read:

"To the voters of the class towns of Mt. Desert, Southwest Harbor, Tremont, Lamoine, Cranberry Island, Swans Island and Long Island Plantation:

"I expect to be a candidate in the June primaries for the Republican nomination as representative from my district. This is the first time that Long Island Plantation has ever offered a candidate for this office; I trust that the voters will give consideration to this fact if they find the qualifications of the candidate equal to the duties of the office.

"I am a fisherman, and I should like to represent this district at the next legislature simply as a working man, there to benefit my fellow workers, as a boon to the common good of all. I expect the voters to select the candidates who, in their opinion, are best fitted to fill the offices to which they aspire: this is real democracy, and I shall be well satisfied with the decision when the elections are over. "At the present time there is a real need to aid the fishing industry. In my opinion, the way to a successful business is to adopt constructive policies and maintain them, which has not been the rule in the past.

Too long these interests have been exploited and laws enacted to benefit a few. One by one Maine's great industries have been shrink-

Courtesy of Ella V. Lunt

*Gertrude Lunt (left), Marjorie Dalzell, Rita Hughes, Raymond Teel, 1920s.*

ing away, and fishing is no exception to the rule.

"It would please me greatly to have an opportunity to offer some constructive suggestions to promote the State fisheries industry. I really have a sincere desire to be of service to the business of which I am a small part. However, this decision rests with the voters at the coming elections held during the year."

## *Frenchboro Historical Society*

The Frenchboro Historical Society was organized in late 1979, not long after publication of Vivian (Davis) Lunt's *History of Long Island Plantation, Frenchboro*. That book helped generate interest in island history and spurred the identification and collection of many important artifacts, especially photographs. From the beginning, Vivian and her sister Lillian served as the society's driving forces.

The first goal was to create a museum. The Historical Society museum opened for the first time in the summer of 1980 in the basement of John and Rebecca Lunt's house. In 1981, the museum moved across the road to John's small workshop.

Also in 1981, the society started a fundraising campaign with a goal of $3,500. As part of that effort, the society began collecting photographs for a pictorial history.

By 1984, the museum operated at the former Brook Hill General Store on the harbor's east side.

In 1985, Margaret "Peggy" Rockefeller Dulany donated land for a museum across from the current schoolhouse. The site was once occupied by the island's second schoolhouse. When the building fund surpassed $6,000, construction was set to begin in the spring.

The new museum opened in 1986. It has evolved into a focal point for island visitors and developed as an important site for the islanders as well. It serves as the fourth building in a cluster with the school, church and parsonage.

The museum building has grown steadily and now houses the town library and computer center.

## *Outer Island Seafood Co.*

The short but eventful life of Outer Island Seafood began in 1985 when the company was officially organized as a corporation with shareholders and an idea.

Based at the Lunt & Lunt wharf, Outer Island Seafood was driven by David L. Lunt and Eric Jacobssen of New York. Jacobssen started Maine Marketing Co., which operated the joint venture with OIS. The company made lobster sauces, jarred them in Bell canning jars and sold them mostly at upscale or gourmet food stores. A 16-ounce jar sold for $22.

The sauces came in four styles. They were: Lobster American, which included lobster, mussels, tomato sauce, garlic, onions and fennel; Lobster Curry, which included lobster, fish, and chicken stocks with onions, mussels, raisins, coconut and sea salt; Lobster Saffron, which included lobster, roasted red peppers, egg yolks, saffron, chicken and fish stock; and Lobster Chowder, which included lobster, potatoes, onions, peas and corn.

The hearty, thick sauces with chunks of lobster meat were essentially heat and serve sauces that could be served alone, over rice or pasta or as a base for stew. It was almost universally acknowledged that the four sauces were delicious, and they sold well. However, the product had one fundamental flaw: it spoiled quickly. The company never resolved the conflict between a desire for maximum freshness and the need for longer shelf life. That conflict caused the company's relatively quick demise.

But the idea struck a chord that generated even more media attention for the island. Press highlights included an important mention in *The New York Times* Food Notes column. In addition, *The Ellsworth American* ran a photo spread of Tina M. Lunt, Debbie A. Lunt and Lillian J. Lunt cooking the sauces and John R. Lunt Jr. picking lobsters.

One highlight was a weekend trip in March 1986 to Bloomingdale's in New York City. The famed department store devoted a corner of its fresh food section to Outer Island Seafood. While a gourmet chef heated and served the fresh lobster product to customers, David L. Lunt answered questions from Big Apple natives and tourists. Bloomingdale's cast him as an honest-to-gosh island fisherman and lobster expert.

## Lobsterman's Lunch & Lunt's Dockside Deli

In the same small building on the Lunt & Lunt wharf where Outer Island Seafood operated, two seasonal restaurants have also operated.

Lobsterman's Lunch ran for several years in the 1970s, operated by Sandra and David L. Lunt and including Lillian J. Lunt as a cook. The restaurant served many residents, area natives and the summer yachting crowd before closing down.

*Tina M. Lunt at the Lunt & Lunt wharf, 1989.*

The restaurant was reincarnated in 1987 as Lunt's Dockside Deli by Dean L. Lunt and Tina M. Lunt. It is still operated by Tina, Debbie, David L. and Sandra Lunt. Since 1987, the take-out restaurant, open from July 5 to the end of August, has grown dramatically. It now employs additional workers.

The restaurant helps lure the yachts that now fill the harbor on many summer evenings. Several yachting clubs make reservations to ensure food and moorings. A Bass Harbor tour boat company, operated by brothers Kim and Eric Strauss, makes daily sightseeing runs, which include lunch, to the island during the summer months.

## Great Duck Island

While Long Island does not have a lighthouse on its shores, the town of Frenchboro has two: Great Duck Island Light and Mount Desert Rock.

Mount Desert Rock, a mere outcropping of ledge located about 15 miles from Long Island, is one of the state's most remote lighthouses and is now fully automated.

However, Great Duck actually hosted a small community. The island was so named because a large pond once attracted thousands of ducks each spring to hatch their young, according to Robert Thayer Sterling in *"Lighthouses of the Maine Coast and the Men Who Keep Them."*

Great Duck is about six miles east of Long Island. It has no harbor, making landings on its rocky shore difficult and sometimes impossible.

Great Duck was settled in the early 1800s. The Federal Census lists 19 people and two families on the island in 1820. John Crane and John Hamilton headed the two households.

William Gilley, a former lighthouse keeper on Baker Island, moved to Great Duck in 1849, according to Rita Johnson Kenway in *"Gotts Island, Maine: Its People 1880-1992."* Gilley purchased Great Duck in 1837, but the earliest recorded deed is in 1846 when he purchased the entire island from the executors of William Bingham's estate, Kenway said.

Gilley, 65, built a house and raised sheep on the island pretty much alone because his wife, Hannah, refused to move onto the small island. Gilley stayed on the island for about 15 years until he returned to Baker Island. He died at 92.

Charles Harding, a carpenter in London, and his wife, Mary, a seamstress, purchased the island, more than 100 sheep and a house for $2,200 in 1866, according to Kenway. The Hardings were alerted by a nephew that the island was for sale. They jumped at the chance to buy it. After Mary landed on Great Duck she didn't leave again until her house burned down in 1882.

Charles and Mary Harding had no children, but their nephew William Harding lived with them for awhile. In addition, Jennie H. Lawson, an orphan, moved to Duck Island with them when she was 12.

Another man, Dennis Driscoll, purchased a share of the tiny island in 1871 and lived there as well.

The fire that destroyed the house and other belongings on Duck Island occurred between Christmas Day 1882 and New Year's Day 1883. The families were driven to find shelter in the boathouse until they could be rescued.

Residents in Southwest Harbor saw the flames and a schooner soon reached Great Duck to rescue the Hardings. After the fire, everyone left the island. Most moved to Gotts Island, but Charles Harding moved to Cranberry Island by himself.

Relatives of the Harding family, including Clarence Harding, continued to tend sheep on Great Duck into the 1940s.

During the 1800s there were several shipwrecks on Great Duck. They included *Piciune* at Mers Point, *Edward DesLyle* at Seal Cove and *Ellen* near Eastern Cove. Clarence Harding in *"Gotts Island"* said the *Ellen* ran ashore on Dec. 22, 1878 in a gale and snowstorm. Two men on the ship were saved but four others drowned. The four men were buried in a marsh near Eastern Beach; it was the only spot islanders could dig through, given the frozen ground.

Later, family members removed three bodies, but the fourth man remained after his mother visited the island and felt the oceanside marsh was a good place to remain at rest.

Great Duck Island Light was built in 1890 with a tower that extended about 67 feet above the water. Its flashing red light marks the entrance to Blue Hill Bay and lights a path toward Frenchman's Bay. It was among the loneliest outposts on the coast.

"One who happened to be stationed at this severe outpost before the World War (WWI) knew what it was to be entirely isolated away from friends and the voice that tells what's going on in the world," Sterling wrote.

Three one-and-one-half story houses were also built about 250 feet north of the tower. Two of the three were nearly identical. The third was rectangular in design and designated as the main keeper's house. A 30-foot by 40-foot boathouse was built about 1,500 feet northeast of the dwellings, sometimes called "the reservation." In 1895, the West boat-house was built and in 1901 a stone oil house was built.

After World War I started, the government installed telephones and radios in lighthouses. In part, the government wanted to give lightkeep-ers the ability to immediately report submarine activity.

According to Sterling, a lobsterman with 12 children moved onto the island in the early 1900s. At the same time, two lightkeepers also had chil-dren. After a plea for help, the Lighthouse Service agreed to build a small school. For a short time, a lightkeeper's wife kept school, but later a teacher was hired. Residents provided her with board.

Because of difficult landings and rough seas, it was often impossible to deliver mail for stretches of three or four weeks.

"At times it was like a football game, with plenty of interference," Sterling wrote about mail delivery. "Everybody was anxious, for a letter did mean so much. Relatives and friends might be dead and buried and only the letter would tell the story."

From 1923 to 1941, three keepers were stationed at the lighthouse, including the family of Leverett Stanley. His four children attended school on the mainland and lived on Duck Island when class was not in session.

One of the children was Maxine Stanley Clark of Southwest Harbor. She lived on Duck Island until she was 16 years old.

For a 1988 article in the *Linking the DOTS* newsletter, Vivian Lunt wrote: "Maxine remembers: fishing for cod and mackerel, which her father salted and dried for future use; bird hunting with her brother Perley, who was thoroughly disgusted when she scared the birds; picking wild strawberries, cranberries and shore greens; and searching for pitch gum on spruce trees. She collected the gum in a can and took it home to chew at her leisure.

"There was an old crank record player and that was the source of entertainment. The battery radio was reserved for newscasts and Amos & Andy."

Great Duck Island light was automated in the 1980s. The island is now deserted, but the red glow of the light remains a beacon when crossing Blue Hill Bay between Black Island and Long Island.

## Pond and Placentia Islands

In addition to Long Island, Great Duck Island and Black Island (see Chapter Twelve), Pond and Placentia Islands have also supported year-round communities.

Details of the small communities that existed on Placentia and Pond Islands are provided in Charles B. McLane's *"Blue Hill Bay: Islands of the Mid-Maine Coast"* and *"Islands of the Mid-Maine Coast: Penobscot Bay,"* respectively.

Placentia — pronounced locally as "Plasench" — was likely inhabited during the Revolutionary era, according to McLane. A dwelling is shown on Atlantic Neptune maps of that era. Placentia, like Black Island, maintained strong ties to Long Island. Many of its early residents or their children eventually moved out the bay to Long Island. In 1820, Placentia residents included John Davis, Eben Lane, Robert Mitchell, Elias Rich, Joseph Remick and John Walls. In 1840, residents included Abner Lunt, William Rich, Thomas Rich, Daniel Hamlin (Hamblen), Robert Mitchell and George Twist. At least half of those last six moved to Long Island.

The population dwindled from a high of about 40 in 1830 to just the family of Robert Mitchell by 1860. In 1880, Simson or Simeon Butler and his family, who came from Long Island, lived there. They were probably the last year-round residents of that era, according to McLane.

One couple lived on Placentia Island by themselves starting in 1949. They rowed back and forth to Bass Harbor when necessary for several decades.

No school or any other public structures were built on the island. However, the graves of some early settlers, including some Mitchells, are on the island.

Placentia Island also served as the official poor farm for Tremont during part of the 1800s.

Meanwhile, Pond Island was inhabited sometime before 1810 by the family of William Wells and then before 1820 by Prescott Powers. One of the island's largest landowners was Nathaniel Allen, who acquired Pond Island from agents of Col. James Swan in 1835. Allen, one of the first officials of Long Island Plantation in 1840, operated a large farm on Pond Island (see Chapter Nine).

Like Placentia, Pond Island probably never developed any public infrastructure. Pond Island never grew beyond one or two families. By the late 1800s, absentee ownership tried to run a farming operation there by hiring people from nearby islands, according to McLane. Over the years, other ventures came and went on the island, including weir fishing and later a sportsman club in the 1950s.

At one point, children from Pond Island attended school on nearby Opechee Island or Calf Island in the early 1900s. Opechee, originally part of Long Island Plantation, was given to Swans Island in 1901.

## *The Town Library*

The island's first library, the Long Island Seamans Library, was started in the late 1830s or early 1840s by Rehoboth Hannah B. Lunt. Eventually, the library was probably based at the original school/Baptist church building. However, Hannah started the library before the school was built and before any other public structures existed. The original library was probably based either at Hannah's house or at Israel B. Lunt's store.

The library loaned books to residents and visiting fishermen. Given Hannah's dedication to religion and education, many books probably included Christian themes and the library existed as a combination education/missionary-style endeavor.

Despite that early start, no formal library existed for decades. Island books were stored at the schoolhouse. During the early and mid-20th century, the Maine Sea Coast Missionary Society brought boxes and boxes of magazines for islanders.

In 1969, Isle au Haut residents donated about 135 books to establish a new library. The island's "Womens' Group" donated bookshelves and set them up at the Parish House for want of a better facility. Various people donated books over the years, but the library suffered for lack of a storage and display area.

The island's first dedicated library began to take shape in the late 1980s.

The Frenchboro Historical Society helped raise the money and added a room to its existing museum. Vivian Lunt and Donna (Howard) Hasal helped collect books and donations from island residents while summer visitors began regular book and monetary donations. The library was opened seven days a week in the summer and by appointment in the winter.

Shortly, Donna Forsgren became librarian. She began organizing the collection and streamlining the library's operations. She also developed a children's section, and summer programs such as story hour. Burr Bost also helped out in the 1990s, while Ruth Davis headed the library committee and began computerizing its contents with the help of Joan Daigneault.

In the late 1990s, the library installed a computer with Internet access. In 1998, the library was enlarged, insulated and a heater installed. Marissa Rozenski continues to organize fundraisers and expand the library and computer center.

## Fire Department

Islanders have always worried about a potentially devastating fire and have maintained some type of fire department for more than 100 years.

As early as July 1892, Hiram A. Lunt Sr. was appointed forest fire warden for Great Duck Island, Little Duck Island, East Black Island and Placentia Island. Calvin C. Lunt was appointed warden for Pond, Calf and West Black Islands. William Van Norden was appointed forest fire warden for Long Island, Crow Island, Harbor Island, Eastern and Western Sister Islands and Johns Island.

Presumably, men visited these islands to check for fire hazards or other problems. Each spring, they probably burned the dead grass on some islands, a common seasonal practice.

Despite attention, few advancements occurred in actual fire protection. Several houses burned to the ground during the late 1800s and early 1900s. Those fires, some allegedly set for insurance money, unfortunately are a key reason why few of the island's nicer 19th century houses still stand.

In 1969, the island acquired its first fire truck. Peggy Rockefeller donated a 1936 model truck and islanders raised about $600 at the annual Lobster Festival to buy the hose. Twelve Indian Pumps — metal water containers that strap onto a person's back with a hose, hand pump and nozzle — were also purchased.

In 1987, the town built its first community house, which also serves as a fire station. That building was the first public structure built since the Parish House in 1918. John R. Lunt Jr. served as the fire chief for many years.

## *Medical Care and the early Midwives*

Long Island has never had dedicated medical attention. Islanders tended to the sick using experience and tradition, which sometimes was not enough.

When advanced emergency care was needed — and if weather permitted — doctors came from Swans Island, Tremont or other coastal towns on sloops and other sailing vessels. With no way to contact a doctor in advance, combined with the often unpassable ocean, doctors rarely came until the 1900s. The distance could indeed be difficult. In February of 1923, Alphonso "Fon" Lunt, Eugene Harding and another man rowed more than four miles to Joyce Beach on Swans Island to get medication for Edna (Lunt) Rich. That is likely the beach closest to where the doctor lived. Edna, who suffered a stroke, died two days later.

Midwives represented the most experienced island assistance during the island's first 100 years. Since founding, experienced island women served as unofficial midwives helping deliver babies as safely as possible. Still, during the 19th century many problems arose and some babies died at birth or lived only a short time. Some young women also died during childbirth.

By the early 1900s, two women competed to offer midwife services, receiving $2 for each birth. The best known was Emily S. (Davis) Gilman, the daughter of James T. and Abigail (Milliken) Davis. Emily owned one of the island's grandest homes standing in what was commonly known as the Gilman Field or The Grove, next to the Israel B. Lunt cemetery. Where she got her money has long been a matter of speculation on the island. The Gilman field now contains three houses built as part of the town's Homestead Project. The other midwife was Rebecca N. (Davis) Robinson, daughter of William Davis and Elizabeth Dawes. She died in 1922.

*Courtesy of Frenchboro Historical Society*

*Frank Thurlow and Emily Gilman, 1890s.*

Dr. Howard W. Small signed this statement for Emily on June 11, 1900. "This is to certify that I consider Mrs. Emma (sic) Gilman as a suitable and trustworthy person to attend cases of midwifery and confinement on Long Island in the said state of Maine.

"At this place where confinements often occur when it would be impossible to get the services of a physician and where some trustworthy person is absolutely needed. One who is intelligent, has read and studied suitable books upon the subject and informed herself by experience so as to be able to act in an emergency and so well informed that when a case occurs when a physician is required or any danger to the mother or child is threatened, she will without delay notify those interested of the danger and advise the services of a physician when possible."

Emily Gilman's final delivery was Verna "Bunny" Mitchell on May 20, 1919. Emily died that September.

Throughout the 1920s, 1930s and even into the 1940s, many island women "took sick" and delivered babies in their island homes. All 15 children born to Flora E. "Mammie" and John R. Lunt Sr., stretching from 1905 to 1930, were born in her house. Mammie's first delivery was with a midwife, a stillborn baby girl in 1905. A Swans Island doctor delivered her final baby, John Lunt Jr., in 1930. During that span, three of her children died during childbirth, one died as an infant and another as a toddler.

Starting in the 1920s boats improved, making it easier to bring doctors when needed. However, since the island remained without electricity into the 1940s, night deliveries still occurred by candlelight and oil lamps.

The doctors who did come, came from Swans Island and were rousted in the night if necessary by men in a hurry to shuttle them back to Long Island.

"One night we were having popcorn and were all sitting around eating. We went home and in the middle of the night Momma started having labor pains (with Rosetta Davis). Vincent, I think, went up to Mammie's house to get someone, and that is when Dick and Clarence Howard went after the doctor," said Vivian Lunt.

Sanford "Dick" Lunt added: "Yes, it was in February, and we had to cut for an hour to get the boat clear off the harbor there was so much ice. We had to break a road from his boat to the end of the point to get out."

By the 1920s and 1930s some women also left the island to give birth, often at maternity houses established for pregnant women near their due dates.

When Vivian Lunt gave birth to David L. in May of 1938, she stayed at a maternity house in Manset. She and a woman from Cranberry Island delivered only hours apart. Vivian traveled across eight miles of ocean in a small, open boat at 5 a.m. and delivered David that afternoon at 3 p.m. As was customary in those days, she remained at the maternity house for two weeks.

Even years later, it sometimes remained a rocky ride to delivery. In 1958, Sandra Lunt, pregnant with her first child, David W., rode across the bay in nasty winter storms on the old *SeaWind*. And in the winter of 1960 while pregnant with Daniel L., she spent some rides huddled over a bucket aboard the *Kiboko*.

During the first half of the 20th century, islanders also relied on the Maine Sea Coast Missionary Society for health care. The Mission regularly brought dentists, doctors and nurses to the island for clinics.

## *Island Baseball*

During the early and mid-part of the century when baseball was the nation's true pastime, the island maintained its own baseball team.

The first era of island baseball was in the 1920s and 1930s when enough men gathered to play games on the island and occasional games against other islands or towns.

The second era, mostly during the 1950s and early 1960s, was more ambitious. The island team frequently played teams from Swans Island, and also traveled to Ellsworth, Southwest Harbor, Waltham and other towns.

The second lineup included: John R. Lunt Jr., Carroll W. Lunt, David L. Lunt, Robert A. Lunt, Richard "Sam" Davis, Ben Davis Jr. and men from the original team as well.

As the second baseball era wound down, Frenchboro sometimes picked up players from Swans Island to fill out its roster.

Courtesy of Frenchboro Historical Society

*Island Baseball Team, 1930s. Front row: Guy Lunt (left), Clifton Lunt, Clarence Lunt, John R. Lunt Sr., Tommy B. Lunt Sr., Malcolm Lunt, and Willard Osier.*
*Back row: Everett "Ebbit" Dalzell Jr., Hiram A. "Doonie Hum" Lunt Jr., Sanford "Dick" Lunt, unknown, Vernon Dalzell, Vincent Davis, K. Gardiner Lunt, Frank Dalzell, Irving "Pean" Lunt, Cecil Lunt and Tommy B. Lunt Jr.*

## Radio and Television

In an island community that lived without electricity, ferry service and running water for decades, the first television and radio sets were major events.

Like men and women across the country, islanders gathered around radios to hear ballgames, radio shows and boxing matches. Only a handful of people actually owned battery operated radios in the early days. Men gathered at Eugene Van Norden's store to hear boxing matches featuring such legends as Jack Dempsey and later at Nardy's store to hear Rocky Marciano, Joe Louis and the Friday night fights.

"There were not that many radios around in the very early days. People couldn't afford them because it required buying these dry cell batteries, and they were not long lasting if you had your radio on a lot, and most of them did. You ordered new batteries from the catalog as a rule," said Marjorie Giamo.

Groups of men spent summer afternoons sitting on Marjorie's porch listening to Boston Red Sox and old Boston Braves games. And at night they might listen to country and western music.

"It was big gathering in the summer for ballgame time out on the front porch. The men were there with their 10-cents-a-pack cigarettes, and we would make lemonade for them, or coffee or tea," Marjorie said.

"One of the announcers on the radio at that time was Jim Britt. We called my grandfather Jim Britt as a nickname. They listened to anything. Sometimes they listened to Red Sox games and sometimes they listened to Braves games. We could always get good stations out here in the middle of the ocean. One show, called "The Barn Dance," came on Saturday night about 10:30. It was this country and western music came on from Wheeling, West Virginia.

"Lincoln [Lunt] would come and visit a lot too, he liked radio. They would say 'Lincoln, when you go, just lock the door.' Everyone would go to bed, and he turned the radio off when he went home."

The Maine Sea Coast Missionary Society actually installed the island's first radio at the Parish House sometime before 1920. But the first television sets brought Hollywood and New York to Frenchboro in a whole new way.

Because the island was without electricity until 1956, most early television sets were adapted to operate on battery power, meaning they were converted from AC to DC current.

Charles B. Hooper purchased the island's first television set on Feb. 8, 1953. After his purchase, others quickly followed. Six days later Guy Lunt bought the second set on Feb. 14, 1953, and the very next day, Ben Davis Sr. bought the third set.

"When television came in, people gathered," said Vivian Lunt. "Not everyone was able to get a television right off, so you would go to someone's house and watch. I used to go to Lillian's a lot. She had a television before we did. I used to go up there and watch Fibber McGee and Molly, and there was Burns and Allen, and different groups like that. Little comedies. Every night there was something good on. I would go up at a certain time just like you go to the theater."

## *Pulpwood*

Just as island timber helped lure the first settlers, it also brought pulpwood operators to the island in the 20th century.

Pulpwood companies built many of the roads that still run to such places as Eastern Beach and Southern Cove so they could haul out logs to the ballfield, which served as the central storage area. Throughout the woods on the island's east side, remnants of abandoned roads and discarded truck parts can still be found.

The first pulpwood was cut in 1920 at Richs Head and Southern Cove. That operation was fairly small and lasted about a year.

Roy Allen of Sedgwick and James Mattertall of Ellsworth ran the largest operation in the late 1930s and early 1940s. Allen and Mattertall purchased a large tract of land from Thomas Proctor that started behind

*Courtesy of Frenchboro Historical Society*

*The Ballfield filled with pulpwood, 1940s.*

the ballfield and included most of the land owned today by Peggy Dulany. For five summers, workers cut and hauled and shipped about 3,000 cords of pulpwood from Long Island.

The timber, mostly spruce, was peeled, cut into four-foot lengths and loaded aboard schooners in Lunt Harbor before it was taken to a pulp and paper mill in Brewer.

Earl Bragdon spent his teenage years working in island lumber camps, including one year on Long Island in the 1930s. In an article titled "Boyhood Memories of Pulpwood Cutting on the Islands," he included this account:

"My job at the lumber camp was that of cookee or cook's helper. We worked in a tarpaper shack on the edge of an open field. The cook shack served both as a dining area and as a social gathering place after the evening meal and on weekends. Included in my chores were chopping wood for two insatiable cookstoves, carrying water from the spring in giant metal teapots and waiting on tables. I had to arise at 3 a.m. to build fires in the stoves. Shortly after daybreak the woodsmen filed in silently for breakfast. The men remained silent for breakfast as they did for every meal. No talking was a cardinal rule for every lumber camp so that less time would be spent eating, fewer arguments would arise and the cook could more easily get through his work."

*Courtesy of Frenchboro Historical Society*

*Loading pulpwood at Lunt Harbor, 1942.*

"Wood was hauled out of the forest by a Model A Ford by cutting off the drive shaft and inserting a second transmission. This modification made it possible to utilize the two transmissions for tremendous hauling power at low speeds. We called the contraption a 'jitterbug.'"

Once the pulpwood operation ended, the land was sold to R.K. Barter of Stonington, who in turn sold it to David Rockefeller.

## Electrical Problems

An underwater electrical cable running about five miles from Duck Cove on Swans Island to the Western shore of Lunt Harbor supplies the island's electricity. During the 1980s, scallop draggers repeatedly severed the cable, leaving islanders in the dark and cold for days, sometimes in the dead of winter.

Even though it is illegal to drag within a closed cable zone, scallop draggers swept across the beds in the dead of night for the illegal but bountiful scallops. For some time, relatively lax enforcement existed. That changed as problems increased and repair costs moved into the tens of thousands of dollars.

Eventually, islanders videotaped draggers in the closed areas, and wardens cracked down, even confiscating boats and taking captains to court.

One early incident occurred in December 1982. Islanders lost power for four days until the 2,400-volt cable could be spliced back together. Even then David Honey, manager of the Swans Island Electrical Co-op, said, "They ain't going to leave it alone until we make it expensive."

The state did act. It passed a law calling for mandatory license suspensions and a $1,000 fine.

In the meantime, seven men were charged with dragging in a closed area relating to that incident. The men included two from Tremont, three from Deer Isle, one from Bucksport and one from Stonington.

Despite fines and court appearances, scallopers were not dissuaded. In fact, some scallopers tried to argue it was their fellow draggers who were damaging the cable.

In April 1984, the cable was severed again and the island lost power for four more days. In response, the Army National Guard was called out and the Maine State Ferry Service enlisted to deliver an emergency 440-volt, 100,000-watt generator to provide temporary power. It took two weeks to repair the increasingly worn cable.

During the initial power blackout, islanders rotated a handful of small private generators to keep freezers cold and goods from spoiling.

In April 1985, the island lost power for the third time in four years. After two days, selectmen called a state of emergency as poor weather prevented repair efforts.

April was a predictable time for power outages. The Maine scallop season ends April 15. Each year as the season drew to an end, draggers moved into the forbidden zone.

Finally, in the fall of 1985, the state expanded the zone. That December, Gov. Joseph E. Brennan sign a bill making it a criminal offense to drag in a closed area. Violation brought fines and potential jail time. Wardens said such teeth were needed because the previous $500 fine was a small deterrent when a person could make $2,000 in only a few hours by dragging in the cable area.

Still they came. Wardens boarded one Little Deer Isle boat three times during the first month of the new law. The third time the man was jailed and his boat confiscated. Others were charged and some forfeited their scallops.

Still, the cable was parted again in February. That month, one of Frenchboro's own fisherman was one of the people charged with dragging in the area, causing a great deal of consternation.

By 1988, the Marine Patrol moved into full crackdown mode. Officers seized thousands of dollars worth of scallops and issued frequent summons. At least thirteen fishermen were set for arraignments that January.

However, one fisherman immediately challenged the new law in court. A Little Deer Isle fisherman, who was arrested, fined a total of $2,250 and had his boat impounded, fought his conviction. His lawyers called the law unconstitutionally vague and an improper exercise of the state's police powers. He got nowhere. In a unanimous decision in 1990, the Law Court found no merit in any of his arguments.

Eventually, in the 1990s, a new cable was laid and buried, so far ending the problems. Scallop beds are now open to divers only.

## *The Strange Case of Dan Blaszczuk*

Perhaps the most bewildering island scandal — and certainly its most high profile one —involved Daniel Blaszczuk.

Blaszczuk arrived for a short visit in the early 1980s and stayed for the next eight years. Dan's mother lived in Connecticut and Dan attended Emerson College in Boston where he allegedly roomed with Henry Winkler.

During his stay on Long Island the hulking but easy-going and helpful man quickly became an important part of island life. He babysat children, was a talented quilter and was generally well liked. He became involved not only in large island projects, but also with smaller projects such as clearing underbrush from old cemeteries. He became intimately involved in town affairs, serving as town treasurer for five years and as assistant to the Board of Selectmen. He also became a key figure in the town's attempt to attract new settlers, serving as treasurer of the Frenchboro Future Development Corp., which administered the program to build houses and lure settlers.

Then in late January 1988, Blaszczuk, 44, disappeared.

He left the island in December 1987 to spend the holidays with his mother. He returned to Maine and stayed at a hotel in Ellsworth — some-

*Courtesy of The Bar Harbor Times*

*Lillian J. Lunt (left), an island visitor, Dan Blaszczuk, an island visitor, and Rebecca J. Lunt at Norma Teel's post office, 1980s.*

thing he often did. This time he stayed for weeks. In late December, he failed to bring supplies for Tina Lunt's Christmas party and didn't return telephone calls.

A group of islanders found him at the Eagle's Nest hotel in Ellsworth. He assured them he was fine and would return to the island. But islanders grew concerned. Town officials told a local bank not to honor any town checks with his signature.

The concerns were justified.

On Jan. 28, Dan missed a FFDC meeting, and this time when Tina Lunt went to find him, he was gone. And despite the town's warning to the bank, Dan easily cashed a town check made out to himself for more than $5,200, according to police. He was last seen in Ellsworth on Jan. 26, when he checked out of the Brookside Motel. He allegedly took a taxi to a bus station in Bangor and left. He has never been seen again. An audit of Frenchboro's town books later found nearly $11,000 missing, a large percentage of the town budget.

Dan's disappearance and alleged embezzlement shocked and saddened islanders. At the cabin he rented on Long Island, he left nearly everything he owned: his CD player, his CDs, books, magazines, his sewing machine, handmade quilts and clothes.

In February 1988, he was indicted by a Hancock County Grand Jury and charged with theft.

Rumors about why he left, what he was involved in and where he might have gone have swirled for the last decade. Many speculate he became very sick. It is widely rumored he may even have died. Although no islanders have seen him since 1988, his identification and some personal items were later found on a man in Alaska.

### *Frenchboro Lobster Festival*

The first annual Frenchboro Lobster Festival took place August 15, 1962 and has occurred every summer since. The annual festival, usually held the second Saturday of August, is the largest fundraiser for the Congregational Church. It draws more than 500 people who come by private boat, Maine state ferry and the Maine Sea Coast Missionary Society's *Sunbeam*.

The festival celebrates the signing of the Atlantic Charter by President Franklin D. Roosevelt and British Prime Minister Winston Churchill. The

*Lilla (Lunt) Stanley (left) and Alma Lunt preparing for the annual Lobster Dinner, 1970.*

two leaders signed the charter in Placentia Bay off Newfoundland in August 1941, but the fleet apparently dispersed in Blue Hill Bay near Frenchboro.

Islanders remember the inspiring and awesome sight of the great warships steaming just off the shores of Long Island. According to Dick Lunt, some ships ran halfway between Green Island and Northeast Point.

"The bay was full of ships," he said. "We couldn't imagine what was going on."

Residents boarded lobster boats for a closer look, but the smaller attendant ships travelling in support of the great vessels kept them away.

According to Vivian Lunt, ships included the *USS Augusta, USS Potomac, EMS Prince of Wales, Duke of York, USS North Dakota* and *Repulse*.

## *"Nuckie" or The Legend of Nuckie's Father*

Another island mystery is the origin of the nickname "Nuckie." For several decades during the early and mid-1900s, "Nuckie" became a general nickname for many Long Islanders — "those Nuckies." The nickname even survived on rare occasions into the 1970s and 1980s. No one knows what exactly it means or specifically where it came from. In fact, some people think the name is harmless, while others consider it derogatory and take great offense. In the past, it was sometimes a topic of controversy on the island.

Only this much is known: "Nuckie" was Grant H. Lunt. Grant died April 10, 1924. From Grant's nickname came the legend of "Nuckie's father," Joseph Warren Lunt Sr., the civil war veteran who died Jan. 18, 1891.

Over the years, some islanders told Bunyanesque tales about Nuckie's father and his derring-do.

Many of the stories were told — and in all likelihood created — by Hiram Albert Lunt Jr., better known as "Doonie Hum."

Doonie Hum was Grant Lunt's nephew and Joseph Warren Lunt's grandson. Hiram Jr. was born 14 years after Joseph's death and was only 19 when Grant died. Doonie Hum is remembered for two key reasons: he was one of the island's storytellers and one of its hardest drinkers.

On the island, the stories about Nuckie's father recounted by Doonie Hum — and later by the late Vincent A. Davis — were considered "putdown" stories and insults by some, and amusing tall tales by others.

Doonie spun such tales while sitting around Nardy's store, while resting on the banks of the harbor or, of course, while drinking. Few actual stories are still remembered, and even those that are contain few details.

The following two stories, which reflect much author's license, provide the gist of stories told by Doonie and Vincent.

"One late fall afternoon, Nuckie's father finished up a day of lobster fishing in the waters off Long Island. After storing his lobsters in crates, he sailed his sloop to his mooring in Lunt Harbor. He moored his boat and waited for his brother to pick him up and set him ashore. His brother forgot.

Nuckie's father waited and waited as the sun set, the air grew chilled and his supper grew cold on the table. And still no one came. Nuckie's father, never one to wait long for anything, grew very impatient. He looked around for a way to get ashore, but all he had on board his sloop were two empty half barrels.

"With supper waiting and his anger building, Nuckie's father took the half barrels, put one on his left foot and one on his right foot, stepped over the side of the boat, and walked down the harbor."

Another story:

"One spring day, Nuckie's father was plagued by a toothache. The pain just wouldn't go away no matter what he tried. Medicine didn't work, ice didn't work, nothing worked. His agony grew worse and worse. No one could help him.

"Finally, after spending another day in pain, Nuckie's father jumped to his feet in his old house, put on his boots and walked down to his wharf on Lunt Harbor. He rummaged through his tools until he found a pair of old pliers.

"He put the pliers in his mouth, clamped them on his throbbing tooth and yanked. Out came the tooth and away went the pain. Nuckie's father looked at the extracted tooth for minute, cursed it, and then stepped out onto the end of his wharf. 'Good Riddance, you blasted tooth, you won't bother me again.' He took the tooth and heaved it. The tooth flew up over the trees on the East Side, past the cow fields, past the Beaver Pond and landed in the deep water just off Eastern Beach. The tooth sank to bottom where it started to grow.

"The next day, Nuckie's father was sailing to Richs Head to haul his lobster traps when suddenly his boat slammed into a ledge in the once open water between Northeast Point and Yellow Head. 'What, in the world?' Nuckie's father said, as he ran to the bow.

"He looked down and knew in an instant what had happened. He sat high and dry on his once-aching tooth.

"And that is where Eastern Beach Ledge came from."

## *Joseph W. "Innie" Lunt*

While Doonie Hum and others spun tall tales, Joseph W. "Innie" Lunt was known as the island poet. Most of the time the former Navy man created his poems on the spot. Often the poems told a story, whether it was about someone running liquor, an island field day, a house under construction or alleged wrongdoing. Many times they were told at Nardy's store. Unfortunately, like much other oral history, nearly all of his creations have been lost. A few that he did write down, usually those that were considerably more tame, have survived.

One went like this:

### The Nurse and Her Kettle

God has sent a worthy servant
to this lonely little isle
to render success to the ailing
and to make the weeping smile.
Every day as I see her passing
with that kettle in her hand
with an air of grace and splendor
and a smile so broad and grand.

She lives up to true traditions
as her kind have done before
on the battlefields of Flanders
where the cannons used to roar.
Often to the village schoolhouse
we will see her gently go
to take refreshments to the scholars
who have learned to love her so.

How it thrills my soul with pleasure
to pen down my thoughts in verse
to extol the sterling virtues
of this precious Red Cross nurse.
On our isolated island
when a neighbor's taken ill
how we need a one so sacred
qualified with craft and skill.

To this lonely little Island
God this worthy servant sent
to spread sunshine to the weary
and to fill them with content.
And I know we all consider
her to be His richest gift.
For she takes a part in church work,
tries our morals to uplift.

May her task on here be pleasant,
lots of joy and not all woe.
To reflect the people's friendship
in her mind, where e'er she'll go.
May her days on earth be lengthened
till her worthy mission's done.
Then, may she find a life of sunshine
in the land of never setting sun.

We must act for time is fleeting,
do kind deeds while we are here
and when time comes for our parting
let us leave devoid of fear.
When we cross the crystal river
over to fair Jordan's strand,
let's hope to meet her with her kettle
on that beach of golden sand.

## The Demon Rum

Few things had greater impact on the island, or Maine itself for that matter, in the later 19th century and early 20th century than alcohol. It was a part of island life. And some islanders were, quite frankly, alcoholics. Even from the days of the earliest missionaries, some young men and at least a few women had problems with alcohol. It remained so through the first half of the 1900s despite Prohibition until 1934.

Drinking binges, often lasting days or weeks, remain the stuff of island legend. When all else failed, some men drank vanilla or other cooking liquids with alcohol content. Sometimes they used these cooking liquids to slowly sober up.

Alcohol came from numerous places. Some coastal residents rendezvoused with Canadian ships offshore to load rum and run it along the coast. Rum Cove Point on Black Island is a name from those days. Lopaus Point in Bernard was a well-known landing place for bootleggers.

Those involved in bootlegging needed men with good reliable boats and often tried to recruit islanders. Marjorie Giamo said her grandfather, Frank W. Ross, was approached at least once and asked if he would run rum. He refused, but others with boats were also approached and unquestionably some agreed.

One rum ship anchored three or so miles off Long Island in international waters. The smaller running boats often took off rum in five-gallon cans and ferried it to points and coves along the coast.

In one story, a man from another island, his boat loaded with cans, found himself chased by the law. As officials closed in, the man smashed his cans open. By the time he smashed the last one, he stood deep in rum as it washed over the deck. As the precious alcohol ran out the scuppers into the Atlantic, he picked up speed and avoided capture.

On Long Island, at least a handful of islanders journeyed out for their own supplies. In one tale, an island fisherman or two would run out to fishing grounds located near the Canadian ship, set trawls in the morning, then board the boat during the day for breakfast and a few drinks. Then they got back in their own boats to haul back their trawls.

In the early part of the century, fishing vessels also brought alcohol into the harbor and spread it around the island during layovers.

Homebrew also made an occasional appearance during the first half of the century, including a well-known operation by Jasper Lunt. Jasper made beer near his house above the head of the cove. Jasper, who was not a big drinker, sold his brew. He lived in a house located near the Myron and Sarah Lenfestey house in 1999. He lived with his mother Harriet "Hat" (Davis) Lunt, the widow of George Colliver Lunt. Hat didn't approve of liquor and didn't like the guys coming around to get it. However, she was hard of hearing. So, Jasper had the men stand in the woods above his house and throw rocks on the roof when they wanted some beer. He would hear it, but Hat couldn't.

Some enterprising islanders also made money on spirits. One or two houses served as local bars for visiting fishermen. One even doubled as a brothel. Island legend says that during summer and fall nights in the late

1800s, fishing vessels lined the length of Northeast Point where fishermen frequented a bar and brothel, which operated beyond Whale Beach. In *Biography of an Island*, Perry Westbrook, perhaps referring to Northeast Point, wrote that Long Island was once known as a place where fishermen could put in for a good time.

But it wasn't all fun and games along Northeast Point. It is also part of legend that on one summer night, the mistress of the house smashed a fry pan across the head of a rowdy sailor and tossed his body into the waters off Northeast Point.

## Mobile Homes

Islanders, by necessity, were a thrifty lot, including when they built homes. At times they tore down old houses for the lumber and used it for new houses. In some cases, they tore off a section and moved it for a new house. And sometimes they moved entire houses to new locations.

Such actions were a chore, given the lack of heavy machinery. They sometimes floated the house or raised it and rolled it on logs.

The house now owned by Ben Davis Jr. was actually built on Harbor Island. It was rolled off Harbor Island, floated to Long Island and then rolled to its current location on Lunt Harbor.

Islanders also floated at least one house out from Richs Head to Lunt Harbor around the turn of the century as the community on the Head was being abandoned.

Harold and Evelyn Burr's house was originally a wing attached to Israel B. Lunt's house. It was detached and moved across the road for Israel's daughter, Hortense, after she married William Van Norden.

Tommy B. Lunt's old fishhouse was originally part of a large wharf on the harbor. Again, part of it was torn off and floated across the harbor for Tommy.

Several Long Island houses are built from lumber torn off Black Island houses as that community was dismantled.

Tommy's house, now owned by Robert Roxby, came from lumber torn off a Black Island house and brought to Long Island as did the house now owned by Dick and Vivian Lunt and the house owned by Rod and Donna Forsgren.

Sylvester Morse built the house now owned by Marjorie Giamo, in part using lumber and other materials from Black Island. The old Dalzell house now owned by Richard Hamblen Jr. includes parts from the old Abbie Rich house.

Even into the 1980s, islanders occasionally moved houses. David W. and Debbie Lunt dragged their house across the road to where it now sits beside the Butler Road.

## Island Trails

Above nearly all other reasons, visitors come to Long Island for its unspoiled beauty. The working harbor itself is sheltered, peaceful and picturesque, while the backshores are rugged and sometimes breathtaking. The paths to reach them cut through silent, undisturbed woods. You may find rare orchids, stumble across white-tailed deer or perhaps just soak in the quiet.

For decades, these major paths and dirt roads were maintained by Clifton Lunt. Clifton, who married Ella V. Lunt in 1924, worked daily for David Rockefeller cutting, maintaining and marking trails. Since Clifton's death in 1984, the trails have grown in some, but most are still visible and walkable.

*Courtesy of Ella V. Lunt*

*Clifton Lunt (1900 - 1984)*

## Summer Ministers and Visitors

Starting in 1957, the Maine Sea Coast Missionary Society began supplying ministers for two months each summer. One minister and his family spent July on the island and another spent August there. They taught Sunday School, held Sunday services and sometimes repaired the church and parsonage. The summer ministers lived in the parsonage. For many years, families filling that role were among the island's only summer visitors.

During the program's first decade, ministers changed regularly. Then starting in the mid-1960s, two men became island staples and its longest serving ministers.

Rev. James D. Miller of Pennsylvania and Rev. John D. Stewart of North Carolina have spent parts of 30 summers on the island.

Rev. Miller first came to Frenchboro in 1967. He and his family — wife Janet, and children Jane, James and Jennifer — have spent parts of every summer since that time on Long Island and have become an important part of island summers and church life. Jim and Janet purchased land and built their own island house in 1999. Their son James P. Miller and his wife Susan bought a house on the island in 1998.

Photo by Lillian J. Lunt

*Back row: Janet and Rev. Jim Miller. Front row: Jane and Jim Miller, 1967.*

Rev. Stewart first came to the island in 1968. He has served nearly every summer since, missing only a year or two during that span. Frequently, his family — wife Freda, and children Mary, Margaret and Carrie — have also made the trip.

John Stewart recently purchased the house near the ferry pier originally built by Paul "Rusty" Crossman.

Current summer visitors who have been coming to Frenchboro for many years include: Frank and Marge Mancuso, who own a house on the west side; Harold and Evelyn Burr, who own the old Van Norden house on the east side; and Rod and Donna Forsgren, who own a house and wharf on the west side and the Walter Wolf family with a house on the east side.

More recent summer visitors with island homes include Duncan and Gretchen Bond, Chuck and Marlys Amos, Rod and Burr Bost, David and Pat McEachern, Janneke Neilson and Robert Roxby, a long-time visitor who recently moved to the island.

## Of Names & Places

One feature of a town or island is the historic or traditional names of people, places and homes. Long Island has many, although some are now forgotten or changed. The following are some popular island sites and land marks:

*Flat Point* — The point on Richs Head that forms the southern side of Western Cove.

*Lunt Harbor* — The main harbor on Long Island.

*Gully Road* — A path running from Steamboat Beach to the head of Lunt Harbor.

*Western Point* — The point that ends the west side of Lunt Harbor, directly across the channel from Harbor Island. Known in the early 1800s as Allen's Point.

*Lookout Point* — The point, mostly ledge actually, between Western Point and the Salt Ponds.

*Aunt Rose house* — A house owned by Adelbert W. and Rose (Murphy) Lunt located just above what is now the Lunt & Lunt wharf.

*Will Lunt house* — The homestead of Hezekiah W. "Will" Lunt Jr. and his wife, Cora, located just below the house owned in 1999 by James and Susan Miller. The cellar is still visible. Hezekiah W. Lunt Sr. owned a house located just south of that house or closer to the Butler Road.

*Alec Davis Homestead* — The house where Valeria and Alexander "Alec" Davis raised nine children, including Vivian and Lillian. The house sat on a wharf just below the house formerly owned by their son, the late Vincent Davis. According to legend, Ted Morrill lived there at the turn of the century. One night a schooner broke from is mooring and the bowsprit crashed through his window. Unperturbed, Teddy took out his saw and each time the bow pushed further through the window, he sawed it off and tossed it on the fire.

*Bartholomew Lunt house and jail* — Bartholomew Russell "Judge" Lunt lived in a house that stood just above the Alec Davis house and north of the old Vincent Davis house. The Alec Davis house originally served as both Bartholomew's wharf and an island jail.

*Doonie Hum road* — Doonie Hum's camp was located on the hill just north of the Butler Road and below the path that leads to David L. Lunt's house. For years, Doonie walked from his house over the hill to the back-shore, wearing a path that served as the main route for years.

*Salt Ponds* — The Salt Ponds are two natural saltwater ponds on the shore facing Swans Island. For years, the ponds were deep enough to float rafts and serve as skating ponds. During the past decade, the shifting beach has exposed the ponds and lowered the water level.

*The Old Salt Ponds Road* — Before the Butler Road, the main route to the Salt Ponds was a path starting near Frank and Marge Mancuso's house and running down through the woods to the ponds.

*Millie's or the Capt. Davis House* — Millie (Davis) Hunton owned a house just below the Osier house. It was also the original homestead of Capt. William Davis, who passed it on to his son, Leaman T. Davis. It was torn down in the 1970s.

*The Old Sand Pit* — Located behind the Dick and Vivian Lunt house. Sand from the old pit was used to build roads on the west side.

*Joseph Warren Lunt Homestead* — The deteriorating house — more frequently called the "Old Homestead" — located across the road from Vivian and Dick Lunt's house. It overlooks the inner harbor. In the mid-1800s, Joseph and his wife, Alice, raised nine children there, and took in many relatives over the years. The house was passed on to John R. and Flora E. "Mammie" Lunt, who then raised 12 children there, including two children who died very young. Flora and her daughter Alma were the last to live in the house during the 1970s. They also ran a store there.

*Almy's Hill* — The steepest hill on the west side running past the Joseph Lunt house. Alma was born and raised in the house and lived there into the 1970s.

*Kai Lunt house* — A house near John and Rebecca Lunt's house owned by Hezekiah E.S. "Kai" Lunt.

*Kai Davis and George Butler camps* — Two small camps owned by Hezekiah Davis and George Butler located past the head of the cove.

*Bennie June Road* — The road to Gooseberry Point, named after Ben Davis Jr., who built it in the 1960s to provide better access to his land.

*Schoolhouse Hill* — Self-Explanatory.

*Jake Siegal's store* — One of the island's more famous stores. It was located on the road between Derry Rundlett's house and the Dan and Tina Lunt house.

*Joe Lunt's store* — Joseph W. "Joe" Lunt and his wife, Minnie Cross, operated a store and wharf on Western Point.

*The Meadow* — Essentially a bog today. The meadow once served as a skating pond located between the head of the cove and Little Beach.

*Thurlow homestead* — The house of James H. and Lizzie (Lunt) Thurlow located behind the old Brook Hill General Store and between the low and high roads. It was owned for several years by Winston and Harriet Harmon and earlier by Charles Hooper.

*Brook Hill* — The hill below Marjorie Giamo's house.

*The Spring* — A natural spring on the east side located on the shore below Marjorie Giamo's house.

*Israel B. Lunt Homestead* — The house, formerly owned by Norma Teel, purchased in 1999 by Paul Charpentier. The Israel house, built in the 1840s, is probably the oldest house left on the island.

*The Green House* — A house once located between Billy Wolf's house and the Mildred Onyett house. Once owned by Clarence McIntire.

*The Lincoln Road* — A path from the Northeast Point road to the Ferry Pier. Used by Lincoln Lunt when he lived near there in a camp.

*The Ball Field or The Head of the Field* — The field, the island's only baseball field, near the Community Building.

*Gertrude's house* — The Gertrude Lunt house, along the high road, was built in the 1800s. Once occupied by Sadie and Alphonso "Fon" Lunt and their daughter Gertrude Lunt. It is owned in 1999 by Marcia Murphy.

*Abbie Rich house and Abbie Rich field* — House and farm owned by William S. and Abbie (Davis) Rich. The farm was on the left side of the road to the Gilman Field, just beyond the turn off the dump hill. The house and barn were on the right side.

*Courtesy of Frenchboro Historical Society*

*The Emily Gilman House, 1911. The Gilman house formerly located in The Grove or Gilman Field. Woman on porch is Lida (Lunt) Higgins.*

*The Grove or Gilman Field* — Once an open field used for camping and sometimes games such as volleyball. There are now three houses built there as part of the island's Homestead Project. Originally called the Gilman Field because it was owned by Emily S. Gilman. She lived in a large, beautiful house there. The house burned down or, as legend has it, was burned down in the early 1900s.

*Beaver Pond* — The island's largest natural pond.

*Burnt Hills* — The highest point on the island, along the path to Richs Head. Named after a fire that burned through there in the 1800s.

*Yellow Head* — The point between Eastern Beach and Richs Head. Named after the stands of yellow birch trees.

*Richs Head* — The Southeastern part of the island, connected to the island by a narrow strip of beach rocks sometimes called the Carrying Place. The Head was named after the Rich family who originally settled there and built a farm. At one time the Head contained several houses, a fishhouse and even a school. It survived as a community for about 80 years. The Rich family sold their last claims to the Head in the late 1800s.

*Bluff Head* — Steep bluffs between Southern and Western Coves.

*Brandy Rock* — Rock at Big Beach named after bootleggers hid liquor there during Prohibition.

*House Point* — Plot of land between Big Beach and Middle Beach. A house once stood there.

*Steamboat Beach* — Located between the Salt Ponds and Gooseberry Point. Has had the name since at least the mid-1800s.

*Gooseberry Point* — Also named in the mid-1800s likely because of the preponderance of gooseberries. Provides spectacular views of both sunsets and winter storms.

## *Fishing Grounds and Marks*

*Abner Grounds* — Fishing grounds between Long Island and Duck Island and Mount Desert Rock.

*Israel Grounds* — Now known as the Blueberry Hill piece. It is located about three miles south of the backside of the island.

*Ricochet Landing* — Site of a shipwreck between Big Beach and Southwest Point. The wreck, a coal freighter, remains sunken there.

*Butler's Reef* — Off the southwest side of the island. About one mile west of the Israel Grounds.

*Southwest Point Shoal* — Just off Southwest Point.

*Pinnacle* — About three miles off the southern side of the island. East/northeast of the Blueberry Hill piece.

*Horse Reef* — A reef also located about three miles to the east of Long Island, toward Mount Desert Rock.

*Schooner Head Mountain Piece* — About two miles south of the island, inside the Pinnacle. Found by lining up Schooner Head over the Head.

*Milliken* — Off backside of the head. About one mile east/southeast.

*Noble's Reef* — About one-half mile south of Bluff Head.

*Spring Grounds* — Just outside of Noble's reef.

*Lighthouse Piece* — Halfway to Swans Island. Found by lining up Bass Harbor Head Light between the Sister islands. Generally considered the dividing line between the Swans Island and Long Island fishing grounds.

## Nicknames

One island practice that caused confusion while writing this book was the reliance on nicknames, some of which even show up in official town books. Frequently, islanders used their middle names instead of first names. Such was often the case with Bartholomew Russell Lunt, Hezekiah

*Courtesy of Frenchboro Historical Society*

*Thanksgiving Dinner, 1950s. Irving "Pean" Lunt (left), Ben S. Davis Sr., Millie (Davis) Hunton and Leonard A. "Nardy" Lunt.*

Wills Lunt Jr., and Joseph Warren Lunt Sr.. They were more commonly known as Russell, Will and Warren. In other cases, nicknames were simply unique and colorful. Following is an effort to clarify some of those names.

*Dib* — Benjamin S. Lunt

*Innie* — Joseph Warren Lunt, although not the son of either Joseph Warren Lunt Sr. or Jr.

*Doonie Hum* — Hiram Albert Lunt Jr.

*Nuckie* — Grant H. Lunt

*Nuckie's Father* — Joseph Warren Lunt Sr.

*Pean* — Irving Lunt

*Hud* — Llewellyn Lunt

*Nardy* — Leonard A. Lunt

*Squire Lunt* — Israel B. Lunt Sr.

*Bert* — Israel B. Lunt Jr.

*Dimp* — Ellen Nickerson

*Rusty* — Paul L. Crossman

*Dick* — Sanford L. Lunt

*Tar* — Charles R. Mitchell

*Ebbit* — Everett E. Dalzell Jr.

*Seen* — Asenath (Lunt) Wallace

*Courtesy of Frenchboro Historical Society*

*Camilla Lunt (left) and Asenath (Lunt) Wallace near the junction of Butler Road and the Main Road. Will Lunt house at left and Calvin "Cade" Lunt house at right.*

*Hite* — Hiram A. Lunt Sr.
*Birge* — Orrin Lunt
*Scotty* — Frank W. Ross
*Manny* — Erland Dalzell
*Goog* — Elmer Davis
*Sim* — Grandville Davis
*Kai* — Hezekiah Davis and Hezekiah (H.E.S.) Lunt
*Sabe* — Sabra (Lunt) Rice and Sabra Lunt
*Aunt Rose* — Rose (Murphy) Lunt
*Fon* — Alphonso Lunt
*Robbins* — Milton Dalzell
*Del* — Adelbert Lunt
*Whit* — Henry Whitfield Lunt
*Happy Jack* — Ethel Lunt
*Mammie* or *Eva*— Flora Eveline Lunt
*Bud* – Emily Thurlow
*Rose* — Rosanna (Murphy) Lunt
*Ski* – Roman Rozenski

*Henry Whitfield "Whit" Lunt (1853 - 1934) and Gladys Lunt, around 1915. Whit was one of the last people to live on Richs Head in the late 1800s.*

# Chapter Seventeen

# Ebb and Flow

## Generations Past

Every generation considers itself the end of an era. And usually each can make a solid case. At Frenchboro, Long Island, my ancestors forged a community with little more than determination and will from an isolated island eight miles out in the Atlantic. And each generation since has seen dramatic change both good and bad.

My great-grandparent's generation – Alexander and Valeria Davis and John and Flora Lunt — was the last to live without a graded or even regular school system, the last without daily mail service and the last to grow up using only rowboats and sailboats for transportation.

My grandfather and grandmother — Dick and Vivian Lunt — were among the last to grow up as the classically "rural poor," although some economic hardship remained into the 1940s and 1950s. They lived through the nation's Great Depression and the island's own even longer economic struggles which forced them to scrape a living by any means necessary. They were born in island homes without doctors and were never guaranteed an education beyond eighth grade. They were the last to run open boats, and the last truly rooted to the island. My grandmother washed clothes on scrub boards and still boiled her whites.

My father's generation — David and Sandra Lunt — was the last to grow up without electricity; they lugged water from hand-dug wells and

*Alexander P. Davis (left) (1888 - 1968) and John R. Lunt Sr. (1876 - 1951)*

lived without indoor plumbing. His was the last generation without some type of regular ferry service.

Milestones all, and the examples could go on and on.

But in many ways my brothers, David W. and Daniel L., and I, the eighth generation of Lunts on Long Island, were the generation to witness the island's final transformation as Frenchboro shook off the last vestiges of true isolation and poverty.

Not that island life is not still different. Certainly, those from mainland cities and towns will argue that Long Island remains removed and tiny. It has no stores, only one mile of paved road and streetlights you can count on one hand. It doesn't have daily ferry service like Swans Island, Islesboro or North Haven. The one-room school with its two students is among only a dozen or so such schools left in the state.

So certainly island life is unique. It is different. It is less convenient. It takes a commitment to adapt. But truly isolated? I don't think so.

Maybe on winter days when storms roll up like thunder out of the Northeast or when thick vapor from the bone-chilling cold numbs Lunt Harbor. But it quickly passes.

Clearly, island life is not meant for everyone, but neither is a small mainland town or Maine itself. The closeness can be suffocating if you let it be. There are trade-offs for the rewards of living in a true community.

But is Frenchboro more isolated than Jackman or Prentiss or Pembroke? I might argue less so. Is isolation defined only by the inability to drive a car to a store? To go to the movies on a whim? Today's boats can run to Bass Harbor in most any weather in less than 30 minutes.

Certainly, Long Island no longer trails the mainland in basic technological advances or modern conveniences as it did during much of the twentieth century. When you can sit on the couch and watch MTV and CNN or dial into the World Wide Web, life is no longer radically different.

Most importantly, any inherent economic disparity that lured missionaries and state workers to island shores has vanished from Long Island. Indeed, with a strong lobster economy during much of the past decade, the island's per family income exceeds most Maine towns, and islanders now live far better than the majority of rural Mainers. It is now a town of Dodge Rams, 40-foot fiberglass boats and Loran systems. As recently as the early 1960s, my father fished, as a married man with two children, using a 13-foot skiff and outboard. Today, teenagers own full-sized lobster boats.

Of course, the economy is better everywhere. Look around Bass Harbor and Southwest Harbor and Swans Island, all of which struggled economically, and you will see much the same thing. Should the lobster industry collapse, the story will be different, but for the moment, money is not a major problem.

Even in the 1960s and 1970s, while my brothers and I were certainly not lavished with gifts or luxury items — my parents would never pay for overly expensive sneakers, designer clothes or useless toys — we never truly wanted for anything. Those days were long gone for us. We traveled to California and Florida and Canada on family vacations.

I was born in 1966, and perhaps the biggest change to occur since my childhood is the perceived distance of Long Island. Those eight miles of Atlantic seem a lot shorter than they once did. Even into the 1970s, visitors rightfully said the ride seemed to take 20 years to cross — both physically and culturally.

Indeed, into the mid-1970s, we rarely "went ashore" during the fall, winter or spring. Boats remained small enough or slow enough that weather mattered. There was no radar, and no telephones.

We left infrequently enough that Ellsworth seemed like a real destination even if it was just Britt's or Zayre's or Woolworth's. Bangor, with its Airport Mall, was a rare trip. Few people had second homes on the mainland.

Still, it remains difficult to accurately characterize the change. Much of it's simply progress, as seen in many other places in Maine, and the rest so subtle as to be imperceptible, but no less real.

In those days, people gathered daily at Norma Teel's waiting for the mail boat to arrive and for her to sort over the letters and packages. Sears, Roebuck and Montgomery Ward catalogs were still a important sources of supplies.

Arrival of the twice-a-week ferry served as a major event. Many islanders either waited on the pier or watched through binoculars to see who came and went.

Visitors remained sparse. The harbor did not fill with yachts every night; there were no tourists and few summer people other than friends or relatives. In fact, the entire island was mostly relatives. Today, I do not bat

*Courtesy of Vivian D. Lunt*

*Lunt & Lunt wharf, early 1980s.*

an eyelash at seeing strangers on the road. As a kid, that was an event.

Lunt Harbor remained lined with the rundown houses, the fallen wharves and the ghosts of a different era. Buildings sat filled with the clothes, letters and belongings of people either dead or removed. Window curtains fluttered through the broken window panes, and dishes often filled an abandoned cupboard.

Island stores still operated. Men still hired young, old or poor to bait pockets. Some adults still fished using a skiff and outboard.

Money remained tight. Wharves stood stacked high with wooden lobster traps. Trucks were still beat-up.

We still used mostly hand-me-down gear. My brothers rowed to haul their traps when they were just 7 or 8. My first skiff was nearly 30 years old. My father used it, my uncle used it, my brother used it and then I used it. When it leaked, I bailed it out. When it was damaged, my grandfather fixed it.

We still fought island stereotypes when visiting mainland schools. I clearly remember visiting Tremont School one day during middle school when a teacher during math class condescendingly asked if I had learned about fractions — islanders were all backward, you know. I said "yes," but I wanted to say, "Yeah, two or three years ago."

I am not saying the old days were all better, not at all.

Who wants to be poor?

Who wants isolation?

Who wants to lug water or empty slop pails?

Or be unable to make telephone calls? Or even watch three channels of snowy television?

Not me.

But surely that old life had easy charms.

As I slipped through my 20s and worked at jobs across New England, the old days mostly disappeared. And frankly, I am not sure the island community could have survived if they did not.

If asked to mark three things during my lifetime that to me completed the transformation from past to present, I might pick the *Starburst*, the telephone and Cecil E. Lunt.

The *Starburst* was my oldest brother Dave's first good boat in 1977 and the family's first fiberglass one. It just seemed to make travel easier and faster and more comfortable and bring the mainland that much closer.

Other new boats, ever bigger, ever quicker, soon followed with radar and other technological advancements.

The first off-island telephone call in December of 1983 connected the island and mainland to a previously unknown degree. It opened up regular daily contact. I don't think it is possible to overstate how much the telephone lifted the sense of remoteness.

My great uncle Cecil or "Ceece" — the man who dug clams at picnics and whittled airplane and windmill propellers from laths — died in 1992.

His death did not represent any dramatic overall change for the island in and of itself. But to me it ended what remains one of the most indelible memories of my childhood: old fishermen sitting endlessly on the family wharf always watching, always talking, always there as fixed as the tide, living the often-stereotyped unhurried life.

Even more significantly, with Cecil gone, with Clarence Lunt having died a few years earlier and with Vincent Davis soon to leave, the three men I tied to a certain way of life were gone. Other generational figures such as Manny Dalzell, Helen Lunt and Clifton Lunt had also died. As a result, the balance shifted from those rooted in island ways and in the island's more isolated, hardscrabble past, to a more mobile generation.

And you know, even though I love the island and the family and all the positive changes that may have saved Frenchboro, occasionally down at my dad's wharf around dusk as the sun sets over the spruce trees on a still summer evening, or on a raw winter's day huddled by the workshop stove, I do sense a strange loneliness.

Like waiting for an echo that doesn't return.

⎯⎯◆◆◆⎯⎯

## Long Island Timeline

| | |
|---|---|
| 1524 | First Europeans visit the Maine coast. |
| 1604 | French explorer Samuel de Champlain explores coast of Maine. Names "l'Isles des Monts-deserts" or Mount Desert Island and "Ille Haute" or Isle au Haut. |
| 1620 | The Mayflower lands at Plymouth, Massachusetts. |
| 1624 | The first Lunt, Henry, lands in America from England and helps settle what becomes Newburyport, Massachusetts. |
| 1720s | "Long Isle" is first named on charts by Capt. Cyprian Southack. |
| 1740 | Maine's European population reaches 12,000, most live in Southern Maine. |
| 1761 | Abraham Somes and James Richardson establish the first permanent settlement on Mount Desert Island at what becomes Somesville. |
| 1769 | Abner Coffin Lunt, 18, leaves Newburyport, Massachusetts. Lands in Scarborough, Maine. |
| 1771 | Abner Coffin Lunt marries Elizabeth Hodgdon. |
| Aug. 8, 1772 | Amos Coffin Lunt born in Scarborough. |
| 1776 | J.F.W. DesBarres publishes detailed charts — *Atlantic Neptune* series — of Blue Hill Bay. |
| July 4, 1776 | The Declaration of Independence is approved. |
| 1783 | Slavery is abolished in Maine and Massachusetts. |
| June 1785 | Abner Coffin Lunt moves family to North Fox Island, now North Haven. |
| 1786 | Col. James Swan, a wealthy Revolutionary War veteran, buys Burnt Coat Island, now Swans Island, and 24 others, including Long Island, from the Commonwealth of Massachusetts. |
| 1789 | George Washington is elected first U.S. President. |
| 1789 | Abner Coffin Lunt moves family to Pretty Marsh, Mount Desert Island. |
| May 4, 1792 | Abner Coffin Lunt, 39, dies on Deer Island after spending two years working on York Island off Isle au Haut with his son, Amos Coffin Lunt. |

| | |
|---|---|
| Mid-1790s | Amos Coffin Lunt marries Mary Bartlett, daughter of Christopher Bartlett, the first settler of Bartlett Island. |
| May 16, 1796 | Israel B. Lunt born in Pretty Marsh. |
| 1797 | Possible first temporary settler — William Davis — on Long Island. |
| Mar. 15, 1798 | Amos Coffin Lunt Jr. born in Pretty Marsh. |
| 1804 | Lewis and Clark begin exploration of West. |
| 1809 - 1812 | On Long Island, John Walls stakes claim to 75 acres in 1809. William Post may have staked a claim even earlier. |
| 1812 | John Perkins and Jacob Lunt stake claims to 100-acre lots. |
| 1820 | Maine becomes a state and officially separates from Massachusetts. |
| 1820 | Long Island is permanently occupied. U.S. Federal census lists three households on Long Island and a population of 19. These settlers, the first known to live on the island year round, are: Asa Smith, William Pomroy (A.K.A. Pumroy and Pomeroy) and Thomas Pomroy. All three men left by 1830. |
| 1821 | Maine's first high school established in Portland. |
| 1822 | Israel B. Lunt and Amos Coffin Lunt Jr. move to Long Island essentially establishing Long Island as a long-term, viable community. Israel and Amos soon marry Nancy and Eliza Pomroy, respectively. They are both daughters of William Pomroy. Amos and Israel's father Amos Sr. and their Uncle Abner soon follow them onto Long Island. These four Lunts produced 52 children between them. Jacob Lunt, who never marries, also lives on Long Island. |
| 1823 | Israel B. Lunt starts island's first major business, shipping fish, wood and stones to Boston and other ports. His business establishes the island's economic backbone and spurs its growth for the next four decades. |
| 1823 | Israel B. Lunt purchases the 100-acre claim of William Stevens. |
| 1827 | Israel B. Lunt purchases the 100-acre claim of John Perkins. |
| 1827 | First known death on Long Island. Mary Lunt, the 22- |

|  |  |
|---|---|
|  | month-old daughter of Amos C. Lunt Sr. |
| 1827 | First schooner known to be built either for or on Long Island, the 79-foot *Arcade* by Israel B. Lunt. It may have been built on Swans Island. |
| 1830 | Federal Census lists six island households and a population of 42: The households are: Israel B. Lunt, Amos C. Lunt Sr., Amos C. Lunt Jr., Abner Lunt Sr., Thomas Rice and William Rich. Placentia Island has seven households and Black Island has six. |
| 1834 | Swans Island Plantation formed. |
| 1835 | Israel B. Lunt buys Long Island from former agents of Col. Swan for $600. His purchase follows a court battle against a Swan agent. Israel later purchases Johns Island, Harbor Island, Crow Island and the Sister Islands. |
| Late 1830s | Baptist missionaries visit Long Island. |
| Oct. 24, 1840 | Long Island Plantation is organized. The new plantation includes the inhabited Long Island, Black Island, Placentia Island, Pond Island, Great Duck Island, Calf Island and Harbor Island near Naskeg Point. |
| 1842 | The first schoolhouse is built. The building also serves as a church and community building. |
| Feb. 1843 | Baptist Church of Long Island officially organized with 45 members. |
| 1844 | Samuel F.B. Morse invents the telegraph. |
| 1851 | Maine becomes the first state to prohibit the manufacture and sale of alcohol. |
| Oct. 1851 | Capt. John Walls dies with his entire crew aboard the Henry Clay. He is caught in the infamous "Yankee Gale" in the Bay of Chaleur off Canada. More than 100 ships are wrecked and possibly 300 fisherman die. Deaths on Henry Clay include 16-year-old Edward P. Lunt, son of Israel B. Lunt, and Joshua Trask of Swans Island. |
| 1852 | Amos Coffin Lunt Sr. dies. |
| Feb. 11, 1857 | Long Island Plantation officially incorporated as town of Islandport. |
| Mar. 27, 1858 | Islandport dissolved. Long Island Plantation restored. |
| 1858 | First known Congregationalist missionary, Joshua Eaton |

|  |  |
|---|---|
| | of Isle Au Haut, visits Long Island. |
| 1861 | The Civil War begins. |
| Oct. 2, 1861 | Israel B. Lunt dies. The first era of Long Island ends. |
| 1864 | At least seven island men serve in the Civil War. They are: Joseph Warren Lunt, Hezekiah Wills Lunt Sr., George Colliver Lunt, Samuel Rich, William Rich, George R. Rich and William Davis. Davis had joined the fight in 1862. In addition, William T. Lunt, Daniel S. Lunt, Jacob Lunt, James H. Lunt and Henry Lunt, who all were either born or lived on Long Island, also serve in the war. William T. Lunt is killed in action. Daniel S. Lunt dies from a war-related illness in Boston. All others survive. |
| 1870s | Second schoolhouse built. |
| 1875 | First lobster pound is established in Vinalhaven. |
| 1875 | New Maine law requires children between 9 and 15 to attend school at least 12 weeks per year. |
| 1880 | Eight of the island's 41 fishermen fish for lobsters. |
| Summer 1880 | Capt. George W. Lane, a Sunday school missionary, begins summer visits to the island. |
| March 1883 | The town elects its first road surveyor, George Rich. |
| 1885 | Prototype of the modern automobile is invented. |
| 1887 | Phonograph invented. |
| Fall 1888 | Rev. Jonathan Edwards Adams, secretary of the Maine Missionary Society, visits the island to decide how he can help spur a religious revival. |
| Dec. 1, 1888 | Alexander P. MacDonald, a Bowdoin College sophomore, is sent to Long Island by Adams. |
| 1889 | Baptist Church of Long Island is officially dissolved. |
| July 23,1889 | Congregational Church of Outer Long Island is officially organized. Church starts with 27 members and regular attendance of about 50. |
| Sept. 10, 1890 | The island's first chapel is built and officially dedicated. |
| 1891/1892 | First Post Office is established. Post office is named Frenchboro after Bass Harbor lawyer E. Webster French. |
| 1900 | Long Island has 34 households and a population of 159. Island remains in the midst of economic depression that will last for nearly four more decades. |

| | |
|---|---|
| Feb. 22, 1901 | Calf Island and Western Black Island are set off to the town of Swans Island. |
| 1904 | Church Parsonage built. Cost: $1,100. |
| 1905 | Alexander P. MacDonald starts Maine Sea Coast Missionary Society. |
| 1907 | Current schoolhouse is built. |
| 1910 | Sanford L. "Dick" Lunt is born. |
| 1912 | Long Island Elementary School becomes a graded school. |
| 1914 | Parish House is added to church. |
| 1915 | Vivian Davis is born. |
| 1915 | First transcontinental telephone call placed from New York to California. |
| 1919 | Lafayette National Park, later renamed Acadia, is established on Mount Desert Island. |
| 1919 | Maine Missionary Society turns over care of island church to Maine Sea Coast Missionary Society. |
| 1920 | Long Island's population is 137. |
| 1920 | First Sigma Kappa sorority-sponsored mission worker, Lucy Allen King, arrives at Frenchboro. |
| 1920s | Daily mail service begins. |
| 1922 | Alexander P. MacDonald dies aboard the original *Sunbeam*. |
| Oct. 29, 1929 | Stock market crashes. The Great Depression begins. |
| 1932 | Gladys Muir arrives to teach school and church. She stays a record 24 years. |
| 1934 | Prohibition in Maine is repealed. |
| 1938 | David L. Lunt is born. |
| 1939 | Long Island fishermen begin to fish for herring by stop or purse seining during summer and early fall. Over the next two decades herring will help bring the island out of its depression. |
| 1939 | First commercial quality television is introduced by RCA. |
| 1940 | After six years of work, the first state aid road is completed around the harbor. |
| 1940 | Island population at 119. |
| Dec. 7, 1941 | Japan attacks Pearl Harbor. U.S. enters World War II. |
| 1940s | Some islanders build personal power plants using banks of |

|  |  |
|---|---|
|  | batteries and gasoline generators to provide DC power to individual homes. |
| 1945 | World War II ends. The lobster economy begins its slow recovery. |
| 1950 | Bay Ferry Corp. is formed and the passenger boat *SeaWind* provides first ferry service to Long Island. *SeaWind* is discontinued July 1, 1960. |
| 1951 | A lighting plant is installed at the church. |
| 1951 | Dick Lunt starts S.L. Lunt Lobsters, which soon becomes Lunt & Lunt Lobster Co. Lunt & Lunt remains the island's only year-round island business and the longest running business in island history. |
| Feb. 8. 1953 | Charles B. Hooper buys and installs the island's first television set. |
| Mar 18, 1956 | Electrical service is provided to Long Island via an underwater cable from Swans Island. Raymond Teel is the first to turn on lights at his house on Western Point. |
| 1960 | Island population drops to 57. |
| April 1960 | Islanders meet to discuss lobbying state for car ferry service. |
| Oct. 1960 | *Kiboko* begins temporary passenger ferry service to island. Service ends April 1961. |
| Oct. 12, 1961 | *William Silsby* makes first run to Frenchboro, establishing the first car ferry service. |
| August 1962 | Long Island holds the first lobster festival to celebrate the signing of the Atlantic Charter by British Prime Minister Winston Churchill and President Franklin Roosevelt. |
| 1963-1964 | School dwindles to two students: Barbara Lunt and Cheryl Hooper. The next year the school is set to stay at two children: Hooper and David W. Lunt. Island petitions state for foster children. |
| 1964 | The "high road" is finished. |
| August 1964 | The first two foster children arrive on island. Phoebe and Lilly Leach live with Lillian and Cecil Lunt. Two more children, including Anthony W. Brown, arrive in the fall. Eight brothers and sisters, all members of the Holland family, arrive in the winter of 1965. |

| | |
|---|---|
| 1968 | The first streetlight is installed on Long Island, below the house of David L. Lunt. Five more streetlights are installed in 1970. |
| 1969 | Neil A. Armstrong lands on the moon. |
| March 1, 1971 | Ben Davis Sr. and Clyde Onyett die after their car drives off the ferry pier and into the harbor. |
| Aug. 1973 | Jeffrey Webber starts island-only telephone company. |
| 1976 | Inner part of Lunt Harbor is dredged to provide a deep-water channel and anchorage. |
| 1976 | Rebecca Lunt starts writing Frenchboro News for *The Bar Harbor Times.* |
| Feb. 1979 | The island school dwindles to one student, Dean L. Lunt. Classes are moved to a private house, marking the first time in history the schoolhouse is not used during the winter. |
| 1979 | Town of Frenchboro is incorporated. Town encompasses all islands of the former Long Island Plantation. |
| 1979 | Frenchboro Historical Society is started by Vivian and Lillian Lunt. |
| 1980 | Island population dips to 43. |
| 1980s | State approves grant to begin Homestead Project. Frenchboro Future Development Corporation is organized. |
| 1983 | Brook Hill General Store, the last long-running island store, closes. |
| Dec. 22, 1983 | Telephone service to mainland is officially established. |
| 1986 | The Frenchboro Historical Society Museum is built. |
| 1987 | Community building is built in ballfield. |
| 1987 | Lorena and Wyatt Beal move to Frenchboro. They are among a group chosen as the original Homesteaders. They soon buy a house on the harbor and still live on the island. |
| 1987 | Lunt's Dockside Deli opens. |
| 1987 | Seven houses are built for the town's Homestead Project, six for new residents and one for the schoolteacher. Five other lots are set aside for outright sale. Twenty-eight current residents are directly or indirectly linked to the program. |

| | |
|---|---|
| 1990s | Power cable from Swans Island to Frenchboro is buried, virtually eliminating the power outage problems caused by cable breaks that plagued the island throughout the 1980s. |
| 1990s | The first satellite television service is installed on the island. Maine State Ferry service adds a third weekly ferry trip on Sunday afternoon. |
| 1997 | A seasonal passenger-only ferry service begins providing round trip service on Fridays. |
| 1998 | Island Internet service is established in town library. |
| 1998-1999 | For part of the school year, Mariner Beal is the only pupil. |
| 1999 | The Israel B. Lunt Sr. homestead is sold for the first time to Paul and Kay Charpentier. |
| Fall 1999 | Peggy Rockefeller Dulany puts her 900 acres of island land up for sale. The property, which stretches from Northeast Point to Little Beach, excluding the village and Richs Head, carries a price tag of nearly $3 million. Worries begin that the pristine land, which includes 5.5 miles of shoreline, will be bought and developed. |
| Spring 2000 | A coalition of non-profit organizations led by the Maine Coast Heritage Trust purchases the Dulany land. The deal also sets aside land to accommodate future village growth, includes an endowment fund to aid community organizations and provides roughly $300,000 to renovate the island chapel, school, parsonage and library. The Maine Sea Coast Missionary Society, The Island Institute and the Frenchboro Future Development Corp. also participate in developing the plan and helping raise the nearly $3 million necessary to fund it. |
| 2003 | Frenchboro preschool begins with five children. |
| 2003 | Molly Elizabeth Lunt is born, representing the first tenth generation Lunt on Long Island, followed by Tyler in 2006 and Breanna in 2007. |
| 2007 | Frenchboro Elementary School boasts 13 pupils. |
| May 2007 | Island population stands at approximately 70. |

*Appendix A*
# Selected Bibliography

### Books

*Bangor Historical Magazine. 1885 - 1887.* Bangor, Maine (Reprinted by Picton Press, Camden, Maine).

Beattie, Donald W., Rodney M. Cole, and Charles G. Waugh. *A Distant War Comes Home: Maine in the Civil War Era.* Camden: Down East Books, 1996.

Maxfield, Albert. *The Story of One Regiment, the Eleventh Maine Infantry Volunteer in the War of the Rebellion.* New York: J.J. Little & Co., 1896.

Binnewies, Esther, and Muriel Davisson. *A History of Bartlett's Island Mount Desert, Maine.* Bartlett Island: self-published by Peggy and David Rockefeller, 1981.

Bishop, W.H. "Fish and Men in the Maine Islands." *Harper's New Monthly Magazine,* 1880.

Boatner, Mark M. III. *The Civil War Dictionary.* New York: Vintage Books. 1959. Revised edition printed 1991.

Clark, Calvin Montague. *History of The Maine Missionary Society, 1807 - 1925.* Portland: The Southworth Press, 1926.

Currier, John J. *History of Newbury, Mass., 1635 - 1902.* Boston: Damrell & Upham, 1902.

Davis, Walter Goodwin. *The Ancestry of Abel Lunt 1769-1806 of Newbury, Massachusetts.* Portland: The Anthoensen Press, 1963.

Duncan, Roger E. *Coastal Maine: A Maritime History.* New York: W.W. Norton & Co., 1992.

Goode, George Brown. "Fishery Industries of the United States." United States, 47th Congress, first session (1881-82), *Miscellaneous Documents,* Vol. 7, Sect. II.

Judd, Richard W., Edwin A. Churchill, and Joel W. Eastman. *Maine: The Pine Tree State from Prehistory to the Present.* Orono: University of Maine Press, 1995.

Kenway, Rita. *The History of Gotts Island Maine: Its People 1880 - 1992.* Penobscot Press, 1993.

Long, Alice MacDonald. *Vital Records of Mount Desert Island Maine and Nearby Islands, 1776-1820.* Camden: Picton Press, 1990.

Lunt, Thomas S. *A History of the Lunt Family in America.* Salem: Salem Press Co., 1913.

Lunt, Vivian D. *Long Island Plantation: History of Frenchboro, Maine.* Frenchboro: self-published, 1976.

Martin, Kenneth R., and Nathan R. Lipfert. *Lobstering and the Maine Coast.* Bath: Maine Maritime Museum, 1985.

Maxfield, Albert and Robert Brady Jr. *Roster and Statistics of Company D of the Eleventh Regiment Maine Infantry Volunteers, With a Sketch of Its Services in the War of the Rebellion.* New York, 1890. Reprinted by Union Publishing Co., 1994.

McLane, Charles B and Carol E. McLane. *Islands of the Mid-Maine Coast, Vol. 1: Penobscot Bay.* (revised editions). Gardiner, Maine: Tilbury House and Rockland, Maine: The Island Institute, 1997.

McLane, Charles B. *Islands of the Mid-Maine Coast: Blue Hill Bay.* Woolwich, Maine: The Kennebec River Press Inc., 1985.

Millet, Rev. Joshua. *History of Baptists in Maine.* Portland: Charles Day and Co., 1845.

Mitchell, Edwin Valentine. *Anchor to Windward.* New York: Coward-McCann Inc., 1940.

Morison, Samuel Eliot. *The Story of Mount Desert Island, Maine.* Boston:

Little, Brown and Co., 1960.

Norton, Lemuel. *Autobiography of Lemuel Norton.* Concord: Fogg, Hadley & Co., 1864.

O'Leary, Walter M. *Maine Sea Fisheries: The Rise and Fall of a Native Industry, 1830 - 1890.* Boston: Northeastern University Press, 1996.

Richardson, Eleanor Motley. *Hurricane Island: The Town That Disappeared.* Rockland: Island Institute, 1989; reprinted 1997.

Robbins, Raymond E. Jr. *A History of the Houses of West Tremont, Maine.* Tremont: self-published, 1998.

Rolde, Neil. *Maine: A Narrative History.* Gardiner: Tilbury House Publishers, 1990.

Small, Dr. H.W. *A History of Swan's Island, Maine.* Ellsworth: Hancock County Publishing Co., 1898; reprinted in 1975 by Gelvert Associates of Quakerstown, Pa.

Snow, Dean R. "Eastern Abenaki" in *Handbook of North American Indians, Vol. 15.* Washington: Smithsonian Institution, 1978.

Sterling, Robert Thayer. *Lighthouses of the Maine Coast and the Men Who Keep Them.* Brattleboro: Stephen Daye Press, 1935.

Street, George E. *Mt. Desert: A History.* (edited by Samuel A. Eliot). Boston: Houghton Mifflin, 1905 (revised 2nd edition, 1926).

Thornton, Nellie C. *Traditions and Records of Southwest Harbor and Somesville, Mt. Desert Island, Me.* Auburn: Merrill and Webber, 1938.

Wasson, George S. *Sailing Days on the Penobscot: The Story of the River and the Bay in the Old Days.* New York: W.W. Norton & Co. Inc., 1932.

Wasson, Samuel. *A Survey of Hancock County, Maine.* Augusta: Sprague, Owen and Nash, 1875.

Westbrook, Perry D. *Biography of an Island.* New York: Thomas Yozeloff, 1958.

Whitman, William F.S. and Charles H. True. *Maine in the War for the Union: A History of the Part Borne by Maine Troops in the Suppression of the American Rebellion.* Lewiston: Nelson Dingley Jr. & Co., 1865.

Williamson, William D. *The History of the State of Maine; from its first discovery, A.D. 1602, to the Separation, A.D. 1820, Inclusive.* Hallowell: Glazier, Masters and Co., 1832, 2 volumes.; reprinted by the Bond

Wheelwright Co., Freeport, Maine, 1974.

## Newspapers and Magazines

*Bangor Daily News.* Daily newspaper published in Bangor, Maine.

*Bar Harbor Times, The.* Weekly newspaper based in Bar Harbor, Maine.

*Christian Mirror, The.* A weekly newspaper once published in Portland.

*Down East* magazine. Monthly magazine published in Rockland.

*Eastern Argus.* A daily newspaper once published in Portland.

*Ellsworth American, The.* Weekly newspaper based in Ellsworth, Maine.

*Hartford Courant, The.* Daily newspaper published in Hartford, Conn.

*Republican Journal, The.* Newspaper published in Belfast, Maine.

*Triangle, The.* Publication of the Sigma Kappa sorority. A collection is kept at Colby College.

## Manuscripts, Documents and Records

Adjutant General for the State of Maine. Annual reports of Adjutant General from 1861 to 1866 detailing the actions of Maine's Civil War soldiers.

Dalzell Papers. Deeds and business agreements related to Israel B. Lunt Sr. Donated to the Frenchboro Historical Society by Marjorie (Dalzell) Giamo.

Frenchboro, Town of. Town records of Frenchboro from 1979 to present.

Hancock Baptist Assocation. Annual reports and meeting minutes from the 1800s.

Hancock County Registry of Deeds. Various island deeds. All deeds recorded in Hancock County since 1789 are located in Ellsworth.

Long Island, Plantation of. Records of Long Island Plantation to 1979 at which time Long Island Plantation was incorporated as the town of Frenchboro.

Lunt, Cyrus King, papers. Collection of journals and workbooks kept by Cyrus King Lunt and his father, Amos Coffin Lunt Sr. Includes poems written by other family members. Part of the Maine Historical Society collection.

Lunt, Israel B. Papers. Journal kept by Israel B. Lunt Sr. Part of the Maine

Historical Society collection.

Maine Baptist Convention. Annual reports and annual meeting minutes from the 1800s.

Maine Public Documents. Annual or biannual collection of reports from state agencies, including the old Sea and Shore Fisheries commision.

Maine Register or Yearbook. Published annually or biennially by the state of Maine.

Maine Sea Coast Missionary Society, The. Bulletins and Annual Reports of the Maine Sea Coast Missionary Society.

Maine Missionary Society. Annual reports from the 1800s.

Maine State Archives. Various state records including U.S. Census Records, Civil War records, court documents, political papers and official town letters.

Map 1721. Southack, Cyprian. "New England Coasting Pilot from Sandy Hook to Cape Canso (Nova Scotia)."

Map 1776. Des Barres, J.F.W. "Charts of the Coasts and Harbours of New England, composed and engraved by Joseph Frederick Wallet Des Barres, Esq., in Consequence of an Application of the Right Lord Viscount Howe, Commander in Chief of His Majesty's Ships in North America — from the Surveys taken by Samuel Holland, Esq." London, 1776, first publication.

Map 1860. Walling, H.F. (surveyor). "Topographical Map of Hancock County," New York: Lee & Marsh. (A copy is located at the Maine State Library in Augusta. Includes names of settlers and approximate house location).

Map 1881. Colby, George N. (compiler). Atlas of Hancock County, Maine. Ellsworth, Me: S.F. Colby & Co., 1881. (A map shows settler's names on Swans Island and house locations on Long Island. Copy obtained from Saco Valley Printing, Fryeburg, Me).

Massachusetts, Commonwealth of. Archives. Documents and papers dealing with Maine before statehood, including the "History of the Land Office: 1780-1820," an unpublished 23-page history of the Land Office and an overview of the Eastern Lands documents.

Penobscot Marine Museum. Applebee papers. Records of vessel registrations kept by Robert Applebee.

State Superintendent of Common Schools. Annual reports from the superintendent on the condition of Maine's schools and educational efforts.

Tremont, Town of. Town records of Tremont, Maine.

U.S. Census records. Exhaustive census of Maine towns conducted every 10 years. The latest complete census records released to public is for 1920. Also, U.S. Agricultural Census for 1860 and 1870.

### *Interviews*

Davis, Bennie Jr. Born and raised on Long Island. Son of Ben Davis Sr. and Lillian Bridges.

Dobson, Verna B. Born and raised on Long Island. Daughter of Charles R. Mitchell and Jen Rice.

Giamo, Marjorie. Born and raised on Long Island. Daughter of Milton Dalzell and Vera Ross.

Hall, Mable. Born and raised on Long Island. Daughter of John R. and Flora E. Lunt.

Holland, Michael. Moved to the island as a four-year-old in 1966 and spent several years there as an adult. Raised by Lillian J. Davis and Cecil E. Lunt.

Horton, Phoebe. Moved to Long Island in 1965 and spent part of both childhood and adulthood on island. Raised by Cecil E. Lunt and Lillian J. Davis.

Lunt, A. Sandra. Born on Mount Desert Island. Married David L. Lunt and moved to Long Island in 1958. Daughter of William Morris Jr. and Bessie Farley.

Lunt, Carroll W. Born and raised on Long Island. Son of Wallace L. Lunt and Lenora Higgins.

Lunt, David L. Born, raised and still lives on Long Island. Son of Sanford L. "Dick" Lunt and Vivian Davis.

Lunt, Earlene F. Born and raised on Long Island. Daughter of Alma Lunt.

Lunt, Ella V. Born, raised and spent most of adult life on Long Island. Daughter of William Sanford Lunt and Edna F. Rich.

Lunt, John R. Jr. Born, raised and still lives on island. Son of John R. and Flora E. Lunt.

Lunt, Lillian J. Born, raised and still spends summers on Long Island.

Daughter of Alexander P. Davis and Valeria Lunt.

Lunt, Rebecca J. Married John R. Lunt and moved to Long Island in 1949. Still lives on Long Island.

Lunt, Robert A. Born and raised on Long Island. Son of Wallace L. Lunt and Lenora Higgins.

Lunt, Sanford L. "Dick." Lived entire life on Long Island. Son of John R. and Flora E. Lunt.

Lunt, Vivian D. Born, raised and still lives on island. Daughter of Alexander P. Davis and Valeria Lunt.

Sawyer, Barbara. Born, raised and still lives on Long Island. Daughter of Cecil E. Lunt and Lillian J. Davis.

Thompson, June Elizabeth. Born and spent part of childhood on Long Island. Daughter of Grandville "Sim" Davis and Violet Thurlow.

# *Appendix B*
# Census of Long Island

***Note on Federal Census***

The federal census is an important, not always accurate description of a town's population. Census takers, especially during the 19th century, listed names as they were told. Thus nicknames may appear in one census, but not the next. Likewise, middle names were sometimes listed as first names in one census, but not the next. In addition, some names in the handwritten census are illegible. Also, ages sometimes seem wrong.

As a result, the following census records provided are not straight transcriptions of the federal records. Instead, I have followed some family threads through the different census records, consulted town records, the works of other historians and family records to reconstruct the true names and make them uniform where possible. I have made no attempt to check or correct the ages or birthdates. I urge anyone with further details or corrections to contact me or the Frenchboro Historical Society.

Furthermore, all census records for 1890 were destroyed in a fire. I have provided three lists of names from that era, one from the church and two from militia records, to provide some accounting of residents. Also, the 1910 census for Long Island is largely illegible and thus I have not attempted to reconstruct it here. An * means the name presented has been changed from the original census record.

# 1820

| Head of Household | Male 0-16 | Male 16+ | Female 0-16 | Female 16+ | Total |
|---|---|---|---|---|---|
| **Long Island — Population: 19** | | | | | |
| 1. Thomas Pomroy | 0 | 1 | 0 | 2 | 3 |
| 2. William Pomroy | 2 | 1 | 6 | 2 | 11 |
| 3. Asa Smith | 3 | 1 | 0 | 1 | 5 |
| **Placentia Island — Population: 39** | | | | | |
| 1. John Davis | 3 | 1 | 4 | 1 | 9 |
| 2. Eben Lane | 2 | 1 | 3 | 1 | 7 |
| 3. Elias Rich | 5 | 1 | 2 | 1 | 9 |
| 4. Robert Mitchell | 0 | 1 | 0 | 1 | 2 |
| 5. Joseph Remick | 3 | 1 | 4 | 1 | 9 |
| 6. John Walls | 1 | 1 | 0 | 1 | 3 |
| **East Black Island — Population: 9** | | | | | |
| 1. Benjamin Dawes | 2 | 3 | 3 | 1 | 9 |
| **Pond Island – Population: 10** | | | | | |
| 1. Prescott Powers | 1 | 3 | 3 | 3 | 10 |
| **Duck Island — Population: 19** | | | | | |
| 1. John Crane | 4 | 3 | 3 | 1 | 11 |
| 2. John Hamilton | 4 | 1 | 2 | 1 | 8 |

# 1830

## *Long Island — Population: 42*

| Head of Household | Ages (Male/Female) | | | | | | |
| --- | --- | --- | --- | --- | --- | --- | --- |
| | 0-15 | 15-40 | 40+ | 0-15 | 15-40 | 40+ | Total |
| 1. Israel B. Lunt | 0 | 1 | 0 | 0 | 0 | 0 | 1 |
| 2. Abner Lunt | 4 | 5 | 1 | 3 | 0 | 1 | 14 |
| 3. Amos C. Lunt Sr. | 3 | 0 | 1 | 2 | 2 | 0 | 8 |
| 4. Amos C. Lunt Jr. | 2 | 1 | 0 | 0 | 1 | 0 | 4 |
| 5. Thomas Rice | 2 | 1 | 1 | 3 | 3 | 0 | 10 |
| 6. William Rich | 1 | 2 | 1 | 0 | 0 | 1 | 5 |

## *Placentia Island — Population: 39*

| Head of Household | 0-15 | 15-40 | 40+ | 0-15 | 15-40 | 40+ | Total |
| --- | --- | --- | --- | --- | --- | --- | --- |
| 1. Daniel Hamblen | 1 | 1 | 0 | 0 | 2 | 0 | 4 |
| 2. Robert Mitchell | 1 | 1 | 0 | 3 | 1 | 0 | 6 |
| 3. Francis Gilley | 0 | 1 | 1 | 2 | 2 | 0 | 6 |
| 4. "Usher" Parker | 0 | 1 | 0 | 2 | 2 | 0 | 5 |
| 5. Nathaniel Richardson | 2 | 0 | 1 | 1 | 1 | 0 | 5 |
| 6. Elias Rich | 1 | 2 | 1 | 4 | 2 | 1 | 11 |
| 7. Thomas Rich | 0 | 1 | 0 | 0 | 1 | 0 | 2 |

## *Johns Island — Population: 8*

| Head of Household | 0-15 | 15-40 | 40+ | 0-15 | 15-40 | 40+ | Total |
| --- | --- | --- | --- | --- | --- | --- | --- |
| 1. David Carter | 1 | 0 | 1 | 2 | 1 | 1 | 6 |

## *Pond Island — Population: 14*

| Head of Household | 0-15 | 15-40 | 40+ | 0-15 | 15-40 | 40+ | Total |
| --- | --- | --- | --- | --- | --- | --- | --- |
| 1. Prescott Powers | 5 | 1 | 1 | 2 | 4 | 1 | 14 |

## *Black Island — Population: 30*

| Head of Household | 0-15 | 15-40 | 40+ | 0-15 | 15-40 | 40+ | Total |
| --- | --- | --- | --- | --- | --- | --- | --- |
| 1. Benjamin Dawes | 0 | 2 | 1 | 0 | 1 | 1 | 5 |
| 2. Joseph Dawes | 0 | 1 | 0 | 2 | 1 | 0 | 4 |
| 3. Jonathan Dawes | 0 | 1 | 0 | 1 | 1 | 0 | 3 |
| 4. George Butler | 1 | 1 | 0 | 1 | 1 | 0 | 4 |
| 5. Reuben Davis | 1 | 1 | 0 | 5 | 1 | 0 | 8 |
| 6. John Walls | 3 | 0 | 1 | 1 | 1 | 0 | 6 |

## *Calf Island — Population: 13*

| Head of Household | 0-15 | 15-40 | 40+ | 0-15 | 15-40 | 40+ | Total |
| --- | --- | --- | --- | --- | --- | --- | --- |
| 1. Kimbal Herrick | 0 | 1 | 0 | 2 | 1 | 0 | 4 |
| 2 Moses Bridges | 2 | 2 | 0 | 4 | 1 | 0 | 9 |

# 1840

## *Long Island — Population: 115*

| | Name, Age | Males<br>0-20 | 20+ | Females<br>0-20 | 20+ | Total |
|---|---|---|---|---|---|---|
| 1. | Israel B. Lunt, 40s | 3 | 1 | 3 | 4 | 11 |
| 2. | Amos C. Lunt Jr., 40s | 4 | 1 | 2 | 1 | 8 |
| 3. | Thomas Rice, 40s | 1 | 1 | 1 | 1 | 4 |
| 4. | Jacob Rice, 20s | 2 | 1 | 0 | 1 | 4 |
| 5. | Gilbert Rich, 20s | 1 | 1 | 2 | 1 | 5 |
| 6. | John Rich, ? | 1 | 1 | 1 | 1 | 4 |
| 7. | William Rich, 60s | 0 | 1 | 0 | 1 | 2 |
| 8. | Ezra Davis, 20s | 2 | 2 | 5 | 1 | 10 |
| 9. | Amos C. Lunt Sr., 68 | 6 | 2 | 1 | 3 | 12 |
| 10. | Abigail Walls | 2 | 0 | 5 | 1 | 8 |
| 11. | George B. Lunt, 30s | 3 | 2 | 0 | 1 | 6 |
| 12. | Bartholemew R. Lunt, 20s | 2 | 1 | 3 | 2 | 8 |
| 13. | Abner Lunt Sr., 50s | 4 | 4 | 1 | 1 | 10 |
| 14. | Jacob Lunt, 30s | 5 | 1 | 1 | 1 | 8 |
| 15. | Jonathan Tinker, 20s | 0 | 1 | 1 | 1 | 3 |
| 16. | Samuel Alley, 30s | 2 | 1 | 3 | 1 | 7 |
| 17. | William McCready, 30s | 0 | 1 | 3 | 1 | 5 |

## *Black Island — Population: 30*

| | | | | | | |
|---|---|---|---|---|---|---|
| 1. | Joshua Murphy, 40s | 5 | 1 | 3 | 1 | 10 |
| 2. | Benjamin Dawes, ? | 0 | 2 | 0 | 4 | 6 |
| 3. | Jonathan Dawes, 20s | 3 | 1 | 2 | 1 | 7 |
| 4. | Joseph Dawes, 30s | 2 | 1 | 3 | 1 | 7 |

## *Placentia Island — Population: 34*

| | | | | | | |
|---|---|---|---|---|---|---|
| 1. | Abner Lunt Jr., 30s | 0 | 1 | 2 | 1 | 4 |
| 2. | William Rich, 20s | 1 | 1 | 1 | 1 | 4 |
| 3. | Thomas Rich, 30s | 3 | 1 | 1 | 1 | 6 |
| 4. | George Twist, 20s | 0 | 1 | 0 | 1 | 2 |
| 5. | Daniel Hamlin, 30s | 3 | 1 | 3 | 1 | 8 |
| 6. | Robert Mitchell, 40s | 2 | 1 | 4 | 3 | 10 |

# 1850

## *Long Island — Population: 152*

|     | Name (maiden name), Age | Job | Real Estate |
| --- | --- | --- | --- |
| 1. | Israel B. Lunt, 54 | Trader | $1,600 |
|    | Nancy P. (Pomroy) Lunt, 44 | | |
|    | Albion K.P. Lunt, 26 | Mariner | |
|    | John R. Lunt, 19 | Sailor | |
|    | Amanda S. Lunt, 18 | | |
|    | *Edward P. Lunt, 14 | | |
|    | Mary A. Lunt, 12 | | |
|    | *Rhoda Z.M. Lunt, 10 | | |
|    | Hortense B. Lunt, 9 | | |
|    | Nancy H. Lunt, 7 | | |
|    | Freelove Lunt, 6 | | |
|    | Israel B. Lunt Jr., 5 | | |
|    | *A. Victoria Lunt, 4 | | |
|    | Fannie E. Lunt, 2 | | |
|    | John Turner, 38 | Shipcarpenter | |
|    | Abner Pomroy, ? | Mariner | |
|    | *John Walls, 24 | Sailor | |
|    | Matilda (Clark) Lunt, 22 | | |
| 2. | Thomas Rice, ? | Fisherman | $50 |
|    | Mary (Rich) Rice, ? | | |
|    | Samuel Rice, 22 | Fisherman | |
|    | George W. Twist, 30 | Sailor | |
|    | Mary (Rice) Twist, 28 | | |
|    | John H. Twist, 8 | | |
|    | Alice A. Twist, 8 | | |
|    | Sally Twist, 3 | | |
| 3. | Jacob Rice, 36 | Fisherman | $45 |
|    | Dorcas Rice, 32 | | |
|    | *Abraham Rice, 12 | | |
|    | Timothy Rice, 10 | | |
|    | Emeline Rice, 8 | | |
|    | Angeline Rice, 2 | | |
| 4. | William Rich, 31 | Fisherman | $35 |
|    | Eleanor (Rice) Rich, 40 | | |
|    | George Rich, 13 | | |

Margaret Rich, 11
Sarah Rich, 9
Ann Rich, 7
*William Samuel Rich, 5
Eleanor Rich, 3

5.  Gilbert Rich, 34                 Mariner          $25
    Caroline Rich, 18
    Mary Rich, 14
    Gilbert Rich Jr., 13
    Elizabeth Rich, 10
    William J. Rich, 5

6.  John Rich, 40                    Mariner          $45
    Jane (Lunt) Rich, 36
    Henry Rich, 15                   Sailor
    Mary J. Rich, 8
    Nancy Rich, 3

7.  Amos C. Lunt Jr., 52             Fisherman        $65
    *Eliza P. (Pomroy) Lunt, 40
    Joseph W. Lunt, 22               Sailor
    William P. Lunt, 13
    *Maria L. Lunt, 11
    Hiram H. Lunt, 9
    Caroline M. Lunt, 6
    Mary A. Lunt, 5
    *Lucretia Lunt, 3
    George W. Lunt, 2

8.  William Davis, 28                Fisherman        $20
    Polly Davis, 30 (Mary Dawes?)
    Melissa Davis, 10
    Caroline Davis, 8
    Charles Davis, 6
    Betsy Davis, 5
    William Davis Jr., 2

9.  Joseph Davis, 34                 Fisherman        $15
    Betsy Davis, 26
    Jane Davis, 12
    James Davis, 9
    Henry Davis, 6
    Ezra Davis 2nd, 3

| | | |
|---|---|---|
| 10. Ezra Davis, 36 | Fisherman | $25 |
| Rebecca Davis, 30 | | |
| William Davis 3rd, 13 | | |
| Levi Davis, 6 | | |
| Joseph Davis 2nd, 4 | | |
| Hezekiah Davis, 1 | | |
| | | |
| 11. Andrew P. Lunt, 27 | Sailor | $35 |
| *Laurania M. (Pomroy) Lunt, 23 | | |
| Lucy A. Lunt, 5 | | |
| *Laurania N. Lunt, 3 | | |
| Mary B. (Beal) Pomroy, 66 | | |
| John McLaine, 15 | | |
| Abram P. Bridges, 10 | | |
| | | |
| 12. Francis Pomroy, 38 | Fisherman | $45 |
| *Jerushia B. (Lunt) Pomroy, 24 | | |
| Ebeneezer Walls, 7 | | |
| John Pomroy, 5 | | |
| Amanda Pomroy, 2 | | |
| | | |
| 13. Joshua Sylvester Lunt, 21 | Sailor | $50 |
| Rebecca Lunt, 19 | | |
| Sylvester Lunt, 3 mos. | | |
| | | |
| 14. Richard H. Lunt, 36 | Fisherman | $45 |
| Abigail (Davis) (Walls) Lunt, 50 | | |
| Hannah Walls, 10 | | |
| Lafayette Walls, 5 | | |
| | | |
| 15. James T. Davis, 34 | Fisherman | $15 |
| Abigail M. (Milliken) Davis, 43 | | |
| | | |
| 16. Rebecca Davis, 67 | | |
| Nancy Walls, 16 | | |
| | | |
| 17. Polly Lunt, 28 | | |
| Rosamah Lunt, 5 | | |
| Roxana Lunt, 1 | | |
| Charles Davis, 25 | Fisherman | |
| | | |
| 18. Amos C. Lunt Sr., 78 | Fisherman | $75 |
| Priscilla (Butler) Lunt, 47 | | |
| Rufus B. Lunt, 18 | Sailor | |
| Roland H. Lunt, 16 | Sailor | |
| *Daniel Baron Stow Lunt, 14 | | |

<table>
<tr><td>19.</td><td>Abner Lunt, 69</td><td>Fisherman</td><td>$20</td></tr>
<tr><td></td><td>Jane (Dawes) Lunt, 63</td><td></td><td></td></tr>
<tr><td></td><td>Juliann (Lunt) Tinker, 32</td><td></td><td></td></tr>
<tr><td></td><td>Jacob Lunt, 65</td><td>Fisherman</td><td></td></tr>
<tr><td></td><td>Israel Lunt, 24</td><td>Sailor</td><td></td></tr>
<tr><td></td><td>Huldah Walls, 11</td><td></td><td></td></tr>
<tr><td>20.</td><td>William D. Lunt, 27</td><td>Sailor</td><td>$50</td></tr>
<tr><td></td><td>*Mary Elizabeth (Allen) Lunt, 27</td><td></td><td></td></tr>
<tr><td></td><td>William D. Lunt Jr., 11 mos.</td><td></td><td></td></tr>
<tr><td>21.</td><td>George B. Lunt, 36</td><td>Fisherman</td><td>$35</td></tr>
<tr><td></td><td>Miriam H. Lunt, 48</td><td></td><td></td></tr>
<tr><td></td><td>Noel Byron Lunt, 13</td><td></td><td></td></tr>
<tr><td></td><td>*George Colliver Lunt, 11</td><td></td><td></td></tr>
<tr><td></td><td>*Freelove Lunt, 8</td><td></td><td></td></tr>
<tr><td>22.</td><td>Bartholomew R. Lunt Sr., 36</td><td>Fisherman</td><td>$60</td></tr>
<tr><td></td><td>Asenath (Allen) Lunt, 38</td><td></td><td></td></tr>
<tr><td></td><td>Hezekiah W. Lunt, 16</td><td>Sailor</td><td></td></tr>
<tr><td></td><td>*Sabra A. Lunt, 11</td><td></td><td></td></tr>
<tr><td></td><td>*Amos Allen Lunt, 13</td><td></td><td></td></tr>
<tr><td></td><td>Augustus S. Lunt, 5</td><td></td><td></td></tr>
<tr><td></td><td>Calvin C. Lunt, 3</td><td></td><td></td></tr>
<tr><td></td><td>David N. Lunt, 3</td><td></td><td></td></tr>
<tr><td></td><td>*Apipzubath Lunt, 1</td><td></td><td></td></tr>
<tr><td>23.</td><td>Jacob Lunt Jr., 43</td><td>Fisherman</td><td>$50</td></tr>
<tr><td></td><td>Sally (Allen) Lunt, 42</td><td></td><td></td></tr>
<tr><td></td><td>*Joseph Medbury Lunt, 16</td><td>Fisherman</td><td></td></tr>
<tr><td></td><td>Abner Lunt 2nd, 14</td><td></td><td></td></tr>
<tr><td></td><td>Jacob Lunt, 3rd, 12</td><td></td><td></td></tr>
<tr><td></td><td>*Henry Lowell Lunt, 10</td><td></td><td></td></tr>
<tr><td></td><td>Timothy G. Lunt, 9</td><td></td><td></td></tr>
<tr><td></td><td>Mercy L. Lunt, 9</td><td></td><td></td></tr>
<tr><td>24.</td><td>Joseph D. Lunt, 28,</td><td>Fisherman</td><td>$75</td></tr>
<tr><td></td><td>Rehobeth Hannah Lunt, 39</td><td></td><td></td></tr>
<tr><td></td><td>*Benjamin F. Stinson Lunt, 8</td><td></td><td></td></tr>
<tr><td></td><td>*Zaphnath Lunt, 3</td><td></td><td></td></tr>
<tr><td></td><td>Lucy B. Lunt, 6</td><td></td><td></td></tr>
<tr><td>25.</td><td>Moses Pomroy, 28</td><td>Fisherman</td><td>$25</td></tr>
<tr><td></td><td>Caroline Pomroy, 26</td><td></td><td></td></tr>
</table>

Nancy Pomroy, 4
Ichabod Walls, 34        Sailor

## *Pond Island — Population: 10*

1.   Nathaniel Allen, 53      Farmer      $1,250
    Ruth Allen, 56
    Eben Allen, 23      Farmer
    Eliza Allen, 21
    George Allen, 19      Farmer
    William Allen, 16
    Nancy Allen, 13
    Vesta Allen, 11
    Madison Babson, 35      Mariner
    Edward Allen, 14

## *Placentia Island — Population: 13*

1.   Daniel Hamblen, 49      Fisherman      $400
    Rhoda Hamblen, 50
    Walter B. Hamblen, 22      Sailor
    John Hamblen, 18
    Lucinda Hamblen, 15
    (Female) Hamblen, 13
    Daniel Hamblen Jr., 10
    Huldah Hamblen, 7

2.   Robert Mithchell, 61      Farmer      $480
    Lydia Mitchell, ?
    Judith Mitchell, 18
    May A. Mitchell, 16
    Robert Mitchell Jr., 14

## *Calf Island — Population: 7*

1.   Benjamin Cole, 44      Farmer      $750
    Mary A. Cole, 40
    Edwin Cole, 15      Farmer
    Benjamin Cole Jr., 13
    Joseph Cole, 8
    Mary S. Cole, 6
    Mary H. Herrick, 18

## *Black Island — Population: 25*

1.   Joseph Dawes, 52      Fisherman      $150

Mary Dawes, 47
Susan Dawes, 20
Margaret Dawes, 18
David Dawes, 14
Joseph Dawes Jr., 12
Samuel Dawes, 10
Mary E. Dawes, 8
Elinda E. Dawes, 6
Nancy C. Dawes, 4

2.　Jonathan Dawes, 50　　　Fisherman　　　$100
　　Charlotte Dawes, 49
　　George Dawes, 21　　　Sailor
　　Emeline Dawes, 18
　　John Dawes, 16　　　Fisherman
　　Mary Dawes, 14
　　Lydia M. Dawes, 12
　　Susan Dawes, 10
　　Joseph E. Dawes, 8
　　Johnathan Dawes Jr., 6

3.　George Butler, 57　　　Fisherman
　　L. Butler, 31
　　George Butler Jr., 6
　　Albion Butler, 4
　　Rhoda Murphy, 8

## *Duck Island — Population: 11*

1.　William Gilley, 70　　　Fisheman　　　$125
　　Hannah Gilley, 69
　　Samuel Gilley, 24　　　Sailor
　　(Female) Gilley, 22
　　Harrison Gilley, 2

2.　William Gilley Jr., 40　　　Fisherman　　　$100
　　Rhoda Gilley, 41
　　Frances Gilley, 14
　　Ruth Gilley, 12
　　Betsy Gilley, 9
　　Thomas Gilley, 6
　　Hannah Murphy, 50

# 1860

### *Long Island — Population: 153*

| | Name (maiden name), Age | Job | $REstate | $PEstate |
|---|---|---|---|---|
| 1. | Hezekiah W. Lunt Sr., 27 | Fisherman | $175 | $50 |
| | Lydia M. (Dawes) Lunt, 17 | | | |
| | Adelbert W. Lunt, 8 Mos. | | | |
| 2. | Bartholomew R. Lunt Sr., 46 | Fisherman | $350 | $100 |
| | Asenath (Allen) Lunt, 48 | | | |
| | Gilbert L. Rich, 22 | Fisherman | | |
| | Sabra A. (Lunt) Rich, 22 | | | |
| | Amos Allen Lunt, 23 | | | |
| | Augustus S. Lunt, 15 | | | |
| | Calvin C. Lunt, 13 | | | |
| | Bartholomew Russell Lunt 2nd, 9 | | | |
| 3. | (Capt.) William Davis, 42 | Fisherman | | |
| | Mary T. (Rice) Twist, 38 | | $700 | $125 |
| | Joseph W. Lunt, 32 | Fisherman | $30 | |
| | Alice A. (Twist) Lunt, 19 | | | |
| | John H. Twist, 16 | Fisherman | | |
| | Sarah Twist, 13 | | | |
| | (Female) Twist, 6 | | | |
| | Almena Twist, 3 | | | |
| | (Male) Twist, 4 mos. | | | |
| 4. | William D. Lunt, 37 | Fisherman | $100 | $40 |
| | Mary Elizabeth (Allen) Lunt, 37 | | | |
| | William D. Lunt Jr., 11 | | | |
| | *Henry Whitfield Lunt, 7 | | | |
| | Hezekiah E.S. Lunt, 2 | | | |
| 5. | George B. Lunt, 49 | Fisherman | $100 | $20 |
| | Miriam H. Lunt, 57 | | | |
| | Noel Byron Lunt, 25 | Fisherman | | |
| | George C. Lunt, 20 | Fisherman | | |
| 6. | Israel Lunt, 34 | Fisherman | | |
| | John Rich, 51 | Fisherman | $200 | $225 |
| | Jane (Lunt) Rich, 46 | | | |
| | Nancy A. Rich, 13 | | | |
| | Eliza Rich, 3 | | | |

|   |   |   |   |   |
|---|---|---|---|---|
|   | Jane (Dawes) Lunt, 73 |  |  |  |
|   | Francis A. Vautier, 22 | Fisherman | $40 |  |
|   | Mary Vautier, 17 |  |  |  |
|   | John F. Vautier, 2 |  |  |  |
| 7. | Joseph D. Lunt, 39 | Fisherman | $250 | $350 |
|   | Rehobeth Hannah B. Lunt, 49 |  |  |  |
|   | Benjamin F. Stinson Lunt, 18 | Fisherman |  |  |
|   | Lucy B. Lunt, 16 |  |  |  |
|   | Zaphnath P. Lunt, 13 |  |  |  |
| 8. | Gilbert L. Rich, 46 | Fisherman | $100 | $25 |
|   | Mary (Walls) Rich, 29 |  |  |  |
|   | William Rich, 14 |  |  |  |
|   | Isora M. Rich, 6 |  |  |  |
|   | Mary A. Rich, 5 |  |  |  |
| 9. | Richard H. Lunt, 48 | Fisherman | $100 | $60 |
|   | Abigail (Walls) (Davis) Lunt, 58 |  |  |  |
|   | Jacob Lunt, 76 |  |  |  |
|   | Abner Lunt Jr., 50 | Fisherman |  |  |
|   | Hannah Walls, 22 |  |  |  |
|   | Gilbert L. Walls, 16 | Fisherman |  |  |
|   | Henry Lunt, 15 |  |  |  |
|   | Benjamin F. Lunt, 3 |  |  |  |
| 10. | Henry Murphy, 32 | Fisherman | $75 |  |
|   | Nancy J. Murphy, 20 |  |  |  |
|   | Mary Lunt, 31 |  |  |  |
|   | (Female) Lunt, 11 |  |  |  |
|   | Rebecca Davis, 75 |  | $200 | $100 |
| 11. | Joshua Sylvester Lunt, 30 | Mariner | $75 |  |
|   | Rebecca Lunt, 28 |  |  |  |
|   | Amos C. Lunt, 10 |  |  |  |
|   | Charles E. Lunt, 6 |  |  |  |
| 12. | James T. Davis, 42 | Fisherman | $500 | $80 |
|   | Abigail (Milliken) Davis, 52 |  |  |  |
|   | Emily S. Davis, 7 |  |  |  |
| 13. | Jonathan Dawes, 60 | Fisherman | $250 | $1,200 |
|   | Charlotte Dawes, 52 |  |  |  |
|   | George Dawes, 28 | Fisherman |  |  |
|   | Andrew C.A. Stover, 31 | Fisherman |  |  |
|   | Mary Stover, 19 |  |  |  |

Susan Dawes, 14
Joseph Dawes, 12
Rodney Dawes, 10
Catherine E. Dawes, 7
John H. Stover, 1

14. George Butler, 46     Fisherman    $75      $25
     Lois Butler, 55
     Phebe Murphy, 18
     George W. Butler, 14
     Albion K.P. Butler, 12

15. Israel B. Lunt Sr., 64     Trader     $600
     Nancy P. (Pomroy) Lunt, 54
     John R. Lunt, 28     Master Mariner   $600     $1,000
     Rhoda Z.M. Lunt, 21
     Hortense B. Lunt, 19
     Nancy E. Lunt, 17
     Freelove Lunt, 16
     Israel B. Lunt Jr., 14
     Adelaide Victoria Lunt, 13
     Francis E. Lunt, 11
     Reuben P. Joyce, 23     Master Mariner
     Mary A. (Lunt) Joyce, 22
     James Hamilton, 16     Mariner

16. Amos C. Lunt Jr. 61     Fisherman    $200      $50
     Eliza (Pomroy) Lunt, 50
     William P. Lunt, 22     Mariner
     Maria L. Lunt, 20
     Hiram H. Lunt, 19     Mariner
     Caroline M. Lunt, 16
     Mary A. Lunt, 15
     Lucretia Lunt, 12
     George W. Lunt, 12
     Emma F. Lunt, 9

17. Ezra Davis, 44     Fisherman    $30
     Rebecca Davis, 45
     William Davis 2nd, 22     Fisherman
     Emeline (Dawes) Davis, 21
     Levi Davis, 18     Fisherman
     Joseph Davis, 16     Fisherman
     Hezekiah Davis, 10
     Harriet Davis, 8

|  | | | |
|---|---|---|---|
| 18. Betsy Davis, 38 | | $35 | $20 |
| Sarah J. Smith, 22 | | | |
| James Davis, 18 | Fisherman | | |
| Henry Davis, 16 | Fisherman | | |
| Robert D. Davis, 8 | | | |
| A. Davis, 5 | | | |
| Asa Smith, 5 | | | |
| Oliver Smith, 3 | | | |
| Alexander Smith, 1 | | | |
| 19. Mary Davis, 46 (Polly?) | | $100 | $30 |
| Caroline Davis, 19 | | | |
| Charles Davis, 17 | Fisherman | | |
| Betsy Davis, 15 | | | |
| William Davis, 13 | | | |
| Rebecca Davis, 10 | | | |
| Abraham Rice, 25 | Fisherman | $25 | |
| Melissa (Davis) Rice, 21 | | | |
| Emily Rice, 2 | | | |
| Mary Rice, 1 | | | |
| 20. William Rich, 42 | Fisherman | $800 | $225 |
| Eleanor (Rice) Rich, 49 | | | |
| George Rich, 22 | Fisherman | | |
| Margaret Rich, 20 | | | |
| Sarah Turner, 18 | | | |
| Ann Rich, 14 | | | |
| Samuel Rich, 12 | | | |
| Eleanor Rich, 10 | | | |
| Martin H. Rich, 8 | | | |
| 21. Thomas Rice, 80 | | $350 | $150 |
| Mary Rice, 66 | | | |
| Sarah Twist, 13 | | | |
| David R. Barbour, 50 | Wagon Maker | | $25 |
| Olivia Barbour, 43 | | | |
| James Barbour, 16 | | | |
| Galen Barbour, 6 | | | |
| Mary Barbour, 4 | | | |
| 22. Jacob Rice, 46 | Fisherman | $30 | $30 |
| Dorcas Rice, 38 | | | |
| Emeline Rice, 19 | | | |

*Placentia*

23.  Robert Mitchell, 70          Farmer
     Lydia Mitchell, 63
     Charles Mitchell, 41        Farmer          $1,200          $300
     Marietta Mitchell, 26
     Judith A. Mitchell, 8
     Charles B. Mitchell, 3

24.  Henry Burns, 57             Farmer                          $60
     Comfort Burns, 35
     David H. Burns, 16          Fisherman
     Benjamin Burns, 11
     Sophronia F. Burns, 7
     William Burns, 5
     Warren Burns, 1

*Black Island*

25.  Joseph Dawes, 62            Farmer          $1,000          $200
     Mary Dawes, 56
     Joseph Dawes Jr., 22        Fisherman
     Samuel Dawes, 19            Fisherman
     Mary E. Dawes, 17
     Elinda E. Dawes, 14
     Nancy C. Dawes, 12
     Susan Hodgdon, 28
     David Hodgdon, 5
     Franklin Hodgdon, 2

*Calf Island*

26.  Benjamin Cole, 54           Farmer          $1,500          $1,000
     Mary A. Cole, 50
     Benjamin W. Cole Jr., 22    Farmer
     Joseph W. Cole, 18          Farm Laborer
     Mary Cole, 15
     Henry Cole, 10
     Elmeana Cole, 10

*Pond Island*

27.  Nathaniel Allen, 62         Farmer          $2,500          $750
     Ruth R.Allen, 66
     Nancy R. Allen, 22
     Adelbert A. Gott, 17        Farm Laborer
     Alphonso (Cousins?), 14

# 1870

## *Long Island Plantation — Population: 176*

| | Name (Maiden name), age | Job | Real Estate | P. Estate |
|---|---|---|---|---|
| 1. | Eliza P. (Pomroy) Lunt, 60 | K. house | $400 | $100 |
| | William P. Lunt, 32 | Seaman | | $500 |
| | Mary A. Lunt, 24 | At-home | | |
| | George W. Lunt, 22 | Seaman | | |
| | Emma Lunt, 19 | At-home | | |
| 2. | Jonathan Dawes, 69 | Fisherman | $200 | $100 |
| | Charlotte Dawes, 63 | Keeping house | | |
| | Rodney Dawes, 20 | Fisherman | | |
| | Augustus S. Lunt, 25 | Fisherman | | |
| | Susan E. Dawes) Lunt, 25 | Keeping house | | |
| | Winnie D. Lunt, 2 | | | |
| 3. | Mary E. Davis, 50 | Keeping house | | |
| | Rebecca Davis, 18 | At-home | | |
| | Abbie Davis, 26 | At-home | | |
| 4. | Betsy Davis, 40 | Keeping house | | |
| | Irene Davis, 15 | | | |
| 5. | Reuben P. Joyce, 31 | Master Mariner | $600 | $400 |
| | Mary A. (Lunt) Joyce, 31 | Keeping house | | |
| | Agnes T. Joyce, 9 | | | |
| | George W. Joyce, 6 | | | |
| | Reuben B. Joyce, 4 | | | |
| | Alden Joyce, 1 | | | |
| 6. | Abraham Rice, 32 | Fisherman | $100 | $100 |
| | Melissa (Davis) Rice, 30 | Keeping house | | |
| | Emily Rice, 12 | | | |
| | Mary Rice, 10 | | | |
| | Sanford Rice, 8 | | | |
| | Samuel Rice, 7 | | | |
| 7. | Lafayette Walls, 24 | Seaman | $150 | — |
| | Caroline Walls, 27 | Keeping house | | |
| 8. | Richard H. Lunt, 56 | Fisherman | | |
| | Abigal (Davis) (Walls) Lunt, 63 | Keeping house | | |
| | Benjamin Lunt, 13 | | | |

9.  *Benjamin F. Stinson Lunt, 26     Fisherman    $600      $100
    Ann (Rich) Lunt, 24             Keeping house
    William S. Lunt, 9
    Ada V. Lunt, 2

10. John Rich, 63                 Fisherman    $200      —
    Jane (Lunt) Rich, 55            Keeping house
    Charles Reeves, 36           Fisherman
    Sarah W. Reeves, 5
    Martha J. Reeves, 2
    Elizabeth Rich, 14

11. Gilbert Rich, 56             Seaman      $200      $100
    Mary (Walls) Rich, 40          Keeping house
    Isora M. Rich, 17             At-home
    Mary A. Rich, 15
    Edna F. Rich, 1

12. Bartholomew R. Lunt Sr., 56    Fisherman    $200      $100
    *Aseneth (Allen) Lunt, 58      Keeping house
    *Amos Allen Lunt, 34         Fisherman
    Calvin C. Lunt, 23           Seaman
    Bartholomew R. Lunt Jr., 19     Fisherman

13. Robert Ross, 55             Fisherman    $200      $100
    Mary Ross, 47                Keeping house
    Rebecca Davis, ?
    William Davis, 22           Fisherman
    Terisina Davis, 22          Keeping house
    Robert Davis, 4
    William Davis, 1

14. Augustus Leland, 28        Seaman      $100      —
    Elizabeth Leland, 24        Keeping house

15. James T. Davis, 55         Fisherman    $600      $150
    Abigal W. Davis, 62        Keeping house
    Emily S. Davis, 17          At-home
    James H. Thurlow, 2 mos.

16. Henry Murphy, 40           Fisherman    $100      —
    Nancy Murphy, 29           Keeping house
    Rosanna Murphy, 8
    Phebe Murphy, 5
    Rhoda Murphy, 4
    James Murphy, 7 Mos.

17. George Butler, 50 — Fisherman $150 — —
    Lois Butler, 60 — Keeping house
    George F. Butler, 24 — Fisherman
    Albion Butler, 22 — Fisheman

18. Dorcas Rice, 41 — K. House $200 — $100
    John S. Rice, 11

19. *Noel Byron Lunt, 35 — Fisherman $100 — —
    Ellen F. (Rich) Lunt, 19 — Keeping house
    Gardiner Lunt, 5 mos.

20. William Rich, 52 — Farmer $1,500 — $470
    Eleanor (Rice) Rich, 58 — Keeping house
    Martin H. Rich, 18 — Fisherman
    William S. Rich, 22 — Fisherman
    Abbie Rich, 16 — Keeping house
    Levi Davis, 28 — Fisherman
    Sarah Davis, 28 — Keeping house
    Rosa A. Davis, 3

21. Edgar Davis, 30 — Fish Dealer $2,000 — $1,000
    Etta Davis, 27 — Keeping house
    Frank L. Davis, 3
    Harry S. Davis, 1
    William J. Teel, 35 — Store clerk
    Willie W. Teel, 4

22. George B. Lunt, 59 — Fisherman $250 — $100
    George C. Lunt, 30 — Fisherman
    Harriet (Davis) Lunt, 18 — Keeping house
    Angeline Lunt, 2

23. William Davis Jr., 32 — Seaman $100 — —
    Emeline (Dawes) Davis, 35 — Keeping house
    Charlotte Davis, 9
    Perry W. Davis, 4
    John Davis, 2
    Lydia Davis, 2 Mos
    Margie Davis, 2 Mos

24. William D. Lunt, 47 — Fisherman $150 — $100
    Mary Elizabeth (Allen) Lunt, 47 — Keeping house
    Henry Whitfield Lunt, 17 — Seaman
    William D. Lunt Jr., 20 — Fisherman

Hezikiah E.S. Lunt, 12
Merritt W. Lunt, 9

25. Joseph W. Lunt, 42 — Fisherman — $200 — $150
    Alice A. (Twist) Lunt, 27 — Keeping house
    Atwood L. Lunt, 10
    Hiram A. Lunt, 8
    Joseph W. Lunt Jr., 7
    Elizabeth B. Lunt, 4

26. William Davis, 53 — Fisherman — $500 — $1,000
    Mary T. (Rice) Davis, 48 — Keeping house
    Almena Davis, 12 (Listed as a Twist in 1860)
    Albertie Davis, 9
    Rubie Davis, 7
    Leaman T. Davis, 5
    Mary E. Davis, 3

27. Joseph Cousins, 67 — Fisherman — $100 — —
    Hannah Cousins, 30 — Keeping house
    Laura Cousins, 3

28. George R. Rich, 32 — Seaman — $100 — —
    Lucy B. (Lunt) Rich, 26 — Keeping house
    Joseph F. Rich, 5
    Lemuel L. Rich, 3
    Zaphnath Rich, 1

29. Joseph D. Lunt, 48 — Fisherman — $400 — $225
    Rehobeth Hannah B. Lunt, 59 — Keeping house
    Zaphnath P. Lunt, 23 — Seaman

30. Edgar Davis , 56 — Fisherman — $100 — —
    Rebecca Davis, 50 — Keeping house
    Hezikiah Davis, 21 — Fisherman
    Joseph Davis, 24 — Seaman

31. Nancy P. Lunt, 65 — K. house — $4,000 — $1,200
    Israel B. Lunt Jr., 25 — Farmer
    Francis E. Lunt, 21 — At-home
    Rhoda Z.M. Lunt, 30 — At-home
    Hortense B. (Lunt) Pinkham, 28 — At-home
    George B. Brewer, 27 — Seaman
    Freelove (Lunt) Brewer, 26 — Keeping house
    Byron C. Wilson, 26 — Seaman — $150

Adelaide Victoria (Lunt) Wilson, 23  Keeping house
Israel Wilson, 4 Mos.

*Likely Placentia Island*

| | | | |
|---|---|---|---|
| 32. Henry Burns, 66 | Farmer | $1,200 | $800 |
| Comfort Burns, 46 | Keeping house | | |
| Benjamin Burns, 23 | Seaman | | |
| Augusta Burns, 17 | At-home | | |
| Willie Burns, 15 | | | |
| Warren Burns, 11 | | | |
| Philip Burns, 9 | | | |
| Leonard Burns, 6 | | | |
| Alton Burns, 4 | | | |

*Unknown Location*

| | | | |
|---|---|---|---|
| 33. Abram Morris, 58 | Farmer | $1,300 | $325 |
| Susan Morris, 46 | Keeping house | | |
| James Morris, 33 | Seaman | | |

*Likely Black Island*

| | | | |
|---|---|---|---|
| 34. *Joseph Dawes, 79 | Farmer | $1,00 | $300 |
| *Mary Dawes, 77 | Keeping house | | |
| *Joseph Dawes Jr., 35 | Seaman | | |

*Unknown Location*

| | | | |
|---|---|---|---|
| 35. Simeon Butler, 26 | Fisherman | $500 | $340 |
| Melinda Butler, 23 | Keeping house | | |
| Nancy Butler, 6 | | | |
| Mary Butler, 3 | | | |

*Unknown Island*

| | | | |
|---|---|---|---|
| 36. Elbridge Saulsbury, 53 (Salisbury?) | Farmer | $3,000 | $1,110 |
| (Female) Saulsbury, 55 | Keeping house | | |
| Clara Saulsbury, 21 | At-home | | |
| Kendal R. Saulsbury, 18 | | | |
| Walter D. Saulsbury, 12 | | | |

| | |
|---|---|
| 37. Henry W. Hart, 30 | Farmer |
| Maria Hart, 28 | |
| Frederick Hart, 1 | |

# 1880

### *Long Island — Population: 150*

1.  Betsy Davis, 51, Keeping house, widow
    Irene Davis, 22, Daughter, At-home
    Hiram Davis, 7, Grandson
    Lizzie E. Davis, 5, Granddaugther
    Esther F. Davis, 2, Granddaughter
    Lizzie (Carew?), 22, Boarder

2.  Mary (Polly) E. Davis, 60, Keeping house, Divorced
    Rebecca Davis, 25, Daughter, At-home, Widow
    William Davis, 11, Grandson
    Samuel Davis, 8, Grandson
    Caroline Davis, 5, Granddaughter
    Rosanna Murphy, 18, Boarder

3.  Caroline Merrithew, 30, Keeping house
    George Merrithew, 32, Husband, Fisherman

4.  Levi Davis, 36, Fisherman
    Sarah Davis, 35, Wife, Keeping house
    Georganna Davis, 13, Daughter
    Ann Lewis, 34, Boarder, Widowed
    William S. Lewis, 17, Boarder, Fisherman
    Ada V. Lewis, 12, Boarder
    Alva Lewis, 8, Boarder
    Lucy M. Lewis, 6, Boarder

5.  Byron C. Wilson, 35, Fisherman
    Adelaid V. (Lunt) Wilson, 33, Wife, Keeping house
    Israel B. Wilson, 10, Son
    Hortence P. Wilson, 8, Daughter
    Louis Wilson, 6, Son
    Alexander Wilson, 4, Son
    Mary F. Wilson, 2, Daughter
    Emily F. Wilson, 3 Mos., Daughter

6.  Reuben B. Joyce, 42, Fisherman
    Mary A. (Lunt) Joyce, 42, Wife, Keeping house
    Agnes F. Joyce, 20, Daughter, At-home
    George W. Joyce, 16, Son, Fisherman
    Reuben B. Joyce Jr., 14, Son
    Alden Joyce, 12, Son

7.  Hortence (Lunt) Pinkham, 36, Widow, Keeping house
    Frank Pinkham, 10, Son
    Ellen M. Lunt, 27, Sister
    William Van Nordon, 30, Boarder, Fisherman
    Thomas W. Graves, 28, Boarder, Fisherman

8.  William J. Teel, 40, Fisherman
    Rhoda M. (Lunt) Teel, 40, Wife, Keeping house
    William M. Teel, 14, Son
    *Sophronia Teel, 5, Daughter

9.  *William Samuel Rich, 32, Fisherman
    Abbie E. (Davis) Rich, 25, Wife, Keeping house
    Laforest F. Rich, 9, Son
    Nellie Rich, 7, Daughter

10. James T. Davis, 66, Fisherman
    Abigail M. Davis, 74, Wife, Keeping house
    Frank E. Gilman, 27, Son-in-law, Fisherman
    Emily S. Gilman, 27, Daughter
    Horace K. Gilman, 21, Boarder, Fisherman
    James H. Thurlow, 10, Grandson

11. Israel Lunt, 65, Fisherman
    Dorcas Lunt, 65, Wife, Keeping house

12. Robert Ross, 65, Fisherman
    Mary Ross, 60, Wife, Keeping house
    Robert Davis, 14, Grandson
    Ella Cunningham, 7, Granddaughter
    Albion Butler, 28, Boarder, Fisherman
    George Butler, 32, Boarder, Fisherman

13. Abraham Rice, 41, Fisherman
    Melissa (Davis) Rice, 40, Wife, Keeping house
    Emily Rice, 23, Daughter, Widow, At-home
    Mary O. Davis, 22, Daughter, Boarder
    Edwin Rice, 18, Son, Fisherman
    Samuel Rice, 17, Son, Fisherman
    Granville Rice, 4, Son
    Naomi Davis, 4, Granddaughter
    John L. Davis, 2, Grandson
    Marston Murphy, 2, Boarder

14. Eleanor (Rice) Rich, 69, Widow, Keeping house
    Martin H. Rich, 27, Son, Fisherman.

15. Hannah Lunt, 38, Widow, Keeping house
    (Elma?) C. Lunt, 11, Daughter
    William Murphy, 5, Boarder

16. Richard Lunt, 68, Fisherman
    Abigail Lunt, 81, Wife, Keeping house
    Benjamin F. Lunt, 23, Grandson, Fisherman

17. Gilbert Rich, 66, Fisherman
    Mary Rich, 50, Wife, Keeping house
    Edna F. Rich, 11, Daughter

18. *Israel Bertrand Lunt Jr., 31, Fisherman
    Isora M. (Rich) Lunt, 26, Wife, Keeping house
    Alphonso Lunt, 7, Son
    Minnie G. Lunt, 5, Daughter
    Ellen F. Lunt, 3, Daughter

19. Henry Murphy, 50, Widowed
    Rhoda Murphy, 14, Daughter, At-home
    Edward Murphy, 10, Son
    Hannah Murphy, 8, Daughter

20. George B. Lunt, 69, Widower, Farmer
    George C. Lunt, 40, Fisherman
    Harriet (Davis) Lunt, 26, Daughter-in-law, Keeping house
    Angeline Lunt, 12, Granddaughter
    Edwin Lunt, 9, Grandson
    Daniel Lunt, 5, Grandson
    *Alvina Lunt, 2, Granddaughter

21. Rebecca Davis, 60, Divorced, Keeping house
    Hezekiah Davis, 28, Son, Fisherman

22. Stephen Donham, 66, Fisherman
    Betsy Donham, Wife, Keeping house

23. William D. Lunt, 57, Fisherman
    Mary Elizabeth (Allen) Lunt, 57, Wife, Keeping house
    Henry Whitfield Lunt, 27, Son, Fisherman
    Hezekiah E.S. Lunt, 22, Son, Fisherman
    Merritt W. Lunt, 19, Son, Fisherman

24. Joseph W. Lunt Sr, 52, Fisherman
    Alice A. (Twist) Lunt, 36, Wife, Keeping house
    Atwood L. Lunt, 20, Son, Fisherman

Hiram A. Lunt, 17, Son, Fisherman
Joseph W. Lunt Jr., 15, Son, Fisherman
Elizabeth B. Lunt, 14, Daughter
Henry S. Lunt, 12, Son
Maria A. Lunt, 10, Daughter
Nelson P. Lunt, 5, Son
John R. Lunt, 3, Son
*Cora A. Lunt, 2, Daughter

25.  Thomas N. Osier, 29, Fisherman
Almenia S. Osier, 23, Wife, Keeping house
Mary A. Osier, 5, Daughter
Nathan F. Osier, 2, Son
Frank Copeland, 30, Boarder, Fisherman

26.  Charles Gray, 40, Fisherman
Flora Gray, 27, Wife, Keeping house
Georgie L. Gray, 5, Daughter
Emma Deeker, 22, Boarder, Servant

27.  William Davis, 63, Fisherman
Mary  T. (Rice) Davis, 56, Wife, Keeping house
Ruby A. Davis, 17, Daughter, At-Home
Leaman T. Davis, 15, Son
Mary E. Davis, 14, Daughter

28.  Bartholomew R. Lunt Sr., 66, Notary Public
Asenath A. (Allen) Lunt, 67, Wife, Keeping house
Amos Allen Lunt, 44, Son
Bartholomew Russell Lunt Jr., 29, Son, Fisherman

29.  George R. Rich, 41, Fisherman
Lucy B. Rich, 36, Wife, Keeping house
Frank J. Rich, 15, Son
Lemuel L. Rich, 13, Son
Zaphnath Rich, 11, Son
Mabel Rich, 8, Daughter

30.  Joseph D. Lunt, 58, Fisherman.
Rehobeth Hannah Lunt, 69, Wife, Keeping house
Zaphnath P. Lunt, 33, Son, Fisherman
Athalana Lunt, 17, Daughter-in-law
Addie B. Lunt, 12, Granddaughter
Caleb S. Lunt, 9

# Church Attendees 1888/1889

1. W. Sanford Lunt
2. H. Whitfield Lunt
3. Flora Gray
4. Alphonso Lunt
5. Joseph Warren Lunt
6. Hezekiah Davis
7. Maria Teel
8. Bartholomew R. Lunt
9. Billy Davis
10. Maggie Butler
11. William Lunt
12. Daniel Lunt
13. Capt. William Davis
14. Mary Osier
15. Nellie Rich
16. Abbie Rich
17. Henry Davis
18. Cora Lunt
19. Linnie Rice
20 William M. Teel
21. Leaman T. Davis
22. Agnes Davis
23. Hiram Lunt
24. Frank Ross
25. Will Lunt
26. Grant Lunt
27. Melissa Rice
28. Henry Davis (Betsy's son)
29. Hortense Van Norden
30. James T. Gilman
31. Frank Gilman
32. Emily Gilman
33. Atwood Lunt
34. Angeline Lunt
35. C. Edward Rice
36. Granville Rice
37. Nathan Osier
38. Merrit W. Lunt
39. Hezekiah W. Lunt
40. G. Coliver Lunt
41. Elvina Lunt
42. Polly Ross
43. Robert Davis
44. Isora Lunt
45. Mary Rich
46. Asa Carter
47. Constantine Carter
48. Edna Lunt
49. Ellen Turner
50. William J. Teel
51. Sophronia S. Teel
52. Mr. Anderson
53. James Vinal
54. Martin Hall Rich
55. Flora Rice
56. Rosanna Lunt
57. John R. Lunt Sr.
58. Nelson P. Lunt
59. Richard Lunt
60. Samuel Allen
61. James T. Davis

# Long Island Militia 1893/1897

| *April 18, 1893* | *April 27, 1897* |
|---|---|
| Leaman T. Davis, 28 | Leaman T. Davis, 32 |
| Hezekiah Davis, 44 | Samuel Davis, 25 |
| Robert Davis, 27 | Robert Davis, 31 |
| Samuel Davis, 21 | Franklin E. Gilman, 44 |
| Franklin E. Gilman, 40 | Henry W. Lunt, 41 |
| Henry W. Lunt, 37 | H.E.S. Lunt, 38 |
| Hezekiah E.S. Lunt, 34 | Atwood L. Lunt, 37 |
| Atwood L. Lunt, 33 | Merritt W. Lunt, 36 |
| Merrit W. Lunt, 32 | Hiram A. Lunt, 34 |
| Hiram A. Lunt, 30 | William S. Lunt, 35 |
| William S. Lunt, 31 | Adelbert W. Lunt, 37 |
| Adelbert W. Lunt, 33 | Grant H. Lunt, 29 |
| Grant H. Lunt, 25 | Edwin Lunt, 27 |
| Edwin Lunt, 23 | Hezekiah W. Lunt Jr., 25 |
| Hezekiah W. Lunt Jr., 21 | Alphonso L. Lunt, 24 |
| Alphonso L. Lunt, 20 | Edwin S. Lunt, 22 |
| Edward S. Lunt, 18 | Daniel Lunt, 24 |
| Daniel Lunt, 20 | Nelson P. Lunt, 22 |
| Nelson P. Lunt, 18 | Joseph W. Lunt, 33 |
| Frank W. Ross, 23 | John R. Lunt, 20 |
| Walter M. Robinson, 25 | Frank W. Ross, 27 |
| Martin H. Rich, 41 | Walter M. Robinson, 29 |
| Charles E. Rice, 31 | Charles Robinson, 35 |
| Samuel Rice, 29 | Samuel Rice, 33 |
| James H. Thurlow, 23 | James H. Thurlow, 27 |
| William M. Teel, 27 | William M. Teel, 31 |
| William A. Van Norden, 44 | |
| James F. Vinal, 35 | |
| E. G. Webber, 35 | |

# 1900

### *Long Island — Population: 166*

| | Name, (Maiden Name), age | Desc. | Work | YM | Birth |
|---|---|---|---|---|---|
| 1. | *William Samuel Rich, 52 | Head | Lobster | 31 | Mar. 1848 |
| | Abbie E. (Davis) Rich, 45 | Wife | | 31 | Jan. 1855 |
| | Nellie Rich, 27 | Daughter | | | Jan. 1873 |
| | John R. Robinson, 46 | Boarder | Lobster | | May 1854 |
| 2. | Frank Gilman, 47 | Head | Lobster | 21 | Nov. 1852 |
| | Emily S. Gilman, 46 | Wife | | 21 | Sept. 1853 |
| 3. | Levi T. Davis, 57 | Head | Groceries | Wd | May 1843 |
| 4. | Alphonso L. Lunt, 27 | Head | Lobster | 1 | May 1873 |
| | Sadie L. (McKusick) Lunt, 22 | Wife | | 1 | Jul. 1877 |
| | Leonard Lunt, 4 mos. | Son | | | Jan. 1900 |
| 5. | James H. Thurlow, 30 | Head | Lobster | 10 | Mar. 1870 |
| | Lizzie M. (Lunt) Thurlow, 27 | Wife | | 10 | Apr. 1873 |
| | Frank A. Thurlow, 7 | Son | | | Jul. 1892 |
| | Violet B. Thurlow, 4 | Daughter | | | Oct. 1895 |
| | Emily M. Thurlow, 2 | Daughter | | | Sept. 1897 |
| | Lydia M. Thurlow, 1 mos. | Daughter | | | May 1900 |
| 6. | William Sanford Lunt, 38 | Head | Lobster | 16 | Mar. 1862 |
| | Edna F. (Rich) Lunt, 31 | Wife | | 16 | Jan. 1869 |
| | Everett S. Lunt, 16 | Son | Lobster | | May 1884 |
| | Charles B. Lunt, 14 | Son | Lobster | | Sept. 1885 |
| | *Flora E. Lunt, 12 | Daughter | | | Jul. 1887 |
| | Nellie Lunt, 11 | Daughter | | | Apr. 1889 |
| | Benjamin S. Lunt, 9 | Son | | | Nov. 1890 |
| | Leonard A. Lunt, 6 | Son | | | Mar. 1894 |
| | Lida E. Lunt, 4 | Daughter | | | Aug. 1895 |
| | Irving Lunt, 5 mos. | Son | | | Dec. 1899 |
| 7. | Abraham Rice, 64 | Head | Lobster | 40 | Dec. 1835 |
| | Melissa (Davis) Rice, 61 | Wife | | 40 | Mar. 1839 |
| | Marston Rice, 23 | Adopt Son | Cod | | Jan. 1877 |
| | Elizabeth McIntire, 21 | Boarder | Teacher | | Feb. 1879 |
| 8. | *Everett Edward Dalzell, 34 | Head | Lobster | 10 | Dec. 1865 |
| | Linnie D. (Rice) Dalzell, 27 | Wife | | 10 | Sep. 1872 |
| | Bernard S. Dalzell, 7 | Son | | | May 1893 |

| | | | | | |
|---|---|---|---|---|---|
| | *Milton Dalzell, 4 | Son | | | Apr. 1896 |
| | Hollis P. Dalzell, 3 | Son | | | May 1897 |
| | *Everett E. Dalzell Jr., 11 mos. | Son | | | June 1899 |
| 9. | Charles E. Davis, 57 | Head | Cod | 1 | June 1847 |
| | William Davis, 65 | Boarder | Cod | 45 | Dec. 1836 |
| 10. | *Israel B. Lunt Jr., 52 | Head | Lobster | 28 | Mar. 1848 |
| | Isora M. (Rich) Lunt, 46 | Wife | | 28 | Aug. 1853 |
| | Ellen F. Lunt, 21 | Daughter | | | Aug. 1878 |
| | *Cassie Lunt, 9 | Daughter | | | Mar. 1891 |
| | Mary Rich, 69 | Mom-in-law | | Wd. | Mar. 1831 |
| 11. | Samuel Rice, 36 | Head | Lobster | 10 | Jun. 1863 |
| | Sabra A. (Lunt) Rice, 33 | Wife | | 10 | Jul. 1866 |
| | Pearlie O. Rice, 5 | Son | | | Aug. 1894 |
| 12. | Charles E. Rice, 37 | Head | Lobster | 16 | Mar. 1863 |
| | Flora A. (Lunt) Rice, 31 | Wife | | 16 | Feb. 1869 |
| | Jennie M. Rice, 10 | Daughter | | | May 1890 |
| 13. | Hezikiah E.S. Lunt, 41 | Head | Lobster | | July 1858 |
| 14. | Atwood L. Lunt, 40 | Head | Lobster | 11 | Mar. 1860 |
| | Angeline V. Lunt, 32 | Wife | | 11 | Mar. 1868 |
| | Bertha L. Lunt, 11 | Daughter | | | Jan. 1889 |
| | Joseph W. Lunt, 7 | Son | | | Jan. 1893 |
| | Llewellyn Lunt, 4 | Son | | | Feb. 1896 |
| | Grover C. Lunt, 2 | Son | | | May 1898 |
| | Phillis Lunt, 1 mos. | Son | | | May 1900 |
| 15. | George Colliver Lunt, 60 | Head | Lobster | 33 | Dec. 1839 |
| | Harriet (Davis) Lunt, 48 | Wife | | 33 | Dec. 1851 |
| | Edwin L. Lunt, 30 | Son | Lobster | | July 1869 |
| | Daniel R. Lunt, 26 | Son | Lobster | | June 1873 |
| | Jasper E. Lunt, 18 | Son | Lobster | | June 1881 |
| | Nathan F. Osier, 24 | Boarder | Cod | | Aug. 1875 |
| 16. | George Butler, 59 | Head | Cod | | Sep. 1840 |
| 17. | Henry W. Lunt, 46 | Head | Lobster | 20 | Aug. 1853 |
| | Sadie M. Lunt, 22 | House Keeper | | | Nov. 1877 |
| 18. | Merritt W. Lunt, 48 | Head | Lobster | | Apr. 1862 |
| 19. | Betsy Harvey, 47 | Head | | Wd. | Sep. 1852 |

| | | | | |
|---|---|---|---|---|
| 20. Alice A. (Twist) Lunt, 56 | Head | | Wd. | Aug. 1843 |
| Grant H. Lunt, 31 | Son | Lobster | | May 1869 |
| Nelson P. Lunt, 24 | Son | Lobster | 1 | July 1875 |
| *Alvina E. Lunt, 22 | Daughter-in-Law | | 1 | Mar. 1878 |
| Reuben L. Lunt, 4 mos. | Grandson | | | Jan. 1900 |
| Herman E. Lunt, 2 | Grandson | | | Dec. 1897 |
| John R. Lunt, 23 | Son | Lobster | | Nov. 1876 |
| Reuben L. Davis, 34 | Boarder | Preacher | | July 1865 |
| | | | | |
| 21. Hiram A. Lunt, 37 | Head | Lobster | 14 | Dec. 1862 |
| Mary S. Lunt, 30 | Wife | | 14 | Oct. 1869 |
| Jessie G. Lunt, 9 | Daughter | | | Feb. 1891 |
| Thomas B. Lunt, 7 | Son | | | Mar. 1893 |
| Valeria M. Lunt, 4 | Daughter | | | May 1894 |
| Lula B. Lunt, 3 | Daughter | | | Apr. 1897 |
| Nora E. Lunt, 8 mos. | Daughter | | | Sep. 1899 |
| | | | | |
| 22. Leaman T. Davis, 36 | Head | Lobster | 12 | Apr. 1864 |
| Agnes (Joyce) Davis, 39 | Wife | | 12 | Aug. 1861 |
| Alexander Davis, 11 | Son | | | Oct. 1888 |
| Alden M. Davis, 10 | Son | | | May 1890 |
| Grace H. Davis, 7 | Daughter | | | Nov. 1892 |
| Millie L. Davis, 6 | Daughter | | | Feb. 1894 |
| Abbie F. Davis, 5 | Daughter | | | Apr. 1895 |
| Grandville W. Davis, 3 | Son | | | Mar. 1897 |
| Elmer L. Davis, 1 | Son | | | Jan. 1899 |
| Mary A. Bridges, 15 | Step-Daughter | | | Aug. 1884 |
| | | | | |
| 22. Hezekiah W. Lunt Sr., 66 | Head | Lobster | 41 | July 1833 |
| Lydia M. (Dawes) Lunt, 57 | Wife | | 41 | Oct. 1842 |
| Edwin S. Lunt, 25 | Son | Lobster | | Nov. 1874 |
| Asenath M. Lunt, 23 | Daughter | | | Nov. 1876 |
| Calvin B. Lunt, 21 | Son | Lobster | | Aug. 1878 |
| Charles Lunt, 18 | Son | Cod | | Aug. 1881 |
| Leforest G. Lunt, 11 | Son | | | Dec. 1888 |
| | | | | |
| 23. Hezekiah W. Lunt Jr., 29 | Head | Lobster | 5 | Sept. 1870 |
| Cora A. (Lunt) Lunt, 21 | Wife | | 5 | July 1878 |
| | | | | |
| 24. Martin H, Rich, 40 | Head | Cod | 7 | Aug. 1859 |
| Charlotte L. Rich, 39 | Wife | | 7 | Apr. 1861 |
| *Harry W. Lunt, 15 | Son | | | Oct. 1884 |
| *Clarence A. Lunt, 11 | Son | | | Oct. 1888 |
| *Blanche H. Lunt, 10 | Daughter | | | Apr. 1890 |

| | Name, Age | Relation | Occupation | Yrs. Married | Birth |
|---|---|---|---|---|---|
| | Frank S. Rich, 7 | Son | | | June 1892 |
| | Naomi M. Rich, 5 | Daughter | | | Feb. 1895 |
| 25. | Adelbert W. Lunt, 40 | Head | Lobster | 17 | Nov. 1859 |
| | Rosanna (Murphy) Lunt, 38 | Wife | | 17 | Nov. 1861 |
| | Shirley W. Lunt, 9 | Son | | | Dec. 1890 |
| | Lewis L. Lunt, 7 | Son | | | Dec. 1892 |
| | Sabra A. Lunt, 2 | Daughter | | | Mar. 1898 |
| 26. | Joseph W. Lunt Jr., 35 | Head | Lobster | 1 | Sept. 1864 |
| | Minnie (Cross) Lunt, 27 | Wife | | 1 | May 1873 |
| | Sylvia E. Lunt, 1 mos. | Daughter | | | Apr. 1900 |
| 27. | Charles Bartlett, 35 | Head | Lobster | 0 | May 1864 |
| | Emily O. (Rice) Bartlett, 44 | Wife | | 0 | July 1855 |
| 28. | William M. Teel Jr., 33 | Head | Lobster | 12 | June 1866 |
| | Maria L. (Lunt) Teel, 29 | Wife | | 12 | June 1870 |
| | Clinton B. Teel, 11 | Son | | | May 1889 |
| | Wyman S. Teel, 9 | Son | | | Aug. 1890 |
| | William L. Teel, 8 | Son | | | Sept. 1891 |
| | Raymond L. Teel, 3 mos. | Son | | | Feb. 1900 |
| 29. | William J. Teel Sr., 67 | Head | | 30 | Apr. 1833 |
| | Rhoda M.(Lunt) Teel, 61 | Wife | | 30 | May 1839 |
| | Sophronia Teel, 26 | Daughter | Clerk | | Feb. 1874 |
| 30. | William A. Van Norden, 50 | Head | Lobster | 18 | Nov. 1849 |
| | Hortense B. (Lunt) Van Norden, 58 | Wife | | 18 | Oct. 1841 |
| | Frank W. Ross, 30 | Stepson | Lobster | 5 | Mar. 1870 |
| | Lizzie B. (Lunt) Ross, 33 | Step-daughter-in-law | | 5 | Oct. 1866 |
| | Vera M. Ross, 4 | Granddaughter | | | Jan. 1896 |
| | Alice H. Ross, 2 | Granddaughter | | | Feb. 1898 |
| 31. | Charles Robinson, 38 | Head | Lobster | | Mar. 1862 |
| | Rebecca N. Davis, 48 | Housekeeper | | | Sept. 1851 |
| | Robert Davis, 34 | Boarder | Cod | | Jan. 1866 |
| 32. | Walter Robinson, 33 | Head | Lobster | 8 | July 1866 |
| | Carrie E. Robinson, 25 | Wife | | 8 | Mar. 1875 |
| | Maynard A. Robinson, 8 | Son | | | Jan. 1892 |
| | Albertine E. Robinson, 4 | Daughter | | | Sept. 1895 |
| 33. | Samuel Davis, 29 | Head | Lobster | 7 | Apr. 1871 |
| | Lydia M. Davis, 39 | Wife | | 7 | Mar. 1861 |
| | Lena M. Higgins, 16 | Daughter | | | Aug. 1883 |

|  | | | | | |
|---|---|---|---|---|---|
| | Frederick Higgins, 14 | Son | | | Feb. 1886 |
| | Warren H. Higgins, 11 | Son | | | Mar. 1889 |
| | Carrie Davis, 7 | Daughter | | | May 1893 |
| | Jessie L. Davis, 1 | Daughter | | | Apr. 1899 |
| | Emeline Davis, 65 | Boarder | | Wd. | May 1835 |
| | Minnie F. Davis, 5 mos. | Boarder | | | Dec. 1899 |
| | Hattie M. Davis, 24 | Boarder | | | June 1875 |
| 34. | David Dawes, 69 | Head | Lobster | 13 | Aug. 1830 |
| | Irene Dawes, 44 | Wife | | 13 | Mar. 1856 |
| | Sydney Dawes, 12 | Son | | | Feb. 1888 |
| | Irena M. Dawes, 10 | Daughter | | | Apr. 1890 |
| | Laura L. Dawes, 7 | Daughter | | | Aug. 1892 |
| | Elry Dawes, 5 | Son | | | Jan. 1895 |
| | Goldie Dawes, 2 | Daughter | | | Dec. 1897 |
| | Eugene G. Van Norden, 16 | Boarder | Lobster | | Nov. 1883 |
| 35. | George Marshall, 35 | Head | Lobster | 2 | June 1864 |
| | Villa Marshall, 22 | Wife | | 2 | Nov. 1877 |
| | Eugenie Marshall, 4 mos. | Daughter | | | Jan. 1900 |
| 36. | John T. Murphy, 29 | Head | Lobster | 8 | Oct. 1870 |
| | Viola A. Murphy, 23 | Wife | | 8 | Mar. 1877 |
| | Grace M. Murphy, 5 | Daughter | | | Jan. 1895 |
| | Neal L. Murphy, 2 | Son | | | July 1897 |

## Pond Island

|  | | | | | |
|---|---|---|---|---|---|
| 37. | Colson H. Robbins, 41 | Head | Farmer | 22 | Oct. 1858 |
| | Lizzie A. (Sprague) Robbins, 42 | Wife | | 22 | Aug. 1857 |
| | Chester Robbins, 19 | Son | Farm laborer | | Jan. 1881 |
| | Lottie F. Robbins, 17 | Daughter | | | Nov. 1882 |
| | George Robbins, 15 | Son | Farm Laborer | | May 1885 |
| | Vola M. Robbins, 11 | Daughter | | | Oct. 1888 |
| | Lem Robbins, 9 | Son | | | Nov. 1890 |
| | Jay L. Robbins, 3 | Son | | | May 1897 |

# 1920

## *Long Island — Population: 139*

| | Name (maiden name), age | Relationship | Job |
|---|---|---|---|
| 1. | Leonard A. Lunt, 25 | Head | Fishing |
| | Mildred L. (Davis) Lunt, 25 | Wife | |
| | Joseph Dondis, 36 | Boarder | Store |
| 2. | Warren H. Higgins, 28 | Head | Fishing |
| | Lida E. (Lunt) Higgins, 33 | Wife | |
| | Maynard P. Higgins, 8 | Son | |
| | Lenora L. Higgins, 6 | Daughter | |
| | Leonard W. Higgins, 5 | Son | |
| 3. | Eugene C. Van Norden, 36 | Head | Fishing |
| | Vera M. (Kelly) Van Norden, 27 | Wife | |
| | William Van Norden, 70 | Father | Widow |
| 4. | Iris J.M. Cornetta, 55 | Head | Fishing |
| 5. | Sophronia S. Teel, 45 | Head | |
| | Raymond L. Teel, 19 | Nephew | Fishing |
| 6. | Charles R. Mitchell, 26 | Head | |
| | Jennie M. (Rice) (McKown) Mitchell, 29 | Wife | |
| | Verna B. Mitchell, 1 | Daughter | |
| | Genevieve W. McKown, 4 | Daughter | |
| 6A. | Herman L. Anderson, 27 | Head | Fishing |
| | Emily M. (Thurlow) Anderson, 21 | Wife | |
| 7. | Flora A. (Lunt) Rice, 50 | Head, Widow | |
| | Calvin B. Lunt, 41 | Brother | Fishing |
| | Bertha L. Lunt, 25 | | |
| 8. | Frank W. Ross, ? | Head | Lobster Fishing |
| | Elizabeth B. (Lunt) Ross, 53 | Wife | |
| | Alice H. Ross, 22 | Daughter | |
| 8A. | Milton Dalzell, 23 | Son-in-law | Lobster Fishing |
| | Vera M. (Ross) Dalzell, 23 | Daughter | |
| | Marjorie Dalzell, 1 | Granddaughter | |
| 9. | Granville W. Dalzell, 19 | Head | Lobster Fishing |
| | Lydia (Thurlow) Dalzell, 19 | Wife | |
| 10. | James H. Thurlow, 49 | Head | Lobster Fishing |

| | | |
|---|---|---|
| Lizzie M. (Lunt) Thurlow, 46 | Wife | |
| Edith M. Thurlow, 18 | Daughter | |
| James E. Thurlow, 17 | Son | Fishing |
| Thelma V. Thurlow, 11 | Daughter | |

11. Franklin E. Gilman, 67 — Head — Postmaster
    Emily S. (Davis) Gilman, 67 — Wife

12. Alphonso L. Lunt, 46 — Head — Fishing
    Sadie L. (McKusick) Lunt, 43 — Wife
    Gertrude L. Lunt, 16 — Daughter

13. Jephtha Nickerson, 54 — Head — Fishing
    Ellen (Lunt) Nickerson, 40 — Wife
    Lewis A. Nickerson, 7 — Son
    Esther B. Nickerson, 5 — Daughter
    *Ernest B. Nickerson, 5 — Son

14. Martin H. Rich, 65 — Head, widower — Fishing

15. William S. Lunt, 58 — Head — Fishing
    Edna F. (Rich) Lunt, 51 — Wife
    Benjamin S. Lunt, 29 — Son — Fishing
    Irving F. Lunt, 20 — Son — Fishing
    Orrin C. Lunt, 16 — Son — Fishing
    Virginia M. Lunt, 13 — Daughter
    Ella V. Lunt, 11 — Daughter
    Kenneth Gardiner Lunt, 8 — Son
    Annie M. Lunt, 6 — Daughter

16. Charles B. Lunt, 34 — Head — Fishing
    Edith (Stanley) Lunt, 23 — Wife

17. Everett Lunt, 35 — Head
    Alma (Hall) Lunt, 50 — Wife

18. Everett Edward Dalzell, 50 — Head
    Mildred S. Dalzell, 15 — Daughter

19. Samuel M. Rice, 56 — Head — Lobster Fishing
    Sabra A. (Lunt) Rice, 53 — Wife
    Pearl O. Rice, 25 — Son — Fishing
    Charles Rice, 4 — Grandson

20. Isora M. (Rich) Lunt, 66 — Head, widower

21. Hezekiah M. Davis, 68 — Head, widower — Lobster Fishing

22. George W. Butler, 74 — Head, widower — Fishing

23. *George Colliver Lunt, 81 — Head — Fishing
Harriet (Davis) Lunt, 65 — Wife
*Alvina Lunt, 41 — Daughter, divorced
Edwin L. Lunt, 48 — Son — Fishing
Jasper E. Lunt, 36 — Son — Fishing
Herman E. Lunt, 22 — Grandson — Fishing

24. Henry W. Lunt, 66 — Head — Fishing

25. Charles W. Wallace, 44 — Head — Lobster Fishing
*Asenath M. (Lunt) Wallace, 43 — Wife

26. Grandville W. Davis, 22 — Head — Lobster Fishing
Violet B. (Thurlow) Davis, 24 — Wife
Theda A. Davis, 1 — Daughter
June E. Davis, 3 mos. — Daughter

27. John R. Lunt, 42 — Head — Lobster Fishing
*Flora E. Lunt, 32 — Wife
Alma M. Lunt, 13 — Daughter
Lilla F. Lunt, 11 — Daughter
Sanford L. Lunt, 10 — Son
Marguerite H. Lunt, 6 — Daughter
Cecil E. Lunt, 5 — Son
Mable J. Lunt, 1 — Daughter
Nelson P. Lunt, 44 — Brother, divorced — Fishing
Lincoln R. Lunt, 19 — Nephew — Fishing

28. Thomas B. Lunt, 25 — Head — Fishing
Helen E. Lunt, 16 — Wife

29. Mary S. Lunt, 50 — Head, widow
Marie E. Lunt, 30 — Daughter
*Alice Winifred Lunt, 16 — Daughter
Hiram A. Lunt Jr., 15 — Son — Fishing
Wallace L. Lunt, 31 — Son — Fishing
Everett Dalzell, 21 — Son-in-law — Fishing
Lula B. (Lunt) Dalzell, 22 — Daughter

30. Nathan F. Osier, 41 — Head — Lobster Fishing
Mary A. (Bridges) Osier, 36 — Wife
Willard K. Osier, 16 — Son
Evelyn M. Osier, 14 — Daughter

|  |  |  |  |
|---|---|---|---|
| 31. | Leaman T. Davis, 55 | Head | Fishing |
|  | Agnes F. (Joyce) (Bridges) Davis, 59 | Wife |  |
|  | Elmer S. Davis, 20 | Son | Lobster Fishing |
|  | Floyd O. Davis, 17 | Son | Fishing |
|  | Bennie S. Davis, 15 | Son | Fishing |
| 32. | Hezekiah W. Lunt Jr., 48 | Head | Mail/Fishing |
|  | (Cora?) Blanche E. Lunt, 43 | Wife |  |
|  | Cora B. Lunt, 7 | Daughter |  |
| 33. | Alexander P. Davis, 21 | Head | Lobster Fishing |
|  | Valeria M. (Lunt) Davis, 23 | Wife |  |
|  | Vincent A. Davis, 6 | Son |  |
|  | Vivian M. Davis, 4 | Son |  |
|  | Elmer C. Davis, 2 | Son |  |
|  | Lawrence H. Davis, 1 | Son |  |
| 34. | Rosanna A. (Murphy) Lunt, 58 | Head | Widow |
|  | Shirley W. Lunt, 29 | Son | Lobster Fishing |
| 35. | Grant H. Lunt, 51 | Head | Fishing |
|  | Lena M. (Higgins) Lunt, 38 | Wife |  |
|  | Almena A. Lunt, 13 | Daughter |  |
|  | Samuel Lunt, 9 | Son |  |
|  | Lena M. Lunt, 7 Mos. | Daughter |  |
| 36. | Joseph W. Lunt Jr., 55 | Head | Store |
|  | Minnie V. (Cross) Lunt, 46 | Wife |  |
|  | Sylvia E. Lunt, 19 | Daughter |  |
|  | Etta E. Lunt, 17 | Daughter |  |
|  | Hazel B. Lunt, 13 | Daughter |  |
|  | Herbert O. Lunt, 10 | Son |  |
| 37. | Atwood L. Lunt, 59 | Head |  |
|  | Angeline Lunt, 50 | Wife |  |
|  | Bertha L. Lunt, 30 | Daughter | Servant |
|  | Llewelyn Lunt, 23 | Son | Fishing |
|  | Alva Lunt, 18 | Daughter | Fishing |
|  | Edwin L. Lunt, 15 | Son | Fishing |
|  | Thurza M. Lunt, 2 mos. | Granddaughter |  |

## *Great Duck Island — Population: 17*

1. Vinal O. Beal, 50 — Head
   Nettie E. Beal, 40 — Wife
   A. Beal, 11 — Son
   R. Beal, 8 — Daughter
   R. Beal, 6 — Son
   V. Beal, 4 — Daughter

2. Harvard R. Beal, 22 — Head
   Alva Beal, 22 — Wife
   Nettie F. Beal, 2 — Daughter
   Vera Beal, 1 — Daughter

3. Myrick Morrison, 40 — Head
   Elva Morrison, 39 — Wife
   Willard R. Morrison, 8 — Son
   Norman L. Morrison, 6 — Son
   Foster G. Morrison, 4 — Son
   Harold Morrison, 3 — Son
   Frieda Morrison, 1 — Daughter

# Long Island Births

## 1820 — 1829

| Name | (# Children/Mother) Parents | Birth Date | Source |
|---|---|---|---|
| Abner Pomroy | (x)William Pomroy & Mary Beal | Dec. 10, 1920 | D |
| Albion K.P. Lunt | (1)Israel B. Lunt & Nancy Pomroy | Dec. 29, 1823 | I |
| Mary Lunt | (12)Amos C. Lunt Sr. & Priscilla Butler | April 10, 1825 | A |
| Charles H. Lunt | (1)Amos C. Lunt Jr. & Eliza Pomroy | March 3, 1826 | I |
| Jerushia B. Lunt | (13)Amos C. Lunt Sr. & Priscilla Butler | July 11, 1827 | A |
| Joseph W. Lunt | (2)Amos C. Lunt Jr. & Eliza Pomroy | April 27, 1828 | E |
| (BI)Mary Walls | (x)Mr. Walls & Abigail Tinker | March 1829 | F |
| John Sylvester Lunt | (14)Amos C. Lunt Sr. & Priscilla Butler | Dec. 18, 1829 | A |

## 1830 — 1839

| Name | (# Children/Mother) Parents | Birth Date | Source |
|---|---|---|---|
| Caroline Pomroy | (x)William Pomroy & Mary Beal | 1834 | D |
| Freeborn G. Lunt(dy) | (3)Amos C. Lunt Jr. & Eliza Pomroy | Feb. 22, 1831 | I |
| John R. Lunt | (2)Israel B. Lunt & Nancy Pomroy | Dec. 30, 1831 | I |
| Rufus B. Lunt | (15)Amos C. Lunt Sr. & Priscilla Butler | April 13, 1832 | A |
| Hezekiah W. Lunt Sr. | (1)Bartholomew R. Lunt Sr. & Asenath Allen | July 26, 1833 | I |
| Amanda S. Lunt | (3)Israel B. Lunt & Nancy Pomroy | August 3, 1833 | I |
| Roland H. Lunt | (16)Amos C. Lunt Sr. & Priscilla Butler | March 23, 1834 | A |
| Elizabeth J. Lunt | (2)Bartholomew R. Lunt Sr. & Asenath Allen | March 28, 1835 | I |
| Noel B. Lunt | (1)George B. Lunt & Miriam Lunt | March 31, 1835 | I |
| Caroline Rich | (x)Gilbert Rich & Pauline | May 9, 1835 | D |
| Edward P. Lunt | (4)Israel B. Lunt & Nancy Pomroy | Oct. 11, 1835 | I |
| William P. Lunt | (4)Amos C. Lunt Jr. & Eliza Pomroy | Nov. 3, 1836 | D |
| Amos Allen Lunt | (3)Bartholomew R. Lunt & Asenath Allen | Dec. 4, 1836 | I |
| Daniel Baron Stow Lunt | (17)Amos C. Lunt Sr. & Priscilla Butler | Feb. 18, 1837 | A |

| | | | |
|---|---|---|---|
| Micajah Lunt | (2)George B. Lunt & Miriam Lunt | June 17, 1837 | I |
| Mary A. Lunt | (5)Israel B. Lunt & Nancy Pomroy | Jan. 11, 1838 | I |
| Sabra A. Lunt | (4)Bartholomew R. Lunt & Asenath Allen | April 22, 1838 | I |
| Angeline V. Lunt | (3)George B. Lunt & Miriam Lunt | Oct. 10, 1838 | I |
| Maria L. Lunt | (5)Amos C. Lunt Jr. & Eliza Pomroy | April 27, 1839 | A |
| (Boy) Rich | (x)John Rich & Jane Lunt | April 28, 1839 | A |
| Rhoda Z.M. Lunt | (6)Israel B. Lunt & Nancy Pomroy | May 15, 1839 | A |
| George Colliver Lunt | (4)George B. Lunt & Miriam Lunt | Dec. 28, 1839 | I |

## 1840 — 1849

| | | | |
|---|---|---|---|
| Rehoboth B. Lunt (dy) | (5)Bartholomew R. Lunt Sr. & Asenath Allen | Feb. 21, 1840 | I |
| Hiram A. Lunt | (6)Amos C. Lunt Jr. & Eliza Pomroy | April 1, 1841 | I |
| Alice A. Twist | (x)George Twist & Mary T. Rice | Aug. 25, 1841 | E |
| Hortense B. Lunt | (7)Israel B. Lunt & Nancy Pomroy | Oct. 20, 1841 | I |
| Jonas Holman Lunt (dy) | (6)Bartholomew R. Lunt Sr. & Asenath Allen | Feb. 1, 1842 | I |
| Freelove E. Lunt | (5)George B. Lunt & Miriam Lunt | June 10, 1842 | I |
| Benjamin F. Stinson Lunt | (1)Joseph D. Lunt & Rehoboth Hannah B. Lunt | July 6, 1842 | I |
| Nancy H. Lunt | (8)Israel B. Lunt & Nancy Pomroy | March 21, 1843 | I |
| Addo K. Lunt (dy) | (7)Bartholomew R. Lunt Sr. & Asenath Allen | Aug. 26, 1843 | I |
| Caroline Lunt | (7)Amos C. Lunt Jr. & Eliza Pomroy | Nov. 18, 1843 | I |
| (BI)Lydia M. Dawes | (x)Johnathan Dawes & Charlotte Langley | Oct. 1843 | F |
| Lucy B. Lunt | (2)Joseph D. Lunt & Rehobeth Hannah B. Lunt | Feb. 20, 1844 | I |
| Freelove Lunt | (9)Israel B. Lunt & Nancy Pomroy | May 1, 1844 | I |
| Mary Ann Lunt | (8)Amos C. Lunt Jr. & Eliza Pomroy | April 16, 1845 | I |
| Augustus S. Lunt | (8)Bartholomew R. Lunt Sr. & Asenath Allen | April 17, 1845 | I |
| Matilda Lunt | (9)Amos C. Lunt Jr. & Eliza Pomroy | 1845-1848 | I |
| Emma Frances Lunt | (10)Amos C. Lunt Jr. & Eliza Pomroy | 1845-1848 | I |
| (Louisa?) Lucy A. Lunt | (1)Andrew P. Lunt & Laurania Pomroy | Jan. 29, 1846 | I |
| Israel B. Lunt Jr. | (10)Israel B. Lunt & Nancy Pomroy | March 11, 1846 | I |
| Zaphnath P. Lunt | (3)Joseph D. Lunt & Rehobeth Hannah B. Lunt | April 23,1847 | I |
| A. Victoria Lunt | (11)Israel B. Lunt & Nancy Pomroy | Aug. 16, 1847 | I |
| Fannie E. Lunt | (12)Israel B. Lunt & Nancy Pomroy | Feb. 7, 1849 | I |
| Calvin C. Lunt | (9) Bartholomew R. Lunt Sr. & Asenath Allen | March 24, 1847 | I |
| David N. Lunt (dy) | (10)Bartholomew R. Lunt Sr. & Asenath Allen | March 24, 1847 | I |
| William S. Rich | (x)William Rich & Eleanor Rice | March 1848 | C |
| George W. Lunt | (11)Amos C. Lunt Jr. & Eliza Pomroy | May 23, 1848 | I |
| Laurania M. Lunt | (2)Andrew P. Lunt & Laurania Pomroy | Oct. 21, 1848 | I |
| Apipzubath Lunt (dy) | (11)Bartholomew R. Lunt Sr. & Asenath Allen | April 28, 1849 | I |

## 1850 — 1859

| | | | |
|---|---|---|---|
| Harriet Davis | (x)Ezra Davis & Rebecca Davis | Dec. 1851 | F/B |
| Bartholomew R. Lunt Jr. | (12)Bartholomew R. Lunt Sr. & Asenath Allen | June 8, 1851 | I |
| Martin Hall Rich | (x)William Rich & Eleanor Rich | March 1852 | F |
| Emily S. Davis | (x)James T. Davis & Abigail Milliken | Sept. 11, 1852 | F/B |
| Isora M. Rich | (x)Gilbert Rich & Mary Walls | Aug. 10, 1853 | G |
| Henry Whitfield Lunt | (x)William Dow Lunt & Mary Elizabeth Allen | Aug. 1, 1853 | F |

| | | | |
|---|---|---|---|
| Rebecca N. Davis | (x)William Davis & Mary Elizabeth Dawes | 1853 | G |
| Mary A. Rich | (x)Gilbert Rich & Mary Walls | 1854/55 | |
| Hezekiah E.S. Lunt | (2)William Dow Lunt & Mary Elizabeth Allen | July 1858 | F |
| Abbie E. Davis | (x)William Davis & Mary T. Rice | Jan. 26, 1858 | F |
| John F. Vautier | (x)Frank Vautier & Mary F. Rich | Sept. 24, 1858 | E |
| Almena Davis | (2)William Davis & Mary T. Rice | 1858 | E |
| Adelbert W. Lunt | (1)Hezekiah W. Lunt & Lydia M. Dawes | Nov. 3, 1859 | I |
| Alma Cousins | (x)Charles Cousins & Hannah Walls | Oct. 1859 | F |

## 1860 — 1869

| | | | |
|---|---|---|---|
| Agnes F. Joyce | (x)Reuben B. Joyce & Mary A. Lunt | July 4, 1860 | F |
| Atwood L. Lunt | (1) Joseph W. Lunt & Alice A. Twist | March 4, 1860 | I |
| Lottie L. Davis | (x)William Davis & Emeline Dawes | April 12, 1861 | C |
| Ada T. Lunt | | Aug. 10, 1861 | E |
| Albertie M. Davis | (3)William Davis & Mary T. Rice | 1861 | E |
| Merritt W. Lunt | (3)William D. Lunt & Mary Elizabeth Allen | April 1861 | F |
| (BI)Rosanna Murphy | (x)Henry Murphy & Nancy J. Tinker | Nov. 4, 1861 | F |
| William Sanford Lunt | (1)Benjamin F.S. Lunt & Ann Rich | March 24, 1862 | E |
| Charles E. Rice | (x)Abraham Rice & Melissa Davis | March 28, 1862 | G |
| Zerelda E. Rich | (x)Gilbert R. Rich & Lucy B. Rich | Aug. 19, 1862 | G |
| Hiram A. Lunt | (2)Joseph W. Lunt Sr. & Alice A. Twist | Dec. 17, 1862 | E |
| Rubie Davis | (4)William Davis & Mary T. Rice | 1863 | E |
| Samuel Rice | (x)Abraham Rice & Melissa Davis | June 1, 1864 | F |
| Joseph F. Rich | (x)George R. Rich & Lucy B. Lunt | March 21, 1865 | C |
| Joseph W. Lunt Jr. | (3)Joseph W. Lunt Sr. & Alice A. Twist | Sept. 27, 1865 | E |
| Leaman T. Davis | (5)William Davis & Mary T. Rice | 1865/April 1866 | E/G |
| William M. Teel | (x)William J. Teel & Rhoda M. Lunt | June 7, 1866 | F/G |
| Elizabeth B. Lunt | (4)Joseph W. Lunt & Alice A. Twist | Oct. 21, 1866 | E |
| Lester P. Rich | (x)George R. Rich & Lucy B. Lunt | Nov. 28, 1866 | C |
| Angeline V. Lunt | (1)George Colliver Lunt & Harriett Davis | March 30, 1868 | C |
| John G. Davis | (x)William Davis & Emeline Dawes | May 2, 1868 | C |
| Grant H. Lunt | (5)Joseph W. Lunt Sr. & Alice A. Twist | May 5, 1868 | F |
| Mary Etta Davis | (6)William Davis & Mary T. Rice | 1867/July 13, 1868 | E/F |
| Edna F. Rich | (x)Martin H. Rich & Mary A. Rich | Jan. 2, 1869 | F |

## 1870 — 1879

| | | | |
|---|---|---|---|
| Frank W. Ross | (1)Alexander C. Ross & Hortense B. Lunt | March 28, 1870 | F |
| Maria L. Lunt | (6)Joseph W. Lunt Sr. & Alice A. Twist | June 22, 1870 | E |
| Samuel F. Davis | (x)James Davis & Rebecca Davis | 1871 | |
| Edwin L. Lunt | (2) George C. Lunt & Harriet Davis | July 8, 1869 | C |
| Eugene B. Brewer | (1)George E. Brewer & Freelove Lunt | Dec. 18, 1871 | E |
| Hortense B. Wilson | (x)Byron C. Wilson & Adelaide Victoria Lunt | January 1872 | F |
| Sophronia S. Teel | (2)William J. Teel & Rhoda M. Lunt | Feb. 1, 1873 | F |
| Alphonso L. Lunt | (1)Israel B. Lunt Jr. & Isora M. Rich | May 4, 1873 | G |
| Mary Abbie Osier | (2)Thomas Osier & Almena Davis | July 27, 1874 | E |
| Nellie Rich | (x)William S. Rich & Abbie E. Davis | Jan. 26, 1873 | C |

| | | | |
|---|---|---|---|
| Carrie Elizabeth Davis | Rebecca Davis | March 11, 1875 | E |
| Daniel R. Lunt | (3) George Colliver Lunt & Harriet Davis | June 21, 1875 | C |
| Addie M. Davis | (x)William Davis & Emeline Dawes | June 24, 1875 | C |
| Nelson P. Lunt | (7)Joseph W. Lunt Sr. & Alice A. Twist | July 23, 1875 | E |
| Lizzie Emma Davis | (2)Irene Davis | Oct. 2, 1875 | E |
| Granville Rice | (x)Samuel J. Rice | Aug. 21, 1876 | E |
| John R. Lunt | (8)Joseph W. Lunt Sr. & Alice A. Twist | Nov.1, 1876 | F |
| Alexander K. Wilson | (4)Byron C. Wilson & Adelaide Victoria Lunt | June 23, 1876 | E |
| Alvina Lunt | (4)George Colliver Lunt & Harriet Davis | March 18, 1877 | C |
| Ellen F. Lunt | (5)Israel B. Lunt Jr. & Isora M. Rich | July 1877 | F |
| Cora A. Lunt | (9)Joseph W. Lunt Sr. & Alice A. Twist | July 31, 1878 | I |
| Nathan F. Osier | (x)Thomas N. Osier & Almenia Davis | Aug. 2, 1878 | E |

## *1880 — 1889*

| | | | |
|---|---|---|---|
| Emily F. Wilson | (6)Byron C. Wilson & Adelaide Victoria Lunt | March 10, 1880 | F |
| A daughter | (x)James Turner & Ellen Turner | May 31, 1881 | J |
| Maud E. Lunt | (x)Israel B. Lunt Jr. & Isora M. Rich | 1882 | G |
| Gertrude M. Osier | (x)Jacob Osier & Irene Davis | May 1, 1882 | F |
| A daughter | (x)Calvin C. Lunt & Catherine Dawes | June 4, 1882 | J |
| A daughter | (x)Byron Wilson & Adalaide Victoria Lunt | Sept. 22, 1882 | J |
| Harold Allen | (x)Samuel Allen & Ruby Davis | Oct. 30, 1882 | J |
| A daughter | (x)Peter Higgins & Ellen Higgins | Dec. 7, 1882 | J |
| Charlotte E. Lunt | (x)Calvin C. Lunt & Catherine Dawes | June 4, 1883 | F |
| Jasper Lunt | (x)George Colliver Lunt & Harriet Davis | June 8, 1882 | C |
| Eugene C. Van Norden | (x)William A. Van Norden & Hortense B. Lunt | Nov. 2, 1883 | F |
| Fatima Allen | (x)Samuel Allen & Ruby Davis | Jan. 11, 1884 | J |
| Everett S. Lunt | (1)William S. Lunt & Edna F. Rich | May 29, 1884 | I |
| Harry Winford Lunt | (x)Bartholomew R. Lunt Jr. & Charlotte Davis | Oct. 4, 1884 | E |
| Ernest Powers | (x)Peter Powers & Ellen Rich | Nov. 11, 1884 | J |
| Bessie Osier | Jacob Osier & (5)Irene Davis | Dec. 2, 1884 | E |
| Unnamed daughter | (13)Hezekiah Wills Lunt Sr. & Lydia M. Dawes | June 1885 | F |
| Charles B. Lunt | (2)William S. Lunt & Edna F. Rich | Sept. 2, 1885 | G |
| Clarence A. Lunt | (1)Hiram A. Lunt & Mary Lunt | March 13, 1886 | I |
| Mary Lunt | (x)George C. Lunt & Harriet Davis | Feb. 1887 | F |
| Flora E. Lunt | (3)William S. Lunt & Edna F. Rich | July 16, 1887 | I |
| Edith Bell Lunt | (2)Hiram A. Lunt & Mary S. Lunt | Sept. 20, 1887 | I |
| A son | (x)Irene Davis | Feb. 24, 1888 | J |
| A son | (x)Charles V. Grey & Flora Grey | March 21, 1888 | J |
| Nellie Lunt | (4)William S. Lunt & Edna F. Rich | April 13, 1888 | E |
| Clinton B. Teel | (1)William M. Teel & Maria L. Lunt | May 11, 1888 | E |
| Alexander P. Davis | (*)Leaman T. Davis & Agnes F. Joyce | Oct. 11, 1888 | E |
| Laforest Glendon Lunt | (14)Hezekiah W. Lunt Sr. & Lydia M. Dawes | Dec. 10, 1889 | C |
| Fred C. Carter | (1)Constantine Carter & Susie M. Butler | 1889 | E |
| Bertha L. Lunt | (1)Atwood L. Lunt & Angeline Lunt | Jan. 15, 1889 | I |
| Zula M. Lunt | (3)Hiram A. Lunt & Mary S. Lunt | July 25, 1889 | I |

## 1890 — 1899

| | | | |
|---|---|---|---|
| Ruel Powers | | March 19, 1890 | J |
| Irene Mary Dawes | (*)David Dawes & Irene Davis | April 7, 1890 | E |
| Blanche Helen Lunt | (x)Bartholomew R. Lunt Jr. & Charlotte E. Dawes | April 27, 1890 | J |
| Jennie M. Rice | (1)Charles E. Rice & Flora A. Lunt | May 20, 1890 | E |
| Benjamin Stinson Lunt | (5)William S. Lunt & Edna F. Rich | Nov. 17, 1890 | E |
| Shirley W. Lunt | (1)Adelbert W. Lunt & Rosanna Murphy | Dec. 16, 1890 | E |
| Jessie G. Lunt | (4)Hiram A. Lunt & Mary S. Lunt | Feb. 19, 1891 | E |
| Samuel F. Gray | (14)Charles V. Gray & Flora E. Dresser | July 29, 1891 | E |
| Frank L. Rich | (1)Martin H. Rich & Lizzie L. Davis | June 8, 1892 | E |
| (BI)Stillborn female | (1)Adelbert E. Nice & Laura E. Hessey | July 20, 1892 | E |
| Frank R. Thurlow | (1)James H. Thurlow & Elizabeth M. Lunt | July 26, 1892 | E |
| Laury L. Dawes | (8)David Dawes & Irena Davis | Aug. 29, 1892 | E |
| Grace Hester Davis | (3)Leaman T. Davis & Agnes F. Joyce | Nov. 2, 1892 | E |
| Lewis LeRoy Lunt | (2)Adelbert W. Lunt & Rosanna Murphy | Dec. 21, 1892 | E |
| Joseph W. Lunt | (3)Atwood L. Lunt & Angeline Lunt | Jan. 15, 1893 | G |
| Thomas Burton Lunt | (5)Hiram A. Lunt & Mary S. Lunt | March 21, 1893 | E |
| Maynard A. Robinson | (2)Walter M. Robinson & Carrie E. Davis | April 24, 1893 | E |
| Sylvester Dalzell | (2)Everett E. Dalzell & Linnie D. Rice | May 8, 1893 | E |
| Perry Rich | (2)Martin H. Rich & Lizzie L. Davis | Nov. 21, 1893 | E |
| Millie Leah Davis | (4)Leaman T. Davis & Agnes F. Joyce | Feb. 9, 1894 | E |
| (BI)Edith Anne Silver | (1)George W. Silver & Elizabeth M. Leith | March 2, 1894 | E |
| Leonard A. Lunt | (6)William S. Lunt & Edna F. Rich | March 25, 1894 | E |
| Lydia Thurlow | (2)James H. Thurlow & Elizabeth M. Lunt | July 2, 1894 | E |
| Pearl Davis | (1)Georgia Davis | Aug. 19, 1894 | E |
| Pearl O. Rice | (*)Samuel Rice & Sabra Lunt | August 1894 | B |
| David Dawes Jr. | (9) David Dawes & Irene Davis | Dec. 4, 1894 | E |
| Naomi M. Rich | (3)Martin H. Rich & Lizzie L. Davis | Feb. 2, 1895 | E |
| Abbie Florence Davis | (5)Leaman T. Davis & Agnes F. Joyce | April 19, 1895 | E |
| Olitty Davis | (3)Samuel F. Davis & Maria Norwood | Aug. 18, 1895 | E |
| Violet S. Thurlow | (3)James H. Thurlow & Elizabeth M. Lunt | Oct. 11, 1895 | E |
| Vera Maria Ross | (1)Frank W. Ross & Lizzie B. Lunt | Jan. 19, 1896 | E |
| Llewellyn Lunt | (4)Atwood L. Lunt & Angeline Lunt | Feb. 8, 1896 | E |
| Milton S. Dalzell | (3)Everett Edward Dalzell & Linnie D. Rice | April 26, 1896 | E |
| Valeria May Lunt | (6)Hiram A. Lunt & Mary S. Lunt | May 8, 1896 | E |
| Ethel Lida Lunt | (7)William S. Lunt & Edna F. Rich | Aug. 20, 1896 | E |
| Rebecca Davis | (4)Samuel F. Davis & Maria Norwood | Jan. 17, 1897 | E |
| Grandville W. Davis | (6)Leaman T. Davis & Agnes F. Joyce | March 27, 1897 | E |
| Lula B. Lunt | (7)Hiram A. Lunt & Mary S. Lunt | April 16, 1897 | E |
| (PI)Jay L. Robbins | (6)Colson H. Robbins & Lizzie A. Sprague | May 23, 1897 | E |
| Stillborn female | (1)Calvin C. Lunt & Addie M. Davis | Aug. 9, 1897 | E |
| (BI)Stillborn female | (1)Judson A. Webber & Odessa Barbour | Sept. 22, 1897 | E |
| Emily Maud Thurlow | (4)James H. Thurlow & Elizabeth M. Lunt | Sept. 28, 1897 | E |
| Stillborn male | (6)Thomas N. Osier & Almenia S. Davis | Dec. 10. 1897 | E |
| Herman Lunt | (1)Alvina Lunt | Dec. 14, 1897 | E |
| Goldie Dawes | (10)David Dawes & Irene Dawes | Jan. 21, 1898 | E |

| | | | |
|---|---|---|---|
| Hollis Dalzell | (4)Everett E. Dalzell & Linnie D. Rice | Jan 30, 1898 | E |
| Alice Hortense Ross | (2)Frank W. Ross & Lizzie B. Lunt | Feb. 13, 1898 | E |
| (BI)Stanley J. Silver | (2)George W. Silver & Elizabeth M. Lieth | Feb. 24, 1898 | E |
| Unnamed daughter | (4)Walter M. Robinson & Carrie Davis | Feb. 25, 1898 | E |
| Sabra A. Lunt | (5)Adelbert W. Lunt & Rosanna Murphy | March 3, 1898 | E |
| Grover C. Lunt | (5)Atwood L. Lunt & Angeline Lunt | May 19, 1898 | E |
| Cora Thurlow | (5)James H. Thurlow & Elizabeth M. Lunt | Sept. 24, 1898 | E |
| Elmer S. Davis | (7)Leaman T. Davis & Agnes F. Joyce | Jan. 7, 1899 | E |
| Nettie Nelson | (1)John Nelson & Lottie E. Lunt | March 4, 1899 | E |
| Jessie Florence Davis | (5)Samuel F. Davis & Maria Norwood | April 21, 1899 | E |
| Stillborn male | (6)Samuel F. Davis & Maria Norwood | April 21, 1899 | E |
| Everett E. Dalzell Jr. | (5)Everett E. Dalzell Sr. & Linnie D. Rice | June 16, 1899 | E |
| Nora Evie Lunt | (8)Hiram A. Lunt & Mary S. Lunt | Sept. 19, 1899 | E |
| Florence Davis | (1)Charles E. Davis & Addie M. Davis | Dec. 1, 1899 | E |
| Irving F. Lunt | (8)William S. Lunt & Edna F. Rich | Dec. 14, 1899 | E |

## *1900 — 1909*

| | | | |
|---|---|---|---|
| Lincoln R. Lunt | (2)Nelson P. Lunt & Alvina E. Lunt | Jan. 5, 1900 | E |
| Alphonso Leonard Lunt | (1)Alphonso L. Lunt & Sadie L. McKusick | Jan. 21, 1900 | E |
| Raymond L. Teel | (4)William M. Teel & Maria L. Lunt | Feb. 9, 1900 | E |
| Sylvia E. Lunt | (1)Joseph W. Lunt Jr. & Minnie V. Cross | April 15, 1900 | E |
| Phillis L. Lunt | (6)Atwood L. Lunt & Angeline Lunt | May 18, 1900 | E |
| Lydia M. Thurlow | (6)James H. Thurlow & Elizabeth M. Lunt | May 27, 1900 | E |
| Granville Dalzell | (6)Everett E. Dalzell & Linnie D. Rice | July 31, 1900 | E |
| Helen C. Lunt | (6)Adelbert W. Lunt & Rosanna Murphy | Sept. 29, 1900 | E |
| Clifton M. Lunt | (3)Nelson P. Lunt & Alvina E. Lunt | Dec. 30, 1900 | E |
| Gertrude L. Lunt | (2)Alphonso L. Lunt & Sadie McKusick | Jan. 17, 1901 | E |
| Carrie D. Dawes | (11)David Dawes & Irene Davis | Jan. 23, 1901 | E |
| Flora Davis | (9)Leaman T. Davis & Agnes F. Joyce | April 9, 1901 | E |
| Elva (Alva?) Lunt | (7)Atwood L. Lunt & Angeline Lunt | April 30, 1901 | E |
| Edith M. Thurlow | (7)James H. Thurlow & Elizabeth M. Lunt | Aug. 15, 1901 | E |
| Marie Lunt | (9)Hiram A. Lunt & Mary S. Lunt | Nov. 30, 1901 | E |
| Guy E. Lunt | (9)William S. Lunt & Edna F. Rich | Jan. 3, 1902 | E |
| Ella L. Dalzell | (7)Everett E. Dalzell & Linnie D. Rice | April 5, 1902 | E |
| Hyman W. Lunt | (8)Atwood L. Lunt & Angeline Lunt | May 11, 1902 | E |
| Jamie E. Thurlow | (8)James H. Thurlow & Elizabeth M. Lunt | Oct. 2, 1902 | E |
| Etta E. Lunt | (2)Joseph W. Lunt Jr. & Minnie V. Cross | Nov. 20, 1902 | E |
| Unnamed | (1)Grant H. Lunt & Lena M. Higgins | Dec. 15, 1902 | E |
| Orrin C. Lunt | (10)William S. Lunt & Edna F. Rich | March 7, 1903 | E |
| Alice W. Lunt | (10)Hiram A. Lunt & Mary S. Lunt | March 15, 1903 | E |
| Willard K. Osier | (1)Nathan Osier & Mary A. Bridges | March 17, 1903 | E |
| Carrie Helen Dalzell | (8)Everett E. Dalzell & Linnie D. Rice | May 29, 1903 | E |
| Edwin Lunt | (9)Atwood L. Lunt & Angeline Lunt | Aug. 31, 1903 | E |
| Ethel Lunt | (4)Alvina Lunt | Nov. 20, 1903 | E |
| Stillborn male | (9)James H. Thurlow & Elizabeth M. Lunt | April 25, 1904 | E |
| Bennie S. Davis | (10)Leaman T. Davis & Agnes F. Joyce | June 1, 1904 | E |

| | | | |
|---|---|---|---|
| Christie Davis | (7)Samuel F. Davis & Maria Norwood | May 26, 1904 | E |
| (BI)Walter Morrill | (1)Sumner Morrill & Lottie L. Davis | Aug. 5, 1904 | E |
| Mildred S. Dalzell | (9)Everett E. Dalzell & Linnie D. Rice | Sept. 12, 1904 | E |
| Hiram A. Lunt Jr. | (11)Hiram A. Lunt & Mary S. Lunt | Oct. 2, 1904 | E |
| Unnamed boy | (5)Alvina Lunt | March 1, 1905 | E |
| Stillborn girl | (1)John R. Lunt & Flora E. Lunt | March 12, 1905 | E |
| Otis Lunt | (10)Atwood L. Lunt & Angeline Lunt | May 30, 1905 | E |
| Maud E. Osier | (2)Nathan Osier & Mary A. Bridges | June 4, 1905 | E |
| Gladys M. Lunt | (1)Charles K. Lunt & Mary E. McFarland | June 18, 1905 | E |
| Hazel B. Lunt | (3)Joseph W. Lunt Jr. & Minnie V. Cross | Jan. 7, 1906 | E |
| Daryl E. Thurlow | (10)James H. Thurlow & Elizabeth M. Lunt | Feb. 27, 1906 | E |
| Wallace L. Lunt | (12)Hiram A. Lunt & Mary S. Lunt | April 24, 1906 | E |
| Margaret Virginia Lunt | (11)William S. Lunt & Edna F. Rich | July 1, 1906 | E |
| Marina Everett Lunt | (11)Atwood L. Lunt & Angeline Lunt | Aug. 4, 1906 | E |
| Maria Almenia Lunt | (2)Grant H. Lunt & Lena M. Higgins | Aug. 11, 1906 | E |
| Alma M. Lunt | (2)John R. Lunt & Flora E. Lunt | Nov. 14, 1906 | E |
| Stillborn female | (11)James H. Thurlow & Elizabeth M. Lunt | April 22, 1907 | E |
| (Illigible) female | (2)Charles K. Lunt & Mary E. McFarland | Nov. 1, 1907 | E |
| Clyde Lunt | (13)Hiram A. Lunt & Mary S. Lunt | Jan. 2, 1908 | E |
| Louisa Lunt | (3)Grant H. Lunt & Lena M. Higgins | Jan. 7, 1908 | E |
| Thelma Thurlow | (12)James F. Thurlow & Elizabeth M. Lunt | March 15, 1908 | E |
| Ella V. Lunt | (12)William S. Lunt & Edna F. Rich | June 10, 1908 | E |
| Harold Lunt | (12)Atwood L. Lunt & Angeline Lunt | June 14, 1908 | E |
| Lilla F. Lunt | (3)John R. Lunt & Flora E. Lunt | July 8, 1908 | E |
| Neal E. Stewart | (2)John J. Stewart & Lottie E. Lunt | Sept. 2, 1908 | E |
| Stillborn female | (3)Alphonso L. Lunt & Sadie L. McKusick | Sept. 25, 1908 | E |
| Doris E. Robinson | (1)Walter M. Robinson & Irene M. Dawes | Dec. 19, 1908 | E |
| Herbert O. Lunt | (4)Joseph W. Lunt Jr. & Minnie V. Cross | Jan. 16, 1909 | E |
| Roy Thurlow | (13)James H. Thurlow & Elizabeth M. Lunt | April 26, 1909 | E |

## 1910 — 1919

| | | | |
|---|---|---|---|
| Charles E. Lunt | (3)Charles K. Lunt & Mary E. McFarland | April 7, 1910 | E |
| Samuel G. Lunt | (4)Grant H. Lunt & Lena M. Higgins | May 11, 1910 | E |
| Sanford L. Lunt | (4)John R. Lunt & Flora E. Lunt | May 30, 1910 | E |
| Stillborn boy | (14)Hiram A. Lunt & Mary S. Lunt | July 2, 1910 | E |
| Rubie M. Thurlow | (14)James F. Thurlow & Elizabeth M. Lunt. | Feb. 17, 1911 | E |
| Tina Bernice Lunt | (13)Atwood L. Lunt & Angeline Lunt | April 11, 1911 | E |
| Kenneth Gardiner Lunt | (13)William S. Lunt & Edna F. Rich | Aug. 13, 1911 | E |
| Edna Geneva Lunt | (5)John R. Lunt & Flora E. Lunt | Feb. 28, 1912 | E |
| Marion E. Teel | (1)William L. Teel & Annie Hall | April 16, 1912 | E |
| Cora B. Lunt | (4)Charles K. Lunt & Mary E. McFarland | Aug. 16, 1912 | E |
| Lewis A. Nickerson | (1)Jephtha Nickerson & Ellen F. Lunt | Nov. 27, 1912 | E |
| Marguerite H. Lunt | (6)John R. Lunt & Flora E. Lunt | March 22, 1913 | E |
| Lenora L. Higgins | (2)Warren T. Higgins & Lyda Lunt | May 8, 1913 | E |
| Unnamed girl | (1)Winfield H. McKown & Jennie Rice | July 11, 1913 | E |
| Jeanette R. Teel | (3)William L. Teel & Annie Hall | Aug. 2, 1913 | E |

| | | | |
|---|---|---|---|
| Annie M. Lunt | (14)William S. Lunt & Edna F. Rich | Aug. 26, 1913 | E |
| John Walter Robinson | (2)Walter M. Robinson & Irene Dawes | Oct. 7, 1913 | E |
| Vincent Alden Davis | (1)Alexander P. Davis & Valeria M. Lunt | Nov. 2, 1913 | E |
| Ralph W. Thurlow (SB) | (15)James H. Thurlow & Elizabeth M. Lunt | Nov. 25, 1913 | E |
| Carrie A. Elliot | (9)Orrin S. Elliot & Bessie Roberts | April 18, 1914 | E |
| Leonard W. Higgins | (3)Warren T. Higgins & Lyda Lunt | July 20, 1914 | E |
| Ina Beatrice Lunt | (5)Charles K. Lunt & Mary E. McFarland | Oct. 2, 1914 | E |
| Cecil E. Lunt | (7)John R. Lunt & Flora E. Lunt | Nov. 11, 1914 | E |
| Stillborn boy | (4)Alphonso L. Lunt & Sadie L. McKusick | Dec. 31, 1914 | E |
| Flora F. Lunt | (14)Atwood L. Lunt & Angeline Lunt | Jan. 4, 1915 | E |
| Charles K. Rice | (1)Pearl O. Rice & Lorena Birch | Jan. 19, 1915 | E |
| Vivian M. Davis | (2)Alexander P. Davis & Valeria M. Lunt | April 17, 1915 | E |
| Leslie C. Elliot | (10)Orrin S. Elliot & Bessie Roberts | June 21, 1915 | E |
| Stillborn girl | (16)James H. Thurlow & Lizzie M. Lunt | Aug. 9, 1915 | E |
| Esther Nickerson | (2)Jephtha Nickerson & Ellen F. Lunt | Sept. 17, 1915 | E |
| Ernest Nickerson | (3)Jephtha Nickerson & Ellen F. Lunt | Sept. 17, 1915 | E |
| Maurice Kendall Teel | (1)William M. Teel & Marie McLaughlin | April 14, 1916 | E |
| Genevieve W. McKown | (2)Winfield McKown & Jennie M. Rice | May 6, 1916 | E |
| Blanch A. Elliot | (12)Orrin S. Elliot & Bessie Roberts | Aug. 17, 1916 | E |
| LaForest G. Lunt Jr. | LaForest G. Lunt & (6)Mary E. McFarland | Sept. 3, 1916 | E |
| Elmer C. Davis | (3)Alexander P. Davis & Valeria M. Lunt | Feb. 4, 1917 | E |
| Stillborn male | (8)John R. Lunt & Flora E. Lunt | July 17, 1917 | E |
| Stillborn female | (1)Milton Dalzell & Vera M. Ross | Aug. 17, 1917 | E |
| Mable Lunt | (9)John R. Lunt & Flora E. Lunt | July 1, 1918 | E |
| Theda A. Davis | (1)Grandville W. Davis & Violet B. Thurlow | July 26, 1918 | E |
| Marjorie R. Dalzell | (2)Milton Dalzell & Vera M. Ross | July 30, 1918 | E |
| Verna B. Mitchell | Charles R. Mitchell & (3)Jennie Rice | May 20, 1919 | E |
| Naomi B. Davis | (1)Forrest Stanley & Flora O. Davis | May 23, 1919 | E |
| Lawrence H. Davis | (4)Alexander P. Davis & Valeria M. Lunt | Sept. 21, 1919 | E |
| June Elizabeth Davis | (2)Grandville W. Davis & Violet B. Thurlow | Oct. 7, 1919 | E |
| Thursa Lunt | (1)Thomas B. Lunt & Elva Lunt | Oct. 29, 1919 | E |

## *1920 — 1929*

| | | | |
|---|---|---|---|
| Vernon E. Dalzell | (1)Everett E. Dalzell Jr. & Lula B. Lunt | April 18, 1920 | E |
| Thomas B. Lunt | (1)Thomas B. Lunt & Helen Dalzell | Nov. 17, 1920 | E |
| Catherine B. Lunt | (10)John R. Lunt & Flora Eveline Lunt | Feb. 27, 1921 | E |
| Kermit B. Lunt | (1)Llewellyn Lunt & Alice Winnifred Lunt | May 25, 1921 | E |
| Ganiel L. Perkins | (1)George Perkins & Marie Lunt | June 14, 1921 | E |
| Ronald E. Mitchell | (4)Charles R. Mitchell & Jennie M. Rice | Aug. 1, 1921 | E |
| Calvin B. Lunt Jr. | (3)Calvin B. Lunt & Bertha Lunt | Aug. 7, 1921 | E |
| Frank W. Dalzell | (3)Milton S. Dalzell & Vera M. Ross | March 20, 1922 | E |
| Marilyn B. Davis | (3)Grandville W. Davis & Violet B. Thurlow | Aug. 27, 1922 | E |
| Clarence Lunt | (11)John R. Lunt & Flora E. Lunt | July 29, 1922 | E |
| Freda P. Lunt | (2)Llewellyn Lunt & Alice W. Lunt | Dec. 23, 1922 | E |
| Rose Mary Dalzell | (2)Everett E. Dalzell Jr. & Lula B. Lunt | Sept. 4, 1923 | E |
| John K. Mitchell | Charles Mitchell & (5)Jennie Rice | Feb. 22, 1924 | E |

| | | | |
|---|---|---|---|
| Malcolm Lunt | (1)Clifton M. Lunt & Ella V. Lunt | Aug. 26, 1924 | E |
| Pauline M. Lunt | (12)John R. Lunt & Flora E. Lunt | April 22, 1925 | E |
| Erland H. Dalzell | (3)Everett E. Dalzell Jr. & Lula B. Lunt | June 16, 1925 | E |
| Geraldine Dalzell | (1)Grandville Dalzell & Lydia Thurlow | Nov. 3, 1925 | E |
| Lillian J. Davis | (5)Alexander P. Davis & Valeria M. Lunt | Nov. 16, 1925 | E |
| Norma B. Lunt | (2)Thomas B. Lunt & Helen Dalzell | Feb. 5, 1926 | E |
| Stillborn male | Charles Mitchell & (6)Jennie M. Rice | April 18, 1926 | E |
| Roy R. Dalzell | (2)Granville Dalzell & Lydia Thurlow | Nov. 2, 1926 | E |
| Betty Ruth Dolliver | (2)Hiram S. Dolliver & Flora Davis | March 17, 1927 | E |
| Priscilla Jean Howard | (1)Clarence Howard & Alice H. Ross | May 6, 1927 | E |
| Thelma B. Davis | (4)Grandville W. Davis & Violet B. Thurlow | June 9, 1927 | E |
| Merrill Irving Lunt | (14)John R. Lunt & Flora E. Lunt | Jan. 10, 1928 | E |
| Herbert Orville Mitchell | Charles R. Mitchell & (7)Jennie M. Rice | April 29, 1928 | E |
| Edna Carolyn Lunt | (2)Clifton M. Lunt & Ella V. Lunt | Oct. 23, 1928 | E |
| Basil Dempsey Lunt | (3)Thomas B. Lunt & Helen Dalzell | May 18, 1929 | E |
| Dalton Granville Dalzell | (3)Granville Dalzell & Lydia Thurlow | Oct. 7, 1929 | E |

## 1930 — 1939

| | | | |
|---|---|---|---|
| Ramona Madeline Davis | (3)Elmer S. Davis & Ella N. Tinker | Jan 27, 1930 | E |
| Rosetta Marion Davis | (6)Alexander P. Davis & Valeria M. Lunt | Feb. 17, 1930 | E |
| Louise Madelyn Dalzell | (4)Milton S. Dalzell & Vera M. Ross | Aug. 12, 1930 | E |
| John Rodney Lunt Jr. | (15) John R. Lunt & Flora E. Lunt | Nov. 3, 1930 | E |
| Hilda Louise Lunt | (1)Wallace L. Lunt & Lenora L. Higgins | Feb. 24, 1931 | E |
| Ruby H. Davis | (7)Alexander P. Davis & Valeria M. Lunt | March 5, 1931 | E |
| Janet M. Davis | (4)Elmer Davis & Ella Tinker | Dec. 18, 1931 | E |
| Carolyn Marie Davis | (8)Alexander P. Davis & Valeria M. Lunt | May 14, 1932 | E |
| Elizabeth C. Dalzell | (5)Milton S. Dalzell & Vera M. Ross | May 19, 1932 | E |
| June Davis | (1)Bennie S. Davis & Lillian M. Bridges | Aug. 5, 1932 | E |
| Donald Elmer Lunt | (3)Otis M. Lunt & Doris G. Wilson | Nov. 17, 1932 | E |
| Richard Earle Davis | (9)Alexander P. Davis & Valeria M. Lunt | May 26, 1933 | E |
| Dorothy Avis Davis | (5)Elmer Davis & Ella N. Tinker | June 16, 1933 | E |
| Carroll Warren Lunt | (2)Wallace L. Lunt & Lenora L. Higgins | Nov. 20, 1933 | E |
| Bennie S. Davis Jr. | (2)Bennie S. Davis & Lillian M. Bridges | May 4, 1935 | E |
| Elmer Leroy Lunt* | (3)Wallace L. Lunt & Lenora L. Higgins | April 15, 1936 | E |
| Raymond Tinker Davis | (6)Elmer S. Davis & Ella N. Tinker | Feb. 10, 1937 | E |
| David Lawrence Lunt | (1)Sanford L. Lunt & Vivian M. Davis | May 18, 1938 | E |
| Robert Alton Lunt | (4)Wallace L. Lunt & Lenora L. Higgins | Dec. 31, 1938 | E |

*Name legally changed from Elmer Leroy to Alfred Wallace on Aug. 25, 1994.

## 1940 — 1969

| | | | |
|---|---|---|---|
| Donald Kenneth Osier | (1)Willard K. Osier & Genevieve W. McKown | Feb. 9, 1940 | E |
| Donna R. Howard | Clarence E. Howard & Alice H. Ross | April 14, 1940 | E |
| Earl Kenneth Awalt Jr. | (6)Earl K. Awalt Sr. & June M. Grindle | Jan. 7, 1941 | E |
| Willard K. Osier Jr. | (2)Willard K Osier Sr. & Genevieve W. McKown | Jan 1, 1942 | E |
| Marilyn Ruth Crossman | (2)Raymond D. Crossman & Lillian J. Davis | Jan. 7, 1943 | E |
| Rosalie Myrtle Stanley | (1)Hugh L. Stanley & Marguerite H. Lunt | Aug. 22, 1943 | E |

| | | | |
|---|---|---|---|
| Paul Lester Crossman | (3)Raymond D. Crossman & Lillian J. Davis | April 6, 1944 | E |
| Mary Ruth Davis | (2)Lawrence H. Davis & Pauline M. Lunt | Nov. 5, 1946 | E |
| Gloria Jean Lunt | (1)Malcolm W. Lunt & Shirley Belle Maddocks | Dec. 1, 1946 | E |
| Jean Louise Stanley | (2)Hugh L. Stanley & Marguerite H. Lunt | Dec. 12, 1946 | E |
| Cary Burton Lunt | (1)Clarence L. Lunt & Elsie V. Reed | May 30, 1947 | E |
| Valeria A. Davis Lunt | Thomas B. Lunt Jr. & (1)Rosetta M. Davis | Oct. 5, 1947 | E |
| Terry Howard Lunt | Thomas B. Lunt Jr. & (1)Priscilla Jean Howard | May 16, 1949 | E |
| Bradley Fay Teel | (1)Raymond L. Teel & Norma B. Lunt | Aug. 22, 1948 | E |
| Russell Bernard Hooper | (1)Charles B. Hooper Jr. & Rose Mary Dalzell | Nov. 6, 1948 | E |
| Sharon Lorraine Stanley | (3)Hugh L. Stanley & Marguerite H. Lunt | Dec. 22, 1948 | E |
| Billy Raymond Teel | (2)Raymond L. Teel & Norma B. Lunt | Aug. 8, 1949 | E |
| Barbara Ann Lunt | Cecil E. Lunt & (4)Lillian J. Davis | Oct. 28, 1949 | E |
| John K. Mitchell Jr. | (2)John K. Mitchell Sr. & Madeleine M. Dee | Oct. 26, 1950 | E |
| Eva Louise Lunt | John R. Lunt Jr. & (2)Rebecca J. Reed | Feb. 21, 1951 | E |
| Carole Linda Lunt | Carroll W. Lunt & (2)Rosetta M. Davis | Oct. 2, 1951 | E |
| Cheryl Elaine Hooper | (2)Charles B. Hooper & Rose Mary Dalzell | July 24, 1952 | E |
| Denise Marie Dalzell | Vernon E. Dalzell & (3)Lernice J. Martis | Sept. 1, 1954 | E |
| David William Lunt | (1)David L. Lunt & Avis Sandra Morris | Dec. 18, 1958 | E |
| Susan Annette Crossman | (1)Marilyn R. Crossman | Feb. 5, 1960 | E |
| Daniel Louis Lunt | (2)David Lawrence Lunt & Avis Sandra Morris | May 10, 1960 | E |
| Kevin Troy Lunt | (2)Robert A. Lunt & Earlene F. Lunt | Sept. 10, 1964 | E |
| Rachel M. Truxes | (1)Raymond J. Truxes Jr. & Nancy J. Maren | Sept. 12, 1965 | E |
| Timothy W. Bergeron | (1)Cecil W. Bergeron & Pamela L. Condon | April 1, 1966 | E |
| Dean Lawrence Lunt | (3)David L. Lunt & Avis Sandra Morris | April 21, 1966 | E |
| Genevieve M. Truxes | (2)Raymond J. Truxes Jr. & Nancy J. Maren | Sept. 5, 1966 | E |
| Amy Adele Bergeron | (2)Cecil W. Bergerson & Pamela L. Condon | Nov. 4, 1967 | E |
| Bobbi Jo Lunt | (3)Robert A. Lunt & Earlene F. Lunt | Dec. 30, 1968 | E |

## *1970 — 1999*

| | | | |
|---|---|---|---|
| Dale Andrew Bergeron | (3)Cecil W. Bergeron & Pamela L. Condon | April 5, 1970 | E |
| Tammy Lynn Crossman | (1)Paul L. Crossman & Judy E. Ober | May 26, 1970 | E |
| Karen Michelle Lunt | (4)Robert A. Lunt & Earlene F. Lunt | July 8, 1971 | E |
| Jennifer L. Crossman | (2)Paul L. Crossman & Judy E. Ober | Feb. 16, 1972 | E |
| Nancy Elizabeth Osier | Donald K. Osier & (2)Carol Ann Morrison | June 4, 1973 | E |
| Corey Everett Sawyer | (1)Randall S. Sawyer & Barbara Ann Lunt | June 16, 1973 | E |
| April Dawn Davis | (1)Kenneth A. Davis & Eva Louise Lunt | Aug. 15, 1973 | E |
| Izaak Michael Giberson | (1)Michael H. Giberson & Marcia M. Murphy | June 18, 1975 | E |
| Christopher H. Sawyer | (2)Randall S. Sawyer & Barbara Ann Lunt | Dec. 31, 1975 | E |
| Aaron Dean Giberson | (2)Michael H. Giberson & Marcia M. Murphy | Aug. 25, 1978 | E |
| Will Rian Teel | (1)Billy R. Teel & Arin McKane | June 23, 1979 | E |
| Jeffrey Scott Webber | (1)Jeffrey V. Webber & Jill S. Hudson | Dec. 7, 1977 | E |
| Aerie Anna Teel | (2)Billy R. Teel & Arin McKane | Sept. 20, 1980 | E |
| Timothy A. Webber | (2)Jeffrey V. Webber & Jill S. Hudson | Oct. 22, 1980 | E |
| Miranda Marin Teel | (3)Billy R. Teel & Arin McKane | Jan. 2, 1982 | E |
| Amanda Sue Farley | David C. Farley & (3)Gail M. Thurlow | Oct. 12, 1982 | E |
| Zachary Daniel Lunt | (1)Daniel L. Lunt & Tina M. LeMoine | Aug. 8, 1983 | E |

| Kelsea Kathleen Teel | (4)Billy R. Teel & Arin McKane | July 3, 1983 | E |
| Kristi Lynn Lunt | (2)David W. Lunt & Debra A. Herbest | Mar. 12, 1985 | E |
| Nathaniel Dean Lunt | (2)Daniel L. Lunt & Tina M. LeMoine | April 19, 1985 | E |
| Joseph William Lunt | (3)David W. Lunt & Debra A. Herbest | June 3, 1987 | E |
| Thomas Paul Crossman | (1)Jon P. Crossman & Deborah E. Harmon | Aug. 31, 1989 | E |
| Mariner M. Beal | Wyatt L. Beal & Lorena F. Lenfestey | June 11, 1990 | E |
| Louis John Beote | Steven & Elaine Beote | June 12, 1991 | E |
| Raymond Jon Crossman | (2)Jon P. Crossman & Deborah E. Harmon | Dec. 15, 1992 | E |
| Katie Lynn Higgins | Warren P. Higgins & (2)Lisa L. Johnston | Sept. 22, 1993 | E |
| Clayton E. Hurlburt | (1)Timothy N. Hurlburt & Heather A. Erickson | Feb. 26, 1994 | E |
| Erin Tyler Hanley | (1)Patrick E. Hanley & Audrey L. Dorval | June 22, 1995 | E |
| Marcus Blake Lyle | (2)Darrell S. Lyle & Tiffany G. Lyle | June 2, 1995 | E |
| Audrey Lynn Beal | Wyatt L. Beal & Lorena F. Lenfestey | April 23, 1996 | E |
| Elijah Wiggins | Timothy Wiggins & (1)April D. Davis | Mar. 6, 1999 | E |
| Amber Lee Wiggins | Timothy W. Wiggins & (2) April D. Davis | June 20, 2000 | E |
| Myron C. Lenfestey III | Myron Lenfestey Jr. & (1) Rebecca A. Smart | July 16, 2000 | E |
| Teressa Rozenski | Roman A. Rozenski & (1) Marissa Goglia | Feb. 2, 2001 | E |
| Isiah Matthew Sawyer | Christopher H. Sawyer & (1) Samantha E. Betts | Jan. 5, 2002 | E |
| Bradley Ryan Lenfestey | Myron Lenfestey Jr. & (2) Rebecca A. Smart | May 13, 2002 | E |
| Marilyn Lianna Saywer | Christopher H. Sawyer & (2) Samantha E. Betts | Nov. 30, 2002 | E |
| John Joseph Rozenski | Roman A. Rozenski & (2) Marissa R. Goglia | May 2, 2003 | E |
| Molly Elizabeth Lunt | (1) Kristi L. Lunt & Benjamin L. Hopkins | Jan. 23, 2004 | E |
| Seth Maurice Lenfestey | Myron Lenfestey Jr. & (3) Rebecca A. Smart | June 21, 2005 | E |
| Tyler Nathaniel Lunt | Nathaniel D. Lunt & (2) KatieLee Wiggins | Jan. 6, 2006 | E |
| Breanna Danielle Lunt | Zachary D. Lunt & (4) Laurette Smart | May 29, 2007 | E |

Source Key:

A = Amos Coffin Lunt journal
B = Federal Census
C = Civil War Records
D = Family Genealogy
E = Public Birth Records
F = Public Death Records
G = Gravestone
I = Thomas Simpson Lunt
J = Vivian Davis Lunt

BI = Black Island
PI = Placentia Island
dy = died young

472

# Long Island Deaths

## 1800 — 1899

| Name, Age | Parents/Notes | Date | Source |
|---|---|---|---|
| *Mary Lunt, 1 yr. 10 mos. | Amos C. Lunt Sr. & Priscilla Butler | Feb. 15, 1827 | ACL |
| *Boy Rich, infant | John Rich & Jane Lunt | May 1839 | ACL |
| *Charles P. St. Clair Rich, 5 | John Rich & Jane Lunt | Jan. 11, 1848 | ACL |
| Cyrus K. Lunt, 31 | Amos C. Lunt Sr. & Mary Bartlett | April 18, 1848 | ACL |
| *Amanda S. Lunt, 17 | Israel B. Lunt & Nancy Pomroy | April 7, 1851 | Stone |
| Amos Coffin Lunt Sr. | Abner Coffin Lunt & Elizabeth Hodgdon | May 18, 1851 | Stone |
| John Walls, 25 | Drown in Yankee Gale | Oct. 4, 1851 | Stone |
| *Edward P. Lunt, 16 | Israel B. Lunt Sr. & Nancy Pomroy | Oct. 4, 1851 | Stone |
| Abner Lunt | | 1855 | EA |
| Charles Davis | | 1855 | EA |
| Ezra Davis, 12 | | Mar. 20, 1859 | EA |
| John Dawes, 21 | Jonathan Dawes & Charlotte Dawes | Feb. 5, 1859 | EA |
| Roseanna D. Downes | Maiden name Pomroy | Dec. 10, 1859 | EA |
| Israel B. Lunt Sr., 65 | Amos Coffin Lunt Sr. & Mary Bartlett | Oct. 2, 1861 | Stone |
| Amos Coffin Lunt Jr., 65 | Amos Coffin Lunt Sr. & Mary Bartlett | Aug. 27, 1863 | EA |
| *Sabra Ann Rich, 26 | Bartholomew R. Lunt Sr. & Asenath Allen | Sept. 27, 1863 | EA |
| Marston W. Pinkham, 29 | Ichabod Pinkham & Elizabeth Pinkham | Jan. 6, 1864 | Stone |
| Miriam H. Lunt, 61 | Amos Coffin Lunt Sr. & Mary Bartlett | Jan. 8, 1864 | EA |
| Zerelda E. Rich, 2 | George R. Rich & Lucy B. Lunt | May 13, 1865 | Stone |
| Thomas Rice, 88 | | Nov. 6, 1867 | EA |
| Nancy P. Lunt, 65 | William Pomroy & Mary Beal | Dec. 7, 1871 | Stone |
| Jonathan Dawes, 74 | Died at Grand Manan, N.B | Jan. 25, 1874 | EA |
| *Freelove Brewer, 29 | Israel B. Lunt Sr. & Nancy Pomroy | April 13, 1874 | EA |

| | | | |
|---|---|---|---|
| *Abraham Rice Jr., 1 | Samuel J. Rice | Jan. 19, 1875 | PDR |
| *Benjamin F. Stinson Lunt, 33 | Joseph D. Lunt & R. Hannah. Lunt | May 1, 1876 | EA |
| Nancy Jane Murphy, 37 | Mr. & Mrs. Tinker; left seven children | Jan. 12, 1878 | EA |
| Stephen Dunham, 66 | | June 17, 1880 | EA |
| Polly Davis, about 60 | 1st wife of Capt. William Davis | June 28, 1881 | EA |
| George B. Lunt, 70 | Abner Lunt & Jane Dawes | Dec. 27, 1881 | EA |
| Sarah Davis, 38 | Daughter of Eleanor Rich | Dec. 28, 1881 | VDL |
| Gilbert Rich, 67 | | Feb. 25, 1882 | EA |
| Rebecca Davis, 69 | | Aug. 13, 1882 | EA |
| *Florence Powers, 4 mos. | | April 7, 1883 | EA |
| Israel Lunt, 57 | Abner Lunt & Jane Dawes | May 2, 1883 | EA |
| Dorcas Lunt, 63 | Widow of late Israel Lunt | Nov. 26, 1883 | EA |
| Charlotte Dawes, 77 | Widow of the late Jonathan Dawes | Feb. 20, 1884 | EA |
| LaForest Rich, 13 | William S. Rich & Abbie Davis | May 19, 1884 | VDL |
| Abigail M. Davis | Milliken; Wife of James T. Davis | April 27, 1885 | Stone |
| *Amos Allen Lunt, 48 | Bartholomew R. Lunt Sr. & Asenath Allen | May 6, 1885 | VDL |
| Abigail Lunt, 89 | Wife of Richard Lunt | May 29, 1885 | VDL |
| *A daughter, 3 mos. | Hezekiah W. Lunt Sr. & Lydia M. Dawes | Oct. 19, 1885 | PDR |
| *Clarence A. Lunt, 1 mos. | Hiram A. Lunt & Mary S. Lunt | April 13, 1886 | PDR |
| Robert Ross | | July 1886 | PDR |
| Bartholomew R. Lunt Sr., 72 | Abner Lunt & Jane Dawes | Dec. 20, 1886 | PDR |
| Asenath (Allen) Lunt, 76 | Wife of the late Bartholomew R. Lunt Sr. | Feb. 14, 1888 | PDR |
| Albion Butler, 39 | | Feb. 25, 1888 | PDR |
| Infant son, 2 mos. | Charles V. Grey & Flora Gray | June 17, 1888 | PDR |
| *William D. Lunt, 65 | Abner Lunt & Jane Dawes | Oct. 31, 1888 | EA |
| *Harry A. Gray, infant | Charles V. Gray & Flora Gray | May 4, 1889 | EA |
| *John R. Gray, infant | Charles V. Gray & Flora Gray | June 5, 1889 | EA |
| Betsy Davis | | July 27, 1889 | PDR |
| Richard Lunt, 78 | Abner Lunt & Jane Dawes | Nov. 13, 1889 | PDR |
| Zula M. Lunt, 6 mos. | Hiram A. Lunt & Mary Susan Lunt | Jan. 24, 1890 | |
| James T. Davis, 76 | Rebecca Davis | April 28, 1890 | Stone |
| *Joseph W. Lunt, 62 | Amos C. Lunt Jr. & Eliza Pomroy | Jan. 18, 1891 | PDR |
| *Bartholomew R. Lunt Jr., 40 | Bartholomew R. Lunt Sr. & Asenath Allen | June 22, 1891 | PDR |
| Mary Ross, 72 | | Aug. 30, 1894 | VDL |
| Perry Rich, 10 | | Sept. 28, 1894 | VDL |
| William Davis, 77 | | Oct. 20, 1894 | VDL |
| Lydia Thurlow, 7 | | Feb. 3, 1895 | VDL |
| *Mary Lunt, 8 | George C. Lunt & Harriet Davis | July 9, 1895 | PDR |
| *Maud E. Lunt, 13 | Israel B. Lunt & Isora M. Rich | Aug. 3, 1895 | PDR |
| Mary E. Lunt, 72 | Amos A. Allen & Elizabeth Lunt | Aug. 14, 1895 | PDR |
| Granville Rice, 20 | | June 15, 1897 | Stone |
| *Edith Bell Lunt, 9 | Hiram A. Lunt & Mary S. Lunt | Aug. 21, 1897 | PDR |
| Aaron Harvey, 63 | | Aug. 24, 1897 | VDL |
| Mary T. Davis, 75 | | Sept. 23, 1897 | VDL |
| Mary Hessey, 52 | | July 25, 1898 | VDL |
| *Calvin C. Lunt, 52 | Bartholomew R. Lunt Sr. & Asenath Allen | Nov. 11, 1898 | PDR |

| | | | |
|---|---|---|---|
| Olitty Davis, 4 | Samuel F. Davis & Maria  Norwood | Sept. 30, 1899 | VDL |
| Rebecca Davis, 1 | | Oct. 3, 1899 | VDL |

## *1900 — 1919*

| | | | |
|---|---|---|---|
| Georgia Davis, 35 | | Sept. 8, 1901 | VDL |
| William J. Teel, 68 | | Nov. 10, 1901 | VDL |
| Lewis Leroy Lunt, 9 | Adelbert W. Lunt & Rosanna Murphy | June 9, 1902 | PDR |
| Joshua Lunt | | June 9, 1902 | VDL |
| Ella L. Dalzell, 8 mos. | Everette E. Dalzell & Linnie D. Rice | Dec. 13, 1902 | VDL |
| *Unnamed boy, 1 mos. | Grant H. Lunt & Lena M. Higgins | Jan 18, 1903 | PDR |
| (DI)Marion Vanhorn, 6 | David W. Vanhorn & Ella Maker | Jan. 29, 1903 | PDR |
| *Merritt W. Lunt, 41 | William D. Lunt Sr. & Mary Elizabeth Allen | April 7, 1903 | PDR |
| *Phillis L. Lunt, 3 | Atwood L. Lunt & Angeline Lunt | June 21, 1903 | PDR |
| *Sylvester Dalzell, 10 | Everett E. Dalzell & Linnie D. Rice | Oct. 16, 1903 | VDL |
| *Maria L. Teel, 34 | Joseph W. Lunt Sr. & Alice A. Twist | Aug. 27, 1904 | Stone |
| *Unnamed boy, 1 mos. | Alvina Lunt | April 24, 1905 | PDR |
| *Ernest Powers, 20 | Peter Powers & Ellen Rich | May 14, 1905 | PDR |
| Alden Davis, 16 | Leaman T. Davis & Agnes F. Joyce | July 6, 1905 | Stone |
| Daryl Thurlow, 4 mos. | | June 10, 1906 | VDL |
| *Alice A. Lunt, 65 | George Twist & Mary T. Rice | June 18, 1907 | PDR |
| Melissa Rice, 67 | | July 7, 1907 | VDL |
| *Marina E. Lunt, 1 | Atwood L. Lunt & Angeline Lunt | Dec. 28, 1907 | PDR |
| Rhoda M. Teel, 68 | Israel B. Lunt Sr. & Nancy Pomroy | Jan. 21, 1908 | VDL |
| *Adelbert W. Lunt, 48 | Hezekiah W. Lunt Sr. & Lydia M. Dawes | June 20, 1908 | PDR |
| William S. Rich | | Aug. 16, 1908 | CWR |
| *Clyde Lunt, 10 mos. | Hiram A. Lunt Sr. & Mary S. Lunt | Nov. 12, 1908 | PDR |
| Unnamed boy, 3 days | Hiram A. Lunt Sr. & Mary S. Lunt | July 5, 1910 | PDR |
| Hortense B. Van Norden, 67 | Israel B. Lunt Sr. & Nancy Pomroy | March 8, 1909 | Stone |
| Frank R. Thurlow, 19 | James H. Thurlow & Lizzie M. Lunt | May 6, 1912 | VDL |
| *Louisa Lunt, 4 | Grant H. Lunt | May 21, 1912 | PDR |
| *Frank S. Rich, 20 | Martin H. Rich & Lizzie L.  Davis | July 17, 1912 | PDR |
| Abram Rice, 75 | | Oct. 9, 1912 | VDL |
| Israel B. Lunt Jr., 66 | Israel B. Lunt Sr. & Nancy Pomroy | Dec. 27, 1912 | VDL |
| Unnamed girl, 1 day | Winfield McKown & Jennie Rice | July 12, 1913 | PDR |
| Wilson G. Carter, 18 | Constantine Carter & Susie Butler | Oct. 29, 1913 | PDR |
| *Hezekiah W. Lunt Sr., 80 | Bartholomew R. Lunt Sr. & Asenath Allen | Jan. 29, 1914 | PDR |
| Charles K. Lunt, 32 | Hezekiah W. Lunt Sr. & Lydia M. Dawes | July 29, 1914 | PDR |
| *Carrie A. Elliot, 1 | Orrin S. Elliot & Bessie Roberts | June 25, 1915 | PDR |
| *Charles E. Rice, 53 | Abraham Rice & Melissa Davis | Jan 22, 1916 | PDR |
| *Cora A. Lunt, 38 | Joseph W. Lunt & Alice A. Twist | Aug. 22, 1916 | PDR |
| *Ruby Thurlow, 5 | James H. Thurlow & Lizzie M. Lunt | Sept. 26, 1916 | PDR |
| *Edna Geneva Lunt, 4 | John R. Lunt Sr. & Flora E. Lunt | Sept. 29, 1916 | PDR |
| Elias T. Cross, 79 | Elias Cross & Nancy Robbins | Feb. 23, 1917 | PDR |
| *Roy Thurlow, 8 | James H. Thurlow & Lizzie M. Lunt | Mar. 7 1917 | PDR |
| John Merchant, 72 | David S. Merchant & Catherine Gross | Mar. 3, 1917 | PDR |
| Lucille Dalzell | | Aug. 17, 1917 | Stone |

| | | | |
|---|---|---|---|
| (BI)Lydia M. Lunt, 73 | Johnathan Dawes & Charlotte Langley | Sept. 15, 1917 | PDR |
| (BI)Mary Rich, 88 | Mr. Walls & Abigail Tinker | Dec. 24, 1917 | PDR |
| *Leonard A. Lunt, 18 | Alphonso L. Lunt & Sadie L. McKusick | April 18, 1918 | PDR |
| *Hiram A. Lunt, 56 | Joseph W. Lunt & Alice A. Twist | Jan. 3, 1919 | PDR |

## *1920 –1939*

| | | | |
|---|---|---|---|
| *Emily S. Gilman, 68 | James T. Davis & Abigail Milliken | Sept. 19, 1920 | PDR |
| *Nelson P. Lunt, 46 | Joseph W. Lunt & Alice A. Twist | July 3, 1921 | PDR |
| Calvin B. Lunt Jr., 8 Mos. | Calvin B. Lunt & Bertha L. Lunt | April 7, 1922 | PDR |
| Louise M. Teel, 11 | William L. Teel & Annie Hall | April 14, 1922 | PDR |
| *Virginia M. Lunt, 15 | William S. Lunt & Edna F. Rich | June 25, 1922 | PDR |
| *Rebecca N. Robinson, 67 | William Davis & Elizabeth Dawes | July 18, 1922 | PDR |
| *Joseph W. Lunt Jr., 58 | Joseph W. Lunt & Alice A. Twist | Oct. 7, 1922 | PDR |
| *Edna F. Lunt, 54 | Martin H. Rich & Mary A. Rich | Feb. 19, 1923 | PDR |
| *Isora M. Lunt, 69 | Gilbert Rich & Mary Walls | June 21, 1923 | PDR |
| *Freda P. Lunt, 9 mos. | Llewellyn Lunt & Alice W. Lunt | Oct. 1, 1923 | PDR |
| *Grant H. Lunt, 55 | Joseph W. Lunt & Alice A. Twist | April 10, 1924 | PDR |
| *George Colliver Lunt, 85 | George C. Lunt & Miriam Lunt | April 29, 1924 | PDR |
| *Kermit B. Lunt, 3 | Llewellyn Lunt & Alice W. Lunt | May 30, 1924 | PDR |
| Samuel F. Davis | | 1925 | Stone |
| *Martin H. Rich, 73 | William Rich & Eleanor Rice | July 14, 1925 | PDR |
| *William M. Teel, 60 | William J. Teel & Rhoda M. Lunt | June 22, 1926 | PDR |
| William A. Van Norden, 76 | John Van Norden & Wealthy Smith | Sept. 21, 1926 | PDR |
| Elidge Lunt, 7 | Calvin B. Lunt & Bertha L. Lunt | Dec. 29, 1926 | PDR |
| Mary S. Lunt, 57 | Hezekiah W. Lunt Sr. & Lydia M. Dawes | July 1, 1927 | PDR |
| *Alma C. Lunt, 67 | Charles Cousins & Hannah Walls | Oct. 3, 1927 | PDR |
| *Merrill Irving Lunt, 9 mos. | John R. Lunt & Flora E. Lunt | Oct. 16, 1928 | PDR |
| Marilyn B. Davis, about 8 | G.W. Davis & V.B. Davis | 1930 | Stone |
| Franklin E. Gilman | | April 29, 1930 | PDR |
| Everett E. Dalzell, 67 | | May 24, 1930 | PDR |
| Meredith Mitchell | | 1931 | Stone |
| *Agnes F. Davis, 70 | Reuben B. Joyce & Mary Ann Lunt | Feb. 4, 1931 | PDR |
| Charles L. Wallace, 67 | Orrin Wallace & Ellen Burns | Feb. 23, 1932 | PDR |
| June Davis, 7 days | Ben S. Davis & Lillian Bridges | Aug. 12, 1932 | PDR |
| Flora A. Rice, 64 | Hezekiah W. Lunt Sr. & Lydia M. Dawes | Nov. 3, 1932 | PDR |
| James H. Thurlow, 62 | Emily S. Davis | Jan. 2, 1933 | Stone |
| *Alice Winnifried Lunt, 30 | Hiram A. Lunt & Mary S. Lunt | Jan. 1, 1934 | PDR |
| *Harry Whitfield Lunt, 80 | William D. Lunt & Mary Elizabeth Allen | March 15, 1934 | PDR |
| *Abbie E. Rich, 77 | William Davis & Mary T. Rice | March 26, 1935 | PDR |
| *Ellen F. Nickerson, 57 | Israel B. Lunt Jr. & Isora M. Rich | July 29, 1935 | PDR |
| *Samuel Rice, 71 | Abraham Rice & Melissa Davis | Sept. 25, 1935 | PDR |
| *Harriet Lunt, 84 | Ezra Davis & Rebecca Davis | Dec. 31, 1935 | PDR |
| Jephtha Nickerson, 70 | Horace Nickerson & Sarah Crowell | Jan. 25, 1936 | PDR |
| *William S. Lunt, 73 | Benjamin F. Stinson Lunt & Ann Rich | March 2, 1936 | PDR |
| *Atwood L. Lunt, 76 | Joseph W. Lunt Sr. & Alice A. Twist | Feb. 23, 1937 | PDR |
| Rita J. Hughes, 19 | Merrill Hughes & Ellen Kelley | July 28, 1937 | PDR |

| | | | |
|---|---|---|---|
| *Angeline V. Lunt, 69 | George Colliver Lunt & Harriet Davis | Dec. 12, 1937 | PDR |
| *Leaman T. Davis, 71 | William Davis & Mary T. Rice | Jan. 24, 1938 | PDR |
| *Alphonso L. Lunt, 65 | Israel B. Lunt Jr. & Isora Rich | April 2, 1939 | PDR |
| *Pearl O. Rice, 44 | Samuel Rice & Sabra A. Lunt | June 17, 1939 | PDR |
| *Everett S. Lunt, 55 | William S. Lunt & Edna F. Rich | Nov. 11, 1939 | PDR |

## 1940 — 1959

| | | | |
|---|---|---|---|
| Bert H. Perkins, 73 | Enoch Perkins & Izora McKown | Dec. 12, 1940 | PDR |
| Sabra A. Rice, 78 | Hezekiah W. Lunt Sr. & Lydia M. Dawes | Oct. 3, 1943 | PDR |
| *Valeria May Davis, 48 | Hiram A. Lunt & Mary S. Lunt | Nov. 22, 1944 | PDR |
| *Rosanna Lunt, 83 | Henry Murphy & Nancy J. Tinker | April 11, 1945 | PDR |
| Daniel W. Malanson, 56 | David Malanson & Rebecca E. Malanson | Nov. 12, 1945 | PDR |
| Lizzie Mabel Thurlow, 73 | Hezekiah W. Lunt Sr. & Lydia M. Dawes | May 24, 1946 | Stone |
| Lena M. Lunt, 64 | Warren Higgins & Maria Norwood | Aug. 22, 1946 | PDR |
| *Valeria Alexis Lunt, 2 mos. | Thomas B. Lunt Jr. & Rosetta M. Davis | Dec. 15, 1947 | PDR |
| Warren D. Stanley, 27 | Derby Stanley & Edith White | April 14, 1948 | PDR |
| Ralph L. Ramsdall, 29 | Almon Ramsdall & Mary Boynton | April 14, 1948 | PDR |
| *Charlotte E. Stewart, 65 | Calvin Lunt & Catherine Dawes | June 30, 1948 | PDR |
| *Frank Warren Ross, 78 | Alexander C. Ross & Hortense B. Lunt | Dec. 18, 1948 | PDR |
| *Daniel R. Lunt, 76 | George Colliver Lunt & Harriett Davis | Nov. 1, 1948 | PDR |
| *Gertrude Mae Gott, 66 | Jacob Osier & Irene Davis | Jan. 3, 1949 | PDR |
| *Hortense B. Wilson, 77 | Byron C. Wilson & A. Victoria Lunt | July 28, 1949 | PDR |
| *Edwin Spear Lunt, 75 | Hezekiah W. Lunt Sr. & Lydia M. Dawes | Jan. 14, 1950 | PDR |
| *John Rodney Lunt, 75 | Joseph Warren Lunt Sr. & Alice A. Twist | Nov. 23, 1951 | PDR |
| *Elizabeth Lunt Ross, 85 | Joseph Warren Lunt Sr. & Alice A. Twist | Jan. 28, 1952 | PDR |
| *Hezekiah E.S. Lunt, 94 | William D. Lunt & Mary Elizabeth Allen | Mar. 23, 1952 | PDR |
| *Milton S. Dalzell, 55 | Everett Edward Dalzell & Linnie D. Rice | April 16, 1952 | PDR |
| *Harry Winford Lunt, 68 | Bartholomew R. Lunt Jr. & Charlotte Davis | Dec. 30, 1952 | PDR |
| Charles R. Mitchell, 59 | Charles Mitchell & Ida Stanley | Mar. 24, 1953 | PDR |
| *Orrin C. Lunt, 49 | William Sanford Lunt & Edna F. Rich | July 25, 1953 | PDR |
| Asenath Maud Wallace, 76 | Hezekiah W. Lunt Sr. & Lydia M. Dawes | Oct. 22, 1953 | PDR |
| *Joseph Warren Lunt III, 61 | Atwood Lunt & Angeline V. Lunt | Aug. 17, 1954 | PDR |
| *Frederick Carter, 66 | Constantine Carter & Susie Carter | Sept. 15, 1955 | PDR |
| *Etta Mary Burns, 87 | William Davis & Mary T. Rice | Nov. 28, 1955 | PDR |
| *Carrie E. Davis, 80 | James Davis & Rebecca Davis | Jan. 2, 1956 | PDR |
| *Jessie L. Perkins, 64 | Hiram A. Lunt & Mary S. Lunt | Jan. 5, 1956 | PDR |
| *Emily W. Stevens, 75 | Byron C. Wilson & A. Victoria Lunt | Feb. 7, 1956 | PDR |
| Vera K. Van Norden, 63 | William S. Kelley & Rita Strout | Aug. 8, 1956 | PDR |
| Ralph Stanley, 39 | Lester Stanley & Helen Borland | Oct. 4, 1956 | VDL |
| *Jasper Lunt, 73 | George Colliver Lunt & Harriett Davis | Jan. 17, 1957 | PDR |
| *Charles B. Lunt, 72 | William Sanford Lunt & Edna F. Rich | May 4, 1958 | PDR |
| *Llewellyn Lunt, 62 | Atwood Lunt & Angeline V. Lunt | Nov. 28, 1958 | PDR |
| Sophronia S. Teel, 86 | William J. Teel & Rhoda M. Lunt | Feb. 12, 1959 | PDR |
| *Irene M. Robinson, 69 | David Dawes & Irene May Dawes | May 3, 1959 | PDR |
| Lillian Davis | Fred Bridges & Belle Rumill | Aug. 10, 1959 | VDL |

## *1960 — 1998*

| | | | |
|---|---|---|---|
| *Susan A. Crossman, 3 days | Marilyn R. Crossman | Feb. 8, 1960 | PDR |
| *Kenneth Gardiner Lunt, 49 | William Sanford Lunt & Edna F. Rich | June 8, 1961 | PDR |
| Edith F. Lunt, 65 | Winslow D. Stanley & Addie Joyce | Aug. 19, 1963 | PDR |
| *Guy E. Lunt, 62 | William Sanford Lunt & Edna F. Rich | Oct. 25, 1963 | PDR |
| *Clinton B. Teel, 75 | William M. Teel & Maria L. Lunt | Dec. 7, 1963 | PDR |
| *Bertha Lunt | Atwood L. Lunt & Angeline V. Lunt | Mar. 26, 1964 | VDL |
| *Leonard A. Lunt, 70 | William Sanford Lunt & Edna F. Rich | Nov. 26, 1964 | PDR |
| *Thomas B. Lunt Sr., 71 | Hiram A. Lunt Sr. & Mary Susan Lunt | Jan. 14, 1965 | PDR |
| *Benjamin Stinson Lunt, 74 | William Sanford Lunt & Edna F. Rich | June 8, 1965 | PDR |
| *Jennie Rice Mitchell, 75 | Charles Edwin Rice & Flora Lunt | Mar. 3, 1966 | PDR |
| *Hiram Albert Lunt Jr., 61 | Hiram A. Lunt Sr. & Mary Susan Lunt | Mar. 5, 1966 | PDR |
| Nathan F. Osier, 88 | Thomas Osier & Almenia Davis | Feb. 21, 1967 | PDR |
| Merrill Hart | | Mar. 15, 1967 | VDL |
| Warren Higgins | | May 20, 1967 | VDL |
| Hyman Lunt, 65 | Atwood L. Lunt & Angeline V. Lunt | May 21, 1967 | VDL |
| Everett Edward Dalzell Jr., 68 | Everett E. Dalzell & Linnie D. Rice | Jan. 20, 1968 | PDR |
| *Irving F. Lunt, 68 | William Sanford Lunt & Edna F. Rich | Sept. 12, 1968 | PDR |
| Sadie L. Lunt, 92 | Samuel D. McKusick & Sarah Witham | Feb. 8, 1969 | VDL |
| *Eugene C. Van Norden, 85 | William Van Norden & Hortense B. Lunt | Aug. 12, 1969 | PDR |
| *Elmer C. Davis, 52 | Alexander P. Davis & Valeria M. Lunt | Oct. 24, 1969 | VDL |
| *Millie Hunton, 76 | Leaman T. Davis & Agnes F. Joyce | Oct. 8, 1970 | VDL |
| Willie A. Gaspar, 61 | Willie E. Gaspar & Evelyn Bemis | Nov. 25, 1970 | PDR |
| Mary Bridges Osier, 86 | Leaman Bridges & Agnes F. Joyce | Jan. 30, 1971 | VDL |
| *Bennie S. Davis Sr., 66 | Leaman T. Davis & Agnes F. Joyce | Mar. 1, 1971 | PDR |
| Clyde V. Onyett, 62 | Ralph Onyett & Sarah C. Onyett | Mar. 1, 1971 | PDR |
| *Vera Dalzell, 75 | Frank W. Ross & Lizzie B. Lunt | April 8, 1971 | VDL |
| *Elmer S. Davis, 72 | Leaman T. Davis & Agnes F. Joyce | Oct. 23, 1971 | VDL |
| *Lincoln Lunt, 74 | Nelson P. Lunt & Alvina Lunt | June 5, 1973 | PDR |
| *Lula B. Dalzell, 78 | Hiram A. Lunt Sr. & Mary Susan Lunt | July 3, 1975 | PDR |
| *Gertrude L. Lunt, 75 | Alphonso L. Lunt & Sadie L. McKusick | Dec. 15, 1975 | PDR |
| *Raymond Leroy Teel, 76 | William M. Teel & Maria L. Lunt | Feb. 20, 1976 | PDR |
| Lilla Stanley, 68 | John R. Lunt Sr. & Flora E. Lunt | Oct. 3, 1976 | VDL |
| *Willard K. Osier Sr., 77 | Nathan F. Osier & Mary Bridges | Nov. 3, 1980 | PDR |
| *Clifton M. Lunt, 83 | Nelson P. Lunt & Alvina Lunt | Aug. 24, 1984 | PDR |
| *Flora E. Lunt, 97 | William Sanford Lunt & Edna F. Rich | Oct. 10, 1984 | PDR |
| Arthur M. Kellam, 73 | Arthur G. Kellam & Catheryn Page | Mar. 28, 1985 | PDR |
| *Erland H. Dalzell, 59 | Everett E. Dalzell Jr. & Lula B. Lunt | May 3, 1985 | PDR |
| *Helen E. Lunt, 82 | Everett Edward Dalzell & Linnie D. Rice | Aug. 4, 1985 | PDR |
| *Clarence L. Lunt, 66 | John R. Lunt Sr. & Flora E. Lunt | June 13, 1989 | PDR |
| Harriette S. Harmon, 68 | Raymond Crossman & Martha Smith | June 22, 1991 | PDR |
| *Malcolm W. Lunt, 66 | Clifton Lunt & Ella V. Lunt | June 27, 1991 | PDR |
| *Cecil E. Lunt, 77 | John R. Lunt Sr. & Flora E. Lunt | July 25, 1992 | PDR |
| Winston Harmon, 76 | Pliney & Helen Harmon | April 22, 1994 | PDR |
| *Vincent A. Davis, 82 | Alexander P. Davis & Valeria M. Lunt | Feb. 20, 1996 | PDR |
| Richard E. Davis, 64 | Alexander P. Davis & Valeria M. Lunt | Dec. 19, 1997 | FG |

| | | | |
|---|---|---|---|
| *Alma M. Lunt, 91 | John R. Lunt Sr. & Flora E. Lunt | May 21, 1998 | PDR |
| *Sanford L. Lunt, 89 | John R. Lunt Sr. & Flora E. Lunt | Oct. 18, 1999 | PDR |
| *Ella V. Lunt, 92 | William Sanford Lunt & Edna F. Rich | June 24, 2000 | PDR |
| Rebecca Jane Lunt, 74 | Ralph E. Reed & Flora Eveline Howard | March 16, 2004 | PDR |
| *Genevieve M. Osier, 90 | Winfield McKown & Jennie M. Rice | March 7, 2007 | PDR |

Abbreviation Key:

| | |
|---|---|
| Amos Coffin Lunt Journal | ACL |
| Gravestone | Stone |
| Ellsworth American | EA |
| Vivian Davis Lunt History | VDL |
| Long Island Death Record | PDR |
| Family Genealogy | FG |

*Born on Long Island

# About the Author

Dean Lawrence Lunt grew up an eight-generation Long Islander.

For nearly two centuries, his ancestors and family have helped build and sustain the island community and fishing village that survive today.

The son of David L. and Sandra (Morris) Lunt, Dean spent eight years in the island's one-room school before attending Tremont Elementary School and graduating from Mount Desert Island High School in 1984.

He lived on Long Island in Blue Hill Bay for nearly 23 years, spending most summers lobster fishing, working the woods or romping across an island playground.

He graduated from Syracuse University in 1988 with dual degrees in newspaper journalism and business.

Following graduation, Dean worked as a reporter for four New England newspapers including the *Portland Press Herald* in Portland, and *The* (Quincy) *Patriot Ledger* and (Springfield) *Union-News*, both in Massachusetts. Following *Hauling by Hand*, Lunt also wrote the book, *Here for Generations*. In 1999, he founded Islandport Press which is dedicated to publishing books about Maine. He continues to serve as publisher. He lives with his wife, Michelle, and daughters Emily and Eliza in Southern Maine.